Voices of the American Civil War

Voices of the American Civil War
Stories of Men, Women, and Children Who Lived
Through the War Between the States

Kendall Haven

2002
Libraries Unlimited/Teacher Ideas Press
A Division of Greenwood Publishing Group, Inc.
Greenwood Village, Colorado

LIBRARIES UNLIMITED
Teacher Ideas Press
A Division of Greenwood Publishing Group, Inc.
7730 East Belleview Ave., Suite A200
Greenwood Village, CO 80111
1-800-237-6124
www.lu.com

Library of Congress Cataloging-in-Publication Data

Haven, Kendall F.
    Voices of the American Civil War : stories of men, women, and children who lived through
the war between the states / Kendall Haven.
        p. cm.
    Includes bibliographical references and index.
    ISBN 1-56308-905-X (paper)
    1. United States--History--Civil War, 1861-1865--Personal narratives. 2. United
States--History--Civil War, 1861-1865--Social aspects. 3. United States--History--Civil
War, 1861-1865--Study and teaching. I. Title.

E655 .H27 2002
973.7'092--dc21
                                                                                    2001054384

Contents

Introduction xi
How to Use This Book xvii

Before the War at a Glance: The Gathering Thunder 1

Free or Slave?: The Bloody Fight for Kansas, 1855–1857 4
    At a Glance...4
    Meet Charles Dickson 5
Free or Slave? 6
    Aftermath 12
    Follow-up Questions and Activities...13
Righteous Raiders: John Brown's Attack on Harpers Ferry, October 17, 1859........15
    At a Glance...15
    Meet Meriam Dean 16
Righteous Raiders...17
    Aftermath 25
    Notes 25
    Follow-up Questions and Activities...25

1861 at a Glance: Passions Boil; the Bloodshed Begins! 29

Dodging the Bullet: President Lincoln Moves to Washington, February 1861 31
    At a Glance...31
    Meet Allan Pinkerton 32
Dodging the Bullet...33
    Aftermath 39
    Follow-up Questions and Activities...40
Growin' Cotton; Killin' Yankees: Southern Prewar Popular Attitudes, April 1861 42
    At a Glance...42
    Meet Thomas Parker 43
Growin' Cotton; Killin' Yankees...44
    Aftermath 48
    Follow-up Questions and Activities...49
Tea Cakes, White Lace, and Bloodshed: First Battle of Bull Run
    (Manassas), July 1861 51
    At a Glance...51
    Meet Ambrose and Abigail Patterson 52
Tea Cakes, White Lace, and Bloodshed 53
    Aftermath 58
    Follow-up Questions and Activities..59

1862 at a Glance: A Deadly Tug of War 61

Supper, Shoes, and Shovels: Supplying a Civil War Army, February 1862............64
At a Glance..64
Meet Captain Walter Huster...65
Supper, Shoes, and Shovels 66
Aftermath 73
Follow-up Questions and Activities...73

Sister Spies: Life in Occupied Winchester, Virginia, March 1862.........................75
At a Glance..75
Meet Rebecca and Hannah Wright 76
Sister Spies 77
Aftermath 83
Follow-up Questions and Activities...84

Turn Coat, Turn Coat: The Civil War in the Far West and the Battle of Glorieta Pass, February–March 1862...86
At a Glance..86
Meet Hector Manuel Alianjo 87
Turn Coat, Turn Coat..88
Aftermath 95
Follow-up Questions and Activities...95

Private Petticoat: Female Army Spy, May 1862..97
At a Glance..97
Meet Sarah Edmonds 98
Private Petticoat...99
Aftermath 103
Follow-up Questions and Activities...104

Patriotic Pride and Prejudice: Northern Blacks' Efforts to Enlist, Summer 1862 106
At a Glance...106
Meet John Mercer Langston..107
Patriotic Pride and Prejudice 108
Aftermath 114
Follow-up Questions and Activities...114

Iron Might: Ironclad Naval Battles on the Mississippi, June 1862..........................117
At a Glance...117
Meet James Brady 118
Iron Might..119
Aftermath 126
Follow-up Questions and Activities...127

"Reporting" for Duty: Civil War Field Reporters, September 1862.....................129
At a Glance...129
Meet George Smalley...130
"Reporting" for Duty 132
Aftermath 140
Notes 141
Follow-up Questions and Activities...141

Ounce of Prevention; Pound of Cure: An Army Field Surgeon, Fall 1862............144
    At a Glance...144
    Meet Thomas Wallsly 145
  Ounce of Prevention; Pound of Cure 146
    Aftermath 152
    Notes 153
    Follow-up Questions and Activities..153

1863 at a Glance: The Tide Turns 157

A Place of Freedom: Southern Slaves' Efforts to Gain Freedom, March 1863.....160
    At a Glance...160
    Meet Ransom Wilson and Elizabeth Wilson 161
  A Place of Freedom 162
    Aftermath 166
    Follow-up Questions and Activities..167
Diary of Death: The Siege of Vicksburg, May–July 1863 169
    At a Glance...169
    Meet Lucy McRae...170
  Diary of Death 171
    Aftermath 176
    Follow-up Questions and Activities..177
Home Town Horror: The Battle of Gettysburg, July 1863...........................179
    At a Glance...179
    Meet Amelia Harmon...180
  Home Town Horror 181
    Aftermath 187
    Follow-up Questions and Activities..187
Striking Out: New York City Draft Riots, July 1863 190
    At a Glance...190
    Meet Michael Ryan 191
  Striking Out 192
    Aftermath 197
    Follow-up Questions and Activities..198
Sounding Battle: The Life of a Drummer Boy at the Battle of Chickamauga,
    September 1863...201
    At a Glance...201
    Meet Ephram Dillard...202
  Sounding Battle 203
    Aftermath 210
    Follow-up Questions and Activities..211
Fast, Dark, and Quiet: Confederate Ships That Ran the Union Naval Blockade,
    October 1863 213
    At a Glance...213
    Meet Captain John Wilkinson...214
  Fast, Dark, and Quiet..215
    Aftermath 222
    Follow-up Questions and Activities..223

1864 at a Glance: The Endless End 225

Southern Shortages: Southern Women's Soldiers' Aid Society Efforts, 1864 228
    At a Glance 228
    Meet Virginia DeLouise 229
    Southern Shortages 230
      Aftermath 236
      Follow-up Questions and Activities 236
Battle "Cries": Women Working in an Army Hospital, May 1864 239
    At a Glance 239
    Meet Sally Tompkins 240
    Battle "Cries" 241
      Aftermath 248
      Notes 248
      Follow-up Questions and Activities 248
Tears of Fear: Army Deserters, May–June 1864 251
    At a Glance 251
    Meet Edward Cooper 252
    Tears of Fear 253
      Aftermath 258
      Follow-up Questions and Activities 259
Unsung Heroes: Black Union Regiments and the Battle of the Crater,
    July 30, 1864 262
    At a Glance 262
    Meet Private Alfonse Mathews 264
    Unsung Heroes 265
      Aftermath 271
      Follow-up Questions and Activities 272
A "Fair" Fight: Northern Women's Efforts to Support the Sanitary Commission,
    September–November 1864 275
    At a Glance 275
    Meet Mary Livingston 276
    A "Fair" Fight 277
      Aftermath 283
      Notes 284
      Follow-up Questions and Activities 284
Sweet Potatoes, Cotton, Tobacco, and Quinine: A Wealth of Smuggling,
    October 1864 286
    At a Glance 286
    Meet Jedediah Turner 287
    Sweet Potatoes, Cotton, Tobacco, and Quinine 288
      Aftermath 296
      Notes 296
      Follow-up Questions and Activities 296

1865 at a Glance: Johnny Comes Marching Home ... .299

United We Fall: Lee's Surrender, April 1865 301
    At a Glance 301
    Meet Captain James Fielder 302
  United We Fall 303
    Aftermath 310
    Follow-up Questions and Activities 310
Skeleton Heroes: Prisoners of War, April 1865 313
    At a Glance 313
    Meet Chester Lumpkin 314
  Skeleton Heroes 315
    Aftermath 321
    Notes 322
    Follow-up Questions and Activities 322

Epilogue: The Road to Reconstruction, April–June 1865 325
Glossary 329
References 333
Index 339

Introduction

The American Civil War was fought on battlefields in 10,000 places spread from Oregon to Florida, from Los Angeles, California, to Vermont. A naval battle was fought off the coast of England, and Confederate and Union ships fired on each other north of the Arctic Circle. There were 5,500 military actions (encounters between opposing forces) during the four years of the war. Nearly a hundred of them were classed as major battles. Yet two states suffered the brunt of the fighting and tramping armies: Virginia and Tennessee. Hardly a day went by that one or more armies were not trampling into mud, camping on, and living off these two states.

In a greater sense, the "real" Civil War was fought in the minds and souls of 40 million Americans. Each person's wrenching, grieving struggle with loyalties and beliefs matched the well-reported bloody, brutal fighting for intensity and importance. These four years of vicious combat shaped our modern America and defined our view of government and society, of who we think we are. More than the revolution that founded our country, more than any other period or movement in our national past, the Civil War was the defining moment in American history.

So what were these people like who split temporarily in two and fought to answer whether parts of the Union could secede, whether the federal government could usurp states' rights, whether slavery could continue?

In 1850 there were 31 states, 16 free and 15 slave. From 1850 to 1861 three free states entered the Union (California, Oregon, and Kansas). No slave states were added. By 1860 the South had lost all hope of gaining voting superiority in the U.S. Senate. After Lincoln, an avowed abolitionist, was elected president (his name didn't even appear on the ballot in 10 Southern states), many in the South felt pushed into the proverbial corner.

South Carolina seceded from the Union in December 1860, followed by Mississippi, Florida, Alabama, Georgia, Louisiana, and Texas in January 1861. That left eight slave states still undecided. By June 1861 four seceded (Arkansas, Tennessee, North Carolina, and Virginia); four did not (Missouri, Kentucky, Maryland, and Delaware), although Maryland came close on several occasions.

The sides were chosen, battle lines drawn. Eleven slave states would battle the 24 remaining states of the Union for the right to secede and to continue slavery. West Virginia, Nevada, and Nebraska were added to the free state column during the war, bringing the final total to 27 free versus 11 slave.

The North had many advantages. In the North were 22 million people and more than 100,000 factories employing over 1 million workers. The North encompassed over 80 percent of the nation's coal mines, over 70 percent of its railroads, and almost 95 percent of its stock of trains and rail cars. The North also had more than 30 percent more land in agricultural production than the South, and it outproduced the South in every agricultural category except for the major plantation crops: cotton, tobacco, indigo, and hemp.

The North exported far more food than the Southern states ever did. The North also controlled more than 80 percent of all U.S. bank deposits and more than 70 percent of all gold reserves. Northern public education was well established throughout the free states, and more than 75 percent of all colleges lay in the North.

The South, by contrast, contained fewer than 9 million people, with more than one-third of them being slaves. It had fewer than 20,000 factories employing well under 100,000 workers. The South had few trains and a widely scattered, unconnected, and uncoordinated rail system.

What the South did have was cotton, and cotton was king. The export value of Southern cotton drove the Southern economy and supported a very gentile and gracious standard of living for Southern white middle- and upper-class citizens. Interestingly, cotton had not emerged as a major plantation crop in the South until 1800. If Eli Whitney hadn't invented the cotton engine (gin), it is possible that it never would have been economically worthwhile for the South to fight a war for independence.

The South also had passion on its side. Southerners boiled with deep, all-powerful loyalty to the South and to their cause that the fractionalized North could not match. When the first shot was fired on Fort Sumpter, citizens in Charleston, South Carolina, swarmed into the streets to cheer. Church bells rang across the South. Parties and celebrations were held in thousands of Southern towns, cities, and villages.

The response was different in the North. There the war was viewed more as a grim and unpleasant necessity, as a nasty duty. There was little joy, no eagerness, just the sad determination that Northerners must march off and teach the fool Southerners a lesson.

Lincoln said that there would be no war unless the South was the aggressor, that the Union would not assail the South. But the South overflowed with fierce and joyous passion and confidence. That enthusiasm and cocky confidence carried the Confederacy a long way in the first two years of the war—almost to victory—before beginning to wane in 1863.

What of the men and boys who slipped on uniforms and fought the war? Approximately 2.5 million had joined the Union's armed forces by the war's end. Some 1.6 million saw combat; 400,000 of those who did so died (either in battle or from disease).

Only 1.25 million joined the Confederate armies and navies. Almost 300,000 of them died (again in battle or from disease). More American soldiers died during the Civil War than in all other American wars combined (the American Revolution through Desert Storm). Furthermore, for every soldier killed on the battlefield, at least two were wounded and maimed.

On the bloodiest single day of the war, 27,000 were killed or wounded along Antietam Creek, Maryland. In the single bloodiest battle of the war, more than 56,000 casualties piled up at Gettysburg, Pennsylvania. More than 7,000 fell in less than 20 minutes at Cold Harbor, Virginia (the fastest slaughter of men during the war). These numbers are almost unimaginable. Such carnage, such devastation is beyond our modern sensibilities. The list of casualties at Gettysburg published after the battle took up more than 20 pages of fine print in the *New York Times*.

Still the men and boys of gray and blue enlisted, marched, ate lousy food, went on short rations, and itched to fight some more. They were not, of course, really the "gray and blue." Many Confederates wore butternut-colored uniforms. Officers usually wore gray. By 1863 many Confederates wore whatever they could find.

Two Louisiana regiments first dressed in blue uniforms, changing to butternut only after having been shot at by confused fellow Confederates. Similarly, regiments from Indiana, New York, and Vermont were dressed in "standard gray." One New Jersey regiment wore yellow uniforms. Several New York (Zoave) units wore red. Early Civil War battlefields were colorful spectacles. By the end of the war, blue and butternut were the colors most often seen. Variety had given way to survival.

Almost half the soldiers in the Federal army were less than 18 years old. Some 150,000 were under 16 when they marched into combat. Only 600,000 were over 21. A 25-year-old was a rare old-timer in the Union forces.

Confederate soldiers were of a wider variety of ages because a greater proportion of the male population was drawn into uniform. Approximately 72 percent were between the ages of 18 and 29. Only 8 percent were under 18 (until the closing year of the war, when many more boys joined home guard units). Sixteen percent were in their thirties, 3 percent in their forties, and about 1 percent in their fifties (nearly senior citizens in that era). Several Confederate privates were well into their seventies.

The war was called by many names in its own time: the War for Southern Independence, the War of States' Rights, Mr. Lincoln's War, the War of Southern Rights, the War of the Rebellion, the War Against Slavery, the War Between the States, the War Against Northern Aggression, the Yankee Invasion, the War for Abolition, the War for Separation, and the War for the Union.

Why did Americans fight? Why did they slaughter each other, bloody the landscape, and destroy the Southern economy? Many historians have claimed that slavery was the central cause of the war, but there were others. Lincoln said repeatedly that he was fighting only to preserve the Union and that, if he accomplished that goal, he didn't care whether he freed the slaves.

From the Southern perspective, a major issue was "preserving states' rights." The federal government had for some time been steadily encroaching on the sovereign turf of states, eroding states' rights and powers. Whether or not that infringement was legal under the Constitution and acceptable to the various states was a valid point of contention. Did the federal government have the authority to tell states what they could do? Could it legally refuse to allow a state to leave the Union?

This was an important question for the states and the federal government to resolve. But was it worth a war? Was that constitutional question worth 700,000 dead? It is highly unlikely that the states' rights issue would have erupted into open conflict had it not been for the powder-keg question of slavery.

The Civil War was fought both to preserve the Union and to defend states' rights against that Union. However, those issues flared into war only because underneath them both lay the issue of slavery. Without slavery there would not have been a Civil War in the 1860s.

Slavery had been a part of Southern culture for more than 200 years by the time the first shot of the Civil War was fired. There were almost 4 million slaves at the beginning of the war. The institution of slavery was viewed in the South as essential to Southern culture and economic success. Slavery had existed in every state in the nation at the time of the American Revolution. Although by 1810 it had been peacefully abolished in every Northern state, its importance in the South grew year after year, as did the political and economic power of large slaveholders. Slavery made the war worth fighting.

The first shots of the war were fired at Fort Sumpter in Charleston harbor by the South Carolina militia. The fort surrendered, and no one was killed.

The first dead in the war were civilians who fell on the streets of Baltimore, Maryland, in early May when a mob armed with stones attacked a Union infantry regiment from Boston as they marched through town on their way to Washington. The soldiers panicked and opened fire, killing 20 in the angry crowd before the rest were able to flee to safety.

The first major battle occurred in early July along a small creek in northern Virginia, Bull Run, near the town of Manassas. However, there had been more than 40 small engagements before that date.

The American Civil War was truly a war of firsts and innovations. It featured the first use of railroad artillery; the first submarine; the first "snorkel" breathing device; the first periscope; and the first land mines, trench warfare, and flamethrowers. Civil War armies used the first military telegraphs, naval torpedoes, aerial reconnaissance (hot air balloons), repeating rifles, breech loading carbine rifles, ironclad ships, steel ships, organized medical and nursing corps, and machine guns.

Even with all these new and improved weapons, Civil War fire was so inaccurate that many soldiers estimated that it took a man's weight in lead to kill a single enemy. A Federal supply expert concluded at the war's end that each Confederate shot had required the use of 240 pounds of powder and 900 pounds of lead.

The Civil War also featured the first military draft (both North and South instituted a draft, with the Confederate draft first) and the first income, withholding, liquor, and tobacco taxes. It saw the first American bread lines and food riots, the first press corps to travel with the armies, and the first battle photographs. (More than 6 million war photos were taken. Ironically, after the war nobody wanted them, and over 99 percent were destroyed.)

The Civil War saw the first use of bugle calls by an army, the first U.S. black officer (Major M. R. Delany), the first American president to be assassinated, the first commissioned army chaplains, the first use of anesthetics for battle wounded, the first Department of Justice, the first use of aerial psychological warfare (copies of Lincoln's Amnesty Proclamation were dropped behind Southern lines from high-flying kites), and the first use of camouflage (the mist-gray and brown paint used to disguise Southern ships used as blockade runners).

Yet these lists and statistics do not convey even a shadow of the terrible, heart-wrenching drama that was the Civil War. The story of the Civil War can only be told by seeing its many facets through the eyes of real people who were forced to endure the conflict.

When we think of the Civil War, we conjure up stirring and thrilling images of long lines of soldiers, shoulder to shoulder, long muskets extended, marching steadily across a deadly space as they close with equally long lines of the opposing army. We imagine the deafening thunder of roaring cannons, the jets of flame and smoke shot into the summer air, the ground-shaking passage of 1,000 horses and mounted cavalry, and fluttering flags snapping in the breeze.

We typically do not picture destructive riots against the war in a dozen major Northern cities, seemingly endless rows of wounded and sick soldiers slowly and painfully dying in pitifully inadequate hospitals, or crowds of desperate women rioting for food on Southern streets. Nor do we think of the Southern economy slowly being strangled to death, children being swept into conflict and battle, and smugglers gaining immense wealth by whisking scarce goods across the undulating border between North and South. We do not picture ironclad riverboats pounding away at each other with deadly cannon fire on the Mississippi or brave and wily Confederate seamen risking life and limb to run the Union naval blockade and deliver goods to keep the Confederacy alive.

Yet these were all part of the Civil War. The stories of these men, women, and children are every bit as much a part of the Civil War as are a soldier's accomplishments on the battlefields.

The Civil War affected virtually every facet of every American's life. Certainly, the battles have always fascinated me: Shiloh, Chickamauga, Fredericksburg, Antietam (Sharpsburg), Bull Run (Manassas), Gettysburg, Vicksburg, Chancellorsville, Petersburg, Cold Harbor, the Wilderness. Each sends a chill down my spine as I try to imagine what it must have felt like to stand in one of the long lines of infantry before the battle, knowing many would die, many more would be wounded and face the terror of a surgeon's knife; knowing there would be no shelter, no cover; knowing that we would have to stand bravely on the field and ignore the deadly musket balls whining past. But not all of the powerful stories of the Civil War happened on battlefields, and every one is worth telling and hearing.

This book presents 27 stories designed, collectively, to paint a broader and more complete image of the war. When selecting individual stories to research and mold for this book, I sought to find voices that lived through that raging inferno that we do not normally hear, voices that we *should* hear to build a more complete image of the war, the period, and its significance in our history. I wanted to focus this book not on tactics and battles (although several are described), but on how the war affected and forever changed the people of America. I chose to select stories to tell that would reveal important themes and trends about how the war changed society, the economy, beliefs, and life. In my research I sought individuals and events whose story I could document that would allow me to tell the story of the effects of the Civil War on the American people. Of course, space limitations have resulted in many worthy stories being omitted: the *Hunley*, the *Alabama*, most of the battles; the Underground Railroad (still active during the war); the political struggles of Jefferson Davis and Abraham Lincoln; the process of forging and forming regiments; the work of Dorothea Dix, Clara Barton, and Elizabeth Blackwell—these and many more have had to be passed by. Readers are encouraged to explore their libraries and the resources at the back of this book to learn more about these topics.

There are thousands of riveting stories from this four-year upheaval. In this book are more than two dozen stories we should all know. All the characters in this book are real and the events are historically accurate; dialogue has been inferred based on known personality traits and outcomes of conversations and events. When they were available, I used actual recorded conversations and statements.

Many names were used for blacks during the mid-nineteenth century; they were all intentionally derogatory. Such terms were part of the effort to belittle and denigrate blacks into a lesser class of humans. These slang terms and names are not used in this book, and although "black" is not a term that was used at that time, it is used in the stories in this book.

The vast majority of white Americans—even most of those favoring abolition—believed that blacks were an inferior race. This deep-seated and insidious prejudice permeated every corner and aspect of life in America in the mid-nineteenth century.

In several stories in this book I have included dialogue for black story characters, most of it presented in dialect. Far from being an attempt to perpetuate racial stereotyping, I was fortunate enough to find black characters to use in my stories who wrote about the events and characters portrayed here. These blacks gave me, in their own words, the speech patterns, dialect, and vocabulary of the story characters I have used. In reading this dialogue the reader must remember that blacks were not allowed to attend school. Imagine how you would struggle with the structure and pronunciation of a foreign language without the benefit of a teacher and formal education.

I owe a deep debt of thanks to many individuals and groups who assisted in my research for this book. In particular, I owe a great debt of thanks to Roni Berg, the love of my life. She graciously spent many hours honing these stories and deserves much of the credit for their clarity and flow. I owe great thanks to Barbara Ittner, who was the guiding force behind the design and content of the follow-up questions and activities in this book as well as in *Voices of the American Revolution*.

I also want to thank the library staffs at the Sonoma State University Salizar Library and the Sonoma County Public Library. They performed heroically in helping me identify and locate many of the references I needed to complete my research. Several of the women's stories in this book are based on stories in a previous book of mine, *Amazing American Women* (Libraries Unlimited, 1996). That book is a good source of additional stories of incredible and unheralded deeds of the women who helped to forge, build, and create this country.

Finally, I owe a great debt of thanks to you, the reader, for being curious enough to venture into these pages and into these histories. Enjoy! Then research and create your own stories of this fascinating period to share.

How to Use This Book

The stories in this book are organized chronologically through the years of the Civil War. They can be used as sources of information about major events of the war and as kickoff points, or inspirations, to lead students to further research on related or suggested topics.

The stories are appropriate for read-alouds with younger children and for silent reading and research by older students. Whether used for story time or as assigned reading, these stories greatly enhance and enliven the study of history by creating vivid, diverse, close-up perspectives on the many different experiences of various groups of Americans during the Civil War.

Each story is self-contained and can be used singly, grouped with other stories with a similar theme, or as part of an extensive study of the Civil War period. It is recommended that readers review the "At a Glance" summaries that precede each year's group of stories as well as the introductory and accompanying material provided with each story. Readers should refer to the glossary to clarify any unfamiliar terms.

A brief summary ("At a Glance") of the major events for each year precedes the two to eight selected stories that take place during that year.

Each unit is divided into five sections:

- **At a Glance**. This section creates background context and perspective for the following story. It includes a brief review of the events and historical figures that led up to, and set the stage for, the events depicted in the story.

- **Meet the Character**. Because most of the characters are not well-known historical figures, this section provides a brief biographical sketch of each story's main character to help students better understand the events of the story and place this story within the context of that character's life.

- **The Story**.

- **Aftermath**. This section quickly summarizes the effect on the overall war of the events described in the story. It also includes summaries of what happened after the story as a direct result of the events described in the story and of what the events in the story meant to the main character's later life.

- **Follow-up Questions and Activities**. Follow-up questions and activities are divided into the following four sections that provide different types of discussions and activities and different levels of complexity. Few of these activities require equipment or supplies. Teachers should feel free to modify and restructure the activities to best meet their own needs and those of their students.

1. *What Do You Know?*—Factual questions for students to discuss and answer that demonstrate their knowledge and understanding of the story and its major historical events and figures.

2. *Find Out More.*—Reading and research questions and topics that extend the events and characters of the story into a wider context and expand student understanding beyond the limits of the material presented in the story.

3. *Make It Real.*—Multidisciplinary learning extension activities for students to undertake that provide demonstration of key concepts and themes of the story.

4. *Points to Ponder.*—Advanced discussion questions and essay themes designed to incorporate student beliefs and values into the discussion of story themes and events.

Before
the War
at a Glance

The Gathering Thunder

When the Constitutional Convention met in 1789, every state in the Union still allowed slavery, and slaves lived in every state. Massachusetts was the first state to outlaw slavery. By 1810, slavery had been banned in every Northern state, but a new cash crop, cotton (made economically possible by Eli Whitney's invention of the cotton engine) made plantation production more profitable than ever before in the South. Plantations depended on slavery, and the Southern economy depended on plantation production of cotton. Even as slavery was outlawed in the North, it was becoming more entrenched in the South.

Even in colonial times a strong distrust and lack of unity existed between North and South. The vernacular, culture, religious origins, and economic development of the two regions differed markedly. Throughout the first half of the nineteenth century, that friction steadily increased as Northern society grew more vehemently anti-slavery and Southern society became more entrenched in the necessity for slavery. In 1820 the Missouri Compromise created a system for ensuring continual political balance between slave and non-slave states and seemed to allow the two cultures to coexist.

However, new Western territories continued to be added to the country. Each addition reopened the fight for political dominance in the U.S. Senate between slave and free states. Every attempt to find a workable compromise seemed to be thwarted by some polarizing event. For example, the decision by the U.S. Supreme Court to return a former slave named Dred Scott to his owner even though he lived in a free state caused outrage among abolitionist groups, who demanded that slavery be abolished everywhere in the nation.

The fight over whether Kansas would be admitted as a free or slave state turned bloody in 1856–1857 when pro-slavery forces poured into the territory from Missouri and abolitionist forces flooded in from free states from Massachusetts to Illinois.

When it became clear that Kansas would be a free state, Southerners howled in protest and began the call to secede from the Union.

In October 1859, fanatical abolitionist John Brown attacked the federal weapons arsenal at Harpers Ferry, Virginia, planning to use the weapons to arm a slave revolt. The raid failed. However, it terrorized Southern slave owners, reopened the bitter dissensions over slavery, and further polarized the nation.

The year 1860 was a busy one for discovery and invention. Louis Pasteur discovered that heat could kill germs (pasteurization). The washing machine was invented, Otis invented his first steam-powered elevator, the world's first oil well was drilled in Titusville, Pennsylvania, and Sir Henry Bessemer invented the process we still use for making steel. However, in the United States all talk seemed to be on politics. In November, Abraham Lincoln, an Illinois lawyer with openly declared abolitionist leanings, was elected president even though his name did not appear on the ballots in 10 Southern states.

Many in the South considered this election to be the final straw, the ultimate insult (and threat) to their culture and way of life. As a group, Southern politicians felt that they had been backed into a corner, losing any chance of gaining future political dominance—even of political survival—in a national Union now led by their philosophical opposite. Southerners felt forced to act.

And act they did. South Carolina seceded from the Union just before Christmas 1860. Most thought this was a political maneuver designed to win important concessions for the South, but then Mississippi, Florida, Alabama, Georgia, Louisiana, and Texas followed suit by February 1, 1861.

Incumbent President James Buchanan felt helpless in the face of this threat and hoped to avoid open conflict before he slipped quietly out of Washington at the end of February 1861. By the time Lincoln was inaugurated on March 4, 1861, the country seemed to be heading unavoidably toward war.

Lincoln tried to smooth the Southern ruffled feathers and especially to appease Virginia politicians. Virginia, he felt, was the key to avoiding open war. Lincoln's efforts, although initially successful (both Virginia and Arkansas initially voted *not* to secede), came to naught when South Carolina (the instigator of the rebellion) fired on Fort Sumpter in Charleston harbor.

Once the firing started, Southern blood, it seemed, was much thicker than Union political water. Between April and June 1861, four more states, including Virginia, seceded, and the war was on.

Key Events Before the War Began

Date	Event
1820	Missouri Compromise is passed.
1850	Compromise of 1850 is created.
1850	California is admitted as a free state.
1855–1857	Bleeding Kansas.
1857	Dred Scott case inflames abolitionists.
1857	Oregon is admitted as a free state.

October 1859	John Brown raids Harpers Ferry arsenal, attempting to start a slave revolt.
December 1859	Brown and his surviving raiders are hung.
November 6, 1860	Abraham Lincoln is elected president.
December 20, 1860	South Carolina secedes.
January 9, 1861	Mississippi secedes.
January 10, 1861	Florida secedes.
January 11, 1861	Alabama secedes.
January 19, 1861	Georgia secedes.
January 26, 1861	Louisiana secedes.
February 1, 1861	Texas secedes.
February 8, 1861	The seven seceded states form the Confederate States of America.
February 18, 1861	Jefferson Davis is inaugurated as president of the Confederacy.
February 28, 1861	President Buchanan leaves office.
March 4, 1861	Lincoln is inaugurated as president.
March 6, 1861	Jefferson Davis, president of the Confederacy, calls for 100,000 men to volunteer for one year of service in a Confederate army.

Free or Slave?

The Bloody Fight for Kansas, 1855–1857

At a Glance

It was all about slavery and political power. In 1819, 11 states were slave states; 11 were free. From that moment on, each side struggled to ensure that the other side never gained a majority in the U.S. Senate. Each new state and territory was bitterly fought over.

The Territory of Nebraska became a focal point of this contention in the early 1850s. In 1854, Senator Stephen Douglas of Illinois proposed splitting Nebraska Territory into two territories: Nebraska and Kansas, in order to break the congressional deadlock. Nebraska would enter as a free state, and, in accordance with the Compromise of 1850, Kansas residents would decide the matter for themselves with a vote.

New England abolitionists saw in the Kansas vote a chance to gain permanent political advantage in the Senate. They created first the Massachusetts Aid Society and then the New England Aid Society that paid settlers to rush to Kansas and stuff the ballot boxes in favor of freedom.

Southerners recognized the danger these new immigrants represented and organized pro-slavery forces in neighboring Missouri to pour across the border to win that vote in any way necessary.

On election day in the spring of 1855, heavily armed Missouri Border Ruffians rode *en masse* into Kansas to flood the ballot boxes with their illegal votes and, more importantly, to prevent at gun point many free staters (those favoring a free Kansas) from voting at all.

4

Pro-slavery forces easily won the election. Their legislature and governor immediately outlawed all opposition to slavery. Kansas free staters howled that the vote was rigged and that the pro-slavery government was a bogus legislature. Free staters refused to accept the new territorial government or its laws.

New England aid changed to Sharps rifles and cannons hoping to win Kansas back. The stage was set for a brutal mini-war that would decide—through new Kansas congressmen once the territory became a state—the critical balance of pro-slavery and anti-slavery power in the nation. It was a time for Kansas to bleed.

Meet Charles Dickson

Charles Dickson was born on a Kansas farmstead along the Kaw River in 1839. His father (Robert Dickson) had also been born on a Kansas farm in 1814. His mother (Abigail Weston) migrated west with her parents in 1829 (at the age of 13) from Indiana when they heard of the opportunities to homestead free land in the territory. Charles and Abby met in 1833 and were married a year later. Their Kansas farmstead produced wheat and corn. They also had chickens, pigs, dairy cows, a small heard of cattle, grew their own vegetables, and tended a grove of apple trees.

Charles had one older sister, Catherine, two older twin brothers (one died of disease as a young child), and one younger brother, Joseph.

Free or Slave?

"**P**eople are going to get theirselves killed tonight. I just know it," muttered 16-year-old Charles Dickson as he squatted in the deep shadows next to a farmhouse in the soft, moonlit night of November 27, 1855, and listened to the gurgling of the Wakarusa River in eastern Kansas. The air felt crisp, but it didn't bite like winter yet.

"Quiet!" hissed Colonel Sam Wood. "Voices carries at night."

Charles hunched tighter to block the cold and stared at the distant ridgeline. Then, well over half a mile away, an object seemed to move. At first Charles thought it was a trick of his eyes. But then another moved, and another.

Charles's heart raced. Perspiration beaded on his forehead. There were riders coming. Over a dozen of them. Charles's breath came in ragged gasps. He knew those riders were heavily armed. If anything went wrong, a lot of them—and a lot of the 15 free state militia hiding here in the dark—would die.

Suddenly Charles didn't feel like a brave militiaman snatching up the sword of freedom. He felt like a little boy stuck in the middle of a shooting war where he didn't belong. Or maybe he was just scared to squat in ambush in the cold, dark night with a loaded gun.

He ground his teeth together, now angry at himself. Maybe his father had been right. Maybe Charles wasn't ready to fight toe-to-toe with an enemy, knowing one of them would die. The thoughts made the young lad even angrier.

Joining the Free State militia had sounded exciting to a 16-year-old Kansas boy who had never seen anything more exciting than the birth of a new calf. The militia leaders had talked of glory and duty and had spun his head full of passion for freedom. They made him feel that he would be shamed if he didn't strike a blow against slavery.

Charles's father said, " 'Tain't any slaves 'round here and twern't no talk of it, neither, 'til those New England abolitionists moved in like they were on a holy mission to save the world and started ranting about blocking slavery." He paused to rub callused fingers across his chin. " 'Course, if slavery *did* come here, that'd be a bad thing."

That was what had made Charles finally decide on this clear morning of November 27 to join the militia and single-handedly keep Kansas free, hoping his father would say, "Bless you, boy. You make me proud." But he hadn't said that at all.

Charles tried to swagger into the barn when he announced, "I'm joining the Kansas militia, Pa."

His father, squatting on a milking stool, didn't even pause to look up. "No you ain't."

Charles spread his feet as if itching for a fight. "You sayin' I can't?"

Mr. Dickson looked up from his milking stool. "I'm saying you're not joinin' the Kansas militia. Yer joinin' the New England anti-slavery militia."

Charles had wanted the reassurance of his father. He hadn't wanted a confusing debate. "We're fighting for Kansas," Charles insisted.

"This isn't a Kansas fight, boy. It's Missouri and Massachusetts fighting, and no reason for you to git involved."

Charles scoffed, "*Somebody* has to be brave enough to save our freedom!"

"We already got all the freedom there is to git," said his father. "This ain't our fight, boy. Let it be."

Charles had felt that he couldn't back down. "Slavery is everybody's fight."

Mr. Dickson sighed. "Remember, boy, every fight's got to be somewheres. Just 'cause they picked *here*, that don't make it your fight." He pointed a warning finger at his son. "Don't go nosin' into fights that aren't yours or you'll get more than you bargained for."

And then Charles had said something he knew he'd regret forever. "You're just *afraid* to stand up and fight."

His father lashed out and hit him—hard. Charles stumbled out of the barn and rode straight to Lawrence to join up with Colonel Wood for this militia assignment.

The bruise on Charles's cheek still throbbed as he squatted in the chill dark. He couldn't decide if it throbbed with pain or embarrassment.

"Steady boy," hissed Colonel Wood. "And be ready! Shoot fast and true at the first sign of trouble. I don't expect that Missouri imposter to give up his prisoner without an argument."

The Kansas pro-slavery government had created counties and made political appointments. One of those counties was called Douglas County. One of those appointments had been to name Missouri postmaster Sam Jones the sheriff of Douglas County. Free state Kansas supporters refused to acknowledge the government, any of their appointments, or even the names they had given to the counties.

Earlier this day of November 27, Sheriff Jones had ridden out to arrest Jacob Branson for the murder of a pro-slavery man who had been shot in retribution for the killing of a free stater—a murder about which Jones had done nothing. This group of 15 free state militia was waiting at Blanton's Bridge on the Wakarusa River to keep the bogus sheriff from unjustly hanging a good-standing free stater.

Charles could hear the creak of leather saddles and could smell pungent horse sweat. He could feel each step of the approaching horses vibrate through the ground.

Militia Colonel Sam Wood was the first to step into the road, blocking the riders' path. The rest of the free staters followed. Most carried Sharps rifles at the ready—rifles provided by the New England Aid Society. A few, like Charles, carried older muskets.

The lead rider, Sheriff Jones, stopped not more than 10 feet from the free staters. He leaned on his saddle horn and scornfully scanned the line of men before him. Behind the sheriff, the other riders hastily slid muskets from their cases and pulled pistols from holsters.

The sheriff said, "Sam Wood. What brings you fellers out on this fine evening?"

"I've come to get my friend, Jacob Branson."

"As legally appointed sheriff of Douglas County I have arrested him."

Colonel Sam Wood scratched his head in mock confusion. "I never heard of a Douglas County, and we don't have a sheriff. But I once heard of a Missouri postmaster name of Sam Jones."

Jones glared at Wood. "I *am* the law, the legal law. Try to stop me and I'll arrest you or shoot you—or both."

Charles realized his hands trembled and his squirrel gun rattled in his grip. Then his stomach dropped as he heard the sharp metallic click of every musket, rifle, and pistol hammer—except his—being pulled back and cocked. Soft moonlight reflected off of the cold, steel barrels of three dozen weapons pointed across the tiny open space between opposing forces. Tension, fear, and anger lay thick as a smothering blanket.

Belatedly Charles realized he hadn't cocked his musket and slowly slid his left thumb back to drag the hammer into the cocked position, hoping no one would notice or hear.

Charles glanced left and right along the line of men around him. Only two had been born in Kansas. Nine were New Englanders who had been in the state less than a year. He studied the faces under the wide brims on the riders across from him. He recognized almost all of them as men from the loosely organized force known as the Missouri Border Ruffians.

"Pa's right," he thought. "It's Missouri and New England that's itchin' to fight. And good 'ole Kansas folks better duck and git out the way. 'Cause blood is surely gonna flow."

One of the free staters called, "Jacob Branson, come on over to our side."

"They'll shoot me," Branson answered from the back of the riders.

Wood answered in a voice calm as a summer breeze, "If they do, we'll shoot every one of them."

Sheriff Jones's gaze settled on young Charles. He growled, "Boy, what are you doin' out of your mama's sight at night?"

"I'm 16 . . ." Charles began.

"Don't interrupt your elders and your betters, boy! You're breaking the law if you don't do exactly what I say. *Right now* you reach over and grab away the rifle of the man next to you and hand it over here."

The sheriff stretched out his hand and glared at Charles.

"Steady boy," hissed Colonel Wood.

The sheriff snarled, "Do it, boy, or I'll hang you."

Colonel Wood said, "Don't listen and don't move, boy."

Arm still outstretched, the sheriff pawed the air with his finger. "What's your name, boy?"

Charles gulped. "Char . . ."

"Don't say a word to this Missouri postmaster, boy," interrupted Colonel Wood. "You just aim at a spot between his eyes."

The sheriff actually smiled as he said, "Last chance, boy. You either help me or you'll be the first to die."

Seconds seemed to stretch into hours. Charles could hear the blood rushing past his young ears as his heart raced. Cold sweat beaded across his forehead. He shivered with dread and cold. His knees wobbled so that he was sure his pants were flapping in the night. He hoped it was dark enough so no one would notice and laugh.

Charles sucked in a breath of bitter-cold air. "I ain't gonna do it!" he yelled at the sheriff. But his voice squeaked some and he blushed a deep scarlet.

Wood and some others chuckled. Charles ground his teeth in frustration. Colonel Wood continued, "Now that that's settled, Jacob, you come on over here on our side."

Step by slow step Jacob Branson walked his horse forward, weaving his way between the gun barrels, his eyes squeezed shut for fear he'd feel a bullet tear into his back at any moment.

When Branson reached the open space between slave and free forces, one of the sheriff's men muttered, "Hell, I ain't a' gonna' shoot. 'Taint worth it."

The tension was shattered. Gun barrels inched lower. Sheriff Jones pointed a gloved finger at Sam Wood. "You are now an outlaw, Sam Wood. And that means I got a duty to come after you. Maybe not today. But you just know that I'm comin'." His voice rose. "All of you! If you don't lay down your weapons and surrender to me right now, I *will* hunt you down and hang you."

Then he pointed at Charles. "Especially you, boy. You just made a big mistake. I'd say you'll live to regret it, but you won't live at all."

Charles's heart felt like ice. It was impossible to breathe. His stomach churned and felt sick. He thought he was about to throw up.

No one moved except for Sam Wood who smiled and bowed, "You come right ahead and try, Postmaster Jones." He patted the side of his rifle. "I ain't fired yet. And I still got a free state bullet right here with your name on it."

Guns were slowly uncocked and reholstered. After the last Missouri rider cleared the bridge, the free staters whooped in a great cheer of victory and relief. Hats sailed into the air. Everyone wanted to slap Jacob Branson on the back and shake his hand.

Charles slumped to the ground, panting. He felt like only the tension had held him upright, and now that it was gone, his legs caved in beneath him.

"Back to Lawrence, boys," called Sam Wood. "We have to build up the town's defenses. There were a dozen of 'em today. But they'll be hundreds of 'em tomorrow!"

Charles rode sullen, quiet, and full of embarrassment and foreboding while the riders around him whooped in wild celebration of their victory. Charles felt that he had failed the test. He felt more like a laughingstock—a fool—than a conquering hero. Charles drifted to the back of the pack and turned west to creep home over eight miles of open Kansas prairie.

Charles dismounted outside the barn just at dawn, knowing his father would already be up and milking inside. Charles hesitated at the double doors, expecting sneers, ridicule, anger, and maybe another hard right fist. Suddenly he felt that he deserved it—deserved it all. His father sat quietly milking while the events of the night poured out of Charles. The boy began to tremble, remembering the sheriff glaring just at him. Then he grimaced, expecting his father to lash out with a vicious "I told you so."

His father asked only, "Did you take your hat off?"

"Did I what?" Charles stammered.

"Take your hat off. Did he see your face?"

"Uhhh, no. I didn't, Pa. And the moon was behind us. No, he never clearly saw me."

Mr. Dickson nodded and wiped his hands. "He was bluffin', just blowing off steam."

"But Pa, he said he'd *kill* me!"

Mr. Dickson rose and placed both hands on his son's shoulders. "He doesn't care about you. He cares about votes in the Federal Senate." He rubbed the corners of his mouth with callused fingers. "Still, may be best you stay tight around the farm this winter. Back off some from your militia duties for a while."

A wave of relief washed over Charles. "Yes, sir!" He already dreaded the thought of reporting for militia duty again and facing the other men from last night's patrol.

Mr. Dickson started out of the barn, then paused. "Oh, and Charles, Kansas will stay free because homebred Kansas folks want it that way. This hullabaloo will blow over and life will go on. You'll see." Then he smiled and softly added, "Let me see your cheek." As his fingers brushed over the bruised flesh, he said, "I'm sorry, son. That weren't right of me. Oh, and I wouldn't mention that business with the sheriff to your mother."

At breakfast, Charles's sister and younger brother demanded to hear every detail of his night's adventure. Charles shrugged, glancing warily at his mother. "We just rode patrol. Nothing exciting happened at all." Charles's father nodded and smiled. His mother suspiciously studied the faces of her husband and son. "Where'd that bruise come from?"

"I bumped a tree in the dark, Ma," Charles answered, but didn't dare look in her direction when he said it.

Winter's bluster and fury hit Kansas hard and cold, locking down the troubled state, shooing everyone inside. Still, the sheriff's threat hung like a crushing weight on Charles's shoulders. At night he could almost feel a coarse rope tighten around his neck. He sometimes woke choking and screaming in a cold sweat.

Charles Dickson drove the family wagon into the town of Lawrence to pick up supplies on the beautiful spring day of April 19, 1856. His mind had begun to ease, to relax, as spring spread its warm enchantment across the rolling Kansas prairie. He no longer peered warily around each corner searching for a sheriff's badge.

Early spring flowers painted the hills around Lawrence. But Charles was more fascinated by the raised earthen forts that had been built at each end of town. Shiny cannon barrels poked through gaps in the heavy earthen walls. The free state Kansas flag fluttered above each stronghold. Men with Sharps rifles paced the walls.

Around 2:00 in the afternoon guards spotted the boiling dust cloud of a large body of approaching riders and sounded the alarm. Tight-faced militiamen snatched up their rifles and rushed into position on roofs or in the forts.

Several recognized Charles as they hurried into position. "Where you been, boy? We could have used you building these forts." "Hey, Charles! Why haven't we seen you this winter?"

Charles blushed and lowered his eyes toward the dust of Massachusetts Avenue. "I—uh—had too much work around the farm this winter. My pa wouldn't let me go."

Colonel Sam Wood strutted down the middle of the street, ensuring that his men were in position and ready. "Glad to have you back, son. Why don't you join A Company in the south fort? We'll need every man today, I think."

"I . . . uh . . . didn't bring my musket, sir. I just rode in for supplies."

Colonel Wood scowled. "Every militiaman, son, is required to be armed and ready at all times." The colonel marched toward the south fort and the growing dust cloud thundering up the road.

Charles's throat tightened. He had struggled all winter to escape this awful dread. With one dust cloud, it tightened again around his young neck. "What's going on?" he asked one of the militiamen.

"It's that Missouri sheriff come to arrest Colonel Wood. We've always shooed him away. But it looks like he brought enough men to mean it this time."

Charles gulped. "Why does he want to arrest the colonel?"

"That business back in November, I think," the militiaman answered.

Charles's stomach dropped. His hands began to shake. Then he hesitated. He had raised his hand and joined the militia. The colonel was right. He had a duty to stay. Besides, he didn't want to look like a coward. Charles pressed his back against a store wall in the deep shadows to watch and wait, and hope for his safety.

Sheriff Jones and his six deputies rode confidently into Lawrence at the head of a U.S. Army cavalry company commanded by Lieutenant McIntosh. The free staters in the Lawrence fortifications paused, unsure of how to react. They were intent on driving Sheriff Jones away. But they were loyal Americans, and none dared fire on the army.

A large crowd poured into Massachusetts Avenue to gawk at the soldiers. Grumblings rumbled through the crowd. All felt cheated and betrayed that the army—*their* army—sided with the bogus government.

Jones announced that he had come to arrest Sam Wood and others wanted for abducting a prisoner from an appointed representative of the legal government of Kansas.

Someone near Charles yelled, "There ain't nothin' legal 'bout that bogus government."

In a flash Jones's pistol was out and pointed at the man. "Lieutenant!" Jones cried. "If that man or any other makes another revolutionary remark against the legal government of Kansas, arrest them. If they resist in any way, shoot to kill."

The lieutenant sat quietly on his horse at the head of his hundred-man column. Charles noted that he hadn't said "yes," but neither had he said "no" to Jones's demand.

Jones and his deputies fanned out through the crowd, surrounded by the angry glares of Lawrence citizens. Many fingers pawed the air next to holstered guns, itching to draw on the Missouri impostors. But the cavalry unit had spread into small clusters scattered up and down Massachusetts Avenue, carbines drawn and resting on their hips.

The crowd slowly grew to fill the street. Muttered, hateful protests rumbled like distant thunder through the crowd. The air felt charged with electric tension. Charles's skin crawled under the fierce pressure.

By 4:00 P.M. Jones had rounded up Sam Wood and six others. Charles's heart ached to escape and also to bravely begin the charge that would free the sheriff's captives. He was afraid he'd be spotted if he ran now. He was afraid he'd be spotted if he stayed, hiding in the shadows by a rain barrel.

Would these militiamen be hanged? Would *he* be arrested and hanged, too? Twice Jones had passed through the crowd near Charles. Once Charles heard him say to his deputies, "There was a boy with them. Keep an eye out for the boy."

Charles's feet felt locked in cement. He couldn't make himself move. He had to struggle to breathe. Would Jones's gun suddenly point at him? What would he do if it did? Faint? Whimper for mercy? Or would he be able to bravely spit back that Kansas was a free state and Jones was a bogus sheriff? Charles sucked in deep breath after breath, trying to draw courage from the tension-filled air.

By 5:00 P.M. Jones called to Lieutenant McIntosh, "We'll camp here tonight and drag these seven prisoners back to Pawnee in the morning." He pointed at one of the houses on the southwest side of the street. "Hold the prisoners in that house and place your tents just behind."

The lieutenant nodded and passed the orders along to his men.

Darkness fell. But the tension continued to mount. The crowd milled about in the street. Jeers, slurs, and curses against Jones and the bogus government echoed across town.

An occasional shot rang out, and Charles, who had now forgotten all about the supplies he was supposed to deliver to his father, tensed at each one, waiting to see if it would start a chain reaction of musket balls blasting across town.

One of the soldiers rushed to the front porch of the commandeered house where the lieutenant perched in a rocking chair. "Lieutenant! The sheriff is dead!"

The news flashed like lightning through the crowd. "He's dead! We killed Jones!" The crowd exploded into a jubilant celebration. The racket of banging on pots and pans, singing, and cheering thundered across the night prairie. Shots were fired into the air.

Lieutenant McIntosh scooped up the sheriff from his tent (badly wounded, but not dead) and ordered his troops to assemble to leave Lawrence. They hastily struck tents, carbines drawn and at the ready. Guards roughly herded the prisoners, tightly roped at wrists and ankles, into a commandeered wagon.

The crowd pressed closer, hornet mad, held off only by 100 gleaming carbine barrels. A shot rang out from a second-story roof. It was followed almost instantly by a dozen jabs of flame and smoke as others in the crowd fired. One soldier and two of Jones's deputies spun to the ground.

The soldiers instinctively fired back, mostly at the roof. People screamed and scattered. Four Lawrence citizens (two militia, one woman, and one civilian man) tumbled to the street. Blood flowed across Kansas dirt.

Lieutenant McIntosh bellowed, "Cease your fire! These are civilians. I will not slaughter civilians." He turned toward the angry crowd. "The sheriff is wounded. One more shot—just one more—and we *will* open fire." The cavalry thundered off into the night before another volley could be organized.

Charles arrived home just before midnight without the supplies he had been sent to buy. A doomed helplessness filled him. Sheriff Jones would be back, maybe with a thousand soldiers next time. How long would it be before his gaze fell on Charles and the spark of recognition lit in the sheriff's frightening face?

Charles wearily climbed onto the porch. A gas lantern burned bright in the sitting room. Charles's father was meticulously cleaning and oiling the family's pistol and two rifles.

He glanced up and solemnly nodded as Charles stepped inside. "Glad you got away, son," was all he said.

"Wha . . . what are you doing, Pa?"

"I was wrong to think the fight would go away on its own, son. They killed good Kansas folk tonight. Now it *is* our fight and we're sure as hell gonna fight it."

The bloody war for Kansas was just heating up.

Aftermath

Three weeks after Sheriff Jones was shot, Lawrence was overrun by pro-slavery militia units. Several office buildings and houses were burned, presses were dumped into the river, two saloons were smashed and looted. Abolitionist reporters inflated the raid into a barbaric and vicious ransacking. Actually, the only person injured was a pro-slavery militiaman struck by falling timbers from a burning building.

One week later John Brown and a unit of 28 free staters dragged seven captured pro-slavery men to Osawatomie Creek and murdered them in revenge for the Lawrence raid. A week later, the free state settlement at Osawatomie Creek was burned to the ground in revenge. A dozen locals were killed. Confrontations—violent and nonviolent—became a way of life. Formal military units were rarely involved. Most clashes occurred between armed gangs and informal militia groups. Property was destroyed or stolen, threats were made, and the killing droned on through 1856 claiming over 200 lives. That period has been called both Bleeding Kansas and Bloody Kansas.

Initially, the military advantage lay fully with the pro-slavery forces who, because they had won the rigged 1855 elections, owned the state legislature. But free state reinforcements poured in from the Midwest via Nebraska. Advantage swung toward free state forces. By mid-September, Federal troops intervened to separate the warring "armies." President Pierce appointed a new territorial governor. Sporadic violence continued until mid-1857 when new, carefully monitored elections were held, and Kansas was declared a free state.

When Nebraska and Kansas both applied to enter the Union as free states, the South felt attacked and cheated. Southern politicians howled their outrage at this Northern "trickery." Southern leaders became far less willing to consider compromises. Their rhetoric and demands grew increasingly hard-line and more repugnant to Northerners. Because of the political debacle of Kansas, the country took a giant step down the path to war.

Charles Dickson lived his entire life in Kansas. His brother and sister both moved west (one to Oregon, one to California), and both urged Charles to follow them to the promised land along the Pacific. Charles married a local Kansas girl in 1861 only weeks before the bombardment of Fort Sumpter started the Civil War, had a large family, and died in 1911, having been a farmer all his life and local Manhattan, Kansas, politician for many years.

Follow-up Questions and Activities

1. **What Do You Know?**

   - Why did the rest of the country care whether Kansas became a slave or free state? What advantage could be gained either way? By whom?

   - Were most of the participants in Bleeding Kansas fighting native Kansans? Where did most of them come from? Why?

   - Who provided the support for the two opposing forces that formed in Kansas?

   - A territorial government for Kansas was elected in the spring of 1855. Why didn't everyone in the state accept the results of that election? Who did accept it? Who didn't? Why?

   - What was really at stake in the fighting in Kansas? Why was it worth fighting over?

2. **Find Out More.** Here are important topics from this story for students to research in the library and on the Internet. The reference sources at the back of this book will help them get started.

   - What did Kansas look like before the mass migrations of the 1850s? Who lived there? What did they do? What did it look like before any white settlers arrived—say, in 1820? Who and what lived there then?

   - Kansas was not the only territory into which white settlers were flowing. Research westward migration during the 1850s and 1860s in America. Which groups or types of people migrated west? Where did they settle?

   - Research the Massachusetts and New England Aid Societies. How many immigrants did they induce to move to Kansas? How much monetary support did they give to these settlers? How much money did they spend on weapons for the free state forces in Kansas?

   - New York newspaper publisher, Horace Greeley, first uttered the famous phrase, "Go West Young Man." What was he talking about and where did he want people to go? Research Horace Greeley's life, work, and political beliefs.

   - One of the three leaders of the Kansas Free State forces, Colonel Sam Wood, is featured in this story. The other two were civilians named Charles Robinson and James Lane. Research these three individuals. Where did they come from? How long had they been in Kansas? What happened to them after the violence settled down in early 1857?

   - Research the pro-slavery Missouri Border Ruffians. Who were they? How many were there in the organization? Who created this military force? Who supported it? What happened to them after 1857?

   - The fanatical abolitionist, John Brown, lived in Kansas for almost 10 years. What is he famous (or infamous) for during the Kansas struggle?

   - Near the end of the Civil War, Confederate Colonel William Quantrill began to attack and raid settlements in and around Kansas. The government labeled him a common criminal with an outlaw gang. He called himself a crusader for

Confederate liberty. For several years, he terrorized the West. Research Colonel Quantrill's life and military career. Find as many men as you can who got their start with Quantrill and went on to become famous Western outlaws.

3. **Make It Real**

- On a map of Kansas locate the free state centers (Lawrence, Topeka, Manhattan, etc.) and the pro-slavery centers (Lecompton, Pawnee, Shawnee Mission, etc.). Which areas of Kansas were controlled by each side of this fight? How many lived in each area in 1850? in 1855? in 1860?

- Draw a map of America in 1855 including all states and the borders of established territories. Shade free states and territories blue. Shade slave states and territories red. Shade those areas green that had not yet been committed to either side.

- Pretend that you are a native Kansas child, then that you are a New England child who has just moved to Kansas from some Northern city. Imagine that it is early 1856 and, as each of these two children in turn, write a letter to the other. What would each talk about? What would each say? What would their vocabulary, diction, and writing look like? How would they feel?

- Can you find examples of other periods in American history when one part of a population refused to accept an election's results? What happened? Compare those cases with what happened in Kansas in 1855 through 1857.

4. **Points to Ponder**

- What makes a government legitimate? Who is to say that one government or election is legitimate and another isn't? What happens when one group refuses to accept an election outcome?

- In this story Charles joined the Kansas militia partly for selfish reasons (to show he was brave, for excitement, to show that he was a man, etc.). Do you think these are legitimate reasons to join a military force? What are examples of good reasons to join? At what age do you think someone is old enough to decide whether to join the military?

Righteous Raiders

John Brown's Attack on Harpers Ferry, October 17, 1859

At a Glance

By the beginning of 1859, "Bleeding Kansas" had cooled down. Public and political tempers still bubbled but were veiled beneath a thin crust of cooperation. President Buchanan hoped for a long-term peaceful compromise on slavery. A sense of peace was on the upswing.

However, rumors had begun to circulate in Washington that a group of radical abolitionists was planning something *big*. The rumors spoke of an army being raised, weapons being stockpiled, and funding being sought for a private war. The names John Brown and Frederick Douglass were quickly linked with the plan, as were those of many notable and upstanding abolitionists. Most denied any knowledge of a planned act of civil disobedience.

In June 1859, President Buchanan and two cabinet members were warned in an anonymous letter that John Brown was planning to attack a federal arsenal in Maryland. They ignored the letter because there was no federal arsenal or armory in Maryland.

It never occurred to Washington politicians that a short two-minute walk across the B & O Railroad bridge over the Potomac River from Maryland stood the federal arsenal, rifle works, and armory at Harpers Ferry, Virginia.

Peace and war hung in a delicate balance as the quiet summer of 1859 rolled by. Still, everyone knew that one violent spark, one dangerous misstep and the country would plunge down the road toward war.

And still no one worried about John Brown or about the frightfully vulnerable federal arsenal at Harpers Ferry.

Meet Meriam Dean

Born a slave on a Georgia plantation in 1823, Meriam Dean seemed destined to spend his life as a lowly field hand. In his spare time, young Meriam helped in the blacksmith's shop and forge. There he quickly gained a reputation for being clever at fixing things, especially the plantation's temperamental cotton gin. When Meriam turned 16 he was pulled out of the fields and made a full-time handyman.

Meriam lost an eye at the age of 18 in a freak accident. The back swing of an over-seer's whip flicked into his face as he walked, unaware, out of the cotton barn. When Meriam turned 22, he wanted to marry one of the house slaves on the plantation, but the owner refused permission.

Deeply embittered, Meriam became a sullen loner. In 1854 he bought his freedom and drifted west to Kansas. There he met John Brown. In 1857 Meriam wholeheartedly joined John Brown's fanatical abolitionist movement and traveled east with Brown and three of his sons to plan the attack on Harpers Ferry.

Righteous Raiders

A crude wooden table separated the two men as they glared at and slowly circled each other in the dim front room of a Maryland ranch house.

"I've seen slavery right up in my face," snarled one, a 37-year-old black man named Meriam Dean. "You don't know nothing' 'bout slavery, white boy."

"I don't need some uppity black telling me what I know and don't know," snapped the other, a strapping youth named Will Leeman. Leeman, at 19 years old, had traveled from Maine to join John Brown's crusade to end slavery and was the youngest of the raiders crammed into this rented ranch house. Outside, drizzling showers had drifted through the afternoon, giving a bleak look to the steep hillsides on this Sunday afternoon of October 16, 1859. Fall had been steadily marching down the mountains the last several weeks, painting colors as it went. The day's rain made the fall brilliance seem drab and forlorn.

Inside the house, 18 men had been holed up for two weeks. Tempers had been rubbed raw by the endless wait to strike, to declare their glorious purpose to the world.

These 18 men represented the bulk of the 21-man force assembled by fanatical abolitionist John Brown to launch his slave revolt that would rid the country of the horror of slavery. Brown promised that the revolution would draw in slaves from every corner of the land, who would throw off their shackles and rise up with a cleansing fire to heal the bitter wounds of a troubled and sinful land.

The men had often heard these passionate words from their leader. Some barely knew what the individual words meant. Most were unable to read or write. Still, they all knew the fierce passion that glowed in John Brown's eyes when he spoke. His raging fire burned bright inside each of them. His energy filled their souls and made them feel bigger and purer, like noble crusaders. They loved the feeling of importance and worthiness that being a part of this great adventure gave them.

But these were simple men of action, and the waiting had taken its toll. So Dean and Leeman slowly circled the rough table—one an older, black man, with a leather patch over his lost eye and flecks of white scattered like fine powder through his hair; the other a white, pale, serious man, with a lumberjack's thick shoulders, arms, and hands. Leeman's right hand flipped open the clasp over his 12-inch knife. "We're here to start some killin'. Might as well start with *you*."

Dangerfield Newby, the oldest raider at 48 and a freed black man from Tennessee, tried to step between the two. "We can't end slavery by killin' each other."

"Out of my way," Leeman snarled. "Or I'll kill you both."

Watson Brown, oldest son of John Brown, also stepped forward. "Put it away, Will. I'll have no fighting among the raiders. Our enemy is out there." He jerked his thumb west across the Maryland border toward Virginia and the town of Harpers Ferry.

Oliver Brown, at 22 the youngest and least broody of the three of Brown's sons who had joined their father's crusade, added, "Father promised we'll strike tonight. Be patient just a little longer."

Will Leeman shrugged and slumped onto a chair. "Been too patient, too long. Got me an itchy trigger finger I hain't used for an over-long time."

White teeth flashed in Dean's deep black face. "Any time, Yankee. Any time."

An hour later John Brown and the final two raiders tied their horses to the house's front rail. Everyone hushed as Brown swept in. He was tall, gaunt, and deeply weathered, and his stringy white hair flowed in wild tangles to his shoulders. Those who met him remembered his fierce wildness, a tangible danger that radiated from this man. His face glowed with boundless hatred and passion that seemed forever to search for targets he could attack and destroy.

"We strike tonight," he announced. "Owen (Brown's other son) and Stewart Taylor (a Canadian) will stay at the Maryland schoolhouse to organize slaves and supporters who join our cause from the east. The rest of us will divide into three groups. Henry Kagi, John Copeland, and Lewis Leavy will hold the rifle works on the Shenandoah River side. Dauphin Thompson, Edwin Coppoc, Aaron Stiven, Jeremiah Anderson, and Charles Tidd will secure the two bridges. The rest of us will secure the armory and arsenal and wait there for the masses to rise up to our battle cry!"

The men pounded tables, rattled chairs, and cheered. Meriam Dean frowned and scratched his head. "Why don't we start down in 'Bama or Georgia where most of the slaves are? Why this nothin' of a town?"

Harpers Ferry was a disheveled collection of ramshackle cabins scattered up a slope called Bolivar Heights from the small flatland where the Shenandoah and Potomac Rivers merged and gurgled leisurely on toward Washington.

That flatland was where the walled federal arsenal compound (musket factory) and armory (weapons storage building) sat. Hall's Rifle Works sat on one of the larger islands that dotted the Shenandoah River side of the peninsula.

Brown's eyes gleamed as he answered. "Because the guns are in Harpers Ferry—a federal arsenal bristling with the weapons our slave army will need. And because there are no troops to guard those weapons. Once armed and deadly, we will sweep south like holy hellfire—50,000, then 100,000, then a million strong to wipe the scourge of slavery from the Earth!"

The men cheered. One fired his rifle up through the ceiling. But Dean still seemed bothered. "So we capture the town tonight, and then . . . what? . . . Just wait? How's that gwine end slavery?"

Brown spread his arms, long bony fingers extended like lightning rods. "We chosen few will ignite the revolution tonight at Harpers Ferry. Five million slaves are the powder that will explode across the country; we are the spark that starts the great fire." He threw back his head. "Rise up, oh, ye oppressed and take my sword! Vengeance will be yours!"

John Brown's raiders left to join destiny at 8:00 P.M. Fifteen rode through the dark in two wagons. Six rode horses.

At 10:00 P.M. the men cut the telegraph wires connecting Harpers Ferry to cities in the East. Two riders peeled off to secure the Maryland schoolhouse. At 12:30 A.M. on the chilly morning of Monday, October 17, in the filtered light of a quarter moon, John Brown's army of 19 (13 whites and 6 blacks including 4 ex-slaves) rode grimly across the Potomac River bridge into Harpers Ferry.

Meriam Dean rode silent and brooding in the wagon. He knew slavery had to end. He believed in John Brown's vision. It was the tactics of this night that made no sense. How could they end slavery in an out-of-the-way town that had few slaves? Dean grunted and figured he'd best shut up, do his job, and hope for the best.

Three guards were posted at each of the two bridges into town. The remaining 13 gathered at the Wager House Hotel, a rambling stone building next to the federal arsenal and armory, that doubled as the train station.

At 1:00 A.M. Brown nodded toward the hotel door. His army rushed to conquer the armory buildings. Two elderly night guards were easily overpowered and tied to the metal arsenal gate.

At 1:30, Kagi, Copeland, and Leavy clattered across town in a wagon to capture Hall's Rifle Works. They sent two more stunned guards as prisoners back to the arsenal. Brown grabbed Barclay Coppoc (one of the Coppoc Quaker brothers who had joined Brown's effort in the early spring), scruffy John Cook, and Osborne Anderson (who was always described as just plain mean) and sent them into the neighborhoods of Harpers Ferry to take hostages.

"Kill someone for me!" Will Leeman called after them eagerly.

"No killing!" Brown shouted. "I want hostages—healthy and unharmed."

"What for?" Osborne asked, obviously disappointed at the restrictions.

"To announce to the world that the messenger of God has arrived and to show that we are serious about our revolution!"

The three men scurried into the deep shadows of night and fanned out to search for anyone foolish enough to be awake and available for kidnapping. They soon returned, herding lines of dumbfounded local citizens before them.

Meriam flopped onto the arsenal's cold cement floor and listened to the deep quiet. A foreboding gnawed at his stomach. *How slaves gonna know we're here? . . . What we gwine do if'n nobody comes?*

At 2:00 A.M. sporadic gunfire signaled the arrival of a few curious townsfolk who sensed something was amiss in their sleeping town. Hayward Sheppard, a respected black man and the railroad night watchman, was gunned down and lay dying on the baggage platform.

"That's jus' great!" railed Meriam Dean. "First thing we do is kill a black man. *Now* what slaves will be willing to join us?"

"Silence!" bellowed John Brown as he herded the last of the hostages into a back room of the arsenal's fire station. "He sided with the plantation owners anyway."

"How do you know *that*?" pressed Meriam.

John Brown stood at the door of the main arsenal building, head cocked to one side, and ignored his irate raider. "It's too quiet." He pointed at meek Will Thompson and at his own son Watson. "Take the wagon. Gather more prisoners. I believe there is a nephew of George Washington living nearby."

"You mean President George Washington?"

"Yes. Bring him."

"Why?"

"To spread the word that we are here and the time of salvation and judgment has arrived! Oh, and free some slaves and bring them, too."

Two raiders stood guard over the bewildered hostages, who demanded to know what was going on. Only six raiders remained in the main arsenal building.

"Well, here we are," Meriam Dean muttered. "But I don't see no revolt happening. All I see is us trapped inside these walls."

"The revolution has already begun!" answered John Brown, eagerly rubbing his hands. "We now own $7 million worth of weapons and the word of our arrival is rippling across the countryside. Woe be unto the slave holder!"

Brown stepped proudly outside the arsenal gate and raised his fists to the sky. "Black men arise! Slaves revolt! Come to me and I will lead you to victory and freedom!"

By 3:00 A.M. the wagon was back, overloaded with five white hostages (including Colonel Lewis Washington) and nine black slaves.

"Arm the slaves and put them on guard duty," Brown ordered.

Watson soon returned, nervous and agitated. "Only two of the slaves will join us, Father. The others insist on being prisoners."

John Brown burst into the back fire house room where the prisoners were crowded together. He pointed at one of the blacks with one long, thin hand and held out a musket in the other. "Rise up, oh, ye oppressed, and claim your rightful freedom."

"No, suh," came the response from a terrified man crouching in the corner.

"You are free. Now rise up and fight for freedom for all!"

"Only Colonel Washington can set me free, suh."

"But he's the enemy, the vile creature that has imprisoned you!"

The voice was almost too soft to be heard. "No, suh."

"Then you," Brown bellowed, offering the musket to another of the slaves.

The man pushed back harder against the wall and lowered his head so he wouldn't have to respond at all.

Exasperated, Brown turned to go. "Watson, stay here with the two blacks who had sense enough to join us. Maybe the others will come around in time."

Dangerfield Newby pointed toward the prisoners' room where seven of the nine "freed" slaves huddled with the other terrified prisoners. "I thought you said all slaves would revolt and join us, Mr. Brown."

"Silence," hissed Brown, listening at the door. "Our word is spreading."

The bells of the Lutheran church at the top of Bolivar Heights began to chime, spreading the alarm across the countryside. Rolling mists gathered thick along both rivers. Osborne Anderson and John Hazelett were sent scurrying to the armory building to stand guard there.

Meriam lingered in the fire house and asked one of the slaves, "Why don't you want to be free?"

"I ain't a' gonna steal it. No, suh."

"Don't call me *suh*," Meriam snapped. "I used to be a slave, jus' like you."

"You steal your freedom?" asked the frightened man.

"No. I bought it. Saved up for 10 years to buy it."

The man nodded. "I'm saving up to do the same. I'm gonna do it legal and be able to walk straight down the sidewalk with my head held high and proud!"

A captured woman asked, "Are we going to be killed?"

"Seems to me, anyone who owns a slave deserves to die," Meriam answered.

The raiders waited. The mists gathered into a thick, cold blanket of fog that covered the flatlands of Harpers Ferry. A reluctant dawn spread gray, ominous light through leaden clouds. Fog and mist swirled through town, making the flatland appear evil and foreboding. And still they waited.

"They ain't comin'!" muttered Dean as he paced. "No one's going to come!"

Leeman barked, "Sit down! You make me nervous."

"Maybe you *should* be nervous," answered Dean. "No one's a' comin'."

John Brown's eyes glowed. "The spark has been lit. Glory and righteousness must follow. They *will* arrive."

Will Leeman, Will Thompson, and Barclay Coppoc climbed to the tiny windows that looked out over the arsenal wall. Each nervously strained to see something through the swirling mist.

But Meriam Dean continued to pace and mutter. "Ain't no sparks. Ain't no slaves pourin' in. I'm afeared no one will even know we *tried* to end slavery."

By 8:30 an angry crowd had edged its way cautiously down Bolivar Heights. "Hallelujah! Throw open the gates," Brown commanded. "Our army of salvation is beginning to arrive."

Two muskets were fired from the mist-shrouded crowd. Both bullets gouged deep chunks out of the brick wall of the arsenal. Brick dust sprayed over John Brown. Oliver rammed into his father, tumbling the old man back inside. "They aren't with us, Father. They're shooting *at* us!"

A crowd of more than a thousand milled about in the open flats near the arsenal compound. Three small companies of militia from nearby towns formed the backbone of the crowd. Locals followed behind the militia, spilling from their houses carrying squirrel guns, axes, knives, and pitchforks.

"But where are the slaves?" demanded John Brown. "Where are our abolitionist supporters?" The old man sank to the floor with a distant look on his face.

"Father? What should we do?"

"How did opposition to our movement form so fast? Why haven't any slaves arrived?"

"Father?!"

The elder Brown stared without seeing the men around him. "This is not how it is supposed to happen."

Dean peered through a smudged window. "Lawd have mercy! I seen crowds like *that* in Georgia. And they done *hang* black folks."

John Brown recovered his composure. "If we must start the war ourselves, then so be it. Break out the top windows and fire at the slavemongers. If we need to escape later, we still hold the bridges."

Time dragged by in the awkward standoff. Musket shots pounded harmlessly into the brick arsenal building and compound walls. Popping sounds and puffs of smoke marked the return fire from the raiders. Two locals were hit. One was already drunk and laughed at the sight of blood flowing from his wounded hand.

Meriam Dean grumbled angrily between his unaimed shots, "Here we are doin' our part. But where is your army, Mr. Brown? Where is your revolt? All I see is a lynch mob."

Watson swung his musket, slamming it into Meriam's back. "Hush up, Dean. You can't talk that a' way to our leader."

Will Leeman unsnapped his long skinning knife. "I should of killed you when I had the chance."

"Any time, Yankee," answered Meriam, rubbing his sore back as he lay on the floor where he had landed after Watson's blow.

At 11:30 A.M. rolling roars of musket fire were followed by cheers from the crowd. Six men scrambled over a back wall of the arsenal compound and into the main building. The guards had abandoned the bridges.

Edwin Coppoc, leader of the bridge guards, sadly shook his head, still panting to catch his breath. "Must have been 80 militia stormed down the bridge from the Maryland side, guns blazing. Weren't no sight of slaves or help. . . . No way we could hold out against so many. We had to beat it back here." He paused to look around the nearly empty room. "Where are the slaves, the army?"

"There aren't any," snapped Meriam Dean. "No one's come."

"No one?" Edwin repeated.

John Brown again slumped to the floor. "We needed the bridges to get reinforcements from Maryland. Where are the slaves? Don't they want to be free?" He sank his head into his hands. "I don't understand."

"We're trapped here, aren't we?" Will Leeman demanded. John Brown vacantly stared back at him.

"The slaves and supporters will come," Brown pronounced, fire again blazing in his eyes. "We simply must hold out until they arrive. Glory comes to those who wait. John Cook and Charles Tidd will take one wagon and speed to the Maryland schoolhouse and bring back whatever reinforcements Stewart and Owen have gathered there."

Cook and Tidd glanced at each other and then eased up to peer through broken windows at the mob. One of their wagons was still parked near the Maryland railroad bridge. That bridge was now undefended because all the militia had gathered in the town's square.

With a fatalistic shrug, the two men slipped out a back window and over the compound wall. They were hurtling across the railroad bridge before anyone in the Harpers Ferry crowd noticed.

At 1:30 John Brown said, "I need to know how our men are holding out in the rifle works." He glanced around the room. "Dangerfield. You go."

"Me? But I'll get killed!"

"Nonsense. Sneak out the back and stay by the river, behind the crowd. You'll get there and back in no time. Besides you're a free black, not an abolitionist. They won't harm you."

Eyes wide with terror, the old black man slid out a back window and crawled crab-like, bent low and out of the crowd's sight.

One of the militia guards shouted, "There goes one of 'em!" and pointed at the black man scurrying along the river's edge down Shenandoah Street. Over 200 shots roared in his direction. Windows were shattered. Doors were chipped and smashed. Dangerfield jerked into the air as he was hit by a dozen bullets, looking as if pulled by hidden puppet strings, and sprawled onto the rocks at the edge of the train track.

The dense smoke from the massed gunfire drifted downriver as the echo of the volley's thunder died against distant hills. Then the crowd went wild, venting their day-long frustration on the poor dead man. By the time they were finished, the mutilated body was an unrecognizable pulp.

Meriam Dean froze in horror, gaping through a corner of one window. He had never seen such brutality, had never dreamed it was possible. "Sweet merciful Jesus! They gwine chop us up! We can't end slavery if'n we's chopped into little pieces!" Watson flung Meriam to the floor. "Hush up, Dean! My father *will* succeed."

"This isn't right . . . ," John Brown repeated as he shook his head as if trying to clear his head of the defeats of the day. "Vengeance is *ours*, not theirs. Perhaps we should pray."

"You better do more than pray, old man," Will Leeman shouted. "You have to get us out of here. Did you see what they *did* to Dangerfield?"

Watson shoved Leeman hard against a wall. "Don't speak that way to my father. He'll tell us what to do." Then Watson turned hopefully to his father, who had dropped to his knees, head bowed.

Volleys continued fast and thick from the crowd. Bullets whined through shattered windows and thudded into the now pockmarked inner walls.

Meriam growled as he reloaded, "What are they waiting for? Why don't they rush us and get it over with?"

"They're afraid we'll kill the hostages," Watson answered. "It was smart to take so many."

John Brown's head snapped up. "You're right, son. We must use the hostages and negotiate. Something has gone dreadfully wrong, I fear. We must leave this place and replan our attack."

Brown's gaze fell on quiet Will Thompson, dutifully loading and then firing high over the heads of the crowd so as not to hurt anyone. "Will, you must negotiate our safe passage. Take one of the prisoners with you as a shield."

At 2:20 P.M. all firing from the arsenal stopped. John Brown cracked open the arsenal building door and waved a white cloth. A moment later Will Thompson fearfully stepped outside and pushed the gate open slightly to negotiate. He carried the white flag in one hand and dragged one of the hostages in front of him for protection.

Shouts and angry confusion met Will's offer to talk. Two dozen beefy fists grabbed Will, beat him bloody, and dragged him to the Galt House saloon to be interrogated by the militia. Cries of "Kill them! Kill them!" rumbled through the crowd.

"Lawdy, Lawdy! You see *that*?" hissed Meriam. An icy panic gripped his stomach. "*That* is what is surely gwine happen to all of us, one by one. . . ."

"The Maryland reinforcements will come," said John Brown to reassure his terrified band. "I am God's messenger. I *will* prevail!"

But Will Leeman would not be calmed. "You've killed us all, you old fool! We're trapped! We'll be torn apart. Well, I'm not going to sit here and die!"

Will raced to a back window, slithered out, and scaled the back wall. He climbed over the B & O Railroad tracks and splashed into the wide, shallow Potomac, hoping to wade and swim across to freedom in Maryland. He was shot a dozen times, his body flailing as it was riddled with musket balls. Then it slid slowly into the river and twisted with the swirling eddies as it drifted toward Washington.

"They're cuttin' us down one by one," Meriam muttered. "One by one."

At 3:00 P.M. a roar of gunfire erupted from the south side of town. "They're storming the rifle works," announced Watson. Each raider felt the noose tighten around his throat as their last outlying group fell to a hail of bullets.

"It is not supposed to be like this," John Brown insisted. "I am not supposed to fail!" He sighed and rubbed his bristly chin. "We will gather those of us that remain in the arsenal's fire engine house with the prisoners in the back room. Osborne and Hazelett will have to fend for themselves in the armory building. It's too dangerous to bring them across open ground to join us."

"I come to end slavery or die tryin'," Meriam said to several slave hostages. "It looks like we're gonna have a bunch of the dying part and none of the ending part. . . ."

One slave asked, "How kin you end somethin' that's always been?"

"'Cause it's wrong!" Meriam answered and stomped into the front room of the fire house.

"Watson, I am going to depend on you," announced John Brown. "You will negotiate our passage. Aaron Stiven and Shields Green will go with you to make sure you are not grabbed."

The fire house door cracked open. Three raiders eased out, waving a white flag of truce. The surly crowd ignored the flag and shot them all. Aaron Stiven dropped dead. Watson, badly wounded, crawled back to the engine house wailing in pain. Shields Green lay moaning in a pool of blood while the crowd cheered and laughed.

The cheers turned again into a rallying chant of, "Kill them! Kill them!"

The dull gray clouds opened into a hard, cold rain as Watson lay moaning in his father's arms. The growling mass of humanity outside lost its enthusiasm and dispersed. But first, as a final blow against John Brown's raiders, they burst into the Galt House, dragged Will Thompson out, and shot him so full of lead that his body sank in the river like a stone.

"One by one . . ." Meriam repeated, wide-eyed in fright.

At 6:30 P.M., Edwin Coppoc cried, "Here they come!"

A large force of militia attacked the armory compound. John Brown bellowed, "Drive them back! Kill them!" His few troopers loaded and fired through the small windows with blurring speed. The deafening roar of gunfire rang in their ears. Thick, choking smoke stung their eyes.

"They're running!" cried Watson with a grand whoop. "We drove 'em back."

One of the two slaves who had joined Brown's crusade burst into the front room. "Most of the prisoners is gone, suh. Them militia snatched 'em out the window, suh."

"We still have some prisoners and we still have the weapons," said Brown. "Our army will come. I know it!"

It was a wild and frightening night for the seven lonely, terrified raiders trapped in the dark of the fire house. Drunken yelling, the steady bark and fireworks-like flash of musket fire, and empty liquor bottles thrown and smashed like missiles kept them from sleeping. Watson slipped closer and closer to death, coughing or gurgling occasionally.

John Brown stood aloof, detached from the others, as if the fire house were a dream. In the real attack (seen so vividly in his mind) a great slave army had rushed to his banner and burned this hateful town to the ground. Oliver Brown, Jeremiah Anderson, Dauphin Thompson, Edwin Coppoc, and Meriam Dean paced, fired, fretted, and in quiet desperation, waited. Before first light, Watson died.

In the pale light of dawn a company of 500 marines arrived from Baltimore led by Colonel Robert E. Lee. The grim-faced, uniformed marines marched off the trains carrying muskets with long, deadly bayonets gleaming in the morning sun. Many also carried sledgehammers to break down any barriers.

"Lawdy! Lookie at them uniforms," murmured Meriam.

"And those bayonets," added Edwin Coppoc.

The mob parted in awed silence as the marines passed through and then closed behind them as they marched to the armory compound. Behind the marines, a great rabble of over 2,000 armed militia and locals aimed every musket and rifle at the small fire engine house in the arsenal compound. Behind them, a larger ring of local citizens craned their necks for a glimpse of the drama and action. Inside sat six lonely, demoralized raiders, the great army of revolution.

At 7:00 A.M. a marine lieutenant carried a flag of truce to the engine house door. He talked briefly with John Brown while the others crowded behind.

"Wha he want?"

"Hush up I can't hear."

"Will they let us leave?"

The lieutenant casually waved his hat. On that cue the marines charged. With one quick flurry of gunfire and a series of shouts, in less than two minutes it was over. Three raiders were captured (John Brown, Meriam Dean, and Edwin Coppoc). The other three were killed in the assault.

In the silence that followed the lightning attack, the crowd began to find its conscience. As if awakening from a dream, people began to remember how bad, brutal, and uncivilized they had been during the past 24 hours, and they were stiffly embarrassed, averting their eyes and dropping their heads in disgrace as they shuffled toward home. The crowd was ashamed of how they had acted and had failed to act. Like bullies and cowards, they had hooted, drunk, and strutted; violated flags of truce; beaten and murdered unarmed men; and allowed a half dozen raiders to hold them all at bay.

Meriam Dean sat in an army wagon in chains—chains he had not known since he was a slave—and he wondered if anyone would ever hear of what they had attempted here, if anyone would take up the cause. John Brown had failed. But slavery still had to end. Meriam rattled his chains, sighed, and wondered, "Will anyone else ever step up to heed the call?"

Aftermath

Nothing was directly accomplished by John Brown's raid. Not one single slave voluntarily joined his army. Most of the slaves the raiders forcibly "freed" refused to join and acted like the white hostages Brown's men had captured. Not one mulatto, free black, or white abolitionist rallied to Brown's cause.

John Brown was hanged by the Virginia authorities. His last words were, "I, John Brown, am now quite certain that the crimes of these guilty lands will never be purged away but with blood."[1]

The raid was a total flop, and a costly one. Two slaves, one free black (Hayward Sheppard, the baggage handler), one marine, three townsmen, and 10 raiders (including two of Brown's sons) died. Six raiders were captured (including three who were caught in the Maryland schoolhouse) and later hanged. Two of the escaped raiders were later hunted down and shot. Three escaped and were never apprehended.

Yet the raid had monumental effects. Fearing that another abolitionist would try to raise a slave army in other locations, militia units were formed and drilled in virtually every Southern community. These units began intense training. Eighteen months after the raid these same militia units would become the backbone of the Southern armies.

At the same time, Northern abolitionists were strengthened and emboldened in their political positions by Brown's "noble" attempt to free the slaves. Congress was further polarized, both sides becoming less willing to compromise and less interested in searching for common ground. At a time when steps toward peace were essential, Brown's raid forced both sides to entrench themselves in their strongest, most uncompromising positions and sent the nation hurtling toward preparations for war.

Notes

1. Joseph Barry, *The Strange Story of Harpers Ferry*, p. 137.

Follow-up Questions and Activities

1. **What Do You Know?**
    - Why did John Brown attack Harpers Ferry? What did he hope to accomplish there?
    - Why didn't he grab the arsenal's guns and leave? Why did Brown feel he had to stay and wait at Harpers Ferry?

- Who were the abolitionists? What did they believe? What were they trying to accomplish?
- Why didn't any blacks join Brown once he took control of the Harpers Ferry arsenal? Why didn't any slaves revolt and join him? Why didn't any other white abolitionists rush to his support?

2. **Find Out More.** Following are six important topics from this story for students to research in the library and on the Internet. The reference sources at the back of this book will help them get started.

- Research the life of John Brown. What jobs had he held? At what had he succeeded? At what had he failed? What event in Kansas made him famous—or infamous? How did he become a radical abolitionist? How old was he when he led the raid on Harpers Ferry?
- Research the American abolitionist movement. When and where did it start? Who were its leaders? How did abolitionists differ from early suffragists? How were they similar?
- Research arsenals, armories, and weapons manufacture in the United States. Where were America's first arsenals? Where were and are weapons stored? How many arsenals now exist? Why did the government want to manufacture weapons instead of leaving it to private manufacturing companies?
- Research the history of Harpers Ferry. When was the town founded? What role did the town play during the Civil War after John Brown's raid? What has happened to the town since?
- Research the origins of slavery in America. When and why did the first slaves arrive in this country? Who brought them? Why was slavery originally permitted? Compare slavery with indentured servitude. Was indentured servitude an established practice in this country? Why and how did it begin?
- John Brown attacked Harpers Ferry with 20 other men. Two were his sons. Who were the other 18? Where did they come from? How many were blacks? How many were whites? Why did they join him and agree to his wild plan? What were their hopes and dreams?

3. **Make It Real**

- Hold a class debate on the "real" causes of the Civil War. Why did the nation go to war? What were the armies really fighting about? Why were those issues worth a war, worth killing 700,000 soldiers? Why couldn't the country hold a national debate or a special election on the issue?
- Make a chart showing the population of whites, slaves, mulattoes, and free blacks in each state and territory just before the Civil War. How many states actually had a minority of whites? Where were the greatest concentrations of slaves?
- Write a profile of John Brown or another abolitionist. Then research Gerrit Smith by visiting the New York History Net (http://www.NYHistory.com/gerritsmith.index.htm) and write an essay comparing Smith and Brown. Or research Frederick Douglass and write about his relationship to Brown.

- Hold a mock trial of John Brown, with students playing the parts of the raiders who survived, witnesses from the town, lawyers, and a judge. The rest of the class can form a jury to decide whether Brown was justified in his actions and what the sentence should be.

- John Brown's raid was in part a protest against slavery. As a class, plan a protest of your own to capture the attention and sympathies of the local community. What will you protest? How can you plan your protest to get noticed but not create an overreaction as did Brown's? (He and his protesters were shot or hanged.) What will you do for your protest? What do you hope to achieve?

4. **Points to Ponder**

- Was John Brown's raid a legitimate form of political action? What do you think would have been legitimate and acceptable for him to do?

- Did John Brown succeed? If he did, in what ways? If not, why not? How would you react today if a group tried to force their way into a national weapons depot for political purposes?

- Why do you think the townspeople reacted so violently to the raid? Do you think they would have been as savage if Brown weren't trying to free and arm slaves but instead was capturing weapons for some other purpose?

- Various people thought Brown was insane, a criminal, a terrorist, a religious fanatic, or a martyr to the cause of abolition. After researching his life, what do you think? Why?

1861 at a Glance

Passions Boil; the Bloodshed Begins!

The American Civil War began on the evening of April 12, 1861, when Southern General Pierre Beaurigard fired his cannons, bombarding Fort Sumpter, which guarded the harbor of Charleston, South Carolina. Church bells rang across the South in celebration. Crowds flocked into the streets of every Southern town, joyously celebrating. By contrast, Northerners grimly set their jaws, determined to snuff out this upstart rebellion.

In 1861 Julius Van Camp first created canned pork and beans. Also in this year the first commercially baked pretzel rolled off the factory line in Litiz, Pennsylvania. Linus Yale invented the pin-tumbler lock, and the first bicycle was introduced to America. This year also saw the beginnings of unimaginable bloodshed in America.

Immediately after the bombardment of Fort Sumpter, President Abraham Lincoln called for 75,000 volunteers to quell the uprising. Virginia, Tennessee, North Carolina, and Arkansas all seceded rather than supply troops to fight against their Southern brothers. Regimental units were quickly formed and armed in every state and community, North and South. Everyone wanted to rush to the front to be part of what they thought would be a very short war. One big battle and the other side would quit; so went the popular wisdom on both sides of the border.

The war's first blood was spilled in Baltimore, a Northern hotbed of Southern support, when a mob attacked a Massachusetts regiment on its way to Washington, D.C. Soon after, forty skirmishes and small battles erupted along a thousand-mile front from the Chesapeake Bay to the Mississippi River.

In July the war began in earnest. Eighty thousand soldiers crashed into each other in northern Virginia along a meandering stream called Bull Run. Thousands died. Thousands upon thousands were wounded. The mighty Union Army of the Potomac fled in shambles and disgrace. The victorious Confederate army lacked the strength and power to pursue and exploit its victory. Both armies staggered back in shock from this crushing encounter.

After Bull Run, Southern and Northern armies eyed each other warily from a distance and concentrated on building their forces before the next bloody battle. The North developed a strategy called the Anaconda Plan, which called for the Army of the Potomac to force its way south toward Richmond and the heart of the Confederacy, for the western Union armies to drive south through Tennessee and (especially) along the Mississippi River, and for the Federal navy to blockade southern ports and strangle the South, like the South American snake for which the plan was named.

The Confederates realized after Bull Run that they lacked the strength for a quick military victory. They developed a "defensive strike" strategy in which Southern armies would wait in defensive positions for Northern armies to attack and would then strike the invaders when and where the greatest advantage lay with the defenders. They hoped to so badly bloody the Northern forces every time they crossed into the South that the Yankees would soon give up and leave the Confederacy alone.

Key Events After the War Began in 1861

Date	Event
April 12	South Carolina Militia fires on Fort Sumpter in Charleston Harbor; 24 hours later, the fort surrenders.
April 15	President Lincoln calls for 75,000 men to volunteer to join the army.
April 17	Virginia secedes from the Union.
April 19	A Baltimore mob attacks a Boston infantry regiment. Two soldiers and 20 civilians are killed, the first casualties of the war.
May 6	Arkansas secedes.
May 14	The first small battle between Confederate and Federal forces occurs in Virginia. The Confederates hold the field.
May 20	North Carolina secedes.
May 25	Northern General George McClellan completes his sweep through western Virginia, clearing the area of all Confederate forces. In two more years, this area will be admitted into the Union as a new state, West Virginia.
June 8	Tennessee secedes, the last state to join the Confederacy.
July 6	Federal naval blockade of Southern ports and shipping routes begins.
July 21	In the Battle of Bull Run, the first major engagement of the war, the Confederacy wins the day.
November 7	Northern General William Sherman captures the South Carolina Sea Islands and the ports of Port Royal and Beaufort as part of the blockade.

Dodging the Bullet
President Lincoln Moves to Washington, February 1861

At a Glance

Abraham Lincoln, whose name had become known through his series of debates with Steven Douglas, was certainly not the favorite of the Republican Party. Lincoln was not well enough known or liked in the East, and certainly not liked at all in the South because of his abolitionist leanings. However, his views were more moderate than several of the better-known Republican hopeful candidates. So Lincoln, a country lawyer from the western frontier of Illinois, got the Republican nod.

The Republicans picked an ex-Democrat from Maine as his running mate, hoping that the East Coast connection would minimize the damage of nominating a western frontier lawyer. Still, Lincoln was not expected to do well in the election.

Imagine the shock when Lincoln won the 1860 presidential election. Southern Democrats were outraged. Lincoln, an avowed abolitionist, had pledged to prevent the spread of slavery to new territories. That debate was still on Congress's front burner. Southerners felt betrayed, cheated, and backed into a corner.

In December, South Carolina seceded from the United States in protest, declaring that it would no longer be a part of the Union. Savvy politicians believed the state would reenter the Union as soon as this dramatic ploy had won them a stronger bargaining position. But in early January, Mississippi and Florida seceded. Alabama, Georgia, Louisiana, and Texas quickly followed, in that order.

31

The Union was disintegrating. President James Buchanan, who wanted only to limp to the end of his term, made no real attempt to patch the crumbling nation together. Long-time East Coast politicians were convinced that Lincoln lacked the experience, finesse, and savvy to serve as president in such a troubled time. He was blasted as being an incompetent country hick.

In mid-February 1861, Lincoln boarded a train in Springfield, Illinois, for a three-week meandering trip that would end in Washington in time for his inauguration on March 4. All eyes, hopes, angers, resentments, and fears were focused on the lanky lawyer.

Meet Allan Pinkerton

Born in Glasgow, Scotland, in 1818, Allan Pinkerton was the son of a police sergeant who was crippled during a riot when Allan was 10 years old. Allan took a job as an apprentice barrel maker to help support the family. He learned the cooperage trade well and decided to emigrate to America when he turned 20. He settled in the town of Dundee, Illinois, a community of Scots. There he set up a successful barrel-making factory (cooperage).

While searching for good wood for his barrels, Pinkerton uncovered evidence of a gang of counterfeiters. He led the sheriff back to the site and helped to capture the entire gang. It was Pinkerton's first taste of detective work and law enforcement, and he wanted more.

Not yet an American citizen, he wormed his way into the position of county deputy sheriff in 1846. Shortly afterward, he sold his cooperage to concentrate full-time on law enforcement. Pinkerton moved to Chicago as Cook County deputy sheriff in 1848. There he became the first detective on the Cook County police force.

Pinkerton's high success rate for tracking down criminals came to the attention of three railroad presidents whose lines were plagued by robberies. In late 1851, Pinkerton quit the police force to found the Pinkerton Detective Agency, the first private detective agency in the country. He initially specialized in railroad security.

Pinkerton was chosen to guard Lincoln on his three-week trip to Washington. After secreting Lincoln to Washington in early 1861, Pinkerton met General George McClellan. When McClellan was named commander of the Army of the Potomac in September 1861, he chose Pinkerton as his chief of intelligence.

For four years and under five commanding generals, Pinkerton served as chief of army intelligence, even though he consistently grossly overestimated Confederate strength.

After the war, Pinkerton moved back to Chicago to pick up the reins of his private detective agency. He married and lived in Chicago, running his agency until he died at age 72 in 1890.

Dodging the Bullet

A short, bald man hunched in the deep shadows at the edge of the Harrisburg, Pennsylvania, train station. He pulled his coat tight around him to ward off the biting cold and drizzle that slickened the train tracks on this bleak night of February 22, 1861. His hands were stuffed into his coat pockets. But his eyes darted left and right, seeming to penetrate the gloom, and missed nothing in the quiet train yard.

Two other men, both armed with rifles and revolvers, jogged over. "Mr. Pinkerton, we've checked with all agents in the area. The train yard is secure and clear."

Pinkerton nodded. "We'll get the man now."

"But, sir, it's only 10:15. He specifically wrote in his schedule that he wanted to mingle until 11:00."

"And that is why we will board him now."

"We've already changed his schedule three times. Must we change it again?"

"Yes," answered Allan Pinkerton, cold and hard. "Mingling with unscreened crowds is dangerous. I would rather be safe than sorry. Get him."

Fifteen minutes later, Abraham Lincoln turned to the man hurriedly pushing him toward a private car hooked to the end of a freight and passenger train in the darkened Harrisburg, Pennsylvania, train station. "Why was I pulled away from dinner 45 minutes ahead of schedule?"

"Because your carriage ride here and this train yard are both far too open for you to arrive when others expect you to."

Lincoln bristled. "You go too far, Mr. Pinkerton. There are not assassins hiding behind every bush."

"Yes, Mr. President. I fear that there might be exactly that."

"And was it absolutely necessary to cut the telegraph lines?"

Allan Pinkerton sighed with exasperation, the strain of his work etched on his face. "Yes, Mr. President. It was. I don't want word leaking out that we have sneaked you out of Harrisburg ahead of schedule."

The smell of grease and damp coal permeated the train yard.

"I'm not the president yet," Lincoln answered as he followed his personal body guard, Ward Hill Lamon, into the waiting car. Lamon was a massive, barrel-chested man armed with four pistols, two knives, a club, and a set of well-used brass knuckles.

The tension between Pinkerton and Lincoln showed in the anger flashing in each man's eyes and in the whiplash sharpness of their words. "And it is my job to get you to Washington safely so that you *can* be sworn in as president in 10 days."

"I don't want to crawl into Washington in the dark like a common criminal."

"Would you rather be carried into Washington as a corpse?"

Lamon turned up the glass-covered gas lanterns in the train.

"Don't touch that light!" Pinkerton bellowed as Lincoln and Pinkerton glared at each other. Pinkerton nodded to one of his agents who pulled the window shades and closed the car's thick curtains over those. "Now, Mr. Lamon, wall lights only. Do not light either desk lamp for they cast shadows outward."

The president-elect entered the richly appointed private car of Samuel Felton, president of the Philadelphia, Wilmington & Baltimore Railroad. Pinkerton had arranged to attach the car to this train due to lurch out of Harrisburg at 11:00 P.M. Three of Pinkerton's operatives—all bristling with weapons—stood inside the car. Countless others were scattered across the train yard.

The front half of Felton's car served as a sitting room. Red-draped window shades covered the two rows of windows and were tied back with yellow cords whose tassels swayed rhythmically when the train was moving. Straight-backed and overstuffed chairs bolted to the floor were scattered in front of a long mahogany desk. Lanterns glowed from the coach walls, flickering shadows across the car. The pungent smell of countless cigars that had been smoked over many miles lingered in the drapes and rich upholstery. The back half of the car was listed as a sleeping car, but it was decked out with chairs and a conference table in addition to twin bunks.

Lincoln's administrative secretary, John Nicolay, sat in a straight chair holding thick bundles of papers. Short, round Nicolay wore a top hat and a heavy black overcoat and walked with a pronounced waddle. He looked like a humorless "bah-humbug" accountant but was really a notorious jokester.

Lincoln again huffed, "And is this secrecy really necessary?"

Scottish-born Pinkerton's bald head barely reached Lincoln's chin. Still, he never flinched or wavered when confronting the newly elected president. "Yes, Mr. President. Seven southern states have already seceded from the union. Eight other slave states may secede at any moment. In the South, citizens scream for your head, since you have publicly avowed your abolitionist leanings. Many there want you dead. Yes, Mr. President, these precautions are necessary. These and many more."

More than 200 railroad guards had been posted at the crossings and stations between Harrisburg and Baltimore. Each was to raise a lantern to signal that all was well as the train rumbled past.

Lincoln sighed and gave in. "Since you will have me reach Washington four days ahead of schedule, John and I have a number of matters to consider tonight."

Pinkerton shrugged. "Just do not touch any of the curtains or press your face near a window."

Lincoln's eyes dimmed. The deep lines in his cheeks seemed to deepen and darken. "At least let me put Tad to bed first."

Lincoln began calling Thomas, his now seven-year-old son, "Tadpole" when he was two. Over the years the name had been shortened to Tad. Tad had been playing in the sleeping half of the train car while Lincoln made a dinner speech in Harrisburg.

Pinkerton grumbled, "And I strongly object to having the child on this trip. He should have stayed home with his mother."

Lincoln's eyes sparkled with amusement. "I thought you, of all people, would appreciate having my son with us. Having family along creates the appearance of unhurried, unworried normalcy."

Without waiting for a reply, the smiling president-elect ducked through the curtain divider. Tad's voice rang out, "A ride, Daddy! I want a ride." The boy's cleft palate gave him a slight lisp when he spoke.

Lincoln's booming laugh rattled the car. "You rascal! I'll give you a ride!" Tad squealed with delight and raced up and down the car, dodging around the scatter of chairs, while the president chased him on hands and knees, laughing. The stern security team arched their eyebrows and thoughtfully puffed on cigars. Pinkerton glanced warily out the window.

It took the president almost an hour to settle Tad into his narrow bunk and return to the front sitting room. Pinkerton glanced at his pocket watch. 11:02. "We should be moving." He turned to an agent. "Get up front and find out—"

His sentence was interrupted as a train whistle screeched into the dreary night. Dogs howled in response. The train jerked forward in fits and starts, its headlamp beaming through the rain. Pinkerton nodded. "Right on time."

Lincoln settled into a high-backed, overstuffed chair. "I don't believe that the threat on my life is that serious, and I resent your overreaction."

"Serious?!" Pinkerton spluttered. "It's deadly serious." Pinkerton pointed at one of his agents who had been standing guard in the shadows by the train door. "This is agent Timothy Webster. He's spent three months penetrating the Baltimore secessionist movement." Pinkerton jerked his head toward the president. "Timothy, tell him."

Agent Webster bowed slightly as he stepped forward. He had a trim beard and pale gray-blue eyes that sparkled in the light of the gas lamps. "Two pro-slavery militia regiments have formed and are secretly drilling in Baltimore: the Palmetto Guards and the Constitutional Guards. Both are pledged to attack Washington once the war starts. There are bands of thugs called Blood Tubs committed to creating riots to disrupt federal communications in the city. There are also at least eight men who have pledged to shoot you dead on your way through Baltimore."

Lincoln seemed to be uninterested, even mildly amused. "Many malcontents make threats. Arrest them if you think they're that serious."

"The police chief, George Kane, is one of the leaders of the secessionists. He has pledged to support and aid the assassins. So have a majority of the state legislature and the Baltimore city council. We can't arrest the entire state government. Anti-Union and pro-slavery sentiment runs rampant in Baltimore. Their plan is to stage riots that will conveniently divert all police protection from your carriage as you pass through Baltimore. That will leave you an easy target for the teams of killers. Secessionist leaders will use your assassination to launch the rebellion that will force Maryland to secede."

Trains from the North arrived at President Street depot in Baltimore, but trains to Washington left from Camden Station. It was during the three-mile carriage ride between the two stations (when Lincoln had planned to greet locals, wave, and shake hands) that the assassins planned to strike.

"Send army units in to secure Baltimore," Lincoln suggested.

John Nicolay shook his head as he shuffled through papers. "I have a report from General Scott. There are only 17,000 soldiers on active duty in the army. Most of those are out West fighting Indians and securing California. Worse, over half the officers and enlisted men have defected to the South. He doubts if he could scrape together one loyal regiment in and around Washington."

"*That's* why I changed your schedule," interrupted Pinkerton. "You will now pass through Baltimore unannounced in the middle of the night and avoid the trap."

Lincoln asked, "And what if the assassins learn of the change?"

Pinkerton dabbed nervous perspiration from his upper lip. "In five hours, Mr. President, we will know."

Lincoln scowled, deep in thought, and drummed his fingers on the mahogany desk. "I still say it looks weak and disgraceful for me to slink into Washington in the dead of night."

Pinkerton tapped his forefinger on the desk for emphasis. "Mr. President," he said, "if the plot against you is successful and Maryland secedes, the Federal capital will be 60 miles deep in enemy territory! The government will collapse. The South will have won before the first shot is fired between armies."

Lincoln seemed unconvinced. "Maryland will follow the lead of Virginia. Virginia is the key. If I can work with the Virginia delegation and get them to lead a compromise proposal, there is still a chance for reconciliation. The South will not go to war without Virginia."

"They will not *need* to go to war if you're killed tonight," Pinkerton snapped.

Again Lincoln seemed lost in thought as the bleak winter landscape rolled by under the watchful eye of Pinkerton's guards.

John Nicolay again politely coughed. "Mr. Lincoln? There are other matters to discuss, sir."

Lincoln merely nodded as he stared at the curtains that gently swayed with the steady rocking of the train.

Nicolay summarized an urgent letter from General Winfield Scott. "General Scott reports that there are fewer than 10,000 in the Federal army you can count on and wants to know if you plan to raise an army to counter the growing Southern military threat."

Lincoln dismissively waived his long hand. "Of course we must protect the Union with a credible army."

"But, sir, raising an army will be interpreted as a provocative act in the South and will encourage them to form their own army."

Agent Webster said, "After the raid on Harpers Ferry in '59, almost every Southern community formed and drilled militia units. Those are now joining into regiments, divisions, and armies. The South already *has* a trained army, even if the federal government doesn't."

Lincoln sighed, "If only the North were as unified and single-minded as the South, my job would be much easier."

"What should I tell General Scott?"

Lincoln pointed a bony finger across the desk. "Tell General Scott that I intend to have 150,000 men armed, trained, equipped, and in uniform by summer, that this Union will not tolerate the secession of any state, and that this army will be empowered to ensure that the Union is preserved."

A deep silence followed, punctuated only by the steady clickity-clack of the wheels and rails, while those in the car absorbed these bold and powerful words.

Nicolay wrote furiously and then shuffled through his stack of reports. "Ummm, pardon me, sir. But I have a report here from the Treasury Department. With revenues no longer flowing from the seven Southern states, they anticipate a dangerous budget deficit by this summer. How exactly will you pay for this grand army?"

Lincoln slammed his fist onto the desk. "I am not in office yet. I do not have a cabinet. I have not yet formed a functioning government. I cannot answer with information I do not possess. But tell General Scott that I pledge that the army will be there! We'll find out *how* later."

Pinkerton and the guards applauded to show their support. Nicolay scribbled quick notes before continuing. "General Scott also wants to know about supplying the garrison at Fort Sumpter, sir."

"Tell him to ask President Buchanan," snapped Lincoln. "I am not the president yet. I have no authority."

Nicolay blushed as he answered, "Buchanan told him to consult you because any resupply effort would arrive in South Carolina after you take office."

Lincoln angrily drummed his fingers on the desk. "Fort Sumpter is the last Federal installation held in South Carolina. Correct?"

"Yes, Mr. President."

"Then we must defend and supply it. I will not abandon Federal property any more than I will allow the Union to be split apart."

"But how, sir? If you send a navy ship to Charleston Harbor, the South will consider it an act of war."

"Use a civilian merchant ship, then," snapped Lincoln.

"President Buchanan already tried that, sir. The ship was turned back by Confederate threats."

Lincoln sadly shook his head and ran his fingers through his unkempt black hair, wondering why leading a nation had to be so difficult. "We cannot abandon Fort Sumpter. Tell General Scott to try again."

Nicolay nodded as he dabbed a quill pen in his ink jar and continued his hasty notes. Then he shuffled deeper through his stack of papers. "Then there is the matter of your cabinet appointments."

"I have already announced my choices for the major posts."

Nicolay cleared his throat and squirmed in his chair. "Yes, sir. However, press editorials over the past week have branded you as 'half-witted,' 'incompetent,' and even called you a 'traitor.' "

Lincoln shrugged and nodded. "The press is free to have their opinions."

"Those opinions, sir, were *given* to the press by some of the very men you have nominated for cabinet positions. If your appointments stay as you have stated, you will be surrounding yourself with enemies."

"But they are the most qualified men for those positions."

"To be qualified, sir," Nicolay continued, "shouldn't they at least *support* their president?"

Lincoln again sighed, "What am I to do? A broken nation, no army, no budget, a hostile cabinet and government. . . . And I haven't even taken the oath of office yet."

The train jerked and squealed as it slid into Baltimore's President Street depot. Pinkerton rubbed his eyes and checked his pocket watch: 3:30 A.M., right on time. Then he nodded to Webster, who dimmed the gas lights. "Just a precaution, sir."

Two other agents rushed out onto the train's rear platform with pistols drawn and cocked. The station platform was deserted except for an official courier from Washington who waited nervously for the train.

As the courier stepped into the car, Pinkerton exploded, "How did you know we were due here at this time?"

The frail-looking man cringed and nervously rubbed his glasses. "An aide to the Speaker of the House sent me."

Pinkerton glared at the president who calmly glared back. "I sent an aide by horseback to where he *could* send a telegraph. There is correspondence I needed to see before I reach Washington."

"You have violated the security I created to safeguard your trip!"

"What good is security if I can't effectively act as president?"

Pinkerton growled in frustration. "Who else must know by this time? . . ." He thought for a moment. "You will not travel by carriage to Camden Station as planned, Mr. President. We will trolley this train car across town. I can defend the train car better." He turned to agent Webster. "I want six horses on this car within 15 minutes. Go!"

Pinkerton lowered all drapes and sashes in the car. "Only one light, Mr. President. I don't want to make this easy for the secessionists."

Nicolay nodded and turned up the gas flame on the one desk lamp.

Lincoln turned to the courier. "What news? Have any new states seceded?"

"No, sir."

Lincoln chortled, "There's some good news."

"I have brought these letters, sir, which have accumulated for you from various political factions. The Speaker thought you should have them before you reach the capital."

Nicolay scanned through the letters. "Here are a series of letters, sir, from Congressmen Horace Vallandigham (Ohio) and his Peace Democrats. They demand that you negotiate a peaceful settlement with the Confederacy and pledge not to go to war. They make no mention of slavery, but, as you know, they are opposed to emancipation."

He scanned the next group as the train car began the slow trip across Baltimore to the clomping sound of horse hooves on the cobbled streets. "These letters are from the Central Democratic Party. They demand that you act immediately to quash the rebellion and preserve the Union. They want a war, sir."

Nicolay continued, "William Garrison and other prominent abolitionists demand that you forbid slavery to expand into any new territories, but that you allow it to die naturally in the South without resorting to war."

Webster stepped back inside the car. "All quiet so far. No sign of any activity."

Nicolay lifted another group of letters. "These are also from prominent abolitionists, led by Frederick Douglass, who demand that you both immediately abolish slavery everywhere in the Union and use armed force to bring the seceding states back under Federal control."

Nicolay flipped to the next bundle and glanced through the letters. "These are letters from Republican congressmen, congratulating you on your election." He read through several of the letters and frowned. "Even though you were nominated by the party because of your moderate views on slavery, they now seem to insist that you adopt a stronger abolitionist view and take some dramatic action to abolish slavery as soon as you take office."

Nicolay went on. "And here is a final group of letters, also from Republicans, mostly it seems from New Jersey, New York, and Connecticut, who insist that you not free the slaves since their immigrant constituents fear a flood of black laborers stealing jobs from recent Irish immigrants."

Lincoln sighed and shook his head. "Why is it that the people of this nation insist on disagreeing about everything?"

At 4:20 A.M. the car reached Camden Station and was attached to a train due to leave shortly for Washington. Pinkerton rubbed his tired face and began to relax. "I believe the worst danger is over, Mr. President."

Tad wandered out, rubbing sleep from his eyes, and climbed into his father's lap. "I'm hungry, daddy."

Pinkerton nodded to one of his agents, who left for a forward dining car.

Nicolay held up the stacks of letters. "What will you do about these opposing demands, Mr. Lincoln?"

A whistle blew like a rooster crowing the dawn and the train began its steady chug toward Washington.

"What will I do?" Lincoln repeated. "I think what I will do is be very careful when dealing with Congress. I *must* preserve the Union. If I can do that and free the slaves, fine. But if I can preserve the Union without freeing a single slave, I will also gladly do that. Virginia is still the key."

"But these letters, Mr. President . . ."

A tray of food was laid on the table in front of Tad and the president. "What am I going to do?" he again mused. "Right now, I think I am going to eat breakfast and play with my son." But a burning question echoed in his mind. "How can I unite a broken nation when there isn't even enough of an army to protect the president-elect from assassins on a simple train trip to Washington?"

Bleary-eyed and bone weary, eyes sunk deep and red-lined from his all-night vigil, Lincoln reached the outskirts of Washington as a pale sun rose over the Maryland countryside. Pinkerton said, "Mr. President, I have some security recommendations . . ."

"Stop!" Lincoln interrupted. "You see too many ghosts and enemies, Mr. Pinkerton. I must embrace this nation, not hide from it. I must see allies when I gaze upon a crowd, not assassins. Thank you for your efforts and good-bye."

As Lincoln stepped off the train, Allan Pinkerton muttered, "That man has no appreciation of the dangers! He won't survive a month."

Aftermath

Lincoln arrived safely, having completely circumvented the Baltimore assassination conspirators. Most of the group actively plotting Lincoln's assassination fled to the South, believing that they would be arrested if they lingered in the North to try to further their cause.

Lincoln began the serious buildup for war after the April shelling of Fort Sumpter with an army of less than 10,000 scattered across the country, with its greatest concentration in the far West. Still, brigade-sized units were actively engaged as early as May, and the Army of the Potomac totaled more than 80,000 before the First Battle of Bull Run (Manassas) in July.

Lincoln had to create this incredible war machine without a unified cabinet (most were still opposed to Lincoln's election and committed to making him fail) and in the face of badly split public opinion. Many wanted to fight; almost as many did not want war. Some wanted to free the slaves. Many did not.

Lincoln took office facing more problems, and more complex problems, than had any president since the nation was created. Serious challenges confronted him on every front, and there existed no solid base of support for him to rely on. No president before or since has faced more daunting tasks.

In May, federal troops arrested 23 members of the Maryland state legislature, most of the Baltimore city officials, and a number of other state and city officials. They were jailed without charges being filed and lived in federal prison for three years without ever standing trial. Maryland never seceded, even when General Lee's mighty Army of Northern Virginia marched north into Maryland in 1862 and again in 1863 hoping to garner popular support for the Confederacy. Maryland (although its support seemed always in doubt) stayed loyal to the Union.

Follow-up Questions and Activities

1. **What Do You Know?**

   - Why was Lincoln sneaked into Washington? Why didn't he use army units to protect himself as he traveled through Baltimore?
   - What does "secede" mean? What does a state give up by seceding?
   - Why did most eastern politicians believe that Lincoln lacked the political savvy to perform adequately as president?
   - Why was Lincoln so worried about Maryland seceding?
   - Why did so many Southern groups and sympathizers threaten to kill the new president?

2. **Find Out More.** Following are six important topics from this story for students to research in the library and on the Internet. The reference sources at the back of this book will help them get started.

   - Research anti-Union sentiment and secessionist leanings in Maryland (and especially Baltimore). Why did so many in Maryland sympathize with the Southern cause? Who were the Palmetto Guards and Constitutional Guards? How much information can you find on them?
   - Research the early history of the U.S. Army. How big was the army during the Revolutionary War, the War of 1812, and the Mexican War? What happened to the army after each war?
   - Research the makeup and location of the American army in 1860. How many soldiers were there? Where were they? How many were infantry? Cavalry? Artillery? How many sided with the Confederates and joined the Southern army?
   - How did Lincoln raise more than 150,000 men to fill out the ranks by the summer of 1861? Where did they come from? Who paid for their uniforms, their equipment, and their training? Who paid the soldiers and who provided for their daily needs?
   - Research detective Allan Pinkerton and his railroad detective agency. Where did Pinkerton come from? How successful was his agency in stopping train robberies?
   - Research the wide variety of Northern sentiments on the two major issues facing the North in the war: slavery and splitting the Union. How many people were on each side of the issue? How did these divisions affect Lincoln's ability to rally the nation and run the government?

3. **Make It Real**

   - Make a chart showing the dates of secession of each of the Confederate states. List the reasons each one gave as the cause of secession. List as many reasons as you can explaining why the four "border states" (slave states that did not secede) remained in the Union. What reasons did they have *to* secede? Which of the four border states were most likely to secede?

- Make a chart of as many threatened, attempted, and successful presidential assassinations as you can. Why do so many people want to kill our presidents? Are there similarities between people on the list and the times they live in? Write an essay comparing two of the individuals on the list.

4. **Points to Ponder**

   - Why did so many want to kill Lincoln before he even got into office? What had he done? What did they hope to accomplish? If Lincoln had been assassinated in early 1861, do you think the war would have turned out differently? Do you think there still would have been a war? Why or why not?

   - Lincoln had to change his plans at the insistence of security staff. Does this sort of thing still happen? How concerned are modern presidents with personal security? What are they worried about?

Growin' Cotton; Killin' Yankees
Southern Prewar Popular Attitudes, April 1861

At a Glance

As late as 1790, cotton floundered as an unimportant, marginal crop in America. The process of separating sticky cotton fibers from the seeds was too slow and labor intensive to be profitable. Then Eli Whitney invented his cotton engine ("gin") in 1794 and revolutionized the Southern economy. One cotton gin could separate cotton fibers as fast as vast teams of slaves could pick. Indigo fields were ripped out and replaced with cotton fields. Slave labor plus cotton gins made cotton the economic giant of the South.

Cotton exports to Northern fabric mills and to European mills skyrocketed. Cotton was king! More than 6 million bales were exported from Southern ports each year by the late 1850s. Millions of dollars flowed into the Southern economy because of cotton. From Maryland and Delaware south, America was a slave and plantation economy, and proud of it.

In 1850 a delicate balance existed in Congress between slave and free states. Northern demands to end slavery were met with Southern cries of states' rights. Through the 1850s these crucial issues broiled together in a raging political storm. By the time Lincoln was elected in November 1860, Southerners had become convinced that he and the Republican Party that elected him were determined to destroy the Southern economy and prosperity by abolishing both slavery and each state's right to choose.

One by one the slave states seceded from the Union, and thoughts turned from compromise to war. The Southern battle cry was "States' Rights!" But the only right they needed to fight for was slavery.

Meet Thomas Parker

Born in 1848, Thomas Parker was the third child of Winfred and May Parker. Winfred Parker was a fifth-generation descendant of English and French Huguenot stock. The family had done well in real estate and law and by 1820 owned a large South Carolina plantation.

Thomas's older brother, Patrick, was killed at the Second Battle of Bull Run (Manassas) two weeks before he would have turned 20. When his father refused to allow Thomas to join the army when he was 15, he ran off to enlist in the infantry in early 1864. He died of disease in the Petersburg trenches less than a year later.

The Parker plantation was looted and burned in February 1865 by Union General William Sherman's army as it turned north from Savannah to meet Grant. Winfred Parker, his wife, and his two daughters survived. When his wife died in late 1865 of disease, Winfred Parker and his daughters moved west to Missouri, where he became a small shopkeeper.

Growin' Cotton; Killin' Yankees

On the muggy spring morning of April 3, 1861, a company of South Carolina militia swaggered proudly along the tree-lined edge of a field, muskets clamped to their shoulders, hats pulled low. Their elongated shadows flowed across the spring green like prancing, long-legged giants.

A large plantation spread before them with its barns, stables, smokehouse, spinning house, and rolling fields of cotton. A shamble of small cabins and shacks was hidden well behind the big house. Cows lazily grazed, children played, and old women gently rocked and watched.

Following the shouted orders of their elected commander, the 60 young men pivoted around a corner of the plantation's peach orchard, down a line of live oaks draped with gray moss, and toward a wide pond surrounded by sloping lawns and graceful willow branches swaying to the ground.

Twelve-year-old Thomas Parker marched, more seriously than any of the soldiers, beside them. Pretending to carry a musket clamped to his right shoulder, the boy inched as close as he dared to the column of soldiers.

A fashionably tailored man galloped his horse past the stately trees lining the plantation's curving drive to intercept the soldiers. Dust billowed behind as his horse raced away from the main house graced by six tall columns lining the front porch that announced the status of the Parker family.

The man reined to a stop, spraying dirt clods next to the column. "Thomas!" he bellowed. "You get away from those soldiers and come back to the house this instant!"

The boy angrily dug his fists into his hips and jerked his head toward the militia. "But Papa, I can march as good as any of them."

The soldiers shuffled to a stop with broad smiles to watch this confrontation.

"I *know* I'd be good at killin' Yankees," Thomas pleaded.

Mr. Parker glared down from his mount and pointed his riding crop at Thomas. "You get home *now*."

Thomas kicked at the grass, huffed, slowly lowered his head, and trudged off to the chuckles and jeers of the soldiers.

Mr. Thomas turned back toward the house. Then he paused and pointed at one of the soldiers. "Patrick! You must *never* allow your brother to drill with you again."

The soldier blushed. "Yes, Papa."

Thomas waited angrily on the wide front porch for his father.

"Why can't I be a soldier, Papa?" he demanded.

Mr. Parker shook his head. "They'll soon be marching to war."

"That's the point, Papa!" The boy kicked at the column's base for emphasis. "If I don't join up *now*, I may not get to the war at all."

Mr. Parker swept his hand around the lawns and bustling fields that rolled away from the big house. "What's important, Thomas, is *here*—our heritage, our livelihood, our way of life."

"Killing Yankees is important. And I want to kill my share before it's all over. Why should Patrick get all the fun just because he's 18?"

Winfred Parker scowled, his eyebrows arching. It was a look intended to silence his son.

But young Thomas would not back down. "And Lewis Tichner told me his daddy—who is now a *colonel*!—said one good shoot and the Yankees will turn tail and run. It'll be all over and I won't have killed *any*."

"No!" Mr. Parker interrupted. "Cotton, not bullets, will win our freedom."

Young Thomas glanced at his father as if he'd lost his mind. "We can't kill Yankees with cotton balls."

Mr. Parker sighed, shook his head, and continued. "Eighty years ago, your great-grandfather changed our indigo fields to cotton because he realized that cotton is power—economic and political *power*."

Thomas was still not convinced. "*Armies* are power."

"War is always dangerous, Thomas. The Yankees have muskets, too. The South will win, of course. Still, there will be killing and suffering on both sides. Your brother will fight because it is the honorable thing to do, and you will stay here with me to ensure the family's power and position."

Thomas began, "But . . ."

His father shouted him down. "No arguing! My mind's made up. Now come along. I want to check the gin before we ride to Sumter for the slave auction this afternoon."

The plantation's noisy cotton gin, short for "cotton engine," had been mounted in a storage barn. Wide leather belts spun the gears, blades, and mesh screens inside the eight-foot-long, five-foot-high, and four-foot-wide metal box. Slaves poured baskets of tough, sticky cotton balls into the top of the gin. Blades and screens ripped the cotton apart to separate the seeds and stems from the valuable cotton fibers.

Mr. Parker patted the metal side of the gin as he spoke. "The world needs—do you hear me, *needs*—this cotton." He had to lean close to be heard over the whining and clanging gin. "No one will dare oppose us if we threaten to cut off their supply of cotton! By staying here to help me run this gin, *you* will win this war."

Thomas hardly heard a word. There was no glory in raising cotton. Dazzling excitement to last a lifetime waited on the battlefield. But how could he say that to his father who had devoted his life to making this plantation the best in the county?

Two slaves pulled the processed cotton fibers from the bottom of the gin and packed them into bales. Two others fed raw cotton balls into the top from loaded wagons pulled in from the fields. A hired white overseer supervised the operation, standing with arms folded across his chest by the gin's control panel. A curled whip and pistol hung from his belt.

Mr. Parker leaned close to the man. "Thomas thinks we'll need more slaves this summer to keep up with the gin's hunger."

"I do?" Thomas stammered.

Mr. Parker winked, then turned back to the overseer. "You agree?"

The overseer thoughtfully rubbed his chin with thick, tough fingers. "Couple more might be useful. Still too early in the year for peak production, though."

Mr. Parker nodded, "I'll let Thomas see what he can get for a couple of those children this afternoon as down payment on new field hands."

"Can I really, Papa?"

Mr. Parker clamped an arm around his son's shoulder. "Might as well start acting like you own the place."

He thought for a moment and said to the overseer, "I'll ask Ludlow to help you load two of 'em in the wagon. Grab any two you like. Chain 'em in tight so they don't try to jump."

The overseer nodded in agreement.

When Mr. Parker and Thomas stepped out of the big house to get into the wagon for their trip to Sumter, two small black girls were tightly chained together in the back of the wagon, streams of tears splashing onto their faded dresses. They helplessly tugged on the thick chains binding their wrists and ankles to the wagon's heavy metal rings.

Two burly overseers stood above the girls in the back of the wagon. A black woman screamed and wailed, lying on the ground and clutching one wagon wheel as if to keep it from moving. "She's my baby. Don't take my baby!"

A tall black man had sprinted in from the cotton fields, also weeping and screaming, "Please, suh. Don't sell my only chil'!" He seemed about to attack the side of the wagon as if to tear the wood apart and free his daughter.

Both overseers held whips at the ready, threatening both the girls and the two adult slaves.

"Why sell children?" Thomas asked. "Wouldn't you get more for an adult?"

Ignoring the piteous pleas of the parents, Mr. Parker pulled himself onto the wagon's front seat. "We don't need young 'uns in the big house and would have to let 'em grow another four or five years before we could put 'em to work in the fields."

Thomas nodded in understanding.

The black man crawled toward Mr. Parker's side of the wagon, his hands clasped in supplication. "Please, suh. Don't take my only chil'. She's barely five, suh. Please don't sell her away!"

Mr. Parker angrily turned to the overseers. "Keep them quiet. I can't hear myself think."

Crack! Both whips lashed out. With yelps of pain the two parents slowly backed away from the wagon. Thomas winced as the whip snapped again across the black man's head and back.

Mr. Parker patted his son's knee. "Don't worry, son. They're used to it. Besides, a little whipping is good for slaves. Keeps 'em on their toes and in line."

He nodded at the overseers, who hopped out of the wagon, whips still cracking the air like thunder.

Mr. Parker slapped the reins and his team of horses started the dusty trot toward town. Continuing the conversation, he said, "I maybe wouldn't sell 'em if it were Benjamin Tucker's child (the plantation blacksmith), or even a child of Mama Cees (short for Cecilia). She runs the kitchen, so her child could be trained into a skilled house servant." He jerked a thumb toward the sobbing girls huddled together in back. "These just came from field hands. Maybe worth something to someone else, but hardly worth spit to me."

Brilliant splashes of color from blooming azaleas and rhododendrons turned the spring green landscape into a bright painting as the wagon rolled toward Sumter. Thomas, deep in thought, hardly noticed the beauty surrounding him or the frightened whimpering from the girls chained in the back. "You say cotton is our power, Papa. Didn't you used to say that *slaves* were our power?"

Mr. Parker shook his head as he snapped the reins to hasten the horses. "Slavery is just the natural order of things, son. That's what the black race was created for. Slaves and the cotton gin combine to create the power of cotton and let us rule the world."

Thomas nodded and wrinkled his brow as he thought, chin perched on the heels of his hands. "We already own over 80 slaves, Papa, and there are only three overseers. If we get more slaves, aren't you worried they might rebel or run off?"

There were over 4 million slaves in the South. Large-scale slave revolts in 1822 and 1831 had made every owner jittery and cautious. But both of those uprisings had happened over 500 miles away in Virginia. True, a slave had tried to start a revolt in Charleston, but that uprising had quickly failed.

Mr. Parker paused to wave at a neighbor riding past on his horse and waited for the dust to settle before answering. "The whip and the gun keep our slaves in line. 'Sides, we treat 'em decent, so they've got no reason to turn against us. And what's a black man gonna do being free? Not good for anything. Can't go anywhere. Slaves are better off staying where they belong, where they know their place, where they're content." He lowered his voice to a growl, "It's those free black agitators and Yankee abolitionists I worry about." He shook his finger as if scolding the horses. "It's that fool Lincoln who's to blame. He's the one who's stealing our property, our rights, our very way of life!"

Thomas brightened, "And *that's* why we're gonna kill all the Yankees. Right, Papa?"

Mr. Parker laughed. "Not you, Thomas. Natural Southern superiority means we can't lose." His voice rose with excitement. "It's a known fact: Yankees are afraid to fight—too cold up North plus their Puritan blood, I reckon. They can talk for weeks or work like machines in dreary factories. But they surely can't fight!"

Thomas had almost forgotten the war in his excitement over his slave sale. "Can't I please go with Patrick and kill some Yankees?"

As they threaded their way through the narrow streets of Sumter toward the market square, Mr. Parker said, "I don't believe there's even going to be a fight, son. The North needs our cotton. So do England and France. Europe will side with us and the Yanks won't dare oppose everyone. As soon as they see a Confederate army in the field, they'll back down right quick and sign a treaty."

Thomas folded his arms sulkily. "Shucks, I never get to do anything important."

Sumter's small market square was packed with a noisy crowd. A few were buyers—local plantation owners or agents planning to transport slaves deeper into the Southern interior to resell at a higher price. Some, like Mr. Parker, had brought slaves to sell. Most had come just to watch, hoot, and be entertained.

Simon and Williams Slave Auction occupied a squat, barn-like building on the square's north side. A fluttering banner tied to the roof announced the day's auction. A three-foot-high platform ran the width of the building's front. Thin Mr. Williams, whose fingers and hooked nose both seemed far too long for his body, stood on the platform, pleading for quiet as the first of the slaves to be auctioned, a spindly male with thick scars across his back from past whippings, was dragged onto the stage, his chains clanking like bells.

Thomas proudly registered his two slaves to sell at a small table next to the stage. Armed guards patrolled the square and stood guard over the line of slaves waiting to be auctioned. Prospective buyers ambled along the line, inspecting the slaves' teeth, feeling their muscles, demanding that they dance or sing to check their attitude.

Both girls still whimpered and sobbed. Mr. Parker hissed to Thomas, "Shut them up. Whining will lower the price we can get."

Thomas bent down and yelled right in the girls' faces. Then he grabbed one by the upper arms and shook her so hard he lifted her clear off the ground. Wide-eyed with terror, both girls fell silent. Thomas nodded and smugly crossed his arms.

Thomas heard a band strike up behind him and wiggled between the shoulders and coats of the auction crowd to peer down a side street to where an army recruiting rally was in progress. Confederate flags flew from the balcony of an office building. A six-piece brass band blared patriotic tunes. Red and blue streamers fluttered in the afternoon breeze like long fingers beckoning young males to the uniformed ranks. An eager crowd milled around the table set up out front where two uniformed officers sat signing up the men.

Thomas reached back through the crowd and grabbed his father's coat. "Papa! Come quick! Look! Look!"

The urgency of his son's voice made Mr. Parker shove through the auction crowd and follow his sprinting son half a block closer to the rally.

Thomas frantically pointed at the line waiting to sign on at the tables. "Look, Papa! *Poor* boys are signing up for the army, too! But why, Papa? They don't own slaves to protect."

A burly recruiting sergeant answered, "Shucks, boy, everyone wants to kill Yankees. They're tryin' to steal our rights. 'Sides, it's gonna be the best turkey shoot ever! Yanks got no passion. All they love is money and work. But they don't believe in anything worth dying for like our good Southern boys do. That means we're gonna whip 'em sure—*if* they even dare show up for a fight."

Thomas turned to his father, his face glowing with excitement. "Can . . ."

"I told you no, and that's final," barked Mr. Parker. "Now git back to the auction where you belong."

Back at the Parker plantation, as the sun dipped to the waving tops of the trees beyond the western cotton fields, Thomas lingered by the tall columns lining the front porch. As his father had told him to do that morning, Thomas gazed out across the family's wide fields.

But Thomas no longer saw quiet plantation fields. He did not see power and wealth.

To Thomas, each puff of growing white cotton was the smoke from a blazing Confederate musket. The muddy water pooled in ditches was spilt Yankee blood. The deep shadows between rows of plants were crumpled Yankee bodies.

Thomas Parker looked at King Cotton, but, as his blood boiled with fierce Confederate pride and passion, what he saw were dead Yankees. It was going to be grand, Thomas thought. And then he smiled.

Aftermath

The views presented in this story were predominant across the entire South as the war approached. Southerners deeply believed in their own military superiority to the North and so were willing to go to war with a nation that had three times the population and 100 times the manufacturing capacity of their own newly created country. Early victories in 1861 and 1862 seemed to affirm this belief. However, the war soon proved that soldiers on both sides of the battle lines were equally skilled and devoted to their cause. The South, badly outnumbered and outgunned, found itself in a war it could not possibly win.

Southerners were also convinced that the world would knuckle under to their demands to keep a steady supply of cotton flowing out of the South. They greatly overestimated the world's dependence on Southern cotton. Europe never came to the South's aid, and Northern economic interests never insisted that the war be ended to reestablish the flow of Southern cotton. Cotton was not quite king, after all.

These two key Southern miscalculations cost the South dearly and virtually ensured that it could not win the war.

Follow-up Questions and Activities

1. **What Do You Know?**

   - What is a cotton gin? What did it do? Why was it so important to the South but not to the North?
   - Why did Southerners in 1861 think they were sure to win the war?
   - Why and how did the Southern economy depend on slaves?
   - What was the Southern view of Northerners? Why did they view Northerners that way?

2. **Find Out More.** Following are seven important topics from this story for students to research in the library and on the Internet. The reference sources at the back of this book will help them get started.

   - Research the inventor Eli Whitney. Where did he come from? What else did he invent? Why did he develop a cotton separating engine?
   - Why did slavery become so important in the South while it quickly and peacefully disappeared in the North?
   - Slave auctioneers and auction companies flourished across the South. Research slave auction companies. How did they get slaves to sell? How did they make money? How were they connected to the shipping companies that brought slaves into America? How did they operate after the slave ships from Africa were stopped?
   - How did slavery and the slave trade in America begin? Who began to capture, transport, and sell slaves? When? Why? Who first bought them? Why?
   - Research Southern beliefs about slaves. How do you think those attitudes came to be? Why did Southerners need to view slaves as less than human?
   - Research cotton and its history. When was it first cultivated? How is cotton harvested and processed now that there are no more slaves? What replaced slave labor in the fields?
   - Research secession. What was the order in which Southern states seceded? Why did the slave states secede? Which ones didn't? Why not?

3. **Make It Real**

   - Cotton is still a vital fiber. Find all the cotton at your school and at your home. Make a chart showing all the possible uses of cotton. How much cotton is harvested and processed each year in this country? In the world? How does that compare with other natural and artificial fibers?
   - Make a map of slavery. Research slavery throughout history and mark on a map where and when slavery was practiced. Which cultures were or are the owners? Which have been forced into slavery? How did slaves gain their freedom?

4. **Points to Ponder**

- Why do you think Southerners were convinced that Northerners were afraid to fight and that Southerners were better fighters? Do you think Northerners felt the same way about Southerners? Why or why not? Do various cultures have similar attitudes about other groups and cultures today?

- How did Southerners justify their reliance on slaves? How did they morally explain their social and economic system? Do modern cultures rationalize immoral practices? Can you find any recent or ongoing examples?

Tea Cakes, White Lace, and Bloodshed
First Battle of Bull Run (Manassas), July 1861

At a Glance

The attack on Fort Sumpter in April 1861 was, in effect, a declaration of war. Both North and South rushed to amass mighty armies. Everyone, North and South, believed that the other side would collapse and run when they faced the pressure of one major battle. In the North volunteers signed on for three-month enlistments. "The war will be won and you'll be home in plenty of time for the harvest," recruiters announced.

In the South new recruits begged their commanders to rush them to the front to make sure they were there for the one great battle during which the Yankee army would surely crumble.

"*One* glorious battle where we kick the tar out of the other side and show them how much better we are!" That was all anyone heard on either side of the dividing line between Confederacy and Federals.

Privately, senior Northern commanders were less confident. Their new army had no battle experience—not the enlisted men that would have to stand in line and slug it outs while shells exploded and musket balls whistled all around them, and not the commanders who would lead the companies, regiments, and most brigades.

Publicly everyone bubbled over with confidence. But behind closed doors, Union army commanders begged for more time for training.

The Southern army harbored no such fears. They were led by most of the experienced officers from the Mexican War and the Western Indian Wars. Their ranks bristled with confidence and pride.

So the great armies gathered and maneuvered between the two capitals—Washington and Richmond—which sat less than 100 miles apart. Everyone knew those vast armies would have to meet soon. And, oh, what a grand show that meeting would be! Everybody who was anybody couldn't wait to ride out and watch this greatest show on Earth.

Meet Ambrose and Abigail Patterson

In the summer of 1861, Ambrose Patterson was a 49-year-old, second-year congressman from Albany, New York. The Patterson family money originated with Ambrose's grandfather who had built a small empire in shipping and lumber. Ambrose served in local and state politics throughout the 1850s as a Whig. When the Whigs disintegrated in 1856, he was one of the first to join the new Republican Party. Unlike most Republicans, Ambrose was not an ardent abolitionist. He was, however, an ardent Unionist and eagerly supported the war effort.

Abigail Patterson married Ambrose in 1848 when she was 18. By 1861 she had grown into the perfect politician's wife, keenly aware of the nuances of social position and status. Abigail, one of seven children of a prominent Albany banker, possessed the political and social aspirations and cunning her husband lacked.

Ambrose served three terms in Congress before retiring in 1866 to his quiet law practice in upstate New York.

Tea Cakes, White Lace, and Bloodshed

Abigail Patterson craned her neck, gazing from their hillside vantage point. "Did they call off the battle, Ambrose? I don't see any soldiers."

Ambrose Patterson chuckled. "Patience, my dear. It takes time to move 35,000 soldiers into battle." He sucked in a great lungful of the oppressive, sticky air on this country hillside. "Ahhh! Such a lovely day to watch our glorious Army of the Potomac knock the stuffing out of the rebels once and for all."

"You know perfectly well there won't be a battle," Abigail insisted. "It makes no sense. War is the failure of diplomacy. They'll stop at the last minute and talk. They always do."

Ambrose answered. "I assure you, Abby. This is not a bluff. Our army is out to teach the rebels they can't destroy the Union!" His pocket watch read 9:00 A.M. on July 21, 1861, but already a fierce sun cruelly flung its heat upon northern Virginia.

Ambrose's wife, 31-year-old Abigail Patterson, had settled onto their picnic blanket under the shade of a beechnut tree, her floral dress spread across the blanket around her. A fan in her left hand lazily pushed air across her face. "This is all much ado about nothing. We should have stayed in Washington and waited for the victory dances this evening."

A number of prominent Washington civilians dotted the hills along the meandering creek called Bull Run. Rolling fields, patches of thick woods, and an occasional farmhouse completed the serene landscape. The clusters of eager onlookers carried parasols for shade, servants for comfort, and fashionable picnics to enjoy while they watched their noble Union army smash the rebels in one great battle. Generals in Washington had been promising for weeks that it would be a glorious show.

"This is history," insisted Ambrose, breathing deep as if he hoped to hold the moment in his lungs. "The greatest battle ever fought and a mighty blow to preserve the Union. And we get front-row seats!"

Quiet Ruth Jacob sat next to Abby. "Do you know what happens in a battle, Abby?"

Abby shrugged as she daintily sliced a wedge of tea cake. "Soldiers march about as they always do. Generals strut and posture. A deal will be negotiated. We'll all go home having wasted the day out here in the heat."

Ruth answered, "No. Men will scream and die. Men will be blinded and crippled and maimed. Horses and hills will be blown apart. That's a battle."

Abby slowly shook her head. "You are positively gruesome, Ruth. I only agreed to come because other Washington dignitaries are here and I might make contacts that will further Ambrose's career."

The congressman nodded as he chewed on a fried chicken leg. "She's always scheming. We should make Abby a general."

Ruth blushed but continued. "If they wanted to talk, they'd meet in Washington. They meet here for a battle—with cannons and muskets and men trying to kill each other."

An anxious look of dismay flashed across Abby's face. "Ambrose, Anthony. Make her stop. She's frightening me with such talk."

"They're coming!" cried Ambrose, eagerly rubbing his hands together. "See that dust cloud? That's troops marching down the road. And we're in the perfect spot."

Ambrose Patterson, second-year New York congressman, his wife, and long-time family friends, Anthony and Ruth Jacob, of Centerville, Virginia, had ridden out early in Ambrose's carriage to watch the spectacle. The foursome forded Bull Run creek at Sudley Springs. There they turned south to find a comfortable hillside a little north of the Warrenton Turnpike.

"How do you know the battle will happen here?" asked Abigail.

Ambrose chuckled, "The power of being a congressman, my dear. I know a colonel on McDowell's staff. He told me last night that the attack will swing around this flank of the rebel army."

"Flank?" asked Ruth, who sat quietly beside Abigail.

"Flank," explained Ambrose. "The side, the edge, the end. If you're going to watch a battle, Ruth, you had better learn military terms."

"The 'term' for today will be death," answered Ruth. "My father died in the Mexican War. More men will die here."

"Nonsense, Ruth," Abby snapped. "I can't believe the politicians will give up their final chance to talk and turn the army loose. This is all for show—just political posturing."

"The rebels had their chance to talk," answered Ambrose. "I assure you, the army is out to crush the rebellion today."

Ambrose scanned the horizon for signs of troop movement and action. He tensed and pointed to a hill half a mile in front of them. "Look! Rebs!"

Abigail began to clap.

"Don't applaud, Abby. Those are the enemy."

"It's like a chess game, each side maneuvering their pieces until one general sees he's at a disadvantage and bows out, taking his army home. Don't you think it's exciting to see how far they'll go before they back down?"

"Will it be exciting to watch them die?" answered Ruth.

Anthony Jacob peered south. His heart pounded and his eyes blazed at the sight of a fluttering Confederate flag. "That's Ed Matthews's place they're lined up on." Living in Centerville, Virginia, Jacob was technically a Southerner and, thus, a Confederate and rebel. While he had always considered himself part of Washington society and did as much business north as south, he felt a sudden stirring of loyalty to Virginia as actual battle approached.

They made an odd-looking foursome spread out for a hillside picnic of tea cakes, egg salad, chicken, bread, apples, cheese, and wine. White-haired Anthony Jacob stood tall, erect, and as stately as a noble plantation owner. His wife, Ruth, was plain and reserved. Squat Ambrose Patterson was a barrel-chested bull of a man with a shiny, domed head who was in perpetual motion. Abigail continually struggled to appear elegant and aristocratic.

"Now those rebs'll get it!" cried Ambrose, pointing back over his left shoulder toward Sudley Ford. A long column of blue had crossed Bull Run, eight men across and undulating miles back as far as the eye could see along the dirt road like a fierce and monstrous snake. Rank after rank of sparkling soldiers marched past the hill where the Pattersons and Jacobs watched. Drums pounded. A band played back near the ford. Ambrose cheered and saluted.

Brilliant flags fluttered. Long musket barrels gleamed in the morning sun. Each uniform was crisp and dazzling blue. The men marched with confidence and pride. None on the hill had imagined such a glorious and inspiring sight. The air reverberated with the sound of 15,000 steadily thumping pairs of boots. The ground vibrated under Abigail from the thunderous might of their passing.

How elegant and powerful they looked. How mighty and ferocious they appeared. Surely, no force on Earth could oppose this heroic onslaught. Surely now the rebels would sensibly ask to talk. . . .

The blue surge swept through a line of trees below the Pattersons' picnic spot and spread into lines for the charge up Matthews's Hill.

"That's General Burnside," cried Ambrose pointing at a mounted officer whose uniform dripped in bright yellow braid. "He's a real fighter. The rebs are in for it now."

Officers drew swords. The 800 muskets of the men in the leading regiment pointed forward. The Union army started up the hill.

Tears rolled down Ruth's cheeks and she turned away. "Can't you make them stop?" she wailed. "You're a congressman."

"Stop? At the moment of victory?" chuckled Ambrose. "I think not!"

Abigail sprang to her feet, caught up in the thrilling pageantry of gathering armies as the regimental colors caught a slight breeze and unfurled over the grassy slope. The lines of blue marched so steady and looked so gallant. Tension grew with the eerie silence on the hill as the two lines of cocked muskets drew closer. Abby's heart rattled. This was no longer an intellectual exercise of political maneuvering. This was raw animal power and emotion such as Abby had never dreamed of in her sheltered world.

"Splendid," murmured Ambrose.

And then the Confederate line opened fire.

The thunder clap of the first volley made Abigail jump. Birds squawked and swooped into the air. The Union flag went down as its holder crumpled to the grass, only to be snatched up by another soldier in brilliant blue.

On they marched uphill into the withering fire of the rebels and into the growing smoke cloud which hung on Matthews's Hill. From half a mile away, the musket fire sounded like a continuous, dull lion's roar.

"So many are down," muttered Abby.

Pain and death had never been a part of the picture of war Washington brass had painted for Abigail Patterson. In her version, war was stirring pageantry, brilliant colors, political maneuvering, backroom secret negotiations, last-minute deals, uniforms streaming across green fields, bands playing rousing songs, men cheering, and victory dances afterward.

Badly mauled by rebel fire, the lead Union regiment stumbled back down the slope.

"Is it over?" gasped Abigail. "Did we lose?"

"Just feeling out the enemy position, my dear," said Ambrose.

"But there are so many dead . . ."

"It's a battle, Abby," Ruth hissed. "What did you expect?"

"Quite normal, I assure you," said Ambrose. "Now Burnside will bring his whole division into the line—several thousand of them—and pound the stuffing out of those paltry few rebs." And he chuckled devilishly.

Fluttering flag after flag, soldier after soldier, unit after unit, line after line marched in regal splendor past the Pattersons's Hill and spread into a vast line of blue that stretched across the whole world at the bottom of Matthews's Hill.

The acid stench of sulfurous smoke from the first attack's firing drifted north to burn Abigail's eyes and throat. The sultry heat beat upon her.

"Patience, my dear," chuckled Ambrose. "The army is about to do all the 'talking' you want with this next charge."

Up the slope marched two new Union regiments, over 1,000 men. Cannons roared from somewhere just behind the Pattersons's Hill. Shells screeched across the sky and blasted into the hill near the Confederate-held top. Dirt and grass exploded in showers across the Confederate line.

Again the Confederates fired. And again the Union soldiers died. And the cannons roared. And the soldiers yelled as they marched into the flaming death. And smoke, thick as fog, flowed across the hillside. And the wounded screamed. And the muskets thundered.

And again the Union advance was pushed back. A new crop of crumpled dead littered the hillside.

"Look at Matthews's Hill now!" called Anthony Jacob.

Reinforcements had swelled the gray line. Thousands of angry rebel muskets now pointed down the deadly slope. But almost 15,000 Federal muskets lined the bottom.

The Confederates charged downhill with barbaric cries. The Union lines fired a monstrous volley that shook the Earth. Gray bodies fell, mingling blue and gray dead on the slope. And now the Confederates retreated and the Union line advanced again.

For two hours the battle for Matthews's Hill raged with a deafening roar of musket, cannon, and human cries before Union forces pushed to the top of the slope and took the hill. Score was kept by the number of mangled corpses in the carpet of dead that covered the hill.

Ambrose leapt and cheered. Anthony ground his teeth and prayed for a counterattack. Both women were stunned into silence. The spectacle had seemed more like a hideous nightmare than a glorious dream.

"Is it over?" whispered Abigail.

"Gather up the food," ordered Ambrose. "Burnside's boys have routed the reb line. We'll follow the army as it roars through the rebel camp and takes the rail center at Manassas Junction. Then its one quick train ride and our army takes Richmond itself!"

Ruth was numbed by the horror of Matthews's Hill. "It was even more dreadful than *I* had imagined . . ." She demanded to leave.

Abigail was mesmerized by the brutal ferocity of the fighting. But, as frightful as the spectacle of Matthews's Hill had been, she couldn't pull her eyes away from the littered field.

"I'll leave with Ruth," Anthony offered. Secretly, he was unwilling to watch his Confederate army disintegrate under Federal assault.

Countless new ranks of blue hurried past the Pattersons' carriage as Mr. Patterson's servant flicked his whip to keep the frightened horse moving. Abigail hardly noticed the flags, uniforms, gleaming muskets, and brave voices raised in regimental songs as they streamed by. The battle still held a grim fascination for her, but the pageantry had lost its innocent charm and sweet romantic blush.

How many of these uniforms rushing past would be shredded by exploding shells and whining musket balls? How many coats of blue would be stained dark with mud and blood before the day was done? How many of these bright young faces would soon be no more than litter on the next hillside?

"We'll search for souvenirs of the victory," declared Ambrose, directing his driver to stop in the middle of the battle-torn slope.

"Ambrose how *could* you? These men *died*!"

"They died to preserve our sacred Union, Abby," he scolded. "And I plan to honor them by tacking some mementos of their victory on my wall."

Matthews's Hill was silent now except for the groans and whimpers of the wounded. The pounding roar of battle already seemed lifetimes away. Union medics drifted from body to body. Stretcher bearers were beginning to cart off the bloody remains.

Abigail was stunned at how such a lovely parade of soldiers could so quickly turn into a mangled and frightful field of death and gore. Trickling streams of blood soaked into her shoes and dress hem as she wandered among the bodies. Looks of terror and suffering were frozen on now silent faces. The smell of death already permeated the field. Muskets, canteens, arms, legs, and lives seemed to have all been thrown away with equally careless abandon.

A pair of rabbits nervously inched out of their burrow, sniffing to see if the roaring monster had gone. Birds circled thick overhead. Massed flies droned everywhere, already feasting on the dead.

Abigail felt hopelessly lost in an endless sea of human destruction that had spread with shocking ease across this hill of horror. From the distance of half a mile, the battle had looked vicious and brutal. Up close the aftermath could only be described as grizzly mayhem and pain-filled misery.

The thought struck her that, while she had watched and eaten chicken from a picnic basket, a thousand children had forever lost their fathers; hundreds of wives had become weeping widows; hundreds of families had been torn apart—all for one patch of sloping grass that had been first trampled into mud and now abandoned as easily as a child tosses aside a broken toy.

"Look at *this*," called Ambrose with a beaming smile as he held aloft two swords and yellow sashes. "Took 'em both off dead Confederate colonels."

Ambrose hustled his wife back into the carriage. "Come along, my dear. We don't want to miss anything."

Abigail rode in silence past Matthews's shattered house and down the south slope of Matthews's Hill. Ambrose rambled on about how glorious a battle it had been and how proud he was to have been here to see it.

The carriage crossed a shallow creek called Young's Branch and reached the Warrington Turnpike, a wide road heading west out of Centerville, and found the great mass of McDowell's Union army bunched just across the road.

Through the trees ahead came the roar of suddenly renewed gunfire. A row of cannons in a clearing to the right erupted into life, thunderous fire and smoke belching across the field. The pounding concussion of each shot beat against Abigail's chest, making it hard to breathe. The unending roar tore painfully at her ears.

The carriage was stopped by a major who barked, "No civilians!"

"I'm a congressman and demand to watch my army in action."

The major shook his head. "Not safe, sir. The fighting's fierce up there."

"Fiddlesticks," Ambrose snapped. "The entire Army of the Potomac stands between me and the rebs. What could be safer, man?"

Still, it was well past 2:30 P.M. when Ambrose and Abigail managed to work their way far enough to the right to get past the trees, past the army guards, and gain a view of the next hillside.

Abigail gasped. Not even the sight of Matthews's Hill prepared her for the sight spread before her. *That* had been a skirmish. This was the raging inferno of battle. Dense lines of soldiers fired at each other from point-blank range. Hundreds sprawled into death throes on each volley. Acrid smoke choked the field with a surreal haze. Broken and blackened bodies of men and horses covered the ground. The din was unbearable. The ground shook hard enough to rattle the carriage.

Abigail felt sick and wanted only to scream and flee. The world had gone mad. How could reasonable men allow *this* to happen? Yet she sat rooted in morbid fascination. Surely, never before on God's green Earth had such a hellish scene been created or witnessed.

Ambrose excitedly pointed to a line of abandoned cannons surrounded by mounds of mangled bodies. "That's the 11th New York Regiment," announced Ambrose pointing at fresh lines of soldiers just wheeling onto the field below the cannons. "They're from my district. They're about to take the cannons back!"

Ambrose rose from his seat and shouted, "Give 'em hell, boys!" and whooped a great cheer.

And then the Confederate line opened fire. In one hideous flash, the orderly rows of soldiers in the 11th New York dissolved. Whole sections of the line seemed to snap into the air before they crashed, lifeless, to the ground. The officers fell. The colonel's horse was shot. The colonel was hit four times while leaping clear of his falling steed. The neat lines of blue were transformed into a mangled pile of death.

The tattered remnants of the 11th crawled and staggered back. So, too, did the 14th Zoauve Regiment from Brooklyn wearing their bright red pants, the next unit to try to climb the hill.

The Confederate line rushed forward with a piercing rebel yell that chilled Abigail's blood. And suddenly the entire right side of the Union army was falling back, not at an orderly walk, not as disciplined units, but like terrified children at a panicked run. The Army of the Potomac disintegrated.

Soldiers streamed back by any path leading north. Muskets, canteens, cartridge belts, and any other equipment that might slow their race to safety were tossed aside like trash. Units that had not yet fought were infected by the spreading terror and fled as if the devil were nipping at their heels, without even knowing why they were running.

Ambrose Patterson erupted from his carriage in a rage. "Stop!" he cried at the routed blue. "You will *not* retreat! You will *not* give up!" His face glowed bright red and his neck veins bulged. "You are *my* army, and you *will* be victorious!"

Now a crazed and rampaging bull, Ambrose snatched up the musket of a fallen soldier. Howling like an enraged bear, Congressman Ambrose Patterson launched a one-man charge up the hill. Amazingly, a number of other Washington dignitaries also held their ground on that bloody field, begging the soldiers around them to stand and fight.

A cavalry captain grabbed Ambrose by the arm and spun him around. "You must leave, sir!"

"But we must win!"

"No. You must leave *now!*"

The Pattersons rode in stunned silence back to Washington over Virginia country roads clogged with troops, littered with countless weapons, tons of valuable equipment, and seemingly endless caravans of army supply wagons.

There was no glory. There was no victory. There would be no courteous conversation to end the war. There would be no victory dance. There was only the shocking reality of the horror of war and the grim realization that the nation had chosen a terrible and bloody path.

Aftermath

The First Battle of Bull Run was a disgrace for Union army commanders and a deep shock for Washington dignitaries and the Northern population. The North came to Bull Run expecting pageantry, valor, and easy victory. They found only the death, terror, and horror of war. More than 8,500 casualties were produced on the field that July day, over 5,000 of them from Northern units. And nothing was gained either way.

Northern soldiers, entering their first combat, fought well enough during most of the day. They suffered, however, from dismal leadership.

Ambrose Patterson felt so ashamed of that defeat that he refused to display his captured Confederate swords until final victory had been won in 1865.

Militarily, the battle accomplished little. Politically, its affects were monumental. Both sides realized that the war could not, and would not, be easily and quickly won.

Lincoln and senior Union commanders realized they lacked skilled generalship and that the South had assembled an efficient and powerful army.

General McDowell was replaced by General George McClellan, the first of a half dozen changes of command in three short years for the Army of the Potomac.

The only real winners at Bull Run were a pair of Washington businessmen who realized the tourist value of the battlefield. Two days after the battle they bought up the fields where the battle had been fought and made a "killing" by charging tourists top dollar for guided tours.

Follow-up Questions and Activities

1. **What Do You Know?**
   - Why did the armies of the Confederacy and Union meet in their first major battle in northern Virginia? What were they protecting and trying to attack?
   - Why did Washington civilians come out to watch the First Battle of Bull Run?
   - Why didn't the larger Union army win this battle? Was it army commanders or the rank-and-file soldiers who failed the test in this battle?
   - How did Abigail Patterson's image of war and battle change over the course of the battle?

2. **Find Out More.** Following are some important topics from this story for students to research in the library and on the Internet. The bibliography at the back of this book will help them get started.
   - Four generals were featured in the fighting at First Bull Run: Northern Generals Irving McDowell (the first commanding general of the Army of the Potomac) and Amos Burnside, and Southern Generals Joe Johnston and Pierre Beaurigard. Research these four men, their previous service, and their accomplishments after this battle in July 1861.
   - Civilians flocked from Washington to watch this battle. Most were horrified by what they saw. Research American public opinions about war, and newspaper editorials about war before the war began. What did these civilians *expect* to see? What did they think battle would *look* like? Did civilians traipse out to watch other Civil War battles? Have civilians been eager to watch battles in other wars over the past thousand years? Are civilians more or less likely to want to watch battles today? Why?
   - Thomas J. "Stonewall" Jackson became one of the most successful of all Southern generals. Research this brilliant but quirky general. Where did he come from? What were his peculiar habits? How and why did he get the name "Stonewall"? When and how did he die? What were his military accomplishments before he died? What effect did his death have on the outcome of the war?

- The First Battle of Bull Run was not the only battle fought near Manassas Junction, Virginia. Research the Second Battle of Bull Run, fought in the summer of 1862. What other smaller engagements occurred in this same area? Why did the armies continually return to this same patch of ground?

3. **Make It Real**

   - Compare and contrast watching a Civil War battle to watching a high school or college football game. Both are combats, both are held in a grassy field. Both feature trained, uniformed warriors who use preplanned strategy and tactics. Both often have cheering spectators. What is different between the two? What are other similarities?

   - Imagine that you are a soldier in the Civil War marching in battle line toward the enemy. Cannon shells explode around you. Musket balls whine past. Your friends are dropping and dying around you. What would make you hold your place in line, face death, and continue your advance? Write a letter to a friend after a battle describing how you felt during an advance into a strong enemy line.

   - At the end of the First Battle of Bull Run, the Union soldiers panicked and fled. Officers could not order, pursue, or threaten them back into the front lines. Reflect on your own life. Write down up to 10 incidents when fear has made you want to run away. Did you run? Why did you run—or not run in each instance? Write down as many reasons as you can. Compare your lists with those of your classmates. Do you think your list of reasons is different than what a Civil War soldier would have felt in the heat of battle?

4. **Points to Ponder**

   - Why do you think both sides believed the other was going to collapse and quit at the first sign of battle? Why do you think each side so badly missed in their evaluation of their enemy? Do you think most wars begin with such false assumptions?

   - Union forces finally collapsed, panicked, and fled at First Bull Run. Why would soldiers panic and run in the face of the enemy? Do you blame them? What made most soldiers in most battles of the Civil War stand and fight, even though they were likely to die? Why would they want to run? If you were in charge of a regiment, what could you do to ensure than no one in your unit broke and ran under fire?

A Deadly Tug of War

In 1862, armies on both sides of the Civil War launched their campaigns into full swing. Ebenezer Butterick created the world's first paper cutout clothes pattern. Pierre Mihaux invented the ball bearing, and Richard Gatling invented the machine gun. In the Civil War, 1862 saw four of the war's bloodiest battles, the final showdown in the far West, the first major evidence of the Union blockade's effectiveness, and lasting changes in naval warfare.

In the East, Union General George McClellan collected a gigantic army of 120,000 and ponderously rumbled south. He could have, and should have, crushed the Confederate force opposing him, which possessed less than a third of his strength. But McClellan was an overly cautious general, and the man who took control of the Confederate forces during this Peninsular Campaign, Robert E. Lee, was not. Lee used bold, swift attacks to drive the Goliath away. McClellan was disgraced by his failure and was relieved of command.

Lee pushed Union troops almost back to Washington, D.C., in his surprise attack leading to the Second Battle of Bull Run. The massive Army of the Potomac shivered in terror of the smaller Confederate forces of Lee and Stonewall Jackson. McClellan was reappointed to command the Army of the Potomac after the debacle of the Second Battle of Bull Run.

In the fall, Lee decided to attack north through western Maryland and take advantage of McClellan's lethargy. Lee's plans were intercepted and handed to McClellan. McClellan pounced and caught Lee unprepared at Sharpsburg, Maryland, along the shore of Antietam Creek. McClellan should have crushed Lee's army; instead, the battle was a draw. Lee escaped back to Virginia.

McClellan was relieved again as a result of his failure to act decisively. General Ambrose Burnside took command and moved the massive Army of the Potomac south into Virginia, attacking Lee through the town of Fredericksburg in mid-December, a disastrous move. Union forces were slaughtered in droves. The Union army fell back. Another Union commander was relieved. No Union general, it seemed, could handle the small Confederate force of Robert E. Lee. In the East, the Southern strategy was working.

In the West it was a different story. Union General Ulysses Grant forced the Confederate strongholds of Forts Henry and Donaldson along the Tennessee and Cumberland Rivers to surrender. Then he pushed south into central Tennessee and survived a near defeat at Shiloh to hold the field, driving off General Joe Johnston's Confederate force. By year's end, Union forces controlled all of Tennessee and were pushing hard down the Mississippi River toward Vicksburg. They seized control of Arkansas. In the West, the Union strategy seemed to be working.

In the far West, two battles in New Mexico settled the question there once and for all. The Union victory at Glorieta Pass drove all Confederate forces back to Texas. Western gold and silver mines were saved for the federal government to use to pay for the war. The Confederacy would have to survive without Western wealth.

The naval blockade also progressed nicely for the Union during 1862. The Savannah River fell to Union control. The Sea Islands of South Carolina and their ports fell. The Lower Mississippi River and New Orleans fell. By year's end, the majority of all Confederate ports were closed by the Union blockade. The rest were tightly guarded by offshore blockade ships so that cargoes had to slip through at a trickle on fast blockade runner ships.

On all fronts except the eastern theater, the Union strategy was advancing as designed. In the East, Robert E. Lee made the giant Union army look inept.

Key Events in 1862

Date	Event
February 16	General Grant captures Confederate Forts Donaldson and Henry in Tennessee. This is the Union's first major victory in the war and destroys the Confederate base in central Tennessee and Kentucky.
February 21	Confederate forces win the Battle of Valverde in New Mexico Territory, threatening to capture the gold-rich West.
February 25	Union forces occupy Nashville, Tennessee.
March 5	Stonewall Jackson defeats Union forces under General Nathaniel Banks in his Valley Campaign, pushing Union forces back to Washington, D.C.
March 8	Union forces win the battle of Elkhorn Tavern in Arkansas.
March 9	C.S.S. *Virginia* (the old *Merrimac*) and the U.S.S. *Monitor* battle to a draw off Norfolk, Virginia. The *Virginia* retreats and never fights again. The era of iron and steel ships begins.
March 27	Union forces win the Battle of Glorieta Pass in New Mexico, the "Gettsyburg of the West," driving invading Confederate forces back to Texas.
April 6–7	General Grant narrowly wins the Battle of Shiloh in Tennessee.

Date	Event
April 10–11	Federal naval forces capture the entrance fort (Fort Pulaski) guarding the Savannah River and close another Confederate port to blockade-running Confederate ships.
April 25	Admiral David Farragut defeats Confederate naval forces on the Lower Mississippi and captures New Orleans.
May 4	Union General McClellan occupies Yorktown, Virginia, as the first step in his Peninsular Campaign.
May 25	Stonewall Jackson defeats Union General Banks at the Battle of Winchester.
May 31–June 1	Union reinforcements stave off disaster from a Confederate attack at the Battle of Seven Pines, Virginia.
June 25–July 1	During the Seven Days Battle smaller Confederate forces under Robert E. Lee push McClellan's giant Union army away from Richmond. McClellan abandons the Peninsular Campaign.
July 11	Lincoln relieves McClellan of command and gives the Army of the Potomac to General John Pope.
August 29–30	Lee outwits Pope, winning the Second Battle of Bull Run.
September 2	Lincoln relieves Pope and reinstates General McClellan.
September 17	The Battle of Antietam (Sharpsburg) is officially a draw between Lee and McClellan. The battle is clearly a defeat for Lee because it stops his invasion of the North. However, McClellan should have easily destroyed or captured Lee's entire army but let Lee slip away back into Virginia.
September 22	Lincoln announces his Emancipation Proclamation, which will become effective on January 1, 1863.
October 8	Kentucky's only battle, the Battle of Perryville, is a victory for Union General Don Buell over Confederate General Braxton Bragg. However, Buell had the opportunity to destroy Bragg's entire army and failed to do it. Lincoln relieves Buell of command.
November 7	Lincoln relieves McClellan again for his failure to act decisively and appoints General Burnside commander of the Army of the Potomac.
December 13	The Battle of Fredericksburg, Virginia, is a disaster for Union forces. Burnside is relieved. General Joe Hooker becomes the new eastern Union army commander.
December 31	The Battle of Stone's River (Murfreesboro) is fought for control of Tennessee. The battle is inconclusive until Confederate General Bragg inexplicably withdraws, leaving Union General William Rosecrans in control of the field and the state.

Supper, Shoes, and Shovels
Supplying a Civil War Army,
February 1862

At a Glance

Everyone thought the Civil War would last a few weeks, maybe a couple of months. One big battle, maybe two, and it would be over. Everyone could go home. With that mentality, neither Northern nor Southern army commanders felt the necessity to develop extensive supply systems.

However, the early battles proved that neither side was going to collapse quickly.

Army commanders were caught completely unprepared. Neither army had developed a formal supply system as it massed vast regiments of infantry, artillery, and cavalry. A 100,000-man army needed 2,500 wagons, 35,000 horses, and 500 mules. It consumed 700 tons of food every day. It often fired 100 tons of powder and ammunition in one day of battle. It demanded steady flows of uniforms, muskets, grease, vinegar, quinine, bandages and lint dressings, pontoon bridges, leather, repair parts, tin cups, cans for cooking, shovels, tents, shoes, blankets, knives, forks, skillets, razors, camp chairs for officers, and much, much more.

Somebody had to find these supplies, figure out where the individual units were that needed them, and find a way to get the wagonloads of goods where they were supposed to go. This was a monumental task. Regiments and brigades were forever on the move. Supply wagons trailed after them, trying to catch up. Roads were often clogged with mud and impassable or were choked with marching troops. Supply wagons regularly took days to travel distances that should have taken only a few hours.

Supplying an army in the field was a nightmarish job. It called for the best and the brightest each army could muster into the thankless job.

Meet Captain Walter Huster

Born during the winter of 1839, Walter Huster grew up as one of 10 children working a Pennsylvania farm southeast of Pittsburgh. When Walter turned four, his mother died giving birth to her 13th child. Walter had a gift for learning and was the only one of his siblings who wanted to go, or seemed capable of going, to college. He graduated at age 20 and took a job as teacher and headmaster of a small school in Cleveland, Ohio, along the shore of Lake Erie. He taught there for two years before feeling compelled to "set a good example for his students." Huster joined the army just as the fall semester was beginning in 1861.

Because of his college education, Walter was snatched out of basic training, promoted to captain, and shoved into the new supply office for McClellan's 100,000-man Army of the Potomac. He never fired a gun, marched with a unit, or witnessed a battle until he was wounded by the Confederate shelling that began the third day's fighting at Gettysburg. Huster was discharged from the army in November 1863, because of this wound and was left with a permanent limp. He returned to teaching and spent most of his life working to educate poor and black children in St. Louis. He never married and died in 1899.

Supper, Shoes, and Shovels

S ergeant Michael Reiley politely coughed, then kicked the cot to stir its sleeping occupant. "Beggin' yer pardon, captain. But the colonel would like to see you, so he would."

Twenty-three-year-old Captain Walter Huster bolted upright, still more asleep than awake. His eyes darted about the pitch-black tent but couldn't quite focus.

"The colonel's callin' for you in his loud voice, captain, don't you know?"

Huster shook his head and rubbed his face. "What time is it?"

"A wee shy of 5:30 in the morning, it is, sir," answered Sergeant Reiley, as if he found something humorous in holding this conversation two hours before dawn. But then Sergeant Reiley's voice always seemed to laugh as if he and his 15 years' experience in the army saw some vast joke that forever eluded Captain Huster.

"The colonel wants to see me *now*?"

"And since his face looked sour as rotten vinegar, I'd rush right over, so I would."

Captain Huster threw off his blanket and fumbled in the dark for his uniform. He splashed water on his face and gasped as its near-freezing cold stung his skin. Finally, he ran his fingers through his mop of sandy brown hair to flatten it down and scratched at his beard. Huster was trying to grow a full, bushy beard to appear older, but it had come in annoyingly spotty.

Adjusting his cap, Walter Huster stepped outside into the moonlit dark on February 18, 1862. Around him sprawled the vast tent city of General McClellan's field headquarters just west of Alexandria, Virginia, while McClellan's divisions and brigades fanned out in a wide protective shield south and west from Washington, and waited. The army trained and waited, waited and trained. Brigades shifted. Regiments darted back and forth in a kind of dance with Joe Johnston's Confederate Army of Northern Virginia. Pickets sniped at each other. An occasional company or regiment mixed it up for a moment with the enemy. But mostly the army trained, waited . . . and ate.

Huster had a half-mile trip through the dark to reach the office tent where he served under Colonel Franklin Ross, chief of supply for McClellan. The thin moonlight made the white canvas tents seem to glow against the dark of rolling fields and trees. A mist hung in the gullies and lowlands, making the tent city seem to float above the clouds.

Huster decided to jog to headquarters. If the colonel wanted him at this hour, something *big* must be happening. Maybe the rumors were true and the entire army was moving out to attack the rebels. If so, the supply office would have lots of work to do today, and Huster was eager to get at it and prove his worth to the army.

Or maybe his transfer to a combat unit had come through. He applied for transfer because he thought he should, because fighting seemed more important than filing papers at headquarters. He wanted to swagger home with war stories that would impress his friends and family. He wanted to be proud of his part in the war. For that, he needed a battle.

He had tried to make himself feel glad he had applied for transfer. But a big part of Walter Huster liked it right here at headquarters. Supply seemed like a giant puzzle, a grand game to figure out. He got to move and arrange the pieces so that they all fit. He was good at this game of paper-shuffling supplies.

But . . . this job felt too safe and somehow cowardly, staying so far from the front and the danger of battle. For weeks, Huster had been unable to settle this turmoil between wanting to stay and needing to go. It hung on him like a giant millstone, like a burden he couldn't shake. He had applied for transfer, but a big part of him—a part that made him feel ashamed—hoped the application would be denied.

Huster easily shook off the morning chill even though it was a damp, bitter cold. He was familiar with soggy cold, having lived in Cleveland where cold rolled in hard and wet off Lake Erie.

What he wasn't familiar with was the army. He'd been in uniform for only four months and could barely identify rank insignia, especially since no two general's uniforms looked alike. Some generals wore coats as plain as corporals', while some majors were gussied up with braid, sashes, plumes, and ribbons like they were the emperor.

Huster mulled over these complexities of army life as he jogged along. Suddenly his arm was taken in an iron grip that almost jerked him off his feet.

"Don't you run away from me, mister," growled a bear-like voice.

Captain Huster squinted at the face and uniform for a clue to this man's identity. To be safe he answered, "Ah, good morning, general."

"Sykes, mister. General Sykes. You remember our conversation of yesterday?"

Huster had held over 100 conversations during the course of the previous day. In each one of them someone had demanded some supply action from him.

General Sykes glared at the young captain while still holding his arm in a vice-like grip that cut off Huster's circulation and made his fingers tingle. "I command a forward brigade, almost down to the Rappahannock, mixing it up every day with the rebs. My men need fresh food, powder, and cartridges."

"Right, sir. I remember. Two wagons filled with food and ammo were sent to your brigade."

"Then why did I get a wagonload of shoes?" Sykes's voice boomed like a cannon and echoed off the hills.

"Shoes, sir? The shoes were sent to the forward depot at General Porter's division."

Sykes yanked Huster up so their faces were only inches apart and growled, "My men can't eat shoes and they can't fire shoes. So you better fix it—before breakfast, Hustle. Understood?!"

Walter Huster had picked up the nickname "Captain Hustle" back around Christmas because he routinely ran through headquarters instead of walking.

"Yes, sir. Right away, sir! As soon as I report to Colonel Ross, sir."

Sykes released the youth and turned away, but then paused. "You like your soft, safe job here at headquarters, captain?"

His voice sounded dangerously calm and friendly. The turmoil boiled furiously inside Huster's mind. All he had to do was answer, "No," and he'd be reassigned to Sykes's brigade. But did he *really* want to serve under General Sykes? If he didn't jump at this opportunity, would he ever make his parents proud? If he *did*, wouldn't Sykes shove him into the front line to be killed in the next battle?

Huster gulped and answered, "I do the best I can at the job I was assigned, sir!" Then he turned and dashed for the army supply office tent, wanting to kick himself for being a mouse, for not being able to bravely volunteer to face danger.

Huster paused outside Colonel Ross's tent office to adjust and smooth his uniform jacket. He tried to knock to announce his presence but, for the hundredth time, was frustrated by his inability to figure out how to knock on a tent flap. He shrugged, sighed, and stepped into the glare of gas lanterns inside. "You wanted to see me, sir?"

Colonel Ross, a plump, red-haired man in his late forties, sat hunched on a stool behind a long table stacked with teetering piles of paper. Maps were pinned to the walls of his tent. Ross glared at his assistant with the piercing gray eyes of a wolf. "Explain yourself, Hustle."

Huster nodded in understanding. Sykes must have seen the colonel. "I know about the shoes, sir, and . . ."

"What *shoes*? I'm talking about McClellan, the man we both work for. He chewed me up one side and down the other at 5:00 this morning because Burnside . . ."

"Burnside, sir?"

"*General* Burnside, II Corps commander, kept McClellan up 'til midnight complaining about the food."

"The food, sir?"

Ross slammed his beefy hands down on the thick table. "Yes, the food. The food that you delivered to his men. What is this new stuff you're trying to make them eat? Desiccated vegetables? Burnside says its terrible. No one can eat it."

"It's ground up, dried vegetables, sir. A wonderful idea."

"Sounds awful," Ross growled.

"You just have to boil desiccated vegetables, sir. Well, actually it's best to simmer them. That reforms the vegetables into a stew-like paste—quite tasty, actually. I thought it was a grand idea. Solves two problems: food spoilage and weight."

"Go on," demanded the colonel.

"Fresh food spoils in the Washington warehouses before it can be shipped out," Huster explained. "They have to throw most of it away. What's left is heavy and bulky to ship. Takes more wagons and more drivers and more teams of horses—all of which we are terribly short of."

"Go on," repeated Colonel Ross.

"If we dry and grind up the vegetables before shipping, then a wagon can carry six times as many rations and they won't spoil. We don't waste food." As an afterthought Huster added, "I find desiccated vegetables are best if simmered with spices and a bit of pork or bacon. . . ."

"Enough!" bellowed the colonel. "This is an army, not a social club. And Burnside's men say this desiccated stuff tastes terrible."

Huster suggested, "Maybe we could offer cooking lessons to show the men how to fix it properly."

Colonel Ross glowered at his assistant. "You want me to tell a corps commander to pull his units out of contact with the enemy to teach them how to cook?"

It sounded like a fine idea to Captain Huster. But obviously the colonel didn't share his enthusiasm. The morning's first rooster crowed somewhere outside. Several dogs barked in response. "Then maybe we could print the recipes and instructions in a manual."

"Are you trying to make me the laughingstock of the army, Hustle?" Colonel Ross almost screamed the words.

"No, sir!" Huster answered, snapping to attention.

"I can't put out a cookbook for the army. This is soldiering, *fighting*, not a garden club."

Huster glumly realized that once again the "army" way of thinking had eluded him. "Maybe just tell them to add salt, sir."

Colonel Ross drummed his fingers on the table and growled, "The commanding general yells at me at 5:00 A.M., and I'm supposed to tell him to have the men add salt? Burnside says they also get moldy bread and maggots in the meat! My God, man! We're only 20 miles from Washington. Can't we supply decent food to our troops 20 miles out in the field?"

Huster heard the nighttime sentries shuffling into camp, having been relieved by the next shift.

"The problem, sir, is in the warehouses themselves. Much of the food spoils before they ship it. I suspect the original supplier is gouging the army, supplying low-grade, improperly prepared meats and charging the government top price for it."

"Of course they are, man," the colonel blurted out. "Suppliers have been doing that to armies for centuries." Ross leaned across the table and lowered his voice. "Now here is what I will tell the general. I will thank him for pointing out the problem to me, and I will tell him that supplying decent food to every unit in the army is our top priority, and that my assistant—*you*—will make solving this vexing problem his top priority and will report to the general's staff regularly with his progress."

"*Me*, sir?"

"Yes, you. I can't have corps commanders in here complaining about food. So you make sure they don't have to." Colonel Ross nodded as if that ended the conversation, but then added, "And what's this about shoes?"

"I sent two wagons with food and ammunition to General Sykes, but he got the shoes I sent to General Porter."

Colonel Ross, who loved to laugh almost as much as Sergeant Reiley, threw back his head and howled, "I would have loved to see the look on Sykes's face when he opened 50 crates of shoes! Both those units relocated early yesterday. Sykes shifted to cover the area where Porter had been. Porter shifted south and west to Morrisville. Your shoe driver apparently thought he *had* found Porter's camp. Lord knows who got Sykes's food. Hope it wasn't the rebs!" And he again let out his booming laugh.

Colonel Ross then shuffled through a fistful of pages to signal that the conversation was over. Huster saluted and had turned to leave when the colonel said, "The army, Hustle, lives on its stomach. If the army is well fed, discipline is better. The lads will fight more willingly. If men are happier, the generals are happier. If generals are happier, then I am happier. And you, captain, do not get to be happy unless I'm happy. Understand? You keep decent food flowing to those troops—all of them!"

"But, sir, I'm short of wagons. We barely have 2,000, but should have over 3,000. We have to deliver over 600 tons of food to over 50 separate sites every day. Medical staffs want wagons. Units want their own wagons. The U.S. Sanitary Commission demands wagons. There just aren't enough wagons. I also need drivers, extra horses, and repairmen."

Colonel Ross sadly shook his head. "You are in the army supply office, Hustle. You *are* the supply office! If you need wagons, horses, and drivers, go out and get them."

"But, sir, the few I can find are of poor quality and grossly overpriced. It galls me to waste the army's money."

"It will 'gall' you much more, captain, if general officers have to complain to me that they aren't getting the supplies they need and deserve."

Huster sighed as he again saluted. He pushed opened the canvas flap between the colonel's inner office and his small outer office and sank into his folding chair at the tiny table he used as a desk. To himself he muttered, "This job is nothing but complaints and impossible problems, problems and complaints."

Maybe I should get transferred, Huster thought. *There's too much responsibility in this job. Maybe I'd be better off where all I have to do is march and stand and shoot.* The simplicity of life in a combat unit suddenly felt like a life of ease and comfort.

The first hint of blue sky appeared over the eastern horizon. It would be clear and cold today. Huster hoped that each unit would be able to find its own firewood and water. Otherwise, he'd surely hear complaints about it tomorrow.

Colonel Ross shoved the flap aside and dropped a short stack of papers on Huster's table. "Take care of these for me."

Irritated at his staggering workload, Captain Huster demanded, "Should I do these before I get Porter his shoes, Sykes his supplies, make desiccated vegetables palatable, straighten out the warehouses, and find 1,000 new wagons, teams, and drivers, sir, or after?"

"Just take care of them!" snapped the colonel.

Huster sighed and glanced at the requisition forms. "Horse feed, sir?"

"Most units are dangerously low."

"Can't the horses eat grass?"

"In winter, Hustle? There are over 35,000 horses in this army—cavalry, your supply wagons, officers' mounts. And we have to make sure they stay healthy."

"Where do I get horse feed, sir?"

"Go to the army supply officer."

"That's you, sir."

Ross smiled and nodded. "And I'll tell you to see my assistant. He'll fix you up with whatever you need."

"But your assistant is me, sir."

The colonel bellowed, "So do it!"

"Can't the combat units do *anything* for themselves?" Huster grumbled.

Colonel Ross paused at his tent flap. "They fight and they die. They do lots of both. And that is why we work round the clock to get them whatever they need!" He stomped inside but then poked his head back outside the flap. "I talked McClellan into throwing out that silly transfer application of yours." He shook his head and chuckled. "Wanting to fight is noble, lad. But you don't know a thing about combat. You don't want to march your feet to blood and blisters just so you can get killed. Your job is here."

Huster started to protest. The colonel cut him off. "We've got a thousand captains who can march into battle, but only a handful who can do your job. I need you here. Request denied." He chuckled again, "Why did you ever ask for such a fool thing, lad?" and disappeared back into the tent.

Because it's easier, more important, and less stressful up there, Huster muttered under his breath to the stacks of forms and requisitions on his desk.

Huster sighed and looked at the next request—medical supplies demanded by three of the divisions. He checked his inventory sheets. The central warehouse was dangerously low on morphine, chloroform, surgeon's saw blades, opium, and suture thread. The next shipment wasn't due for three days.

Next were requests by three different generals for pontoons to be stocked with their units in case they needed to cross a river. There weren't enough pontoons to meet all three demands. Huster tapped his chin while he thought. Wherever he sent them, someone would yell at him for doing the wrong thing.

The next was a complaint about mail delivery. Huster wasn't even sure the army officially handled mail delivery. This army, Huster realized, was like a sprawling city. Like a metropolis, McClellan's army needed everything. But rather than handle each item through different private suppliers and stores, all the army's requests funneled through one desk—his!

The next memo said that General Hunter's division was due to receive 30 new cannons. Huster was to arrange space on a train to deliver them from the factory and horse teams to meet the train at the nearest rail junction when the cannons arrived.

Huster poked his head into Colonel Ross's office. "Does General Hunter have artillery crews for these new cannons?"

"Not our problem, is it, captain? You just make sure cannons and horses reach the rail junction on time." The colonel added, "Oh, and General Keys is wondering why the camp chairs for his officers weren't delivered to his new headquarters."

"Camp chairs, sir? Can't he take care of his own chairs?"

"He *is* taking care of it. He complained to supply—me. So *you* see to it!"

Huster sighed. "Officers' chairs. Yes, sir."

"Oh, you also need to find a new forward storage depot for uniforms, tents, blankets, and mess kits. Ten thousand units of each are on the way."

"Ten thousand?! On the way? Already?"

"Should arrive this afternoon. Be ready."

"This afternoon?" gulped Huster. "That'll take more than 40 wagons!"

"Just be ready to handle them, captain."

Sergeant Reiley was waiting for him back at his desk. "We got 20 scruffy-lookin' lads millin' about outside hopin' to find some work, don't you know, sir."

"Can they handle a team of horses?"

"From the looks of 'em, sir, they're as likely to steal the horses as to drive them. But they are livin', breathin' lads searching for work."

Huster nodded, smoothed his uniform, adjusted his cap, and stepped outside to face the mob of surly young men. "Congratulations. You men now have a chance to serve your country."

"What's the pay?" growled one of them.

"This grand Union and our noble quest for freedom need your help, your service," the captain continued, pacing before the men with his hands clasped behind his back.

"What's da' pay?" demanded another of the youths.

"Food comes with the job, right?" added another.

"And some place to sleep?" asked a third.

"We ain't going to get shot at, are we?" demanded a fourth.

Huster sighed and shook his head. They certainly weren't the quality he was looking for, but they were here, and available. "Sign them up, sergeant."

"Right away, yes I will, sir." Sergeant Reiley led the men away, chuckling to himself. Suddenly he snapped his fingers as he remembered something important. "Maps, sir."

"Maps?"

"You have to make better maps for the drivers. Half of them get lost on a regular basis and waste precious hours wandering around, so they do. They need better maps, sir."

"How can I make maps when I don't know where half the units are or when they move?"

Sergeant Reiley grinned and shook his head. "But the drivers do need good maps, sir."

A mountain of problems buzzed through Huster's head. Which to attack first? Why did every day have to be like this? Wouldn't it be easier in a combat unit?

A lanky, stern-looking major marched in and slammed a paper on Huster's desk, tapping it with one finger for emphasis. "The rebs have pushed up north near Chantilly. We've got two brigades rushing to block them, but they couldn't pack their supplies."

"Is this a big battle?" Huster asked, his eyes widening.

"Not sure yet," answered the major. "Might just be a probe. Still, our brigades need powder and ammo—musket *and* cannon." The major was again tapping the paper as he recited each supply category on the request. "They need food and medical supplies. And they need it by noon today, captain, or they'll be throwing rocks at the rebs."

Huster gulped. "By noon?"

The major added as he tapped the bottom line, "McClellan signed it. And they'll need wagons to fetch the equipment and supplies they left in camp when they marched this morning."

Colonel Ross pushed through his tent flap holding an area map. "Show me where the brigades are, major."

The major scanned the map and pointed at a spot just east of Hopewell Gap. "This is where I left them, sir. But they could have shifted some in the last several hours—depending on what the rebs have done."

"That's 20 miles from here!" Huster gasped. "That's a six-hour trip for wagons."

Colonel Ross dragged out his pocket watch and squinted at its face in the flickering lamp light. "Then you've got 10 minutes to start the wagons moving."

"It can't be done, sir," Huster stammered.

Colonel Ross chuckled and stepped back through his tent flap. "Just take care of it, captain."

Huster sat frozen by the unfair enormity of this assignment. The major again tapped his supply requisition. "What do I tell the general, captain? He wants confirmation that the supplies will be there."

Huster closed his eyes and visualized his network of supply depots—Washington depots, army depots, corps and division depots—and trains of wagons spread across northern Virginia. A forward stock of powder and cannon shells sat at Fairfax. Extra musket cartridges had been sent to a division base at Germantown. More to himself than to the major, he muttered, "We can telegraph to Germantown. And a rider can reach Fairfax in an hour. . . . Food and water can come in a second wave from our forward stores. Then I can replace those supplies tomorrow. . . ."

Walter Huster saw it not as a war, but as a game in which he had to move the pieces like pawns across a giant chessboard. He was good at this game—not just good, better than almost any other soldiers in the army. "We'll have everything on this requisition at this point by noon, sir." He tapped the map to show the delivery spot.

The major slowly nodded. "You do, son, and you'll save a lot of lives."

As the major rushed off with his report, Huster realized just how vital the supply office—his office—was to the army. Supply was far more vital than one more infantry officer firing in a line of battle, more important than 1,000 soldiers in line. That line can't fire at all without a working supply officer.

Supplying the army was a battle every day, a battle of wits and of will. Huster smiled as he dashed out the orders to begin the great rush of supplies. "*This* is my battle."

Huster dispatched his supply orders, grabbed his cap, and headed toward the mess tent for an overdue breakfast. The camp was now buzzing with life. Units drilling; a band practicing far across the compound, its music floating above the tents; officers and enlisted men heading for tents and work. On his way, Huster passed Sergeant Reiley. "And now that the sun is almost up on this fine morning, captain, how is the day treating you, sir?"

Huster scratched his beard. "Generals get the glory, the infantry marches into battle and gets shot at, but it's supply that really runs the army, sergeant. Is this a good day? Unfortunately, so far, it's just about average. Just about average so far."

"By the way, sir, there's a new vendor looking for you. He's got something called 'extract of coffee.' Some sort of instant coffee, so it is. I told him to wait in your office. I'm sure you'll be wantin' to meet with him, sir, so you will."

Captain Huster groaned and jogged toward the telegraph office and mess tent.

Aftermath

Supplying the Union and Confederate armies was a monumental and underappreciated aspect of the war effort. Over 12,000 supply items were handled by McClellan's supply office. They distributed more than 200,000 tons of food a year and cared for over 3,000 wagons and almost 40,000 horses. They provided weapons, clothes, cups, cooking pots, blankets, shoes, razors, and tents to more than 100,000 men. What is most impressive is that no supply system existed at the start of the war. Those few officers in the supply system not only had to provide the goods, they had to create the very system that supplied them.

The same heroic feat was accomplished by the Confederate supply system. Confederate units, however, were encouraged to be more self-sufficient, foraging off the land far more than did the Union army. The South was never able to create a long-term, adequate supply system. By 1864 the Confederate armies suffered from a severe lack of horse feed, ammunition, clothing, powder, and especially food. Lee was unable to concentrate his army in early 1864 because he couldn't provide enough feed for horses and men in one confined location.

By 1864, it was clear that the North's superior ability to supply its army would be the deciding factor in its eventual victory.

Follow-up Questions and Activities

1. **What Do You Know?**

   - Why was it so difficult for Civil War armies to maintain adequate flows of supplies to each unit? Find at least five reasons.

   - How much food would an army of 100,000 men consume in one day?

   - What kinds of supplies were provided to smaller units by the Army of the Potomac? Which supplies and services were provided by volunteer organizations (e.g., the Sanitary Commission) and by donations from home?

   - Why was supply so important to Civil War commanders?

2. **Find Out More.** Following are six important topics from this story for students to research in the library and on the Internet. The reference sources at the back of this book will help them get started.

   - Where did the army get supplies and equipment? How did they pay for them? Was army supply handled differently in the Civil War than it was during the American Revolution?

   - Why was it harder for the Confederate army to buy supplies than it was for the Federal army? How many reasons can you find?

   - The U.S. Sanitary Commission provided vast amounts of aid and supplies to Federal army units. Research the history of this organization. Who started it? How? What services did it provide? How was it funded? What happened to it after the war?

- Desiccated vegetables and extract of coffee are two examples of foods developed specifically for the army. Can you find others? What about Spam®, C rations, and freeze-dried foods? How many can you find? Chart when, by whom, and for whom each food was developed.

- The Federal army during the Civil War was the first field army to make extensive use of the telegraph to communicate with headquarters and with each other. Research the history of the telegraph and, especially, its military applications. Why was the telegraph system run by civilians? Was the telegraph used by the Confederacy as much as by the North? Why would telegraph operators know the most about the commanding generals' plans and thoughts?

- Why was supply such a big issue during the Civil War? Compare supply problems and issues during the Civil War with those in other American wars.

3. **Make It Real**

- Make a batch of hardtack to see what Civil War soldiers had to eat. Mix 2 cups of flour, ¾ cup water, and 6 pinches of salt. Spread the dough ⅜ inch thick in 6-inch squares. Bake at 375 degrees Fahrenheit for 10 minutes. Cut the squares in quarters and poke holes in each smaller square with a dull pencil (or similarly shaped object). Bake them for another hour at 325 degrees. Let them sit for two to three days and you'll have a soldier's lifeline, hardtack.

- Make a detailed inventory of all the supplies that come into your school. Record quantities per day (or week) for each. Remember to include utilities and food. Where do they come from? How are they purchased, transported, and distributed for final use?

- Desiccated vegetables and extract of coffee were early attempts at mass processed food to increase shelf life. Were all foods eaten fresh before the time of the Civil War? How were foods preserved for long voyages and for consumption over the winter? Do we process more or less food now than during the Civil War? Prepare an inventory of your family's pantry, refrigerator, and freezer. How many processed versus fresh foods do you eat?

4. **Points to Ponder**

- Why do you think army food has a reputation for being lousy and tasteless? Why was it so hard to get food to the soldiers during the Civil War? Soldiers had to cook their own food. Do you think that was part of the problem?

- What does this story say about the command structure and relationships in the army, about how the army worked? What kinds of skills were necessary for a position like Captain Huster's? Are those skills needed or used in the military today? Do you think the army of today functions any differently than did the Civil War armies? Do you think that's good or bad?

Sister Spies

Life in Occupied Winchester, Virginia, March 1862

At a Glance

Winchester, Virginia, was a bustling farm town of 2,800 in the northwest corner of modern Virginia. But the town's significance arose from its position as the gateway to the Shenandoah Valley.

Bordered on the east by the Blue Ridge Mountains and on the west by the Appalachian Mountains, the wide Shenandoah Valley stretches 200 miles south-southwest from the mountain gaps just west of Washington. It was the nation's richest agricultural region and the ideal invasion route for Southern forces wanting to slide north past Washington, D.C. Winchester, at the entrance of that valley, was the key to its control.

The Confederacy needed to control the valley to keep the Federal Army of the Potomac away from Richmond, Virginia. The Union wanted to take the Shenandoah Valley to make invading Virginia easier and to prevent General Lee's Southern forces from moving north.

Winchester became the focus of everyone's planning, a strategic prize nestled along the undulating boundary between Federal and Confederate forces. The town changed hands 72 times during three years of fighting and was the sight of seven battles.

Each time control of Winchester changed, a new round of army foraging commenced. Each new controlling army scoured the town searching for spies and informants for the other side whom they could corral and eliminate.

Life was difficult and dangerous in Winchester from 1862 through 1864. An opinion expressed one day could be grounds for hanging as a traitor when the opposing army unit stormed into town. It was a time of suspicious glances, a time for caution, a time when it was exceedingly dangerous for a family's loyalties to be split between North and South.

Meet Rebecca and Hannah Wright

Rebecca Wright was born in rural Maryland in 1838. Hannah was born in 1842. Their parents moved to Winchester in 1844. Amos Wright, a skilled woodcraftsman, took a job working for Oliver Rowe in his furniture manufacturing store on Market Street.

Amos was an outspoken Unionist and helped create the coalition of support in March 1861 that voted to keep Virginia in the Union. A month later, most Virginians changed their vote, but Amos did not. Virginia seceded and joined the Confederacy; Amos Wright did not. He was arrested by General Stonewall Jackson's Confederate forces in March 1862 and died in prison in early 1864.

Mrs. Rachael Wright was a quiet, nonpolitical homemaker, a good mother, and active in her Episcopalian church and in her community. Her daughter Hannah grew into a beautiful Southern belle. She adapted to Winchester and to Virginia quickly and wholeheartedly. Hannah was described as bouncy, emotional, flirtatious, and very popular.

The older daughter, Rebecca, on the other hand, was described as quiet and reserved. She usually wrapped the braids of her chestnut hair up on the back of her head. She had deep, dark eyes and a stern face. Rebecca joined the Society of Friends (Quakers) at age 18 and became a schoolteacher at Powell's Female Academy.

Rebecca, like her father, was a staunch Union supporter and abolitionist. Hannah was an equally ardent supporter of the Confederacy.

After the war, the sisters split. Rebecca moved to Pennsylvania, where she taught and got married. Hannah stayed in devastated Winchester, where she married and raised a large family during the postwar depression.

Sister Spies

"What did you just give to that Negro?" 20-year-old Hannah Wright demanded of her sister from the wide front porch of the family house near the north end of Loudoun Street in rural Winchester, Virginia.

Hannah's 24-year-old sister, Rebecca, blushed and laughed nervously. "Why, nothing at all, Hannah. We were just talking."

Hannah had always been far more excitable than her sister. Her voice rose almost to a shout, so that strollers on this main street of Winchester paused to eavesdrop. Her finger wagged like a schoolteacher's. "I *saw* you slip him something—something small and shiny!"

Rebecca, the quieter and more reserved of the two, turned away from the street with a swish of her skirts and brushed coolly past her sister, "Fiddlesticks, Hannah. I don't know *what* you're talking about."

"Oh, yes you do!"

Rebecca, always stern and solemn in appearance, glared at her sister. "You must be mistaken. And shouldn't you return to your guests?"

Two Confederate captains had spent this bright afternoon of March 8, 1862, regaling Hannah with tales of their exploits while Hannah's golden curls bounced and tossed with delight.

The black man had disappeared down Loudoun Street. Rebecca had marched upstairs to her room. Hannah stomped her foot and turned back toward the parlor where the officers sipped lemonade and munched sponge cake. "I *know* she's up to something."

Upstairs Rebecca collapsed on her bed, hands and heart trembling. That black man was a secret Union army spy. As the driver for a local miller, he was able to pass through Confederate lines and deliver messages to Union army officers.

Rebecca hadn't thought anyone was watching her hand the tiny, tinfoil-covered note to her messenger. Today's note confirmed that Confederate General Stonewall Jackson planned to move his 4,000-man force south from Winchester on the 11th. Rebecca had overheard Hannah's suitors talking about the move earlier in the afternoon and had wrapped her note in tinfoil so that the messenger could carry it in his mouth and not be caught during a search by Confederate pickets.

At their family dinner of steaming beef pot pie and stewed garden greens that night, Hannah glared across the table at her sister. "You're not saying much about *your* day, Rebecca," she taunted.

Rebecca smiled thinly. "In the Society of Friends, we believe it is better for the digestion to eat in silence."

Hannah wouldn't let her suspicions go. "I saw you speaking with Julia Chase this morning."

"She is a friend and lives just across the street. Of course I talk to her."

Hannah pounded her fist on the table so that their mother squealed in surprise. "She is also a known Unionist and abolitionist!"

Their father, Amos Wright, waved his fork. "*I'm* a known Unionist."

"You shouldn't be, Father," snapped Hannah. "We live in *Virginia*. We are Confederates!"

"Poppycock! I'm an American and want to be part of the United States as I always have been. Virginia and this community voted to stay in the Union until mid-April of last year. But I never changed my mind and have regularly said so."

Rebecca, head still lowered, said, "It is dangerous, Father, to openly express yourself so publicly these days."

"Nonsense! America is a free country."

"We live in *Virginia*!" shouted Hannah, "and anyone who doesn't support the Confederacy is a traitor. And awful things happen to traitors!"

An awkward silence followed as the sisters glared across the table at each other. Rachael, the girls' mother, tried to steer the conversation toward pleasanter news. "Mrs. McGuire told me today that poor Emma Reily has decided to leave if the army abandons Winchester and live with her aunt in Lurray."

Mr. Wright nodded and took a forkful of beef pot pie. "Probably a good idea since she lost her parents and one sister to that scarlet fever epidemic this past winter." He pointed his fork at Hannah. "*That* is exactly the sort of thing you get for having armies and war—disease. The Sanitation Commission can't possibly keep up. And so a dear girl has lost her family."

Hannah shot back, "Emma is leaving because she has openly supported the Confederacy and is afraid of what will happen to her if the Yankees march in." With a sly smile Hannah turned to her sister. "You never express your support, Rebecca. Are you a Confederate or Unionist?"

"I am a schoolteacher and member of the Society of Friends. We do not believe that war ever solves problems."

Three days later, on March 11, Jackson's small army, most of whom had enlisted from the Shenandoah Valley region, tramped out of the fields and assembled in long columns in the streets of Winchester. Officers bid farewell to the families that had graciously boarded them. All units faced south and began their slow, dusty trudge. The Confederates were abandoning Winchester ahead of General Banks's army, which was over four times their size.

Winchester streets were lined with weeping, flag-waving supporters. Jackson's scruffy soldiers were caught between bursting pride at this rousing send-off and the knowledge that they were retreating in the face of the enemy. Young women carried pitchers of lemonade and plates of donuts and sugar cakes as a "farewell and hurry back" offering to the troops.

Jackson's one army band played near the head of the column. Music drifted back along the ranks. As the gray column slowly passed south with its cadre of cavalry swinging wide to either side as guards, Winchester citizens felt a deep foreboding, a quiet dread. Grass and fields had been trampled. Rows of trees had been cut for firewood. Certainly, it was always gladly given. But still, the trees were gone. And that had been done by friendly troops. What would the Yankees do?

Knots of worried businessmen clustered along Loudoun Street behind the departing units, conversing in low voices about business under the Yankees. War had been good for local businesses—supplying tobacco, food, jewelry, and watches; making coffins; dying and repairing clothing; taking photographs (called daguerreotypes)—all had prospered with the army in town. What would happen under the Yankees?

The owner of the Union Hotel on Market Street decided to show his Southern support by changing his hotel's name. He chiseled the "U" and "N" from the name carved in stone on the building's front. For 20 years it would be known as the "Ion" Hotel. All across Winchester, Confederate flags were carefully furled and carried to secret cellar hiding places so that they would not be found by the Yankees. Banks closed for fear that there would be a run on cash.

Hannah, in a bright calico dress and slat bonnet to frame her pretty face, stood on the front porch and waved at the officers who had spent so many afternoons in the Wright parlor. She glanced at her sister, stern Rebecca, standing quietly at the north end of the porch. "Why are you looking *north*, Rebecca? Our gallant soldiers are marching *south*."

"I thought I heard something."

"Ha! You were looking for your precious Yankee army to come."

Rebecca blushed because, in truth, she *was* wondering why General Banks wasn't advancing more swiftly, since Rebecca had told him of Jackson's plans.

Hannah jabbed an accusing finger at her sister, her face crimson with anger. "Our glorious army is leaving and all you can think about is . . . is . . . Yankees! You and Mrs. New and Julia Chase, you're all probably *spies*. Someone is going to turn you in and you'll be hanged! That's what we do to spies."

Mrs. Wright also stood on the porch watching the parade spectacle. "Hannah, hush with such talk! You apologize to your sister."

"No apology is needed, Mother," said Rebecca. "I have nothing to worry or feel guilty about."

Jackson's long supply train of wagons, horses, and mules followed the marching troops. The final, rearguard units followed the wagons. These troops scavenged and foraged as they passed through town, stopping at each house to ask for donations, poking through barns and warehouses for supplies the army might need—or at least should keep away from Federal hands. Several warehouses were burned because the Yankees could use the supplies inside and there was no way for Jackson to take them with him on his run south. The owners watched in dismal silence.

Jas Reiley cleared out the cellar under his sprawling house and moved his 12 prize horses down into the dim dark. He covered the floor thickly with hay and straw and wrapped each horse's hooves so they wouldn't make noise. Then he prayed each morning and each evening that they wouldn't be discovered.

The last units to leave were the provost marshals (military police), who swept through town arresting known male Northern sympathizers. James Rea, Charlie Chase, George Aulick . . . and Amos Wright were rounded up on Loudoun Street where they stood and chatted with fellow merchants. The men were marched at gunpoint to wagons that would haul them south to prison.

Rebecca and Rachael, more than a block away on the front porch, screamed and chased the wagon down the street, begging for a chance to at least say good-bye, while neighbors watched stony-faced with raised eyebrows, slowly shaking their heads.

Hannah waited on the front porch for the two women to return. "I told him he was supporting the wrong side. I warned him," she began.

"Stop!" spat their mother. "Your father loves Virginia and this town. And I will not allow him to be spoken poorly of in this house." Mrs. Wright stormed inside, seething with fear and indignation.

With a final, "Serves him right," Hannah swept inside to change into something drab and dreary before the Yankees arrived.

For one day Winchester waited. Townspeople clustered in the street, nervously waiting as if holding their collective breath. On the warm, clear morning of March 13, the ground trembled as 500 Union cavalry thundered through Winchester. Following close behind came the columns of blue. Flags fluttered in the light breeze. Each regiment had its own 18- to 20-piece band and half a dozen drummers. Batteries of cannons rumbled through behind their teams of horses and limbers.

Most Winchester women wore drab black and gray dresses with long "Jeff Davis" bonnets (a style created by President Davis's wife) to express their disgust for the invaders. Most sneered and frowned at the passing ranks of blue and refused to make eye contact with any of the Yankees.

"My, my. Look at how new and lovely their uniforms are," said Mrs. Wright.

"They may have fancy uniforms and bands," chided Hannah, "but they can't fight worth a lick." She swept off the porch and down Loudoun Street toward the courthouse, where the Stars and Stripes was just being raised.

Most local citizens turned away in tears from the flag raising and solemnly walked home. But Hannah, surprisingly, lingered in the grassy park next to the courthouse where a number of Yankee officers had gathered. Watching, spying on her sister from the corner of Market Street, Rebecca saw Hannah actually speak to the Union officers. She seemed to be courteous to these invaders she claimed to hate, as if flirting with them as she had with Jackson's Confederate officers.

An icy shiver crept down Rebecca's spine. Hannah was up to *something*.

A cold rain fell on March 17 from a drab, slate gray sky. A Union cavalry regiment commandeered the use of Mrs. MacDonald's house on the west side of Winchester because her wide lawns were an ideal place to graze their 1,000 hungry horses. Mrs. MacDonald tried to bolt the door. She tried to order them out. But mud-splattered officers marched in to settle in her kitchen and parlor. Muddy boots were propped on her prized ottoman and on her couch. Men scraped mud from their boots and uniforms and flung it on the carpet and floor. Dripping greatcoats were draped across every piece of furniture to dribble their puddles on cushion, carpet, and floor. A steady flow of messengers, dribbling rain, marched through the house.

"Don't fret, ma'am," said a major. "We'll only be here 'til morning. Then the whole regiment's riding out."

By the next morning, no color other than mud brown was visible in any of the MacDonalds' carpets. The couches were slimy with oozing brown goo. Every plate, mug, and pot was covered with greasy, half-eaten food and piled up around the kitchen. The extensive MacDonald pantry was bare, stripped as if by swarming locusts. The brilliant green of the sweeping front lawns had become a sea of mud. Countless horses and mules fed under the trees, most of which had been stripped bare of bark as high as the animals could reach. Countless wagons had rolled through the yard, digging rows of deep ruts.

It would take years for the house to recover. The only comment the officers made as they left was, "Thanks for the hospitality."

Mrs. MacDonald seethed as she marched to General Banks's headquarters to protest. But she was far from alone. Houses all over town had been commandeered. The steady whack of axes reverberated through Winchester as long lines of ornamental trees were cut for firewood, prompting howls of protest. Banks were allowed to open only with military oversight and supervision. Warehouses were raided for grain, flour, and feed. Each Federal action sparked a wave of new complaints from Winchester citizens. Complaints, protests, and proud defiance became full-time occupations for most loyal Confederates in Winchester.

Hannah raced out of the house early on the 18th, as she had every day since the Yankees arrived. Suspicious and curious, Rebecca followed her sister. However, she lost sight of Hannah on Water Street when Colonel Shelby of General Banks's staff called to her from the shadows of the Federal army headquarters. "Miss Wright, a brief word?"

Startled, Rebecca inched closer. "Your past information has been most useful," he said.

"Then why didn't you attack Jackson on the 11th while he was marching south?" Rebecca demanded, trying to whisper so that no passersby would hear.

Shelby shook his head. "It was impossible. But your information saved us *days* in reaching this spot. If you would, please continue your valuable service."

"But what can I tell you now that you're already in Winchester?"

"We will not always be in Winchester," Colonel Shelby answered.

Before Rebecca could ask what he meant, the colonel muttered that they shouldn't be seen speaking together and melted back into the shadows of a narrow alley.

Trembling with intrigue and excitement, Rebecca continued her walk. She hadn't walked half a block when an egg splattered on the sidewalk in front of her. A second missile slammed into her shoulder, splashing yoke and slimy egg white across her face and dress.

Rebecca spun to face her attacker, but saw no one. She carefully scanned the nearby windows but saw nothing to indicate who had taken aim at her. Rebecca's trembling took on a heavy dose of fear. She had to force herself to resume her search for Hannah.

It took half an hour for Rebecca to catch sight of her sister again, just finishing a conversation in an alley off Washington Street. The man ran off as Rebecca approached. "Was that Jackson Tully?" Rebecca demanded of her sister.

Hannah first blushed and then glared at her sister. "Certainly not. Jackson's off with the army, isn't he?"

"*I* heard he was with one of the new partisan units and was sneaking around Winchester as a spy. And that *looked* just like Jackson Tully."

Hannah shook her dress into place and tried to push past Rebecca. "Why would I ever spend time with Jackson Tully?"

Rebecca grabbed her sister's arm. "Were you giving Jackson Tully information on the Union troops? Is that why you've been so pleasant to Yankee officers—to get information?"

"Fiddle dee dee. That would be spying, and spying could get me hanged, sister." Hannah wrinkled her face with disgust. "What happened to you?"

"Some coward threw an egg."

Hannah shrugged. "You're lucky that was all."

Rebecca tightened her grip, squeezing her sister's arm. "What's that supposed to mean?"

"Father claimed to be a Unionist, and he's in prison. Spies get shot or hanged. I'd be careful if I were you, dear sister. Next time it might be a noose or a bullet that comes your way."

"What have you been saying about me?" Rebecca demanded.

Hannah laughed artificially. "Why would I tell anyone about my own sister?" She wrenched her arm free and hurried up Washington Street.

On the morning of March 23, Winchester citizens looked up at a crystal blue sky, wondering where the distant rumble of thunder came from. Then word streaked through town that Jackson was back! He had attacked the Yankees at Kernstown, five miles south.

Eager townsfolk dusted off their Confederate flags, ready to wave banners for the triumphant returning troops. Women raced to their kitchens to bake treats for the conquering gray-clad heroes.

Rebecca's school was closed for the day. She found Hannah gathered with friends on Market Street. "I wonder, sister, who told Jackson it was safe to attack," Rebecca said.

The sisters circled each other like boxers. "*I* wonder," answered Hannah, "who warned General Banks that Jackson was coming."

The other women in the circle giggled. "Armies use cavalry and soldiers to gather information. Why wonder about it?"

"Yes. Cavalry and soldiers," agreed Rebecca, still searching her sister's face for signs of guilt. "Anyone else they used would be a hateful spy."

By noon word had filtered through that Banks was winning the battle. Jackson had been driven off. The only Confederate soldiers who would return to Winchester that day would be prisoners and wounded.

Then the wagons of wounded began to flow in. Endless miles of wagons with as many as a dozen blood-soaked men packed into each one rolled into town. More than 1,600 wounded descended on a town of less than 3,000 citizens. Every church, both hotels, most public rooms, and the lecture halls all became makeshift hospitals. So did many of the larger houses. Union and Confederate wounded were intermingled so that local women wouldn't tend only to the Confederates.

The wounded soldiers died in droves. As many as 60 a day had to be buried. There weren't enough ministers to perform the services or men to carry the bodies and dig the graves. Almost all were buried behind the houses in which they died. Many backyards became instant cemeteries as one by one the wounded succumbed, either to their wounds or to the infections they received on the operating table or in the makeshift hospitals.

Caring for the surviving wounded became full-time work for an army of hundreds of volunteer women. Complaints and defiance were set aside while everyone struggled to preserve life. The Sanitation Commission spread every ounce of lime they had around the hospital buildings and graveyards to control the spread of disease. And still the town trembled, fearing a deadly epidemic.

In late April most of Banks's army moved south, part of a combined force trying to trap Jackson. A small garrison remained in Winchester to maintain the headquarters building and oversee the care of the remaining wounded. The army left acres of stumps that had been thick woods, dozens of damaged houses whose owners had been muscled aside to make room for army officers, many empty barns from which hay and other grain had been confiscated, and a town stripped of many of the basic supplies of commerce and city life.

Five days later, during an April 27th afternoon stroll down Cork Street past the Red Lion Tavern, Rebecca spotted her sister huddled with three friends, all dressed in defiant black. As Rebecca drew near she heard Hannah say, ". . . ugly flag will be burned day after tomorrow. Jackson Tully's unit is . . ."

Hannah stopped, hearing the rustle of Rebecca's dress.

"Is *what*?" asked Kate Sperry, one of the group of young women.

Hannah pushed back her long Jeff Davis bonnet. "Look who's joined us. My sister." She smiled stiffly at Rebecca. "We were just on our way to Mrs. Clark's dress shop. Care to join us?"

"Why go to a dress shop?" asked Rebecca. "All you ever wear is black."

"The Yankees won't be in Winchester forever."

Now Rebecca forced a polite smile. "I was just on my way home." She spun around and hurried up Loudoun Street, thinking, . . . *day after tomorrow* . . . and *Jackson Tully's unit is* . . .

Rebecca scribbled a quick note to Colonel Shelby and raced to Jeffery Legg's flour mill on Market Street, where her messenger worked.

On April 29, the Virginia partisan militia attacked the town. They thundered into Winchester on horseback, 200 strong. The men wore no uniforms, but were armed with modern muskets. Lead riders carried Virginia and Confederate flags. Their commander, Colonel Turner Ashby, wore a brilliant gray officer's uniform with gold scrollwork and gleaming brass buttons. "Citizens of Winchester," he called, "help us rid your town of the Yankees!"

Townsfolk cheered and flooded into the streets to follow the militia. Some marched to the Union army headquarters on Water Street, but they found the 50-man detachment there barricaded inside and heavily armed. The crowd and partisan riders circled widely around the building, not wanting to start a bloodbath by attacking.

Several hundred more Union soldiers were stationed west of Winchester at the Union army camp. A militia screening force rode in that direction to make sure those soldiers didn't try to enter the town. The rest gathered at the courthouse and cheered as the Union flag was lowered and burned.

Confederate flags were quickly hung from balconies and tacked to posts. People sang "Dixie" and danced in the streets as if it were a liberation party.

Three hours later the ground shook and glassware rattled in cupboards as 1,500 Federal cavalry stormed into Winchester. Two regiments of infantry marched close behind the cavalry. The partisan militia fled west and south, racing out of town in small groups.

Hannah burst into Rebecca's classroom without bothering to knock. "How'd the Yankee cavalry know to come here today?"

Rebecca was alone in the room at the time and sat quietly at her desk. "How'd the partisans know it was safe to attack?"

"They can see where the Yankees go," answered Hannah. "They have eyes."

"Yes, they do," said Rebecca. She hesitated for a moment, debating whether she dared say more, then decided she had to add a warning. "Make sure you are very cautious before you let your eyes be their eyes, sister. Jackson Tully was arrested as a spy yesterday. The Union army knows your name."

Hannah cocked her head slightly and answered, "And all Winchester knows your true feelings, sister. Eggs will not be what flies next. You, especially, must be careful."

Deep in thought, walking side by side in silence, the Wright sisters started for home as, to drum and bugle fanfare, the Stars and Stripes was again raised over the Winchester courthouse and as Winchester citizens, in shock, hurriedly pulled down and re-hid their Confederate stars and bars.

Aftermath

Even though they could not consistently hold Winchester, Southern forces were able to hold the Shenandoah Valley until mid-1864. But they were never militarily strong enough to use the valley for an offensive attack against Washington.

Twice (in 1862 and 1863) General Robert E. Lee launched northern swings through the Winchester area. The first was halted at Sharpsburg (Antietam); the second reached Gettysburg, Pennsylvania, before being crushed.

As long as the South held the Shenandoah Valley, it was difficult for the Army of the Potomac to advance far into Virginia. Their advancing flank would be exposed to Confederate attack from the valley.

As the struggle for control of the Shenandoah raged around Winchester, the town was slowly stripped of all its resources by more than three years of occupation by hungry army units—feed, animals, livestock, grain, hay, manufacturing supplies, and materials all were taken. By war's end the town lay in shambles.

Neither Rebecca nor Hannah was ever arrested or charged with spying, although Rebecca remained an active Union informant until late 1864 when Winchester came into Federal hands for the last time. Hannah apparently maintained her contact with Confederate partisan units. However, it is not recorded how much information she provided to the partisans. Southern partisan units slowly folded into the army as casualties created shortages in the main units. Only a few were still active after 1864, most of those acting more like outlaws than guerrillas.

Follow-up Questions and Activities

1. **What Do You Know?**

   • Why was the tiny town of Winchester, Virginia, so important to both the Union and the Confederacy?

   • Why did army units come and go so often there? Why wasn't either side able to hold the area throughout the war?

   • Why was the Shenandoah Valley so important to both sides?

   • What normally happens to spies when they are caught? What is the difference between a spy and a patrol of uniformed cavalry out gathering information?

   • Was it common during the Civil War for local citizens to be used as army informants? Was the Confederacy or Union better able to use local citizens as informants? Why?

2. **Find Out More.** Following are five important topics from this story for students to research in the library and on the Internet. The reference sources at the back of this book will help them get started.

   • Research the town of Winchester, Virginia. Had it been settled by the time of the American Revolution? Research the role of Winchester and its citizens during the Civil War. Did most people in this area favor secession in early 1861? How many maintained close ties with citizens in neighboring Maryland? What happened to Winchester during the war?

   • During this story, a partisan (guerrilla) unit attacks the small Union garrison at Winchester. Where did the word "guerrilla" (meaning a small band of citizen fighters) come from? Who were the first guerrillas? Were they successful? Have other guerrilla units fought in American history? Find other examples in world history of successful guerrilla fighting and campaigns.

   • Winchester suffered as an occupied town during the war. Research at least four other towns or cities that were occupied during the American Civil War. What was the fate of each of these places? How did they survive their occupation? Compare these stories to the fate of towns and cities occupied during twentieth-century American wars.

   • General Stonewall Jackson became famous for his brilliant maneuvering during his Shenandoah Valley campaign of 1862. Research the life and accomplishments of this Confederate hero.

   • Research wartime spies and informants, and especially women spies. Were there other women who spied for the North and South? Who was Belle Boyd, and for whom did she spy? How many were caught? What happened to them? Have nations used women spies during more recent wars? How many examples can you find?

3. **Make It Real**

   • Play an in-class spy game to see how difficult spying really is. Divide the class into three teams. Each team should choose a team captain to create a secret password for the team. The teacher then secretly chooses someone on each team to spy for each of the other two teams. The job of each spy is to pass that password to the captain of the team for whom they are spying.

The spy must slip the information to the captain without getting caught, must do it within a designated time limit (several hours, for example), and must do it in class. Information may not be passed during recess, in the hall, or during lunch. Team captains may designate several guards to protect their areas and to watch for a possible spy slipping information to other teams.

How many spies were successful? How many were caught? Was anyone falsely accused of being a spy? Did others on their team believe them when they claimed to be innocent? How did the spies feel while trying to slip information to the enemy? How distrustful and suspicious did everyone become during the game? Does this give you any insights into what it must have felt like for real spies during a real war when their lives (and the life of their country) were on the line?

- Create a timeline for the occupation of Winchester by the various armies. Also list the dates of all local battles and indicate who won them and the number of casualties in each.

- Make a 3-D map of the Shenandoah Valley. Locate the passes going east from the valley into the eastern part of Virginia. How far north do the mountains along the east wall of the valley extend? Locate Winchester and other Shenandoah Valley cities. Mark the ones that were occupied by Union forces. How many also were garrison sites for Confederate forces? Visit http://www2.cr. nps.gov/abpp/Shenandoah/svs0-1.html. This website illustrates all the battlefields in the valley. How many are there? Choose one site and write a newspaper-type report about what happened there.

4. **Points to Ponder**

- Do you think guerrilla warfare is ethical? Legal? Moral? When are guerrillas really an outlaw gang of criminals? What's the difference? Should guerrilla groups have to follow the same rules of conduct that armies follow? Do they?

- Most people think that spying on some foreign area or people during a war is acceptable. What about spying and informing on your own country? On your own state? On your own community? On your own family? Isn't that what the two sisters in this story did? When is spying not acceptable and justifiable?

- In this story, why do you think the sisters warned each other instead of making public charges? After all, each was spying for what the other sister considered to be the enemy.

Turn Coat, Turn Coat

The Civil War in the Far West and the Battle of Glorieta Pass, February–March 1862

At a Glance

We typically think of the Civil War being fought in the East. Some will remember that Tennessee, Mississippi, and Louisiana also saw their share of epic battles. But few think of New Mexico, Arizona, or Oregon as important battlegrounds of the Civil War.

Battles extended into the new Western territories for two reasons. First, Western mines were the best source of gold and silver with which to finance the war. Second, the West represented new territory that would become either slave or free.

The struggle in the far West was decided early in the war—in 1862. Texas Confederates under General Wilfred Sibley moved north from El Paso in the spring of 1861 planning to capture the major trade routes through northern New Mexico and then turn west to conquer all of the region. Scattered Union troops withdrew from western New Mexico (Arizona) to concentrate their few available forces to repel the rebels.

Arizona citizens (Arizona was at the time part of the New Mexico Territory) promptly declared themselves to be part of the Confederacy and eagerly awaited the arrival of gray-clad forces. In July 1861, Fort Fillmore in southern New Mexico fell to the Confederate invaders. In August, Fort Stanton (the next fort north) was abandoned to the Confederacy. In late 1861 additional Texas troops joined the invasion. By January 1862, over 3,500 Confederates were ready to push farther north. The next Confederate target was Fort Craig along the west shore of the Rio Grande, 40 miles south of Albuquerque, New Mexico.

Meet Hector Manuel Alianjo

Hector's parents migrated from their west Texas home shortly after Texas won its independence from Mexico, fearing harsh treatment from the new white Texans. They, along with several of Hector's uncles and their families, settled in Albuquerque, New Mexico.

Hector was born on a small farm near Albuquerque in 1840, fourth of seven children. His father and two of his brothers also worked on a nearby cattle ranch. The children went to work young as day laborers for larger growers. By the age of eight, Hector was a veteran of long days working in the fields. Hector never attended formal school, but learned rudimentary reading and writing from a neighbor lady.

Hector joined the Federal army in the fall of 1860, a 21-year-old man, hoping to break out of poverty and to give a voice in the new territorial government to his family and to the native peoples of the region.

Turn Coat, Turn Coat

Colonel Canby leaned back from the group of Union army officers huddled around maps spread across the heavy oaken table in his adobe-walled office. "Pedro, fetch some coffee!"

Private Hector Alianjo sat hunched over his tiny desk where he worked as assistant regimental clerk, feeling numb with bitter shock as he reread the letter for the third time. His fists clenched as he sounded out the words scrawled in rough Spanish.

Corporal Charles Reily, the 22-year-old regimental clerk, tossed a wadded-up piece of paper at Alianjo. "Wake up, Mex. Colonel's calling you."

Hector's head snapped up in time to hear the colonel bellow, "Pedro! Coffee!"

Hector clenched his jaw, scraped back his chair, and muttered for the hundredth time, "My name is Hector Manuel Alianjo, not *Pedro*."

Reily laughed at Alianjo's discomfort. "Quit complainin'. The officers call all you Mexicans Pedro."

"I am not Mexican. I was born *here*. I'm a native of New Mexico."

"I don't care if you were born in New York," quipped Reily. "You're *Mexican*."

Hector Alianjo sucked in a slow breath to quiet his anger and stomped out of the Fort Craig headquarters building for his trip to the mess hall. A chill winter wind poured down from distant mountains and moaned across the central New Mexico desert this February 1862.

Hector still clutched the letter and now shook it at the empty New Mexico sky. "They stole my parents' farm," he hissed. "And the army helped the ranchers do it!" The letter was from his younger sister. She could write a limited amount of Spanish—the only other family member who could.

Hector stomped toward the long mess hall muttering, "I can't be in an army that cheats people this way. . . ." He kicked at a rock. "I have to get out of this army." Then he sighed and thought, *But how? I enlisted—volunteered—for three years.*

Hector paused, squinted in the morning glare, and shook his head. Why did the army place a fort *here*, at the ugliest, most worthless spot in all New Mexico? Drab dirt, dust, and spiny tumbleweeds covered the landscape as far as his eye could see. There was nothing here you wouldn't gladly give away, if only someone would take it.

Six miles north, the Valverde River crossing over the Rio Grande was a decent spot. At least there were some trees and grass. Forty miles north at Albuquerque, there were lush, green valleys and tree-covered mesas. It would make sense to put a fort there. But why here?

Hector had decided that, if there was anything uglier than the desert around Fort Craig, it was Fort Craig itself. Rows of drab buildings squatted in the sand and seemed to suffer in both summer heat and winter cold.

Back inside headquarters, Alianjo stepped into the colonel's office with a jug of steaming coffee and a tray of mugs.

"Pour a cup for everyone." The colonel, a trim, clean-shaven man who looked like a college professor, hadn't even glanced up.

"*Si*, colonel," Hector mumbled and began to pour.

Major Brooke, a bear of a man with a bushy black beard, glared at Hector. "These *Mexicans*. You have to tell them every little thing."

"I am *New* Mexican," Hector muttered.

"What's that, private?" demanded Colonel Canby.

"Nothing, colonel." But Hector thought, *Why bother correcting him? These white Americans just want to steal for themselves.*

That evening, as winter's chill seeped into every crack and crevice of the shabby fort, Hector gathered with the three other Hispanic volunteers serving in Colonel Canby's two regiments of regular soldiers. Other Hispanics were at the fort, there as part of the New Mexico volunteer militia that had marched to Fort Craig to swell the ranks of the small garrison of regular army soldiers. A few Colorado Volunteer Infantry under Colonel Christopher "Kit" Carson had also arrived. But the militia and regular army didn't mix much, and the four Hispanics under Colonel Canby felt isolated and alone.

"I hate these blue coats," cursed Hector in Spanish. Officially, they weren't allowed to speak Spanish. But huddled alone at night, the four felt safer talking in their native tongue. "I hate that they won't give us a chance to prove ourselves and I hate that they won't use my real name!"

Armianno Rodriguez shrugged. "They call *all* of us Pedro. I think maybe they can't tell us apart. Besides, it goes with being new in the army. After we're in a while, they'll stop."

"I've been in over a year," hissed Hector.

Jose Lopez, the tallest and strongest of the foursome, laughed and gently punched Hector in the shoulder. "If you hate it so, why'd you enlist for *three* years?"

"Because my family didn't have enough food to eat—and because I wanted to be part of this new Western country and new government." Alianjo snorted and shook his head. "Me and my big plans. . . . They won't let us be part of anything but shoveling up after the mules."

Hector shook his crumpled letter at his three friends. "And now this letter from my sister. A rancher filed a claim—a deed—on land that includes the farm my family has worked for 25 years. A white judge said it was legal so the army—*our* army—forced my family off our land at gun point. They took nothing except the clothes on their backs! No one in my family reads English. They never had a chance!"

He jammed the letter into a pocket. "The army helped steal my family's land."

The others tried to console him and to express their shock and resentment. Hector snarled, "We have to stop the blue coats from stealing all of New Mexico from our people."

"How?" laughed Armianno. "What can the four of us do? They haven't even given us guns yet."

The next day, back at his desk, Alianjo listened to a heated discussion in the colonel's office. An army of Confederates was marching north along the east side of the Rio Grande and would reach Fort Craig in a few days.

Some officers wanted to march out and fight the Confederates. Others wanted to stay in Fort Craig and force the Confederates to attack. Still others wanted to abandon the fort and march north to join other Union forces at Fort Union east of Santa Fe, the territorial capital.

The only thing they *could* agree on was that they didn't trust the New Mexico volunteer militia units. There were too many "Mexicans" in the militia. Every officer in the room seemed to believe that all Mexicans were lazy cowards who couldn't be trusted to stand and fight.

Listening from his desk, Hector ground his teeth and seethed. He had told them when he joined the army 15 months ago that he was a good shot, and excellent with a sword. He expected to be given an important combat position. All he had been allowed to do was fetch coffee, fan away flies, tend mules, and clean out stables.

As if a veil was being lifted from his eyes, Hector suddenly saw the Federal army as cruel invaders—invaders who didn't care about anything except gold from the hills and land for themselves. They had to be stopped. They had to be driven out. Someone had to save New Mexico for his people, for those who were born there, for his family.

Hector realized that that someone would have to be him. But what could one lone man do? One lone man seemed insignificant.

But now the Confederates were coming. And what Hector heard gave him an idea—a wild idea.

That night with his friends Hector hammered again on his theme from the day before. "These new Americans are stealing *our* land and *our* jobs. The army always sides with the whites."

This time he watched closely as the others nodded in agreement, some with resigned indifference, some with anger, all with sadness. "Did you hear that the Confederates are coming?" he asked, trying to sound casual.

Jose said, "I heard we are going to fight them in the next few days."

Hector paused, caught on a terrible moral dilemma. He had a plan for ridding New Mexico of the oppressive Northern whites and Union army. But that plan would force him to break his sacred honor and word. It would force him to become something he and his family had always hated and despised: a liar, a traitor, and a deserter. Yet he could see no other way to save his family, his land, and New Mexico.

Hector glanced over both shoulders, leaned close to his friends, and asked, "Why fight the Confederates . . . when you can *join* them?"

"What?" gasped Armianno. "Defect?"

"Colonel Canby told the other officers that the Confederates will probably win. If we help them win, they will listen to our demands. They will respect our rights."

"No, no, no, my friend," hissed Jose. "Those are *Texans* who are coming north. Texans are *evil*. They are the devils our parents fought 25 years ago. Texans are the ones who stole Texas away from Mexico—away from us—and drove our parents to New Mexico. You can't join *them!*"

Armianno grunted in agreement.

Hector countered, "They're fighting for their freedom from the Union. So are we. We are the same."

"They butchered my family during the war in Texas," Jose growled. "I will hate all Texans forever."

"That was 25 years ago. This is *now*," Hector insisted. "The Union army and the white landowners will make us slaves. Look what they did to my family. If I have to be a turncoat to save my family and land, so be it. I'm going to help the Confederates get rid of the blue coats forever."

But how do I switch sides without getting killed? Hector Alianjo wondered. Pickets and patrols would shoot him dead as a deserter if they caught him wandering through the desert alone. Confederate guards and pickets might shoot him as a spy.

Alianjo glanced over both shoulders again before whispering, "How will I know I've found the Confederates?"

"They wear gray uniforms," answered Jesus.

"Or brown," Jose added.

"Which is it?" demanded Hector.

"The Confederates are the ones wearing anything but blue."

"The New Mexico militia don't wear blue," Hector snapped. "And they're not Confederates."

Everyone thought for a moment. Armianno said, "Confederates love Dixie."

"Who's Dixie?"

"Just wave your arms and shout 'Hooray for Dixie!' "

Alianjo scowled. It seemed too uncertain. Then he smiled. He knew the perfect time and way to defect—the middle of a battle. Confederates would be the ones the blue coats were fighting, and with everyone paying attention to the battle, it would be easy for him to slip across to the Confederate side.

As the next few days dragged by, the electric tension of coming battle hung over Fort Craig like a boiling thundercloud, so thick you could almost touch it. Hector felt anguished and tormented. He longed to curl up with his parents and ask their advice. Saying he'd defect was one thing. Actually doing it was quite another. He would be forever branded a coward, a traitor. He would be hunted and hated. Still, he had to do *something*. Hector felt that the future of his people and his land depended on him.

Early on the morning of February 21, Fort Craig exploded into frantic activity. The waiting was over. Cavalrymen saddled their horses and paraded (assembled) in the dusty open square of the fort. Militia units shuffled into ragged formation carrying muskets and squirrel guns. The regular army (except for the staybacks—those like Alianjo assigned to guard the fort) snapped into line in front of Colonel Canby.

Canby rose in his stirrups. "Men, the rebs are trying to cross the river at Valverde and we're going to stop them! Major Brooke, take the 4th Cavalry Squadron and secure the crossing. Major Willits, take the 6th Squadron to guard the artillery. Place the cannons as far forward as possible. Infantry and militia will march with me. Left by columns . . . March!"

With a great cheer and amid a billowing cloud of dust that was snatched away by a stiff west wind, the infantry units followed galloping horses and clanging, horse-drawn field cannons out of the fort.

From the headquarters porch Alianjo watched the procession fade into the distance. Defecting suddenly seemed so simple. Confederates were on the east side of the river, Union on the west. All he had to do was swim the river and whoever he met should be a Confederate.

Hector raced to the hut where he slept to gather some clothes. Then he eased past the long stables that Jose and Jesus had been assigned to clean while horses and some of the mules were out at battle. This was the moment of truth. Did he really dare to defect and become a Confederate? Was there any other way?

No! No other way!

With a final glance and a subdued wave to his friends, Hector slipped out of the open gate unnoticed and swung south around the fort (since everyone should be looking north). He thought of his family—his sister, his mother, his hardworking father. He felt the awful weight of being a hated defector. He felt the pride of risking his life for his family and people. He felt the fear of not knowing if he would be accepted by the Confederates.

Hector buried his blue coat, pants, and shoes into a shallow hole, pulled on his old civilian clothes, and slipped into the gently flowing green water of the Rio Grande. Like rumbling thunder, he could hear the booming Federal cannons announce that the battle had begun far to the unseen north.

Scrambling up the sandy east shore of the Rio Grande, Hector thought, *I've done it. I have switched sides. I am now a Confederate!* It had been so simple. And yet, it was the hardest thing Hector had ever done.

He jogged north through rolling dunes of dirt, sand, and dust. Somehow, the dirt on this Confederate side of the river seemed less drab. Circling hawks high overhead seemed swifter and more colorful. Alianjo was stopped by a voice hidden in tumbled boulders beside a steep dune. "Halt!"

Hector threw up both hands and shouted, "Hooray for Dixie!" Then he added under his breath, "Whoever she is."

Two gray-clad soldiers cautiously stepped from the rocks, their muskets and bayonets aimed at Hector. "What have we got here?" one asked, glancing behind and beside Hector for signs of trickery.

"Looks like little Mex here wants to express his appreciation for us liberating his stinking desert."

Alianjo nodded and smiled as broadly as he could. "My name is Hector Manuel Alianjo. I am a good shot and am excellent with a sword. I wish to fight for the Confederacy. And I know all about the blue coat forces."

One of the soldiers rubbed his chin and glanced at the other who shrugged. "Hey, Willie!" A third head popped up from behind the rocks. "Run Mex here up to the colonel. He might have some information."

"My name is *Hector*," Alianjo repeated.

The guard shrugged and shuffled back behind his cover.

The Confederate colonel stood peering through binoculars atop a gentle rise overlooking the grassy Valverde River crossing and battlefield. The ground trembled every time one of the Federal cannons fired. Sulfur smoke wafted across the field stinging Hector's eyes and nose. Rows of crumpled bodies on the river's east shore marked where the fighting had been most fierce.

To Alianjo's dismay, it seemed that the blue coats were winning. They held the crossing and had their cannons and lines of infantry on the river's east side. Alianjo began to wonder if he had miscalculated. Lines of stiff blue soldiers, the regulars, spread out on the south side of the artillery pieces. Thick rows of militia spread out on the north side.

Some of the Confederates were crouching in a grove of trees on the southern side of the slope leading down to the crossing, trading musket fire with the Union regulars. Most of the Confederate force—thousands upon thousands, it seemed to Hector—huddled behind a low hill on the north side of the battlefield to escape the Union artillery fire.

"This is not good, not good at all," Hector muttered to himself.

While his guard escort waited for the colonel to turn, Alianjo blurted, "Sir, the units on the north side are new, raw militia. Colonel Canby says that they will never hold in battle."

The colonel spun around and glared at Hector. "Corporal, who is this man?" He was a red-faced colonel whose voice dripped with a thick Texas drawl.

"A local Mex, sir. Says he can help."

"My name is Hector Manuel Alianjo. I am *New Mexican* and a *soldier* and I will serve anyone who fights against the Union army. I am strong, a good shot, and excellent with a sword!"

The colonel glared at Hector for what seemed like an eternity while the Federal cannons boomed away the minutes. "How do you know about those units?" he demanded.

Hector gulped. Maybe he shouldn't admit to being a deserter. "I . . . uh . . . have been in the fort several times, sir."

The colonel snorted, "A deserter. Good." He slowly rubbed his chin. "But can I trust a deserter?"

Hector nodded toward the Union forces. "I have no loyalty there anymore. I want to join *your* army and drive the Union out of New Mexico and win freedom for my people."

The colonel thought a moment, then nodded and turned to his staff officers. "Major, this Mex's intelligence confirms other reports I've heard. I want the 4th Texas Regiment to press the attack from the north. Swing around the far side of that hill and press *hard*."

The major hesitated, "But sir . . ."

"Your goal is to take those cannons. You *must* take them. You hit those troops on the north hard—I mean *hard*, major. If Mex here is right, they'll break."

"With just the one regiment, sir?"

"You collapse that flank, and they *will* break and run."

The major saluted and galloped off. The Union cannons continued to boom. Muskets blazed in rows, sounding like popping corn. And men continued to crumple and scream as they died.

Hector swelled with pride. He had already helped. Now for a uniform and a musket—and maybe a name tag so everyone would know who he was—and he would join the attack!

The colonel called, "Sgt. Jamison?"

"Sir?"

"We have a new recruit here. See if you can find Mex some fitting position."

"My name is . . ." But the colonel had already turned back to watch the battle through his binoculars.

Ten minutes later, Hector Alianjo was shocked to find himself assigned to the sergeant in charge of the mules and supply train. The invading Confederate army depended on over 1,600 mules to pull their supply wagons, their food, repair, water, and ammunition wagons, and their cannons. Without that supply train and those mules, the Confederate army would wither and die in this harsh, hostile desert. But 1,600 mules meant lots of feeding, cleaning, and shoveling— work Hector had risked his life to escape.

Here he stood in a group of blacks and other Hispanics, far away from the action, with no uniform, no musket, and no sword. He held only a shovel and the sergeant had already twice called him Mex, even after he knew Hector's real name.

A black driver lounged in the shade of his wagon near Hector. "Shucks. They didn't whip you, or beat you, or nothing'. You must be somthin' special."

"I'm supposed to be a soldier," Hector replied.

Several black men laughed. "Slaves can't be soldiers."

"I am Hector Alianjo, a native of New Mexico and a free man."

The black drivers laughed. "You's colored. Maybe brown 'stead o' black. But you is surely colored. And in 'dis here army, that makes you a slave."

Another added, "An' that's as good as you ever goin' to get!"

Hector was numb with shock and bitter disappointment. The Confederate victory at Valverde meant nothing to him, even though his information had been instrumental in bringing it about. His dreams of being a respected, regular soldier seemed to be dashed. His eyes blurred as reality crashed about him. The Confederates were no different than the blue coats. There would be no recognition, no advancement, no opportunity. Not for someone whose skin was a shade too dark.

A month later, the Confederate war machine rolled north through Albuquerque and on to Santa Fe. But supplies were running low. Most of the wagons in the long supply train were empty. If they couldn't quickly capture the Federal supply base at Fort Union (just to the east of Santa Fe through Glorieta Pass) they wouldn't be able to feed and water the mules and men of their army.

On March 27, 1862, the Confederate army started into the deep and twisting canyon known as Glorieta Pass. Alianjo, driving one of the wagons in the long wagon train at the rear of the soldiers, heard gunfire echo down the canyon from the front.

A major raced back on his horse to order the supply wagons driven into a side canyon, called Apache Canyon, for safekeeping while the soldiers fought the Fort Union forces in the pass.

Sounding like a distant storm, the battle rumbled and raged all day while Alianjo sat in the shade of his wagon and sadly shook his head. Wounded Confederates stumbled back to carpet the ground near the entrance to the canyon.

Alianjo was struck by a brilliant idea. He rose and jogged along the rows of wagons searching for the captain in charge of the supply train.

"Captain! Captain! I have an idea," he cried.

"Get back to yer wagon, Mex," the captain growled from the makeshift table where he was playing cards with three sergeants.

"I am *Hector*. Hector Manuel Alianjo."

"Just get back to your wagon."

"But I know how to win the battle."

"Why it's Napoleon himself, come to grace us with his genius," sneered the captain. Then he, the sergeants, and the dozen soldiers assigned to guard the supply train all laughed.

Alianjo blushed, but would not abandon his idea. "Captain, there are 300 drivers sitting here doing nothing. Give us muskets and we will circle north to crash into the blue coat flank. I will volunteer to lead the attack. They will surely break."

Hector paused, expecting praise for his brilliant plan. Instead his offer was met with scornful jeers. "Do you think I'm going to take orders from . . . from—a *Mex*?"

"But, sir, my plan *will* work."

"Get back to yer wagon, Mex, or do I have to pull out my whip?" one of the sergeants snarled as the captain turned back to his card game.

Hector felt crushed by this final insult. Blue coat, gray coat. There was no difference. It seemed all white soldiers were arrogant and cruelly smug and superior. Why did it have to be one of these two hate-filled groups who would rule the West?

Word came that the Confederates had won the battle and now controlled Glorieta Pass. Then a Confederate soldier shouted an alarm, pointing into the steep hills above Apache Canyon. A strong Union force charged downhill toward the supply train.

The captain and sergeants shouted for the drivers to hitch their teams and race the wagons up through Glorieta Pass to the protection of the army. Instinctively, Hector began shouting directions to a dozen other Hispanic drivers.

Then he stopped. Why was he helping these hateful Confederates? He drew in a deep breath and, as the pitifully few Confederate soldiers tried to form a defensive line against the Union onslaught, Hector Alianjo nodded to several other Hispanic and black drivers and simply walked away down the canyon. Other drivers followed. Not one single wagon was driven out of Apache Canyon to safety.

Long before Hector and the other Hispanic drivers reached the flatlands beyond the end of Glorieta Pass and the road back to Hector's home near Albuquerque, they saw a dense plume of black smoke rising from Apache Canyon as the entire Confederate wagon train was destroyed.

Hector Alianjo said to the men walking with him, "If they had given me a gray coat, I would bury it deep in the dirt, just as I did the blue one."

Without a glance back, Hector walked home.

Aftermath

The Battle of Glorieta Pass became known as the Gettysburg of the West since it was both the decisive battle in the region and represented the high-water mark of the Confederacy in the West.

Glorieta Pass should have been a Confederate victory: Their forces won the battle. The Confederates were defeated, however, when a small Union force destroyed the entire Confederate supply train, forcing the Confederates into a hasty retreat to Texas. Before another invasion could be organized, the 3,000-man California Brigade reached New Mexico to bolster the Union forces. Also, Admiral David Farragut began his campaign to conquer the Mississippi River. The Texans' attention shifted to the East. The war in the far West was over.

Having cleared all Confederate forces out of the West, the California Brigade attacked Apache, Navaho, and Zuni Indians who had greatly increased their raids when the army withdrew in 1861 to confront the Confederates. The Southwest Indian Wars reached their peak during the last two years of the Civil War.

Hector Alianjo was one of about 50 soldiers who changed sides during the nine months of Civil War conflict in the West. Most switched from Union to Confederate. Hispanics fared little better in the Confederate army than they had in the Union army. Lumped into the catchall category of "colored," they were viewed as inferior soldiers and inferior beings, and were usually relegated to menial duties.

Hector fled west to California in the summer of 1862 to escape being caught as a deserter by whichever army won the war. He worked in California's rich Central Valley as a migrant farmworker for the rest of his life.

Follow-up Questions and Activities

1. **What Do You Know?**

   - Why did both the Confederacy and Union want control of the West? Did they have more than one motive?

   - Why didn't the Confederacy try to recapture the West after their 1862 defeat at Glorieta Pass? What kept the Confederacy form moving another army west through Texas?

   - Why and how did the Federal forces win the battle of Glorieta Pass? Who won the actual fighting?

   - More than 40 Union soldiers switched sides in New Mexico from mid-1861 to mid-1862. Why would they want to switch? How many reasons can you find?

   - Did the population of the far West support the Union or the Confederacy? Where was Confederate support strongest? Where was support for the Union strongest?

2. **Find Out More.** Here are six topics that were important to this story for students to research in the library and on the Internet. The bibliography at the back of this book will help them get started.

   - Research the Civil War in the West. Where were army units stationed at the start of the war? Why were they there? Who started the California Brigade?

What did it accomplish? Who fought? Where? Against whom? What was decided at each encounter?

- Research Native American participation in the Civil War. Which side did most tribes favor? Why? Who had they been fighting before the Civil War began? Who did they fight during the war? Can you find whole Native American regiments who fought in the war?

- This story talks about the experiences of a few men from one minority race. Research the experiences of other minority and immigrant races during the Civil War. Did Chinese and other Asian peoples become involved in the war? What about Irish, German, and other European immigrants? Why would they? What were their experiences? Research other Hispanic units and soldiers from both Union and Confederate armies. What made them willing to fight in a war that really wasn't theirs?

  Why were immigrants willing to fight during the war? How did immigrant regiments fare during the war? How did the returning ethnic or immigrant veterans fare after the war?

- Kit Carson was a colonel of the New Mexico volunteers and fought at both Valverde and Glorieta Pass. Research this famous Western figure and his life on the Western frontier.

- Research other soldiers who have switched sides—defected from one army and joined the opposing army. How often did it happen during the Civil War? Why did soldiers switch? Has this happened during other wars? When? Why?

- Southwest Indian Wars peaked during the last two years of the Civil War. Research the wars between the U.S. Army and the several tribes of the Southwest.

3. **Make It Real**

- Draw a map of the far Western territories (from New Mexico and Colorado west). Mark the population of each territory or state as of 1860 on the map. Then locate and date every Civil War battle or skirmish in this region on your map. Finally, create a timeline for the Civil War in the far West.

- Create a second map and timeline showing battles between the U.S. Army and Southwest Native American tribes during the period of the Civil War. Then compare the two maps and timelines. Where and when was each group of battles concentrated?

4. **Points to Ponder**

- Was treatment of any minorities and ethnic peoples better than that of blacks during the Civil War? How? In what ways was it not any better? Why do you think minorities were badly treated by the armies they joined? Were there exceptions? If you had been a member of a minority in the armed forces during the Civil War, how would you have felt and what would you have done?

- There is an old saying: "The enemy of my enemy is my friend." How do you think this saying describes how Native American and Hispanic settlers in the New Mexico Territory viewed the two sides of the Civil War? How do you think Zuni and Apache viewed the Civil War? Which side do you think they would favor, and why? Why didn't Hispanic settlers in New Mexico side with the Confederacy?

Private Petticoat

Female Army Spy, May 1862

At a Glance

When we think of the Civil War we typically picture long lines of dust-enshrouded soldiers charging through the smoke of a hundred roaring cannons. We think of Lee, Grant, Stonewall Jackson, Lincoln, and Jefferson Davis. We think of men.

But women played a variety of important roles in that great struggle. They provided food, clothes, shoes, and aid for army units. They took up farm, manufacturing, and retail jobs that men abandoned when they went soldiering. They cared for the thousands of wounded and disabled soldiers. They did the fund-raising to support the great armies.

Some women, however, burned with the same fire that sent many men into army uniforms: the need to be part of the great struggle itself. More than 400 women took up arms and fought in the Civil War—a few in infantry units, a few in artillery units, most as medical corpsmen. But women were not allowed to join the army in the 1860s. Each of these women had to disguise herself as a man. They not only had to endure the same horrendous conditions that battered men's minds and bodies during war, they also had to bear the burden of a lonely, secret double life to fight for the causes they believed in.

The most valuable commodity a commanding general could possess was information. Where was the enemy? How strong? What were its plans and intentions? Reliable information was hard to come by. Collecting it involved incredible risks. Gathering that information was the most dangerous assignment an army could give—especially for an invading army that had to deal with a hostile civilian population. This is a story of one of the few women who successfully served both as a soldier and as a spy. She joined the Federal army as a man and served for four years, and she also successfully completed more than a dozen spy missions.

Meet Sarah Edmonds

Born in New Brunswick, Canada, in 1841, Sarah (Emma) Edmondson was the daughter of a farmer, the second of four children. Her older brother, Thomas, had no interest in outdoor activities, so Sarah filled the role he was unwilling to occupy. She became a skilled rider and an expert shot and even wore trousers to try to fulfill her father's desire for a child to share his outdoor interests.

None of Sarah's actions or accomplishments satisfied her harsh, brutal father. By the time Sarah reached the age of 16, she so thoroughly despised her father that she ran away from home and dropped the last two letters from her surname.

Sarah (Emma to her friends) took a job at a millinery shop, but earned such a small wage there that she contemplated turning to prostitution just to survive. Then she had a brilliant idea: If the good jobs went to men, why not pretend to be a man and get one? She cut her hair short, donned men's clothing, and became Franklin Thompson.

Franklin worked first for L. P. Crown & Company in Boston as a door-to-door Bible salesman, then for a larger publisher in Hartford, Connecticut, and finally traveled to Flint, Michigan, in late 1859, still selling books door-to-door.

Sarah (as Franklin) tried to enlist in the army in April 1861 but was rejected for being too short (under 5 feet, 6 inches) and too delicate. She persisted and, on May 17, Private Franklin Thompson joined Company F of the 2nd Michigan Volunteer Infantry and was assigned the position of company nurse.

Sarah was into her fourth year of successful—and undiscovered—army service as a nurse and spy when, in the fall of 1864, she caught malaria. Not daring to enter a military hospital (where she would be examined and her secret would be discovered), Sarah deserted. She reverted to wearing female clothing and spent the last year of the war in St. Louis working for the U.S. Sanitary Commission.

Sarah married in 1867 and spent two more decades in obscurity before her identity as Franklin Thompson was uncovered. Congress awarded her a military pension of $12 per month, the only female so honored for service during the Civil War.

Private Petticoat

Gray-haired Mrs. Butler, wife of the chaplain for the Army of the Potomac, sank into a chair. "Let me get this straight. You're going to *pretend* to be a woman so you can spy on the Confederates?"

"Exactly," nodded the person with sparkling gray eyes standing before her.

Mrs. Butler rubbed her forehead in confusion. "But . . . but . . . how can you pretend to be a woman? I mean, you *are* a woman."

The other woman smiled. "Of course. But you're the only one who knows that."

Mrs. Butler counted on her fingers trying to understand. "So now *you*, a woman who has successfully disguised herself as a *man* named Franklin Thompson so you could join the army, are going to pretend to be this man disguising himself as a *woman* so you can go on a spying mission?"

Sarah (Emma) Edmonds smiled. "Exactly."

The chaplain's wife fanned herself. "It's dizzying! A woman disguised as a man disguised as a woman."

Emma adjusted her red wig and stared into a mirror. "I think I should do pretty well acting like a woman. Do you think I should look plumper? Maybe I should stuff a pillow or two inside my dress."

Mrs. Butler shook her head. "You don't want to wear pillows on a spying mission, Emma. You'll do just fine without."

Emma broke into her mischievous, impish laugh. In a thick Irish brogue she said, "Me name's no longer Emma. Besides, you're the only one in this whole army knows that name. Now me name's Bridget O'Shea."

Mrs. Butler slowly shook her head. "Bridget, Sarah, Franklin. . . . You've got too many names!"

Emma stepped out of the chaplain's small house into a sea of white canvas tents set in neat rows like long waves marching across an ocean. The date was May 20, 1862, and this was the mighty Army of the Potomac, the largest of the Union forces engaged in the Civil War. Endless ranks of blue coats, tall muskets, and gleaming bayonets stretched out like fields of wheat. Rows of carefully aligned cannons and mortars stretched into the hazy blue morning.

Dressed as an Irish peddler woman, with all the swish and sway to match, 22-year-old Emma turned past the hospital tents where she worked as medical orderly Private Franklin Thompson and headed for the command center of the Army of the Potomac.

"Colonel Shrub, sir. There's . . . well . . . a woman . . . to see you."

Major Milton stood nervously just inside the flaps of Colonel Shrub's tent, glancing occasionally over his shoulder at the red-headed woman smiling outside.

Colonel Shrub threw down his pen and growled. "I'm a busy man. General McClellan's taken Yorktown and is eager to attack Richmond. I have to plan the troop movements for 110,000 men. I got no time. Send her away!"

"But sir," pleaded the major, nervously dabbing at the sweat trickling down his neck and under the collar of his stained blue uniform on this muggy Virginia day. "She says she's Private Franklin Thompson."

Colonel Shrub's steel gray eyes glared at his aide; he chomped on an unlit cigar stub. "Well, which is it, major? Is this she really a 'he,' who's a medic in this Army of the Potomac named Thompson, or is this she a 'she' come to pedal her wares?"

Major Milton grimaced, pulling on his muttonchop sideburns. "Well. . . . yes, sir, she is . . . I mean, of course she's a 'she.' Just look at her, sir. But she says. . . . Oh, if you would just see her for a moment, sir?"

Colonel Shrub ran both hands through his short-cropped salt-and-pepper hair. Then he leaned back in his folding chair with a deep sigh. "Send her in, Milton. I guess the attack of the U.S. Army on the capital of the Confederacy will have to wait for a peddler woman."

Before Milton could gratefully salute and step back outside, a slender, red-headed Irish woman swept past him with a gracious smile and curtsied. "Bridget O'Shea, a peddler from County Clare in Ireland, at your service, colonel."

Colonel Shrub's gaze darted between the woman and Major Milton. Milton shrugged. Shrub chewed harder on his cigar and roughly rubbed his unshaved stubble. "How may I help you, madam?"

She laughed merrily. "Why, colonel, darlin', it is I who can help you. Don't you recognize your own spy?"

Thompson suddenly lifted his wig, revealing his own shaggy brown hair, and saluted. Colonel Shrub gasped, almost swallowing his cigar, and doubled over in a coughing fit.

"Thompson?" he wheezed between coughs. "Egad, you look just like a woman. That's a great disguise."

"Thank you, sir," answered the private. "I thought it might fool the Confederates."

Colonel Shrub spat the last of the cigar out of his throat and settled back into his chair. "That disguise would fool Jeff Davis himself, Thompson. But to fool the Confederates you'll have to *act* like a woman."

"I think I can act like a woman, sir," interrupted Thompson with a mischievous grin. Slim for a Michigan farm boy, Thompson was just five and a half feet tall, with brown hair and clear gray eyes.

Colonel Shrub shook his head. "I'm not convinced. You're a medic, not an actor."

"I can do it, sir," insisted Thompson.

"All right. Show me," said the colonel, turning his chair and folding his arms across his barrel chest. "Walk . . . No, no, no. More swish, smaller steps, more graceful, Thompson. Get your skirts flowing like my wife does. Think like a woman, not like a soldier!"

Thompson couldn't hold back a laugh. "I'm trying, sir."

"Concentrate, Thompson. There, that's better. Now sit. No! You sit like a worn-out cow farmer. Use more finesse, man, dainty and helpless, like a woman."

Again Thompson laughed. "Do you really think women are helpless, sir?"

Again and again Colonel Shrub corrected his spy. Finally the colonel shook his head. "I don't think you'll ever look natural as a woman, Thompson. But I'm desperate for information. I'm sending you out anyway."

"Thank you, sir," replied Thompson with a broad smile.

Colonel Shrub rose from his writing desk and fished a fresh cigar out of his coat pocket. He unrolled a large map on the trampled grass floor of his tent. "Memorize this, Thompson."

Stabbing with his cigar at the map, Shrub continued. "We've got 100,000 men slogging their way through these retched Virginia swamps, heading past Yorktown here and up to

Richmond. But in several key areas we don't know what Confederate forces are in front of us. Here," he stabbed the map, leaving a brown smudge from the cigar, "and especially here."

Now the cigar jabbed at a thin blue line called the Chickahominy River. Private Thompson craned his neck to read the name. "Chick—a—home . . ."

"Chickamahoginy, or some such thing," broke in the colonel. "I can't read these Southern names either. But that's where you're going. You'll cross the river here tonight. Find out what units the rebs got in this sector. Find out their plans."

Private Thompson nodded and saluted. "Bridget O'Shea can do that, sir."

"Who?" asked the colonel.

Thompson plopped the wig back on his head. His voice rose an octave. "Why, Bridget O'Shea, darlin' colonel." And she curtsied.

The colonel grunted and turned back to his writing. "Good luck, Thompson. Be back in two days with whatever you can learn—no later. Oh, and I, uh, admire your courage for doing this. If you're caught, you'll be hanged for sure, impersonating a woman. It's mighty brave."

"Oh, not as brave as other things I've done," muttered Thompson.

"What was that?" asked Colonel Shrub.

"Nothing. Thank you, sir." And Private Franklin Thompson backed out of the tent with a mischievous little laugh.

At 10:30 that night the mists began to thicken into dense fog. A lone rowboat softly sculled its way through the pitch-black darkness on the swollen Chickahominy River and silently nosed into the far shore. A trim Irish woman stepped out. The corporal at the oars eagerly pushed back through the dark to the safety and warmth of Union campfires.

Sarah closed her eyes and pictured Colonel Shrub's maps. The road toward Richmond should be off to her right front. She lifted her skirts and pushed her way through soggy underbrush. With each step her heart beat a little faster, a little harder. Her breath came in deep gasps, more from nervous fear than from the effort of walking.

How could she discover the Confederate plans? How could she talk her way into Confederate headquarters? What if they discovered she was a spy? Sarah's dream had never been *just* to join the army. It had always been much more. Sarah dreamed that she would somehow make a greater difference in the outcome of the war than any of the men around her. Now Colonel Shrub had dropped a grand chance in her lap. But how was she supposed to take advantage of it?

The mist thickened into drizzle, the drizzle into sheets of rain. As soon as she stumbled into the deeply worn ruts that were the Richmond road, Sarah sought shelter. An abandoned house with a crumbled porch loomed off to her right. She ran for it.

Forcing open a badly rusted door, she heard a low moan from the kitchen. A Confederate soldier, a captain, lay shivering on the floor, the side of his gray coat stained with a large patch of crimson, his face covered with fevered sweat. In an instant Sarah knew that he was both very sick and badly wounded, and that he was dying.

What could Sarah do all alone in this stormy night? She gave him water and held his hand. Softly she sang to him. As rain and wind howled outside, shutters banged and water streamed through a leaky roof into puddles on the floor around them, Sarah sang, and the Confederate captain died.

Before he died, his trembling hands passed a golden pocket watch to Sarah. In a whisper he begged her to tell Major McKee at General Ewell's headquarters that it came from Captain Hall.

Sarah's heart skipped a beat. General Ewell was the Confederate general whose plans she was supposed to steal. All evening she had struggled to think of how she'd talk her way into Ewell's headquarters. Here was her answer, a lump of softly ticking gold lying heavy in her hands.

Around noon the next day three Confederate sentries escorted Bridget O'Shea through half a dozen security checkpoints to a tall flagpole at the edge of a sea of white canvas tents. To Sarah this tent city looked just like the one she had left the day before. These boys looked no different than the ones she had left on the other side of the Chickahominy River. If it weren't for the color of their coats, she'd never be able to separate Union from Confederate soldiers.

In an orderly semicircle around one side of the flagpole stood larger tents full of bustling activity. There the sentries stopped in front of a lean, kindly looking man with a sad face, soaking in a moment of sunshine.

"Major McKee, sir. This Irish woman says she's lookin' for you."

The sentries saluted, just like Union sentries saluted, then returned to their posts.

The lines in Major McKee's face deepened as he clutched the golden watch and sadly shook his head. "Hall was my nephew and a fine lad." Then he added, "This war will kill us all 'fore it's done."

He clicked his heels and courteously bowed. "I am deeply indebted to you, Mrs. O'Shea. It's a kind and brave thing you've done."

"Not as brave as other things I've done," she muttered.

Bridget O'Shea was given free rein in Ewell's camp. She wandered from company to company, from regiment to regiment. The Confederates were gracious and kind. Many offered her tours of their camp. Soon Sarah had memorized the identity and strength of each unit under Ewell's command. An impish voice inside her was growing cocky. Spying was easy.

But what were their plans? Sarah had less than one day left to uncover the Confederate plans and then escape back across the Chickahominy River.

Major McKee found her talking with several young officers near the camp photographer's tent. He bowed gallantly. "Mrs. O'Shea, ma'am. Would you do us the honor of staying for our victory party?"

Sarah gasped. Was she too late? Had there already been a battle? Had the Union lost without her information? She was barely able to smile as she repeated, "Victory party, major? Has there been a fight today?"

Major McKee's eyes glowed with eager excitement. "Not yet, madam. But very soon. Based on their current distribution, the Yankees will soon have to cross at one of only two possible fords across the Chickahominy River. And I have just placed and fortified two brigades with heavy guns in those dense thickets blocking those crossings. As Federal units come ashore we'll easily drive them into the marshes and swamp to the south. We'll destroy them piecemeal. They won't stand a chance, and we *will* hold a grand victory party."

Sarah trembled with excitement. So that was the Confederate battle plan! But she still had to escape. She curtsied, forced herself to smile, and fluttered her eyelashes at Major McKee. "And at that party I hope you'll save a dance for me, major, darlin'."

Major McKee's face lost its luster. His eyes grew sad. "Before this coming scrap, I'd like to recover Captain Hall's body. Could you possibly ride out with a detachment and show them where that house is?"

Relief swept through Sarah. Riding with this detail would get her through Confederate roadblocks and back near the river. Every time she needed something, the enemy stepped up and offered it. Again she curtsied and smiled at Major McKee. "I would truly be honored, sir."

With a four-man detail, Sarah easily rode through guard posts, sentries, and picket lines that otherwise would have greeted her with that fearful word, "Halt!"

That impish voice inside Sarah laughed mischievously. Spying was exciting and came easily to Sarah. "I'll have to do it again," she told herself.

But still Sarah's heart pounded. How would she get away from these four armed men? If she bolted, they'd surely chase her down. But if she could catch all four off their horses while she was still on hers, she might get enough of a start to get away.

A sergeant leaned nearer Sarah and said, "Mind where you ride, Mrs. O'Shea. Troops are dug in just ahead, itchin' for a fight. If you ride up there, they're liable to think you're a spy."

"I'll remember that, sergeant."

At the crumbling, mournful house the four-man detail dismounted and stepped toward the collapsed porch. Sarah lingered in the saddle. Her blood roared past her ears as the four men pried open the rusted door. A voice inside her screamed, "Now!"

Sarah kicked her horse and bolted, fleeing as fast as she could make the Confederate horse run.

"Mrs. O'Shea, not that way," yelled the sergeant. "It's less than half a mile to the front!"

The detail leapt onto their horses and raced after Sarah.

Ahead Sarah saw three gray-clad riflemen step into the road and wave for her to stop. Again she kicked the horse. "Hee-yaaaw!" she yelled, and leaned down close to the horse's neck. In a frothing fury she thundered forward.

One of the sentries raised his gun to fire. Before he could, Sarah's red wig flew off, spinning through the air, looking as though the whole top of her head had flown off. The sentry stared, too startled to pull the trigger. Sarah smashed through the guard post.

Shots rang after her as she dashed for the river. She clung tight to the horse's neck, tensely waiting for a shot to find its mark. Bullets whizzed past her and thudded into the ground like heavy drops of rain.

Even after she passed beyond the Confederate soldiers' range, danger was not all behind her. Nervous Union sentries and sharpshooters waited just across the Chickahominy River, more likely to shoot at her than not. She splashed her horse noisily into the river, both hands raised high over her head, screaming over and over, "I have important information for Colonel Shrub! I have important information for Colonel Shrub!"

How many Union lives would have been lost the next day had they crossed the Chickahominy without Sarah Edmonds's information? We'll never really know. But history does record that very few were killed, and that the crossing was smooth and bypassed major Confederate resistance.

Aftermath

Before serious illness forced her out of the army, Sarah Edmonds spied for the Union as a contraband slave named Cuff; as the Irish peddler, Bridget O'Shea; as a black washerwoman; as a Southern gentleman and businessman, Charles Maybery; and even as a Confederate soldier from Kentucky, all while posing as Private Franklin Thompson behind Union lines.

In each of these spy disguises Emma collected valuable information for the Union army. But surely her best acting job of all was in fooling that same Union army. For it was not until the war had been over for many years that the army discovered its decorated spy hero, Franklin Thompson, had really been a woman.

The information Sarah Edmonds gathered for the Union army in the summer of 1862 helped, but not enough to save that disastrous campaign. General McClellan's main source of intelligence was detective Allan Pinkerton. Pinkerton's wildly inaccurate intelligence reports froze McClellan into inaction. As a result, McClellan's invasion became mired in failure. With almost three times as many men as Confederate General Joe Johnston (leading the Army of Northern Virginia), McClellan refused to commit his vast army to an all-out attack. McClellan's inaction allowed the Confederates to pick their battles and battlefields.

The defeat of the South was delayed by McClellan's reluctance to act and by Pinkerton's grossly exaggerated estimates of enemy strength. The Civil War should have ended in 1862. However, bad intelligence, accepted and believed by a commanding general, allowed the war to drag on for three more years.

Follow-up Questions and Activities

1. **What Do You Know?**

   - Why was intelligence harder for an invading army to collect than for a defending army in friendly territory?

   - Why was the Army of the Potomac near Yorktown in eastern Virginia in the spring and summer of 1862? What were they trying to do? Why didn't they defeat the much smaller Confederate force?

   - Why didn't each army know the exact strength and location of the enemy? Why was it hard for armies to gather exact information?

2. **Find Out More.** Following are five important topics from this story for students to research in the library and on the Internet. The reference sources at the back of this book will help them get started.

   - Research the life and accomplishments of Sarah Edmonds. She was an amazing woman, not only sneaking her way into the army and admirably performing her duties as a nurse, but also adopting half a dozen disguises and successfully completing various spy missions.

   - Research the Peninsular Campaign of 1862. Robert E. Lee was a prominent Confederate commander during that campaign. How did the Confederates drive off the massive Army of the Potomac? Why didn't McClellan dare to attack forcefully and win the war? What battles were fought? How many casualties piled up during the seven days of fighting?

   - Union General McClellan was the commanding general of the massive Army of the Potomac who repeatedly failed in 1862. Research this controversial figure. How did he rise to be a general? What happened to him after Lincoln relieved him of command?

   - Research the history of women in the army. How many countries and armies have allowed women to fight? Who has used women? Why? What roles have women been allowed to fill in different armies and at different times?

   - Historically, how have armies gathered information as they march into battle? During the Civil War, what was the primary role of cavalry? Of scouts? Of pickets? Of spies? How do nations and armies collect intelligence information today? Do modern nations still use any of the methods used during the Civil War?

3. **Make It Real**

  • Identify 12 famous spies in American history. Make a chart showing the following information: for whom they spied, when, for how long they spied, why they did it, whether they were caught, and what happened to them. Can you draw any conclusions about the dangers and stresses of spying?

  • Imagine that you have a terrible secret that you dare not share with anyone at school, a secret you are afraid will soon be found out. How would that constant worry affect your daily school life? Write a letter to a friend describing how you feel and how the secret has affected your life.

4. **Points to Ponder**

  • Why do you think men didn't want women on the battlefield? Did they not want the competition for their jobs and positions? Did they feel a need to protect women that might jeopardize their own lives? Did men believe that women would be inferior soldiers who couldn't withstand the stress and rigors of battle? Did they think that women were more important to society and so shouldn't be risked in battle? What do you think were the real reasons?

  • Should a woman have been rewarded or punished for lying to get into the army during the Civil War? If women lie about their sex, what else would they be willing to lie about? Could they ever be trusted? How do you feel they should have been treated?

  • Should men and women have separate roles in the military? Why or why not? Does the United States still have gender-specific military functions?

Patriotic Pride and Prejudice
Northern Blacks' Efforts to Enlist, Summer 1862

At a Glance

After the Confederacy's attack on Fort Sumpter (Charleston, South Carolina), patriotic young men flooded into Northern recruiting stations. Fervor ran high to retaliate, to show the upstart Southerners just what it meant to fire on property and soldiers of the United States.

Free Northern blacks rushed to enlist alongside whites—and were summarily and universally rejected. They were told that this was a white man's army and a white man's war. Blacks need not apply. Their help was neither wanted nor accepted.

African Americans were outraged. This was their country, too. The war aimed to free slaves, and it was *their* people who were the slaves. They had a greater stake in ending slavery than anyone.

Frederick Douglass pleaded, lectured, and wrote in impassioned tones. Lincoln remained silent. Black leaders in Massachusetts, New York, and Ohio preached, lectured, and begged. Lincoln, each state's government, and the army remained silent.

During a meeting in Cleveland in September 1861, a congregation of African Americans pledged support for the Union and, in their unanimous declaration, offered "our property, our prayers and our lives to our state and nation."

The nation wasn't interested. The army remained adamant. Most leading abolitionists remained uncharacteristically quiet. Freeing slaves was noble. It was just and right. But arming and training those same blacks and having to treat them as equals was another thing entirely.

Northern blacks were summarily demoted to second-class citizens—or, at least, their noses were rubbed in their second-class status as had never been done before. They faced a new and desperate struggle—one to earn the right to fight and die for their country and their freedom.

Meet John Mercer Langston

Born in October 1822 of free black parents who had immigrated to Cleveland, Ohio, from Buffalo, New York, John was the third of eight children. John's mother took in wash. His father shoveled coal in a factory.

Cleveland had organized black schools by 1820. John excelled at school and won a scholarship to Mercer College. He graduated in 1845 and began a successful business career that elevated him to a leader of the Cleveland African American community.

An outspoken abolitionist and supporter of the Union and the war, Langston led the fight to allow blacks to enlist in Ohio. Langston's own son was one of the first to enlist in Ohio and was killed in action near Petersburg, Virginia, in early 1865. Langston, over 40 when black enlistments began and suffering from asthma, did not serve. He lived in Cleveland, a prominent black businessman, until his death in 1884.

Patriotic Pride and Prejudice

Forty-year-old John Mercer Langston stood in a swirl of dust on Spencer Street in Cincinnati, Ohio, and glanced again at the address scrawled on a scrap of paper in his hand. Then he looked at the sagging, boarded-up building before him and sighed. How could *this* be where he had been asked to meet the secret Cincinnati black militia?

A stingy breeze stirred the oppressive air on this muggy afternoon of July 29, 1862. A dust devil spun up the street, stumbling through deep ruts, and stalled over a mud puddle. Langston hopped onto the warped wood walk, sighed again, and stuffed the paper into a pocket of his fashionable three-piece suit.

He pried several hastily nailed boards away from the entrance, dipped his new bowler low over his eyes, and climbed into the dim room beyond. Slanting beams of sunlight squeezed through chinks in the window boards and gleamed off a thick haze of floating dust.

A voice from deep in the folded shadows that blackened one corner said, "Mr. Langston, please turn all the way around, slowly."

Langston spun to face the voice. "Captain Ballier?"

Langston heard soft voices in a hushed and earnest debate. "He's still an outsider." "*We* asked him to come." "But what if he tells?" Langston squinted past the shafts of filtered light and could just make out four dark shapes huddled in the corner. They, like he, were black men.

Finally one held out his hands to quiet the others and rose. "Yes, I am Captain Jefferson Ballier. We have desperate matters to discuss, Mr. Langston. But we will be arrested if caught here, and think it best if, later, you do not know how you got to where we *will* talk. Would you mind being blindfolded?"

Impressed with Ballier's diction, Langston asked, "Where did you get your education?"

Ballier answered, "I publish a newspaper for the black community in Cincinnati and learned my grammar at Wilberforce College. Over half our militia force are students there."

Langston grunted in surprise. He hadn't expected to meet educated soldiers.

Blindfolded, Langston was led out back to a carriage. After a bumpy ride over uneven fields, the carriage halted and Ballier removed the blindfold in a rolling meadow near a thick tree line. Langston could hear voices beyond.

Ballier led him along a twisting path through the bramble to a small field completely surrounded by dense hedgerows of trees. In that field, 200 black militia drilled in military formation. They wore no uniforms. They carried no muskets, just brooms, poles, or branches that some had whittled into the general shape of a gun.

Most scowled at the outsider as their sergeant called, "Comp-nies! A-tennnnnn—shun!" The sergeant saluted. Ballier saluted back, then said to Langston, "Welcome to the Black Cincinnati Volunteer Militia. You'll have to pardon the men. They don't trust outsiders."

Langston tipped back his bowler, scratched his head, and swatted at a pesky fly. "I'd think you'd want lots of publicity so everyone would notice—photos and articles in your paper—and cheering crowds watching you drill." Then he added, "Your men march very well, by the way."

"That is because they *want* to march—and to serve, and to fight," Ballier answered. "Last year we tried to organize and volunteer. The army wouldn't even talk to us. The police shut us down and boarded up our meeting hall. We moved buildings. They shut us down again and threatened to arrest us for unlawful assembly—threatened us for trying to serve! Now we meet and drill in secret."

"What do you want from me?"

"We want to enlist in the army and fight as soldiers."

Langston laughed. "I have no connections with the army."

"But you know the governor."

"I see . . ." said Langston in sudden understanding. "You want me to talk to Governor Tod about your joining one of the Ohio regiments."

"Not 'talk to,' " Ballier growled. "Persuade."

Langston began, "But I have no real influence . . ."

The drill sergeant bellowed, "Column of two from the left. Quick time. March!"

Another of the company's officers who had joined the conversation said, "You's rich. You's well knowed. You's impo'tant. An' we know you contributed to the gob'ner's campaign. You's got *influence*."

"But I'm also black, which means I can't vote. Votes create political influence," Langston countered. Then he asked, "Why do you want to fight anyway? You'll likely be killed or die of disease."

"Left turn, march!" called the sergeant as the company pounded in rigid, precise steps along the field's far side.

Ballier answered, "If we fight as equal citizens, and win the war as equal citizens, *then* we'll be able to demand equal citizenship after the war."

The four other officers now clustered around Langston solemnly nodded.

Langston countered, "No one gave us equal rights after the Revolution or the War of 1812, and we helped win both of those wars."

"Because our fathers didn't *demand* their rights after they served; they didn't *take* them. But we will."

"Comp-nies, halt! Left face!" the sergeant yelled, marching smartly to the end of the long double line of soldiers.

One of the other black officers added, "Even the Confederacy uses blacks in the army. Some—a few—as soldiers."

"Uncover to the left . . . Preeee-sent!" Two hundred pretend rifles snapped to right shoulders as the men sighted down their wooden weapons.

Yet another officer added, "I hear there's three black regiments in New Orleans already in the Confederate reserve."

The sergeant yelled, "Fire!" Two hundred index fingers jerked back and the men yelled "Bang!" Birds squawked and flapped from the trees at the thunderclap shout. A pair of rabbits bounded across the field away from the line of infantry.

Ballier gripped Langston's arm, his eyes hard and fiery like steel and flint. "We have 300 men training in black units in this city—even though they aren't allowed to join or fight. We use brooms for muskets, sticks for bayonets. You *must* make the governor agree to let us serve. If we don't get to fight in this war, blacks will *never* be treated as equal citizens in this country."

Langston blushed. "I'm not even sure I could get an appointment . . ."

"We *have* to fight in this war," Ballier repeated. "And you are the one who'll get us there." He released his grip, stepped back and nodded.

"Order arms!" cried the soldier. Two hundred right hands slapped their sticks as they slammed into the ground next to right heels.

"We can't do nothin' from here," said one of the lieutenants.

"The battle must be won in the governor's office," Ballier repeated. "Will you do it for us?"

Six eager faces pressed close to Langston, hanging on his answer.

Now, sitting on an uncomfortably hard straight-backed chair in the governor's outer office on the dreary afternoon of August 26, John Mercer Langston realized that it wasn't their specific words he remembered. It was their faces, their desperate looks of hope and pride, which all now rested on his shoulders. To others in the spacious outer office, he appeared calm and confident. Inside he seethed with doubts about his ability to accomplish this awesome mission.

A small bell rang on the secretary's desk, which was connected by pulleys to Governor Tod's inner office. Dorothy Glading nodded at the bell. "You may go in, Mr. Langston."

Langston rose, but paused outside the door to calm himself with a deep breath and to organize his thoughts.

While waiting to ring for Langston, Governor David Tod drummed his fingers on the mahogany desk of his ornate office and then balled those fingers into a fist that he pounded onto the polished surface. Coffee jumped and sloshed in his cup. "This is one fine pickle of a mess!" As if agreeing with the governor, rain drummed on the roof and streaked the windows of the Columbus, Ohio, governor's mansion and made the late summer colors of Columbus look as drab as Governor Tod felt.

The governor sighed and rocked back in his leather chair. Then he wagged his finger at the plump, balding man seated across from him. "I don't know why Dorothy let him make an appointment. Langston is going to march in here and ask—no, he will *demand*—that I allow blacks to serve in Ohio army regiments. What on earth can I tell him?"

Bernard Mason shifted in his chair and poked at a bowl of peanuts on the governor's desk. "Tell him no." Mason had been campaign manager for Governor Tod in the fall of 1861. Now he served as the governor's chief of staff.

"But Langston is a prosperous and prominent businessman. He holds considerable influence in the northern half of Ohio. He contributed to my campaign, for goodness sake."

The office door opened. Fixing a confident smile on his face, John Langston strode in.

The governor's desk sat between two floor-to-ceiling windows framed by red brocade curtains. Before it, the expansive office was sparsely filled with chairs and a modest worktable. Nervously Tod, a thin man in his early forties with delicate, child-like features, plucked a cigar from a box on his desk and rolled it between his fingers before striking a match to light it.

Langston carried a leather briefcase and wore a fashionable top hat and long coat. His curly hair was flecked with white and his skin glowed a deep chocolate brown. He nodded amiably to Mason and extended his hand to the governor. "Governor Tod, I am John Mercer Langston. Thank you so much for agreeing to see me." His voice boomed with conviction and authority.

Without looking Langston square on, Tod took the hand and gestured toward a straight-backed chair. Then Tod sank into his thickly padded leather chair. He gestured toward the cigar box. Langston gave a slight shake of his head. "What brings you to Columbus, Mr. Langston?"

Langston unbuckled his briefcase and drew out a packet of papers. "Governor Tod, we have three companies of black volunteers in Cincinnati ready to serve Ohio and the Union. They are already well trained in marching and battle drill. They are disciplined and motivated.

Half of them are college students at Wilberforce College. That's over 300 eager soldiers ready to serve Ohio if you will but give the word."

Tod pretended to thoughtfully consider Langston's offer. "Interesting, John. Very interesting. But you know my hands are tied. There's nothing I can do."

"Not true, governor." Langston's response came instantly. He had obviously prepared for that argument. "Blacks served with distinction in the Revolutionary War and the War of 1812. There is no law or article of the Constitution that forbids individual states from enlisting blacks."

"It's Washington," whined Governor Tod. "The army headquarters in Washington forbids it. Now, if it were up to me . . ." Tod smiled broadly and stretched his hands in a helpless shrug. "If only it were up to me . . ."

"But it *is*," snapped Langston, leaning far forward in his chair. "General Butler at Fort Monroe, Virginia, has already used the Contraband Acts to free slaves and has enlisted an entire regiment of them in his command with great success." Langston's dark eyes bored into the governor's face. "And now it is up to you. This is *our* country as well as it is the white man's country. It is our brothers who are suffering as slaves in the Confederacy. If you do not act, Ohio's best black citizens will leave for other states like Massachusetts that *will* allow them to serve."

Mason coughed to gain attention. "President Lincoln has recently instructed General Butler to disband his black regiment."

"But Butler *did* form that regiment, and it *is* a success," Langston insisted.

Tod shifted in his chair and tried a new approach. "Blacks already benefit from the war, Mr. Langston. They can get jobs—*paying* jobs—as wagon drivers, muleteers, cooks, laborers. Isn't that enough?"

"No." Langston's voice rang with passion. "Last fall the black community of Ohio pledged their property, prayers, *and lives* to support the war effort. We, as good citizens of Ohio, demand the right to serve our state in its hour of need."

Mason snorted. "*Demand*? What right have you got to march in here and demand?" He paused, smiled, and added, " 'Course, if you had voted for Governor Tod in the last election . . ."

Langston glared at the chief of staff. "You know blacks aren't allowed to vote."

"And they aren't allowed to serve in the armed forces either," snapped Mason, jabbing at the desk with one finger to emphasize his point. "That's just the way it is."

The governor asked, "Why are your black men so eager to get slaughtered in battle?"

Mason glanced at his boss to see if he was serious, then reached for a cigar, lit it, and puffed several times before answering. "If we let blacks into the army as *equals* in combat, they'll want to be treated as equals when asking for jobs after the war. However, the Irish immigrants in Ohio are already stuck grabbing most of the menial, bottom-rung jobs in Cleveland. They're barely hanging on as it is. And they certainly don't want a flood of blacks trying to take their jobs away! And those Irish *do* vote, Mr. Langston. Every election, they *do* vote."

Langston rose to lean over Mason's chair. "But black men have every right to serve their country. These are *free* black men—most of them born right here in Ohio. They didn't just arrive on a boat."

A thin sheen of nervous perspiration glistened on the governor's forehead and upper lip. "There are no states that now enlist blacks, Mr. Langston."

"And you can be the first," answered Langston, sinking back into his chair. "You'll become famous." He lowered his voice as if sharing a dark secret. "Now, governor, you and I both know that Washington is pressuring you to supply additional regiments, and that the 4th Ohio has been rejected by the army because it is too far under strength. Three companies of ready, eager black soldiers will bring the 4th up to full strength and get Washington off your back."

Langston leaned back, crossed his arms, and smiled knowingly.

Tod's glance darted between Langston and Bernard Mason. Mason, suddenly gripped with fear that Tod would cave in and agree, sprang to his feet and dragged his pocket watch from his vest. "I'm afraid the governor is late for a meeting. We'll have to cut this short."

Langston started, "But, governor . . ."

Mason had already extended his hand to Langston and hustled him toward the office door. Before Langston could protest, Mason added, "The governor has heard every word you've said, Mr. Langston, and will carefully consider them. You'll hear from him shortly. Thank you for coming."

Mason forcefully guided Langston into the receptionist's office and shut the door behind him.

Listening to the dreary rain that night in his Columbus hotel room, John Mercer Langston felt like a dismal failure. The meeting swirled through his mind as he tried to decide what had gone wrong. He thought he was making progress—strong, steady progress. Then suddenly he had been booted out. The governor had made no commitments, no promises. How could Langston face the Cincinnati militia with this dreadful news that he had failed?

Langston trudged back home to Cleveland in self-imposed disgrace—and was shocked four days later to receive an invitation for a second meeting in Governor Tod's office.

Bernard Mason was there when Langston marched tentatively in, as was General Lewis (Lew) Wallace, the commanding general of the Ohio militia. Stationed in Cincinnati, he was responsible for Ohio's defense against any Confederate incursion from Kentucky or Virginia.

General Wallace, a mousy-looking man, was a political appointee, not a career soldier. He had never set foot on a battlefield, but had faced numerous political and business fights and always won.

Governor Tod wore a beaming, confident grin. "John, come in! I believe we have a solution to our little problem."

"Problem?" repeated Langston.

Gesturing Langston toward a chair, Tod said, "We've found a way for your black militia to serve."

"They'll serve as soldiers. Right?"

General Wallace spluttered at the suggestion and paced in front of Tod's expansive desk. "First, Mr. Langston" (he counted off his points on his fingers), "black soldiers would drive whites out of the military. Who would be willing to fight next to blacks, for goodness sake? Second, it would destroy unit morale and discipline."

"It would *what*?!" demanded Langston, his fingers gripping the arms of his chair.

Tod interrupted. "Continue, general."

"Third, this is a white man's war. Blacks got no business in it. Fourth, we have to keep our focus on national unity, on the *Union*, and not muddy the waters by bringing in blacks and talking about slavery." He paused and grinned at Langston as if this were the killing blow. "And fifth, Mr. Langston, if we let blacks into the army, the border states will bolt to the Confederacy. It would be counterproductive."

Four slave states (Maryland, Delaware, Kentucky, and Missouri) had not seceded from the Union. In 1862, many on both sides believed that these "border" states *would* bolt if given the slightest provocation. "Losing those four states would be a disaster!"

Langston, seething at the insults, glared at the governor and said through clenched teeth, "You said you have a solution?"

Governor Tod tapped his fingertips together. "You see the problem, John. But we already worked out a solution."

Langston expectantly raised his eyebrows. "They'll join the state militia?"

General Wallace nodded. "They *will* be allowed to serve."

The governor waived his hand, "Oh, there are still a few technicalities to take care of. Nothing that need concern you. The point is, we've worked it out. Tell your militia to be ready to serve."

Mason sprang to his feet and ushered Langston toward the door. "The governor's running late. Now, you get down to Cincinnati and alert the black militia to be ready. Congratulations, Mr. Langston. We'll be in touch."

With a quick handshake, Langston found himself in the outer office with all his swirling questions still unanswered. He should have been warned by the wide grins on the three men's faces. He should have been suspicious. But Langston basked in a flood of joy at the thought of his success.

The Black Cincinnati Volunteer Militia actually cheered when they learned the news and fired three pretend volleys in Langston's honor. He pretended to be embarrassed by the attention. Really, Langston glowed in this celebration of his stunning success.

A week later notices announcing a state of martial law were posted across Cincinnati. The next day squads of soldiers swept through the black neighborhoods gathering males at gunpoint.

"Odd way to enlist new recruits," Ballier said as he huddled in the street in a knot of men, surrounded by soldiers whose muskets pointed at them.

The sergeant scoffed, "You ain't joinin' the army. Now move!"

Shock and anger etched across Ballier's face. "*What*?! We *are* supposed to join."

"Just move!"

Shrieked questions and pleas from the men's families were ignored. The men were marched to General Wallace's fort construction site. For four weeks they worked and strained there like slaves building Wallace's new fort. They lived in open squalor like slaves and were given substandard and inadequate rations—like slaves. They were never allowed to visit their homes or even to write. The men's families had no idea what had happened to them.

Langston stormed into General Wallace's Cincinnati office. "The new recruits are living under intolerable conditions. This violates a dozen sections of military law!"

"What recruits?" sneered Wallace.

Langston felt an icy stab of fear and betrayal. "The three companies of black militia. You promised in the governor's office."

"I said they would *serve* the army, not join it," interrupted Wallace, his pudgy face leering at Langston. "Governor Tod declared martial law at my request. Martial law puts this city under my command and gives me the authority to force anyone I choose to build defenses for the common good." He chuckled. "They *are* serving the military. Isn't that what they wanted?"

Langston protested, "They're not even being paid!"

"Of course not. Under martial law I don't have to."

Langston pressed his face just inches from the general. "You're treating them like slaves!"

Wallace leaned back and sneered, "They wanted to serve . . ."

John Mercer Langston led the black families of Cincinnati in their appeal to Judge William Dickson. He visited the construction site and was instantly appalled and outraged. He ordered the governor and General Wallace to immediately form the black volunteers into a formal army unit and to immediately enlist them as soldiers in the Ohio militia. Wallace's and Tod's plan had backfired.

On September 25, 1862, the Black Brigade of Cincinnati received their uniforms and unit colors (flags and pennants). Though designated as a military labor unit rather than combat unit, the Black Brigade was the first black unit in the Union army.

Aftermath

Two days after the Black Brigade of Cincinnati was formed, Union General Walter Butler (who had been reassigned from Virginia to New Orleans) welcomed the 1st Louisiana Native Guards into the Union army. This was a unit of free blacks that had served in Louisiana since 1803 until the Confederacy disarmed and disbanded them in early 1862. As soon as Union forces captured the city, they formed and marched to General Butler's headquarters. He welcomed and rearmed them, making the 1st Louisiana Native Guards the North's first black combat unit.

After Lincoln issued his Emancipation Proclamation (announced in late September 1862, shortly after the Union victory at the Battle of Antietem), the floodgate opened for states to form and arm black units. The 1st Kansas Colored Volunteers were formed in October 1862. In January 1863, they became the first regiment admitted into the United States Colored Troops (USCT).

The 54th Massachusetts Regiment became the first African American unit to enter combat and fought bravely in South Carolina.

By mid-1863, two black regiments had joined USCT from Ohio. Seventy percent of all eligible Ohio black males had volunteered to serve and fight. USCT trained and sent to the field more than 30 black regiments by early 1864. A total of over 175,000 African American men, many of them former slaves, served in the Union army. That surge of manpower swelling the Union ranks helped turn the tide and seal the Confederacy's doom. These regiments served with valor and distinction—but little recognition—through the end of the war. Many of the USCT soldiers stayed in the army and served in Western Indian Wars through the late 1880s.

Follow-up Questions and Activities

1. **What Do You Know?**

    • Why did blacks want to fight in the Civil War? How many reasons can you identify? How many reasons can you find for why they might not want to join the war effort?

    • Why didn't whites want blacks to join the army? How many reasons can you name? How many reasons can you find for why whites might have wanted blacks to fight for the Union army?

    • Why would a governor worry about letting blacks serve in the Ohio militia?

    • What rights did free blacks have in 1862? What rights didn't they have?

2. **Find Out More.** Here are six topics that were important to this story for students to research in the library and on the Internet. The bibliography at the back of this book will help them get started.

- This story tells of the formation of the first black unit in just one state, Ohio. Research the struggles to form black units in other Northern states. Which states offered the least resistance to forming black regiments? Which states resisted the most? Why?

- Research early black units in the Union army (the First Louisiana Black Infantry, the First Kansas Black Regiment, the 54th Massachusetts Infantry, etc.). Who were their officers? How high were blacks permitted to rise in the army? How did these units fare in their combat?

- Research blacks in the Confederate army. How did the Confederates use blacks to support their war effort? Did blacks ever serve as combat soldiers in the Confederate army?

- The Confiscation Law (commonly called the Contraband Laws), passed in 1861, allowed army generals to confiscate the property of Confederate sympathizers. While it was not originally intended to encourage army units to confiscate (and free) slaves, Generals Butler and Hunter began the practice in early 1862 as Union forces pushed into the coastal regions of South Carolina and North Carolina. Research these controversial laws. How long were they active laws? What happened to them? How much property was confiscated? Was it ever returned?

- General Butler initiated the practice of incorporating black soldiers into his command both while stationed in South Carolina and, later, in New Orleans. Research this Union general. How did he become a general? What did he accomplish during the war? What did he do afterward?

- It may seem surprising that Lincoln never advocated (or ordered) using African Americans in the army. After all, Lincoln desperately wanted a bigger army. He needed men and was paying sizable signing bonuses to new recruits. He was also an abolitionist. So, what were Lincoln's objections to enlisting blacks into the army? Why didn't he advocate using black soldiers from the beginning of the war?

3. **Make It Real**

- Deny access to one basic school function, service, or privilege to some of the students in your class. The group should be arbitrarily picked (those living north or south of the school, those with black hair, those over a certain height, etc.). The privilege lost must be significant (recess, computer or library privileges, etc.) as should the duration of the experiment (one week, for example).

    Each group of students (those losing the privilege and those not losing it) must keep journals. How did you feel? How did your feelings change toward the other group? How well did those losing the privilege accept their fate? What arguments did they make in an effort to regain it? Does this experiment shed any light on the way free Northern blacks must have felt while being rejected for military service during the first two years of the Civil War?

- Frederick Douglass was a famous, articulate, highly intelligent black man who became a national spokesman for abolition and for the war effort. Research this remarkable man. Where did he come from? How did he gain his education? How did he rise to national prominence? Write a biographical sketch of Douglass or make an oral classroom presentation on this great American.

- Compare life for free blacks living in the North in 1860 to life for whites, for recent immigrant groups, for Native Americans, for Southern black slaves. Where did/could each group live? What jobs could they get? How well were they paid? How good was the education provided for each? Which groups could vote and hold public office?

4. **Points to Ponder**

   - Why didn't whites want to use blacks right away in the Union army? Why not send them into battle first and let them get killed first? Why were whites afraid to enlist blacks in the army? Why were they so against it? Do we hold similar fears and prejudices in our culture today?

   - Governor Tod and General Wallace created a plan that was designed to satisfy Ohio voters. Do you think their plan was satisfactory to the blacks forced into labor gangs? Was this plan ethical? Was it justifiable? Why do you think they decided to use it?

Iron Might

Ironclad Naval Battles on the Mississippi, June 1862

At a Glance

For most of us, Civil War naval battles conjure up an image of the *Monitor* and the *Merrimac* blasting each other across the choppy waters of Chesapeake Bay near Norfolk, Virginia. But that six-hour naval slugfest between ironclads failed to accomplish anything for either side—except that every wooden-hulled naval vessel in the world became suddenly obsolete. Ironclads were steam-powered ships armored with thick iron plates over the deck and superstructure to prevent cannonballs from smashing through to wreak havoc inside.

The *Merrimac* (renamed the *Virginia* by the Confederates) sank a month after her battle with the *Monitor* without ever firing another shot. The U.S. Navy immediately retired the *Monitor*. It wasn't stable enough for rough seas and was inadequately ventilated. Over half its engine crew passed out from the heat and foul air during its one battle.

The important naval battles of the Civil War were fought on the Mississippi River. In early April 1862, Federal ironclad gunboats, led by the *Carondelet*, bombarded and captured Island Number 10 along the Missouri shore. On April 24, Admiral David Farragut entered the Mississippi from the Gulf of Mexico and blasted his way toward New Orleans. On the 26th, that city fell to the Union navy and was lost to the Confederacy for the rest of the war.

In early June, Memphis fell to the combined naval fleet under Farragut. By then a massive Union flotilla of almost 50 ships, many new Union ironclads, had swept up and down the Mississippi.

The last Confederate stronghold on the Mississippi River was Vicksburg, Mississippi. Suddenly this sleepy river town was the key to the Western war. As long as the South held Vicksburg, they had access to the rich farmlands farther west. They could still keep the North from freely moving troops up and down the great waterway.

But to hold Vicksburg, the Confederacy had to challenge Farragut's supremacy on the mighty Mississippi. That job fell to a lone Confederate ironclad ram, the *Arkansas*. In the summer of 1862, that one ship had to challenge almost 50 others for its place on the river.

Meet James Brady

Born and raised in rural southern Missouri, James Brady, then 18, enlisted in the Confederate infantry in 1861, two weeks after marrying his childhood sweetheart. He saw his bride only three times during the next four years of bloody fighting.

James volunteered for riverboat duty in early 1862. He was accepted because he had spent several summers shoveling coal on a river steamer and was assigned to the *Arkansas* while it was still under construction in the late spring of 1862. He served faithfully on that ship for all 23 days of its spectacular life. (Only 28 out of a crew of 200 matched that feat. The rest were either killed or severely wounded in action.)

Brady later served aboard the *Little Hattie*, one of the most successful Confederate blockade-running and naval ships during the war. He survived the war and returned to Missouri for a short time before moving west to San Francisco, where he served as first mate and then captain on cargo ships based at that California port. He lived with his wife and three children near Sacramento and retired at the age of 62.

Iron Might

James Brady didn't think much of his new ship when he first saw it. It was a long, squat thing painted reddish mud brown, just like the banks of the Yazoo River in Mississippi where it lay quietly at anchor.

At 6 feet, 2 inches, James was the tallest of the company of infantry soldiers who had volunteered for riverboat duty. He had spent two summers shoveling coal on a river steamer back home in Missouri, and at least knew enough to call it a hatch instead of a doorway and a deck instead of a floor.

The company had marched 20 miles through the stifling June heat, kicking up a sticky red dust cloud that now covered their clothes and skin where it was streaked with sweat.

"That's it?" exclaimed James as they rounded the last bend and approached the dock.

"Sure ain't much to look at," muttered the man next to him.

"I thought we were gettin' ourselves one of them fancy new ships. This looks like a piece of junk."

Captain Isaac Brown, as squat and powerful-looking as his ship, greeted his new company of sailors at the edge of the ship's floating dock. He wore only a dirty undershirt and gray officer's pants with a bright yellow stripe, held up by red suspenders that matched the color of the great handkerchief that bulged from his back pocket.

"Welcome to the *Arkansas*, men," he called, "the finest, toughest, fighting-est ship ever built."

"Well, where is it, captain?" called one of the men. Everyone laughed.

"She may not look like a graceful beauty, gentlemen, but she's got it where it counts. Ten cannons—32 pounders and 64 pounders, four of 'em rifled. Three inches of iron plate cover the slanting casement of the upper decks."

"Why's it's so slanted, captain?" Brady asked.

"So enemy shells deflect off. And she's got 10 inches of solid pine behind the iron. That's 13 inches of protection for the gun crews inside!" The captain rubbed his hands together. "The *Arkansas*, gentlemen, was built to fight! And you are the men who will man her guns, seven to each gun crew. Training begins in the morning. Stow your gear below."

One man called, "Where's the door, captain?"

Brown growled like a menacing bear, "Hatch, man. You're in the navy now. It's aft."

"Aft?" whispered the man next to Brady. "Where's that?"

"The back end," Brady answered.

The vast gun deck was dimly lit by thin rays of light that slithered in around the gun ports. The men's feet crunched on the wooden deck.

"Sand," whispered one of the men, "to absorb blood during a fight."

Ten giant cannons lined the walls, three on each side, two each fore and aft.

James Brady reverently patted one of the shiny black barrels. "These are giants! They'll blast through anything."

The 10-foot-long gun barrels of these monsters gleamed black in the dark and looked deadly dangerous. Each giant cannon rested on iron rails to guide its vicious recoil.

Dropping down the ladder below the gun deck, the men landed in the forward crew quarters. Rows of hammocks were stacked five high from floor to ceiling in the stale, stuffy air. Two sailors shared each hammock—one sleeping while the other stood his duty shift.

One more deck down Brady found the inferno of the boiler room—rows of coal bins with coal dust hanging thick and grimy in the air. Heat radiated from the steam boilers in crushing waves that knocked a man's breath out of him. Every man in the boiler room dripped with sweat and was black with coal dust. This was not like the boiler rooms of the river ships Brady had worked on, where air freely circulated to bathe the workers with relief. This room was like a super-heated coffin.

James Brady scampered back up the ladderlike stairs to the crew deck, shaking his head. "I'd hate to be down there when we're under full steam!"

Reveille blew the next morning by drum and bugle with the 5:00 rising sun. The crew of 200 hastily threw down a breakfast of beans, corn bread, bacon, and coffee, then began their day's work—boiler room crew, deckhands, cooks, medics, stewards, and, of course, the 70 men who would man *Arkansas*'s mighty guns.

For 10 hours a day they practiced the 16 steps for firing one of these giant cannons. James Brady was assigned to the port side forward gun. "At least," he thought, "I'll get to peer forward through the gun port and see where we're going."

Loading and firing proved to be slow, backbreaking work. Six men strained to slide each gun back on its rails so they could reach the muzzle. After each shot the bore had to be swabbed with a wet sponge (mop) to prevent glowing embers left in the barrel by the last shot from igniting the next shot's powder while it was being loaded. The 12-foot-long iron ramrod with swabbing sponge on one end weighed 80 pounds.

Each round cannonball for James Brady's forward gun weighed 64 pounds. The powder was packed in 30-pound bags. The bags and balls had to be separately loaded and rammed down with the ramrod. By the end of the first day the men could pretend-load and fire the mighty gun in six minutes. Their gun officer, Lieutenant Charles Read, a frail-looking, 22-year-old Georgia boy, shook his head and sneered, "Before you're fit for battle, that time better be below two and a half."

The gunners staggered down and flopped into bed, groaning from the throbbing pain in their backs and the endless ache in their arms and shoulders. The crew was lulled to sleep by the steady melody of the crickets that crawled over the ship's hull.

After a week's practice, they fired their first live shells. Brady and his gun mates pulsed with excitement as they rammed real powder charges into the thick barrel and hoisted in a 64-pound iron ball. The cannon's officer adjusted aim for a tall oak draped over the riverbank a quarter mile down stream.

"Ready on one!" cried Lieutenant Read.

"Ready," replied the crew, which meant that they had ducked clear and covered their ears.

"Fire!"

The linstock (a long, slow-burning, match-like rod used to light the cannon) was lowered to the touch hole. Fire sparked down the tiny passageway into the main barrel. A second later Brady's world exploded in deafening thunder and smoke. The giant gun that six men could barely move bucked and slammed back along its rail. Fire roared across the water like the breath of a dragon. Billows of smoke rolled over the gun deck and exploded across the river. James was flattened by the deafening thunderclap.

With a splintering eruption of wood, the oak's thick trunk disintegrated and the tree toppled into the water.

At first the seven-man crew stared in stunned silence, amazed at the destructive power they had unleashed. Then a great cheer rang out. James imagined the tree as the masts of a Federal navy ship, helpless before the mighty *Arkansas.*

Brady felt invincible, tucked inside his iron fortress. Let the Union ships come! The *Arkansas* could fight the war single-handed if she had to.

"Begin loading sequence," called Lieutenant Read as others of the *Arkansas*'s deadly cannons roared into the afternoon. Pastures were ripped into tatters. Cows fled, panic-stricken. Entire woods were splintered and beaten into submission.

Each gun crew fired six shots as hard and fast as they could. The *Arkansas* rocked and trembled. A dense cloud of smoke shrouded the ship. Brady couldn't see across the gun deck, it was so filled with thick smoke. Breathing was difficult and his eyes burned.

Captain Brown leaned down the ladder from the pilothouse, nodding as he studied his stopwatch. "Seventeen minutes. Very good. Congratulations one and all."

No one could hear him. Their ears rang painfully from the endless concussion of the explosions.

A week later, on June 15, the engines were finished being rebuilt and refitted. They had had a nasty habit of shutting themselves down. Chief Engineer George City, a Scottish-born mountain of a man, hoped the refit would calm his jittery machines. Food was stacked on board. Bow and stern lines were cast off. James Brady took a long, final gaze at the dock he had come to call "home." He would never see it again. They were steaming to war.

The word spread, buzzing like a swarm of hornets, that they were sailing down the Yazoo to the Mississippi and then down to Vicksburg to help defend that important city. Along the way, they would face the entire Federal Mississippi fleet. Some said there were 15 ships in that fleet; some said 150.

Brady's stomach sank when he realized that the *Arkansas*—with only her 10 guns and 70 gunners—would sail alone against the entire Federal fleet. How could one ship—even the *Arkansas*—hope to survive?

The *Arkansas* steamed downriver for two days, passing fields abandoned by men gone soldiering, passing river shacks, using the lazy miles for final practice. Each member of the crew was wound tight, twitching for action to relieve the tension.

Every hour the chief pilot called down to the engine room to halt. Two deckhands would scurry forward and drop weighted sounding lines over the bow to measure the depth of the river. The pilot used these readings and nearby landmarks to chart the ship's progress on his maps. Then the engines kicked in again and the *Arkansas* streamed forward toward the waiting Federal fleet.

On the afternoon of the second day Captain Brown spotted smoke rising above the trees far ahead. He shouted down to the gun deck, "Sound battle stations! Open gun ports! Enemy ships approaching!"

Drummer boys stationed on the gun and crew decks pounded out the call to battle stations. Light flooded the gun deck as the armored gun ports were raised and latched back. Extra buckets of sand were spread across the deck. Most crewmen stripped to the waist and tied bandannas around their heads. Officers passed pistols and cutlasses to all the crew to use in repelling any boarders. Water buckets for the swabbers were filled. Powder kegs were rolled into place. Extra rounds of shot were hoisted up from storage.

Brady's heart pounded and his hands trembled as the *Arkansas* rounded a bend and he saw ahead three enemy warships. These were not helpless trees and cows. These were deadly warships.

With a surge of power, *Arkansas* roared straight toward the middle ship. Lieutenant Read stood rock steady next to the round porthole. "Extend the barrel! Prepare to fire!"

The crew eagerly rolled the mighty gun forward on its rails. Lieutenant Read adjusted the sighting screws and raised his saber, waiting for the captain's command.

"Now, Mr. Read," called the captain.

"Fire!" yelled the lieutenant, waving his saber.

One crewman touched the linstock to the touch hole. A second later the mighty gun roared, sending 64 pounds of iron screeching across the water at a thousand miles an hour. Three seconds later the other forward gun erupted in flame, smoke, and deadly iron shot.

The lead ship, a small, fast Federal ironclad ram, trembled from the blows and seemed to jump in the water. Steam escaped from severed burst steam pipes. A giant hole had been bitten out of the front casement.

Brady stared in awe, but also in sadness. He knew what that fearsome hole meant. Many sailors inside that ship had just died, blown apart by the explosion and by the spray of deadly splinters torn loose from the ship's wood planking. The ship turned aside, already beginning to list, and limped toward shore and shallow water.

Brady suddenly viewed Union sailors not as faceless enemies, but as scared, sweating, dry-mouthed men like him. Those sailors were not the enemy. They could just as easily be neighbors or crewmates. The great guns and shells were the real enemy, and poor sailors on both sides were only markers by which the monstrous cannons kept count of who won the day. But there was no time for thought and philosophy. Brady gazed through the forward porthole at the next ship in line, a massive ironclad, easily half again as big as the *Arkansas*. Word ran through the men that it was the famed *Carondelet*, the Federal gunboat that had almost single-handedly conquered Island Number 10 farther upriver, the ship that had won a duel with Confederate shore batteries that were supposed to be invincible.

Three sinister guns poked from its forward gun ports. Eight lined each of the long sides.

Brady gulped, "We're going to fight *that*?"

"Forward and starboard batteries prepare for broadsides!" called the captain. Guns were run out and primed. Crews nervously waited with linstocks poised over touch holes. It seemed to Brady that the *Carondelet* filled the entire river.

The forward guns of *Carondelet* fired. Flame and smoke erupted from the gun ports and hurled a plume of smoke across the river. Brady had time only to suck in his breath before the shells struck. One slammed into the angled casement and bounced with a monstrous "thud" harmlessly over the ship. A second shell hit lower and more solidly, near the waterline. The ship trembled from the blow. Its concussion slammed across the gun deck. Many on the gun crews were knocked to their knees.

The third shell exploded in the pilothouse. Smoke billowed down the ladder; there were gurgled screams. The ship lurched to port, drifting the starboard guns into perfect position to fire.

Fearing that the captain was dead in the wreckage above, Lieutenant Read ordered his number 1 gun to fire. The command rippled the length of the starboard side.

"Reload!"

The frantic crews used every trick and shortcut they had learned during their brief weeks of practice to reload and fire before *Carondelet* could let loose its full power and fury.

The gun deck became a roaring, smoke-filled inferno. A shell blasted through the gun port of one of the starboard guns. The cannon leapt back off its rails and crushed one of its crew. Splinters of wood erupted from the framing timbers around the port like shotgun pellets. Blood oozed across the sandy floor from these first casualties.

"Load and fire!" yelled Lieutenant Read.

For 20 minutes James Brady and the *Arkansas* gun crews blasted their deadly messengers across the water to the waiting *Carondelet*, less than 80 yards away. There was no time for conscious thought, just mindless reflex action. James became a machine. Swab, load, ram, fire!

The sound of explosive shot after shot from the *Arkansas*'s guns rumbled across the Mississippi countryside. Each gun's recoil shook the gun deck so that the sand danced across the wood planks. Incoming shells pounded great dents in the *Arkansas*'s iron plating and bowed and cracked many timbers inside.

"Cease fire!" cried Lieutenant Read. Other officers echoed the call.

The crippled *Carondelet* had turned to flee. But a boiler exploded in the depths of the Federal ship, a final casualty of the last blast from the *Arkansas*. The *Carondelet* jumped in the water and rocked violently. The captain could do nothing but turn his crippled ship toward shore. Eight of *Carondelet*'s 22 guns had been shattered by fire from the *Arkansas*. Over half of her boiler room crew had died in the boiler explosion. Sixty men from her gun crews lay dead and crumpled on the blood-soaked gun deck.

The third Federal ship wheeled about and sped downstream toward the Mississippi, smoke belching from both stacks.

The *Arkansas* had beaten the best the Union navy could put in its path. Brady's mind was a jumbled fog and wouldn't quite clear. Struggle as he might, he couldn't remember anything beyond the first shot they fired at the *Carondelet*. It felt more like a distant dream—a nightmare—than real life. The gun crews' exaltation was dampened by the sight of eight dead shipmates, their bodies sprawled across the sand, their blood staining the deck a dull red.

Brady heard a faint cry for help from the *Arkansas*'s shattered pilothouse. He followed Lieutenant Read up the ladder while the rest of the crew struggled to lift the stricken cannon back onto its rails. Replacement gunners were brought up from the crew deck. Bodies were carted away. More sand was spread. New cannonballs and powder kegs were hoisted up from below.

Half the pilothouse had been blown away. Both the pilot and replacement pilot had died instantly. Captain Brown sat against the iron wall, blood streaming down his face from a wide gash in his forehead.

"Medical officer!" yelled Lieutenant Read.

Brown pointed at Brady. "Can you steer?"

"Me, sir? I guess, sir."

"Get us into center channel."

"Yes, sir!" Brady clutched what was left of the smashed wheel and struggled to turn the ship back on course.

The captain's head was thickly bandaged and he stood up shakily, grasping the handrail for support.

Chief engineer City climbed the ladder, covered with soot, sweat, and grime, his face pale and tired from enduring the intense heat down below. "The port engine has frozen, sir. And there's a nasty steam leak in the starboard drive system."

"We need maximum speed, Mister City," the captain said, his face ashen gray from his wound.

The Scotsman shrugged. "I can't give you more than three or four knots, sir."

Wearily, Brown nodded.

"Do we turn back for repairs, sir?" Brady asked, guiding the battleship back into the central channel.

"If we can move and shoot, we attack, Mr. Brady. Our orders are to reach Vicksburg."

"But, sir, at four knots, we'll be sitting ducks for Federal ships that can make 12 to 15 knots!"

Captain Brown pointed through the gaping hole that had been his pilothouse window. "To Vicksburg, Mr. Brady."

The heat in the engine room had soared to over 130 degrees as sailors furiously shoveled coal into the roaring boilers. Steam leaks had turned it into a hellish sauna. The men staggered onto the deck, drenched with sweat, and collapsed, sucking in sweet, fresh outdoor air.

Captain Brown periodically shook his head to clear his eyes and mind as blood soaked through his thick head bandage and trickled onto his collar. Brady's heart pounded at the pressure of his new job. He had never steered a ship bigger than 26 feet long. He wasn't at all sure he could manage any tricky maneuvers the captain might order.

Brady felt an odd mix of pride and self-conscious terror. The invincible might of all the Confederacy seemed to flow through the ship that rumbled under his feet and obeyed his every command. Yet he also felt that the entire Confederacy was watching *him*, expecting *him*—and him alone—to guide this warhorse to a victory. The fate of his country seemed to lie in his very unsure hands.

The *Arkansas* limped into the great muddy waters of the Mississippi and turned south with the current toward Vicksburg. The great river was deceptively quiet and peaceful. Brady was reminded of leisurely days spent drifting down the river in happier times.

Gradually Brady brightened. Maybe they would reach Vicksburg without additional opposition. Maybe the battle with the three-ship task force led by *Carondelet* was the only fighting they would have to do today.

"Oh, dear Lord," moaned Brady as he steered the wounded ship around a wide turn in the river. The entire Federal Mississippi fleet rested at anchor, blocking the river: 37 warships (including a dozen ironclads) with over 1,000 guns, plus another 30 support ships.

Brady gaped at the forest of masts and the endless rows of smokestacks forming an impenetrable gauntlet for the *Arkansas*. He could suddenly visualize the 12,000 sailors on those ships, all priming cannons and cocking muskets in preparation for the massed fire they would pour onto the *Arkansas*.

"Down the middle, Mr. Brady," said the captain with what feeble enthusiasm he could muster.

"But, sir. They'll be able to fire at us from both sides."

"And we'll be able to fire at them from both sides." Captain Brown sank to the floor and called down to the gun deck. "Lieutenant Read. All guns. On my command. Fire as fast as you can. No need to aim. There are so many Federal ships, you'll never miss."

The gun deck became a frantic flurry of activity as every giant cannon was readied and every sailor steeled himself for the ordeal to come. They had seen what one enemy ship could do from *Carondelet*'s pounding. Now they would feel the bite of 40 times that much firepower.

Over the narrowing distance, Brady could hear Union drummer boys signaling the ship crews to battle stations. He could see the first signs of thin, pale smoke puffing from smokestacks as the Union fleet gathered steam.

Captain Brown grimly chuckled, "They aren't at full steam yet. We've caught them unprepared. Farragut didn't expect us to make it this far."

Union gun ports were thrown open. Cannon barrels ran out, waiting to fire at point-blank range. Brady's hands trembled and his heart pounded. It seemed impossible that *Arkansas* could survive the next few minutes. He was sure they were committing suicide. And yet, it seemed impossible to turn away. The Confederacy—*his* Confederacy—watched, and Brady dared not let his nation see anything less than heroic bravery from their terrified replacement river pilot.

At a leisurely four knots, the *Arkansas* drew even with the first ship in the Union fleet, Farragut's flagship, *U.S.S. Hartford*.

The *Arkansas* fired first with five mighty guns. The ship rocked hard enough to throw Brown to the deck. The upper deck and gun deck of *Hartford* exploded in a mass of splinters. The anchor was cut away. Whole sections of the rail disintegrated. Two cannons were blown out the side and into the river when a powder keg between them exploded. A gaping hole and dozens of bodies were left in its wake. Fires erupted across the deck. The crew scrambled for cover and to fight the fires.

The *Arkansas*'s starboard side guns blasted the *Iroquois* and *Benton*, the first two ships on that side. Firing from less than 40 yards away, it was impossible to miss. Both ships were crippled by the hammering blows but managed to fire back. All of their shells thudded hard into *Arkansas*'s iron casement and bounced over. Two of these ricochets hit the stricken *Hartford*. One shattered the windows of the captain's cabin.

Union gunners responded en masse. Shells smashed repeatedly into the *Arkansas*. The ship shuddered under the raining blows. The smokestack was blasted away. The pointed bow caved in. Water began to pour into the bilge and engine room. Two Union shells simultaneously crashed through an open porthole and into the number 2 portside gun. The metal peeled back along the gun's barrel. The gun bounced off its rail and flipped to its side, crushing five of its crew.

But the *Arkansas* continued to give better than it got. It was impossible for its guns to miss Union ships. Gun crews loaded and fired as fast as new shells could be rammed down the red-hot barrels.

A thick, boiling cloud of smoke shrouded *Arkansas*. Union gunners could no longer see their target and had to aim for the flashes of fire that signaled each deadly shot from the Confederate ship.

The Union gunboat *Sciota* was struck by four shells from a Union sailing warship across the river that had been aiming at the *Arkansas*. The smaller ship began to take on water. Eighteen of its crew had died. The captain had to run the ship aground to keep it from sinking.

And still the *Arkansas* fired as it edged farther into the Union blockade.

And still the Union guns thundered from both sides, battering the rebel ironclad. Four of the *Arkansas*'s 10 guns had been knocked out of action. Fifty of the 70 men in her gun crews lay either dead or too severely wounded to work. The last of the available deckhands had rushed up to take their place and keep up the *Arkansas*'s amazing fire.

The iron casement had buckled in a dozen spots. Wooden timbers underneath were cracked and split. The gun deck sand was awash with blood, but no one could see it through the blinding smoke that filled the ship.

The noise of outgoing blasts and incoming explosions became a horrendous and unending roar. A quarter of the *Arkansas*'s surviving crew went deaf that day.

Through it all, James Brady held the *Arkansas*'s splintered wheel in an iron grip and stared out through eyes too terrified to blink at the awesome spectacle exploding around him.

Suddenly the river cleared ahead of Brady. The *Arkansas* drew even with the last Union ship in the gauntlet, a high-speed but lightly armored river steamer, the *Laurel Hill*.

"Give her a broadside, Mr. Read," called the captain, now huddled in a corner of the shambles that had been the *Arkansas*'s pilothouse, too weak from loss of blood to stand.

Only three of the *Arkansas*'s guns could answer the call. But those three were enough. One shell smashed through the *Laurel Hill*'s hull and exploded against a boiler, sending a billowing cloud of flame, smoke, and steam 100 feet into the air. A second shell tore away the pilothouse, killing the captain. The third ripped through the crew's quarters, killing half a dozen men.

The *Arkansas* was through the blockade and still afloat—badly shattered, but still making steam.

An hour later the *Arkansas* pulled into the protection of Vicksburg's rows of shore batteries (cannons) sitting high atop the rocky cliffs of the rebel stronghold.

Four regimental bands played at the dock. Great crowds cheered and gaped at the battered, twisted, mud-colored, iron scrap barge that had defeated the entire Federal fleet. Medics rushed on board the crippled ship to haul off the dead and dying. Only 28 of the 200-man crew escaped the 10-minute ordeal without injury.

Brady watched the cheering crowds and straightened with pride. They—he—had done well. No. This was something more. *Arkansas*'s incredible audacity and success this day had rekindled a nation's hope, pride, and courage. The fate of the Confederacy *had* ridden on *Arkansas*'s shoulders this day. And, at least for this one day, the Confederacy had triumphed and grown stronger. One Confederate ship had dared to challenge a 50-ship Union fleet and had won the day. The Union navy would forever be haunted by the name *Arkansas*.

James Brady strutted onto the dock, transformed in one day into a conquering hero.

Aftermath

Four times the Union fleet attacked the damaged *Arkansas* as it sat, tethered to the Vicksburg docks. Four times the *Arkansas* drove off the attackers, with heavy losses. On the second of those attacks, the *Arkansas* was defended by a crew of only 28 of its launch strength of 200 men. The rest were all either dead or in hospitals recovering from battle wounds. Yet those 28 pounded the three Union ships that Admiral Farragut sent against the ship. Finally, Admiral Farragut ordered the Union fleet to withdraw, dismayed that all his firepower and all his ships could not sink that one Confederate battleship.

In late July, the hastily repaired *Arkansas* was ordered to steam south to support Confederate troops attempting to recapture Baton Rouge, Louisiana. One-quarter mile before the *Arkansas* would have engaged the Union fleet, both of her temperamental engines conked out. Certain the ship would be captured, the *Arkansas*'s captain ordered all hands to shore and set the ship on fire to keep it out of Union hands. Kegs of exploding gunpowder turned the *Arkansas* into a blazing inferno.

Over its 23-day life span, the *Arkansas* sank or crippled 8 Union ships and damaged 23 others. It landed over 200 cannon shells on target into Farragut's naval force, killing more than 400 Union sailors. For three glorious weeks, one Confederate battleship terrorized the Union fleet. The ship finally sank without having ever been defeated and without having an enemy ever touch its ugly, mud-colored deck.

The *Arkansas* was the Confederacy's last attempt to challenge the Union naval power on the Mississippi. The South had neither the money nor the iron manufacturing capability to produce another functioning ironclad. After the loss of the *Arkansas*, the Union navy was able to bring its firepower to bear in the bombardment of Vicksburg so that that beleaguered city could be attacked from two sides, by land and the river. The loss of the Mississippi River brought defeat a giant step closer for the Confederacy.

Follow-up Questions and Activities

1. **What Do You Know?**

   - Why did Civil War shipbuilders cover the upper decks of ironclad ships with iron plates? Why did they slant the upper deck casement?

   - Why didn't the Confederacy build a whole fleet of ironclads? Why didn't they build any more after the *Arkansas*?

   - Why was the Mississippi River so important to Confederate and Union leaders?

   - Why was the city of Vicksburg so important?

   - Why was the *Arkansas* trying to get to Vicksburg?

   - How was naval fighting in a river more difficult and dangerous than fighting in the open waters of the ocean? In what ways was it safer?

2. **Find Out More.** Following are six important topics from this story for students to research in the library and on the Internet. The reference sources at the back of this book will help them get started.

   - Research the Northern ironclad river fleet. The *Carondelet* was only one of a mighty fleet of Union ironclads. Where were they built? What did they accomplish during the war? What happened to them after the war?

   - How and why did rivers play an important role in the Civil War? On what other rivers besides the Mississippi were battles fought?

   - Why did many shipbuilders add a ram (literally a battering ram) on the front of many ironclads? What did a naval ram look like?

   - The *Arkansas* was one of three Confederate ironclads. The other two, the *Tennessee* and the *Albemarle*, both became famous for their exploits along the Mississippi River. Research these three floating weapons. Where were they built? What armament and protective plating did they carry? How big were their crews? When was each launched? What happened to them?

   - The three Southern ironclad ships that the Confederacy launched into the river war were highly successful. What would the Confederacy have needed (that the South didn't have) to build a real fleet of warships?

   - Research Admiral Farragut of the Union navy, the one admiral in the Civil War who made his reputation fighting along the Mississippi.

3. **Make It Real**

   - The *Arkansas* could not have cleared the Mississippi of Union warships. It had no realistic chance to win its battle against Admiral Farragut's fleet. Should the Confederacy have left the ship in port along the Yazoo River to save it from being destroyed? Was it a wise decision to send the *Arkansas* into battle down the Yazoo River in June 1862? Decide whether you think it was worthwhile to send the *Arkansas* into battle and write a persuasive essay arguing your viewpoint.

- Imagine yourself a sailor on either a Confederate or Union ironclad ship. What job will you have: engine room, medic, pilot, gunner, deckhand, cook, etc.? What do you like about life on board ship? What do you dislike? What are the best and worst aspects of shipboard life on a ship assigned to sail the rivers? Write a letter to your family describing your feelings about your job and life as you cruise the Mississippi River.

  Now write a second letter describing your experience of a battle. Research an actual battle your ship participated in. Did you fight other ships or shore batteries and fortifications? How did it feel to have exploding shells slamming into the upper decks of your ship? What did the battle sound like, smell like, feel like? What did you do? Were you below decks, always wondering if your ship would explode and sink, or on the gun deck, watching the horrors of battle unfold around you?

4. **Points to Ponder**

- Was the assigned mission of the *Arkansas* virtually a suicide mission: 1 ship versus almost 50, 10 guns versus almost 1,000? Do you think the sailors on the *Arkansas* really expected to lose and to die? Why would the captain and crew willingly set out on such a dangerous mission?

- Why do you think the battle between the *Monitor* and the *Virginia* (*Merrimac*) has been given so much attention over the years? Why do you think we always hear about that one inconclusive battle but never about the more important and decisive naval battles along the Mississippi River?

"Reporting" for Duty
Civil War Field Reporters, September 1862

At a Glance

James Gordon Bennett's *New York Herald*, published beginning in 1835, was the first modern American newspaper. It read more like current tabloids than like modern newspapers. In that same year, 1835, Samuel Morse created his now-famous Morse Code. In 1837, Isaac Putnam invented shorthand. In 1839, rolling presses (multiple copy presses) were invented, allowing newspapers to quickly and cheaply roll off the presses. "Penny" papers were created.

Seemingly overnight the number of newspapers in America quadrupled to almost 400 (80 of these published in the South). New York City alone supported 17 dailies. Most papers used a four-page format. A sheet of paper rolled through the presses to print on both sides and was then folded in half to create four pages. A few larger papers used an eight-page format.

In 1844 the telegraph (called the "magnetic telegraph") burst onto the scene, allowing messages to be "instantly" transmitted over long distances. By 1860 there were 1,400 miles of rail lines and 70,000 miles of telegraph lines crisscrossing the United States. The vast majority of the telegraph lines were in the North and West.

By 1860 newspapers were big business. The *New York Tribune* employed 212 workers. The *Herald* had over 250, including field reporters stationed in a dozen cities throughout the country and around the globe. Every newspaper office rang to the constant click of the telegraph keys.

But telegraph messages were expensive. A 2,000-word transmission from Washington to New York cost $100; from New Orleans to New York, $450. A reporter sending in a story typically made $16 a week or less. Still, newspapers were willing to tie up telegraph lines for lengthy reports if it would let them hit the streets sooner with a bigger, more dramatic story than the competition had.

The American Civil War was a great boon to newspapers. The war touched everyone's life, and people wanted to read the latest news from the front. Field reporters of the 1860s were unhampered by any legal, ethical, or traditional restrictions. They could do anything to get a story and to then get it back to their paper. Editors demanded drama, intrigue, patriotism, romance, and excitement—even if they weren't really there. Field correspondents were eager to provide what their publishers wanted.

Yet field reporting was neither easy nor safe. Reporters had to face the same hardships of camp life that plagued the soldiers, without the protections of the army. Correspondents were often harassed by guerrilla bands, local citizens, and patrols from both armies while trying to get their reports to a telegraph office, train depot, or boat dock where they could be sent home. Because the reports often carried important information, reporters were classed as spies when caught by army patrols.

Commanders in both armies despised the press and routinely banned and harassed them at every opportunity. Editors feared that correspondents would gain too much fame and refused to allow articles to be printed under the writer's real name. Copyright protection did not exist, so anyone could steal and use anything written by any reporter.

Correspondents had to endure long marches and dull camp life, and often penned lengthy, cramped accounts by flickering firelight long after midnight, heedless of the thousands of snoring men around them. They still had to be up and ready to go the next morning. Still, the adventure and glory of war reporting drew hundreds of eager young men to its thrilling call.

Meet George Smalley

Born in Boston in 1834, George Smalley was the first son of a prominent local lawyer. Planning to follow in his father's footsteps, George graduated from Yale in 1854 and from Harvard Law School in 1855. In 1858 George broke away from his father's firm. For three years, George ran his own quiet law practice in Boston.

But George Smalley was soon bored with contract law. In the fall of 1861, a family acquaintance, Horace Greeley, lured George away from his practice with promises of adventure and glory as a field correspondent for Greeley's *New York Tribune*. Smalley tagged along behind several other correspondents through the fall and winter of 1861 to get a feel for the work. In the spring of 1862 he was assigned to cover the battles in the Shenandoah Valley between Confederate General Stonewall Jackson and Union General Nathaniel Banks. But George was often lured away from the grind of camp life and marching by the glitter of Washington and the thrill of much larger armies ponderously maneuvering farther east.

In July 1862, Smalley was promoted to chief field correspondent in charge of five other reporters stationed in northern Virginia and western Maryland towns. He himself was assigned to report on the headquarters of the Army of the Potomac and the army's new commander, General John Pope. Smalley wormed his way into this general's good graces, just as he had done with other generals, by writing extremely flattering copy about him and doing small favors for him. Soon Smalley found himself granted unrestricted access to all of Pope's headquarters, the only field correspondent granted such extensive privileges.

George Smalley continued to write for the *Tribune* after the war. In 1868 he was assigned to London as the European chief correspondent for his paper. He transferred to Paris in 1873. In 1880 he returned to this country as the American correspondent for the *London Times*. Smalley roamed America and reported on the events he found until he died in 1895 at the age of 61.

"Reporting" for Duty

George Smalley loved to gallop his horse fast and hard across the countryside. Maybe it was the rushing wind making his eyes water and flapping his coattails or the rhythm of his binocular case slapping against his hip on its leather shoulder strap. Maybe it was just the blur of the trees and the excitement of speed that made him feel the thrill of war—the great war that spun like a tornado everywhere around him. *Around* him, but not ever, as George was painfully aware, exactly where he was.

A 24-year-old rookie reporter for the *Philadelphia Inquirer*, Bernard Calloway, yelled after him, "George! Slow down! Are we being chased?"

Smalley yanked on the reins. His horse jerked to a halt, spraying tufts of grass and soft earth across the Maryland pasture. "We gallant field correspondents are chasing, not being chased," he laughed. "Fame, adventure, glory! They swirl like the wind across the landscape."

The two reporters stopped in a field outside Seneca, Maryland, on the muggy, cloud-filled morning of September 3, 1862. Twenty-eight-year-old George Smalley had recently been promoted to chief field correspondent for the *New York Tribune*, a paper second only to James Gordon Bennett's *New York Herald* for its coverage of the war.

"That's easy for you to say," Calloway complained. "You're a famous field correspondent. But I'm just starting out."

Smalley gestured grandly at the sky. "Ride fast. Stay ahead of the competition. Be in the right place. Get the story. And get your story in first."

Although he said the words, George knew that he had consistently missed being in the right place and had had to fake his stories more than once to make it appear to his paper that he was doing his job.

The Union Army of the Potomac, now gathered near Washington in southern Maryland, was still reeling from the disaster at the Second Battle of Bull Run less than a week before. The air was charged with electric excitement; the very countryside seemed to hold its breath waiting to see what devilment Robert E. Lee and Stonewall Jackson would dream up next to torment the Northern army.

Smalley, a slender man with a lawyer's quick wit and penetrating eyes and sporting a fashionable bushy mustache, itched to be at the heart of some great event before the war ended and history passed him by. He had covered Jackson's valley campaign during the spring and summer before being promoted and assigned to cover the headquarters of the Army of the Potomac. He had seen small encounters and had been *near* major battles. But he had yet to live the events that his articles claimed he had.

"Why are we out here away from Washington?" Bernard asked. "We'll be arrested and banned if we get caught, you know."

At the soft pop of distant musket fire, both men turned their heads, trying to pinpoint its direction. "Just pickets, I think," decided Smalley. "But it tells me we're in the right neighborhood."

"To get arrested," Calloway muttered.

Smalley's dark eyes glowed with eager anticipation. "We're here because the war's out here. The *story's* out here." Again he laughed. "I said I'd show you how the job gets done. Relax, Bernard. I have a friend."

"No friend can help if we're banned from the army," Bernard complained. "McClellan's back in command, you know."[1]

Smalley grimaced as he dug into his shoulder satchel for a flask of whiskey and water. He lifted the flask to the dull, gray sky. "To General Pope." After a long swig, he added, "A good friend and a great source."

Bernard Calloway, who had been nervously scanning the distant trees for signs of cavalry patrol, jerked around in his saddle. "You *know* Pope? You got to actually *talk* to him?!"

A devilish smile danced across Smalley's face. "I did him a couple of favors."

"What kind of favors?" Bernard demanded.

"For one, I gave his good friend, General Fremont, a victory."

"You did *what*?" Calloway interrupted.

"Battle of Cross Keys in the Shenandoah Valley in early June. Actually Fremont botched it and lost. But I reported it as a 'stirring Union victory that proves the merit of this fine commander and should thrill the heart of every freedom-loving American.' "

Calloway stammered, "You actually got to watch a battle—and then *lied* in your report?"

"Actually, I wasn't there. I arrived a day late. But Horace Greeley[2] insists on having stirring, first-person accounts filled with drama and human interest. So I interviewed a couple of people and wrote it as if I had been there. Anyway, Pope is a good friend of Fremont's and appreciated what I did for him."

Calloway slowly shook his head. "That was brilliant! Too bad McClellan's back in command and has banned all reporters from the army camps."

"Actually, it was General Halleck who first wrote that order."[3]

Calloway asked, "Why is Halleck so set against correspondents? We usually write positive, patriotic pieces. He should be happy."

Smalley sipped from his flask, shifted in his saddle, and grinned smugly. "I'm the one who got him mad at us, you know."

"You?" blurted Calloway. "How?"

"I once did a couple of favors for Colonel Alexander, the commander of the hot air balloons. So he let me take a ride last spring. I simply wrote what I saw from the balloon. Unfortunately, what I saw was the placement of most units of the Army of the Potomac. Apparently Halleck was steamed that the *Tribune* openly reported for all the world to see what he considered secret information. He's tried to ban reporters ever since."

Calloway gaped in open wonder. "You're amazing! Do you do favors for everyone?"

But Smalley held up his hand and cocked his head. "I hear horses. Let's make for that tree line." He raked his spurs across the horse's flanks and bolted for the south end of the pasture. They waited among the trees, watching a 12-man Union cavalry patrol pause in the center of the pasture where they had been talking.

"Did they see us?" Bernard asked, his heart pounding.

Smalley focused his binoculars on the patrol's small guideon banner. "Perfect! They're with the 4th Ohio. Let's stroll out and say hello."

Smalley walked his horse back into the field. Behind him Calloway hissed, "No! We'll be arrested and banned!"

The patrol galloped over, carbines drawn and at the ready.

Smalley smiled and extended a hand. "I'm George Smalley, with the *Tribune*."

"Don't tell them you're a reporter," Calloway groaned. Smalley smiled and thumbed over his shoulder toward his companion. "That is Bernard Calloway of the *Inquirer*."

The senior sergeant growled, "By general order, reporters are banned from military areas. You are hereby under arrest. Please follow me."

Smalley meekly fell into line behind the patrol. But Calloway sobbed, "My career's over, and just when I was put on as a staff correspondent."

"You're not freelancing anymore?" Smalley asked. "Congratulations. What's your salary?"

"My salary!?" Calloway bellowed. "After we're arrested, it'll be zero!"

"What's your salary?" Smalley repeated.

Calloway shrugged and shook his head as they walked their horses behind the patrol leader. "$19 a week."

Smalley nodded. "Not bad. I'm only at $28." He leaned far back in his saddle as if confiding a secret. "Did you know that Henry Villard makes $55 a week?"

"That's a fortune!" exclaimed Calloway.

"Of course he's working for three different papers. Personally, I think he's only in it for the money. I don't think he even likes to write and report."

The patrol reached a hastily organized camp and stopped before one of the larger tents. "Dismount here," the sergeant ordered as he swung from the saddle and saluted the bearded man lounging in a folding camp chair. "Sir! We caught these two reporters snooping around the camp perimeter."

Smalley cheerfully jumped to the ground. Calloway slid from his saddle like melting butter and huddled in disgrace.

Major Thomas Woodall glanced at the prisoners and beamed. "George Smalley!" He extended his hand. "What brings you out here in the bush?"

Smalley shook hands and clapped the major on the shoulder. "I got tired of puffing cigars with generals."

"Let's talk inside," Major Woodall began, glancing at the threatening clouds overhead.

"But, sir," the sergeant began. "General orders . . ."

"That will be all, sergeant," said Major Woodall curtly. Then he gestured toward his tent. "Come in, and bring your friend."

"You know him?" whispered Bernard Calloway. "You *knew* he'd be here?"

"In June and July his unit was attached to army headquarters." Smalley grinned. "I did him a few favors. I thought we might be able to find out what Bobby Lee's up to from the frontline cavalry, since McClellan won't breathe a word."

Inside the tent Smalley again warmly greeted the major and introduced Calloway. Then Smalley said, "I haven't seen you since before Second Bull Run. I see you survived intact."

Major Woodall winced and shook his head, "Nasty business. A lot of good men died in that fiasco."

Calloway said to George Smalley, "I hear *you* were in the thick of the action at Second Bull Run."

"Where'd you hear that?"

Calloway answered, "I read your article." He glanced toward the gently flapping tent roof, trying to remember. "Let's see . . . 'I watched the ripened hay mowed flat by rebel volleys so thick I could have walked across them without touching the ground as our noble and unflinching boys in blue stood shoulder to shoulder, badly outnumbered but unwavering in their belief in freedom and the Union, as warmonger Robert Lee sicked his evil hordes upon them.' . . ."[4]

"You liked that piece?" Smalley asked.

"I *loved* it. It . . . it inspired me to be a field reporter and describe the action for myself."

"I never left my tavern in Centerville during that battle. The reports coming into headquarters were so confusing, I didn't know which way to go. By the time I caught a ride out toward the battlefield, all I saw were streams of routed and fleeing soldiers."

Calloway began, "But the article . . ."

Smalley shrugged, "I wasn't there to see it for myself, but I still had to turn in a good story. Remember, Greeley demands eyewitness accounts. I interviewed a couple of captains and then let General Pope 'correct' the story. He wrote lots of it."

Calloway was aghast. "You let a general write the story of his own battle?"

"Pope 'corrected' all my releases. At first he claimed it was for censorship. But I realized that he likes to write. Has a flare for it, actually." Smalley waved his hand. "Don't look so shocked. I could honestly say that my story came from the highest levels, and, in return, he gave me free run of the headquarters—something no other reporter got."

Smalley tapped his forefinger on the major's writing table for emphasis. "But someday I *will* be right there, on the battlefield. I won't need creative invention. Then you'll see what a *real* firsthand report looks like!"

Major Woodall said, "You still haven't told me why the chief field correspondent for a major paper is wandering around way out here getting himself arrested."

Smalley settled himself in his chair and leaned closer to the major. "McClellan is even more tight-lipped than usual. But I can smell that something's up. I'm thinking that Lee's on the move and Little Mac doesn't know where. I thought someone out here with the cavalry patrols might know the truth."

Major Woodall sighed and shook his head. "I don't know any more than you do. But I can say that Stuart's[5] cavalry screen is extra strong and thick as flies to the west."

Smalley jotted down shorthand notes. "Lee's moving *west*? Up into Maryland?"

The major shrugged. "Looks like it. But I've got no proof."

Eagerness flashed in Smalley's eyes. "Can we ride with you? Poke around out toward Winchester, Harpers Ferry, and Hagerstown with your patrols?

Woodall snorted. "First, you'd run into more rebs than you can count going out that far. And second, no. Orders are very explicit this time. No reporters."

Smalley pleaded, "But I *have* to stay with the forward units and see what's going on. I don't want to be a day late again."

Again Woodall shook his head. "No one but staff and aides are allowed in any of the headquarters. Hell, in *any* of the camps, for that matter."

Calloway shrugged, "I guess that's it. Thank you for not arresting us, major. We'll head back now."

But Smalley was lost in thought. "Staff and aides . . . staff and aides." He brightened and gleamed at Major Woodall. "Is General Sedgwick near here?"[6]

"You know I can't reveal unit locations to a reporter."

Smalley closed his notebook and tucked it away, then motioned for Calloway to do the same. "I'm not asking as a correspondent. Just as a friend."

Woodall sighed and rubbed his hands across his face. "He's no more than five miles up the road."

"Can you get me there?"

"Why Sedgwick?" Calloway asked, and then threw up his hands. "I know. You did him a couple of favors."

"Two very complimentary articles, actually," Smalley answered.

Calloway asked, "What are we going to do with General Sedgwick?"

"Not *we*," said Smalley. "Just me. This one I have to do alone."

"But what do I do?"

Smalley grinned. "You figure it out. That's what the *Inquirer* pays you for."

Woodall interjected, "One of my patrols makes regular contact with Sedgwick's nearest brigade. I can get you that far."

"Done!" Smalley exclaimed, slapping the major on the back. "Now I owe you one."

"A nice article about the effectiveness of the cavalry would do."

"In my next courier packet back to New York," Smalley promised.

Calloway departed for Washington, leaving Smalley to wait two days for a patrol that could escort him to Sedgwick's division. He was again arrested for violating McClellan's general order and was marched under armed guard to the general's tent.

General Sedgwick, in uniform pants and white linen shirt, beamed, "George Smalley! Great to see you. What brings you way out here?" Sedgwick noticed the six-man armed guard and laughed. "What'd you do this time? Print more of Halleck's war secrets?"

The grim-faced captain commanding the detail snapped to attention. "Sir! We caught this reporter wandering through camp in violation of . . . "

Sedgwick silenced the captain with a bored wave of his hand.

"I wasn't wandering. I was marching very purposefully to find you, sir."

"*Me?*" Sedgwick repeated skeptically. "You cover army headquarters. Why would you come poking around down at division level?"

Smalley grinned and saluted. "I want to volunteer to be your aide-de-camp."

Startled, Sedgwick repeated, "My aide? I've already got an aide."

"You need another one," Smalley insisted.

Sedgwick suspiciously eyed the *Tribune*'s reporter. "But you're a correspondent. Ah! I see. Sneaking around Halleck's and McClellan's order banning all press. Very clever. As an aide you'll be able to go where press are no longer allowed." The general paused, deep in thought.

"Sir, he's a reporter," insisted the captain, "and should be sent to army headquarters for detention."

"No, he's not, captain. He's my new aide." Grinning, Sedgwick turned to one of his staff officers. "Get this man a sash and side arm. Better get him a uniform, too, to keep him from being arrested again."

The captain started to protest, "But, sir . . ."

"Dismissed, captain." Sedgwick turned to Smalley, his face now hard as flint. "I've liked what you've written in the past. So here's my offer. As my aide you have one duty: special assignment to collect your stories. But you *must* report back to me every day and tell me what you've learned. Fail once and you'll be arrested as a spy."

"Done!" Smalley agreed. He extended his hand, then thought better of it and saluted instead.

Over the next few days George Smalley wandered unchallenged through the various units as they crossed each other in a frantic rush to catch and corner Lee's Army of Northern Virginia. He could feel the tension rise to boiling as Harpers Ferry fell to the Confederates, as Hagerstown was briefly occupied. Everyone knew a major fight was coming. Every soldier seemed to simultaneously anticipate and dread its inevitable arrival. Smalley felt like swaggering past pickets and guards, thumbing his nose at army restrictions and rules. He had found a loophole and was in a position to scoop every other reporter on Earth!

Finally, the armies jostled into position around a small Maryland village, Sharpsburg, along a meandering creek named Antietam. Smalley tingled with excitement the night before the battle, unable to sleep. He wandered through Sedgwick's and other division camps of Hooker's Corps, noting and recording the sights and sounds, which were all surprisingly ordinary and common: men talking about simple things of home and life, men concentrating on cooking an evening meal, men oiling and cleaning their muskets—ordinary men doing a thousand small things trying to block out thoughts of the coming battle.

Smalley swelled with pride, feeling a part of these men and this moment in history—his moment—a moment no other reporter was able to experience and record.

He passed the wagon of famed photographer Matthew Brady with its bright red lettering announcing $.25 photographs. Smalley paused to scoff. Photographs were a cute gimmick, a novelty. But what good were they? The process was too slow to capture movement, and battles were all about movement. There was no way to print a photograph in a newspaper, so they would never be published. Smalley slowly shook his head and thought, "What a useless waste of effort. Give me a good illustrator any day."

September 17, 1862, dawned hazy and hot. Smalley decided to ride with General Joseph Hooker and his staff because he was scheduled to lead the initial attack. No one on the staff knew Smalley. Still, no one asked him why he was there. He simply rode with them, wearing his ill-fitting uniform and aide's sash, in awe of the great vista before him. Some 160,000 men scurried like well-organized blue and gray ants over the fields that sloped to a meandering strip of blue stream.

His missed opportunities to witness battles in the Shenandoah Valley and at Bull Run were forgotten. Those had been mere trifles. This was the greatest gathering of soldiers in history. This *was* history. And George Smalley rode in the very heart of it, able to record it for all time.

The battle opened as two of Hooker's divisions advanced through a cornfield with a roar of cannon and musket fire and a fog of gun smoke. One regiment began to lag and falter. Hooker looked for one of his staff, but all of them had already been sent on other missions. He rode momentarily alone—with George Smalley, whose pencil raced over the pages of his notebook.

Hooker growled, "Who are you?"

"George Smalley of the *Tribune*, sir."

"A reporter?"

"And an aide to General Sedgwick."

Hooker grunted, then thought for a moment. "Can you carry an order?"

"Yes, sir."

Hooker pointed at the faltering regiment. "Tell the commanding colonel of that regiment to get his men to the front and keep them there!"

George Smalley, an untrained civilian, turned and galloped into the heat of battle. He raced through choking smoke and whining bullets, ducked low over his horse's neck. Every detail of battle he had previously invented and reported, he now lived in bigger, bolder, more terrifying and vivid detail.

He reached the colonel and delivered his message.

"Who are *you*?" the colonel shouted over the din of battle.

Smalley answered, "The order comes directly from General Hooker."

"I only take orders from staff officers I recognize."

Smalley asked, "Shall I tell General Hooker you refuse to obey his order?"

The colonel hesitated. "Oh, for God's sake, don't do that. The rebels are too many for us, but I'd rather face them than Joe Hooker!"

Smalley raced back up the slope and reported. Hooker grunted, "Don't let the next man talk so much," and sent Smalley off with an order for a different regiment.

Over the next 90 minutes George Smalley delivered five orders that helped shape the flow of the early fighting at Antietam. He rode through trampled fields where dirt had been churned into red mud with blood. He rode past lines and piles of mangled, broken bodies, so thick they seemed like rows of planted crops in the field waiting for harvest. He rode through the thunder of musket volleys and felt the searing heat of a minnié ball whistle past his cheek. He listened to the cries, screams, and pleas of the wounded. He saw the wide-eyed fear of the soldiers as they stumbled back after a failed attack.

There was no time to write notes, only to race through Antietam Creek's valley of death and pray that the black specks of destruction fired from a thousand rebel muskets never found him as their target. Still he willed himself to impress each sight, sound, and smell into his memory. This story would be—*had* to be—his greatest report!

By 10:00 A.M. the fighting on the northwest side of the field had stopped. The will to fight seemed to have fled across the valley. Exhausted men slumped over hot musket barrels, dazed and vacant stares on their faces. The dead and dying covered the ground.

Smalley surveyed the carnage and felt not the stirring, patriotic elation he always wrote into his articles but rather a deep sadness and sense of futility. So much life and energy expended, and for what? A few hundred yards of meaningless ground had been gained, but the rebel ranks had not been broken. Hooker had been mortally wounded. Thousands of men would never march again. It suddenly seemed to George Smalley that there could be no victory in a giant battle such as this, only loss. The side that lost the least won the battle, but it was still loss that each side accumulated. It was only the loss that would be carried forward by the living.

Smalley rode to McClellan's headquarters at the crest of the eastern slope. Again he was accepted without question. From there he watched the rest of the day's vicious battle unfold: the agonizing slowness of each advance, the brutal power of the guns, the swiftness of death.

All firing had ceased by 5:30 in the afternoon. There was no victor. Both sides simply stopped where they were. It was as if everyone realized there had been enough killing and suffering for one day, and there was no need to inflict any more. They were too worn out to continue.

For the first time in hours, Smalley thought about his story. Other reporters had crowded as close as they could to the battlefield. Many would try to worm their way forward for a quote, an interview. If Smalley was to get his scoop, each minute was now precious. He decided to ride to Frederick, Maryland, the nearest telegraph office, and file his story from there.

But first he had to slow down the competition. He rode the picket line around headquarters and reminded each soldier not to allow any correspondents through. At 8:00 that evening, drained by the emotional roller coaster of the day and bone weary from lack of sleep, George Smalley rode east toward Frederick. Lines of ambulance wagons already carted the wounded back to hospitals. Lines of other wagons rumbled west, bringing new supplies for the army's next effort.

Smalley dismounted at the checkpoint at Crampton's Gap (just east of the battlefield) and approached the captain in charge. "Sir, by order of Generals Sedgwick and Hooker, no reporters or undocumented riders are to be allowed to travel through this gap *in either direction* until noon tomorrow."

The captain shrugged indifferently. "We check documents anyway."

Smalley grabbed the captain's arm. "Especially traveling east."

"Away from the battlefield?" the captain questioned.

"You *must* stop all reporters trying to get out of the battlefield area."

The captain rubbed his face to help scrape away the mind-numbing boredom of road picket duty. "Who are you, again?"

Smalley touched the red sash. "Just an aide. But the orders come from a corps commander."

Smalley remounted and rode east in the dark of night, hoping that he had just given himself an 18-hour head start on any other reporter trying to ride from the battlefield to file a story.

He reached the Frederick telegraph office at 3:00 A.M. and collapsed in the doorway, intending to write the summary and lead of his story. Almost instantly he fell asleep and was awakened only by the telegraph operator stepping over him to unlock the door at 5:30.

The operator said, "You look terrible," as he slid into his swivel chair and adjusted his green visor.

Smalley rubbed his face and grunted, "It's been a busy day." He breathed deep to focus his mind. "I want you to begin transmitting an important report to the *New York Tribune*. Here are the routing codes."

The man began to click on his telegraph key. "Where's the report?"

"I only have the opening line written. 'A fierce and desperate battle between 200,000 men has raged since daylight, yet night closes on an uncertain field. It is the greatest fight since Waterloo, all over the bloody field contested with an obstinacy equal to Waterloo . . .' "

"Is this true?" gasped the operator. "McClellan and Lee had a fight? Who won?"

Smalley ignored the question. "I haven't written the rest. So begin with . . ." Smalley scanned the room and snatched up a Bible. "Begin with Genesis and continue until I give you something else to send."

"This is gonna cost your paper plenty, mister. Why not wait 'til you've got her written?"

"I need to tie up the telegraph line so no other reporter can get a story filed first."

By 6:30 A.M. the summary report had been written and transmitted. Smalley was beginning his main text when the line went dead. The operator scowled and then checked and tested his equipment. "It's the line. Must have been cut somewhere just out of town."

"Another correspondent," Smalley snarled. "What a cheap, low-down trick to pull."

Smalley used the power of his aide's sash to grab space on the first military train to Baltimore, and from there to New York on the express. He wrote the rest of his story leaning against the wall of a train car under the wobbling light of a gas lamp (his third night in a row with little or no sleep). He arrived at the *Tribune*'s offices at 4:00 A.M. and delivered his report to Horace Greeley, who had slept in the office overnight.

Greeley's first two comments were, "Where's the report?" and "You look terrible."

"No sleep," answered Smalley with a yawn and a shrug.

"No, it's more than that," Greeley began, but trailed off as he became absorbed by the text of Smalley's report.

Smalley glanced in the mirror of the staff lounge. He did look terrible. But terrible in a way sleep would not heel. He looked more lined, sadder, older, as if the horror and terrible calamity had etched a pattern forever upon his face. "War is hell," he muttered and wandered back to watch the typesetters at their work.

Four hours later—less than 36 hours after the final shot was fired—the Special Edition of the *Tribune* was on the street with an exclusive in-depth report on the Battle of Antietam.

George Smalley had scooped every other paper in the nation by a full day and become a legend in the small fraternity of field correspondents.

Aftermath

The Battle of Antietam still stands as the bloodiest single day in American history. Some 26,000 died that day; another 35,000 were wounded. Following this battle, General George McClellan was relieved of command for the second and final time for failing to aggressively exploit his chances to achieve total victory and for failing to pursue Lee's fleeing army after the battle. Antietam (Sharpsburg) ended the first of Lee's two northward invasions. The second, a year later, ended at Gettysburg.

Philip Knightley, in a study of war reporting, said, "The majority of Northern correspondents were ignorant, dishonest, and unethical. The dispatches which they wrote were frequently inaccurate, often invented, partisan, and inflammatory."[7] Even highly respected reporters routinely invented eyewitness observations and accounts of battles. (Junius Browne for the *Tribune* invented a detailed eyewitness account of the Battle of Pea Ridge even though he got no closer to the battle than St. Louis and never interviewed any actual participants. Whitelaw Reid was accused of fabricating most of his vivid, on-the-field-of-battle accounts of Shiloh and other Western engagements.)

Top army brass were dismayed at how fast supposedly secret information was discovered and published—and, thus, supplied to the enemy. Robert E. Lee daily read three Northern newspapers and claimed to have learned more about Union plans and troop movements from them than from any other source.

Of course, the information gathered and reported by correspondents was useful to Washington as well. The War Department first learned that Lee was moving into Maryland in September 1862 from an article by *Philadelphia Inquirer* reporter Uriah Painter. The first report received in Washington of the Battle of Antietam was George Smalley's telegraphed article. Reporter Henry Villard provided the first report of the Battle of Fredericksburg to Washington. *Tribune* reporter Homer Byington galloped after Lee following the Battle of Gettysburg and reported better, more accurate information on Confederate troop withdrawals and plans than did Union army scouts. Boston reporter Charles Carelton Coffin was the only person to predict (three weeks in advance) that a major battle would be fought just west of Gettysburg.

Union army brass distrusted reporters and tried at every turn to make their job as difficult as possible. General William Tecumseh Sherman tried one correspondent (Thomas Knox) as a spy for printing details about his troop movements. General George Mead had a sign "libeler of the press" hung around one reporter's neck and marched him through camp while all the soldiers jeered and a few threw stones, because the reporter wrote that Mead had recommended retreat after the Battle of the Wilderness (the report was completely accurate). Generals Halleck, Sherman, McClellan, Sheridan, and Grant (among others) expelled reporters from camp and campaigns on penalty of imprisonment as spies.

Reporters in the South fared no better. They were distrusted by the army and were rarely paid by their papers, and most lost their jobs when their newspapers ran out of paper and money as the war and blockade tightened.

At the Stone Mountain, Maryland, battlefield there is a stone arch memorializing 147 reporters and illustrators who covered the war. There were actually over 280 who covered the war. Each faced extreme risks and paid a high price to bring the war home to every American, North or South. Five correspondents were killed during the war. Twelve died from illness. As many as 30 were jailed as spies at one time.

Notes

1. General George McClellan (affectionately called "Little Mac" by his soldiers) had been in command of the Army of the Potomac for 10 months from August 1861 through May 1862, at which time Lincoln relieved him after his disastrous Peninsular Campaign. Lincoln reinstated McClellan in early September after Pope's dismal failure at the Second Battle of Bull Run.

2. Horace Greeley was the founder and publisher of the *New York Tribune*. An avid abolitionist, Greeley became famous for his quote, "Go west, young man," urging New Englanders to rush west to Kansas to ensure that it would become a free state.

3. General Halleck was commander in chief of all Union armies.

4. From Smalley's *Tribune* article on September 1, 1862, describing the Second Battle of Bull Run.

5. General Jeb Stuart commanded Lee's famed Confederate cavalry division. It was the cavalry's job to ride patrols as a wide screen around the army's moves to shield them from detection by the enemy.

6. General Sedgwick was a division commander in Joe Hooker's 1st Corps of the Union Army of the Potomac.

7. Bernard Weisberger, "Reporter for the Union," in the *South Atlanta Quarterly* 22 (4), p. 401.

Follow-up Questions and Activities

1. **What Do You Know?**
   - What organizations sent field reporters to cover the Civil War?
   - How did field correspondents get their stories back to their home newspapers?
   - Why and how was the telegraph important to field reporters? To newspapers?
   - What rules, regulations, and laws limited what a reporter could do to obtain a story?
   - Why was the Battle of Antietam considered significant in the war?

2. **Find Out More.** Following are six important topics from the story for students to research in the library and on the Internet. The reference sources at the back of this book will help them get started.
   - Photographer Matthew Brady is mentioned in this story. The few remaining copies of his Civil War photographs have become priceless national treasures, even though at the time few people were interested in them and preferred to pay for posed portraits. Research the life of Matthew Brady and the photographic process and technology he used. Why couldn't he shoot action pictures of the war? How has photographic chemistry and technology changed since Brady's day?

- Research Civil War field correspondents. Almost a dozen are named in this story. Which ones became famous? How? Which papers did they work for? How many of the Civil War–era newspapers still exist?

- Compare Civil War journalism with that in more recent wars (e.g., World War II, Vietnam, Desert Storm). Have the lifestyles, pressures, demands on, and tactics of war correspondents changed since the Civil War? How?

- Research the style and development of American newspapers from colonial times to the present. Who have been the "Great Newspaper Men"? How have formats and content changed? How have reporting, editing, and verifying processes changed over the years?

- Research the history of the magnetic telegraph. Who invented it? Who built telegraph lines across the country? Who ran the telegraph stations and trained the operators? Is the telegraph still used today? What has replaced that technology?

- Research the Battle of Antietam. What led up to this battle? Why was it fought at Sharpsburg? What helped McClellan decide his strategy and move boldly into the battle? How "should" the battle have ended? Why was McClellan fired shortly after winning this battle? What was its significance for the Union? For Lincoln? For the war?

3. **Make It Real**

- As a class, put out one issue of a Civil War newspaper. This four-page paper should include illustrated news articles about a recent battle, human interest stories about war figures and personalities, one camp life story, one story about life at home away from the war, a patriotic editorial written by the editor, and one or more letters to the editor.

   As a class, agree on the date of the edition and the events to be covered. Research both the events to appear in that day's edition and the style of writing used by Civil War correspondents. Try to match that style and tone in your various pieces. Assign an editor, assistant editors, illustrators, layout people, typesetters, and field reporters.

- Pick a major Civil War battle. Imagine that you are a field reporter. Research the events of the battle and then write a quick summary press release on that event. What will be your lead (opening paragraph or two to grab the reader)? What facts will you present? In what order? What will be the central theme of your release? What quotes and colorful elements will you include? Keep each release short and succinct, yet still powerful and descriptive. Read your release to other students and compare style, approach, and organization.

4. **Points to Ponder**

- From reading this story, it might appear that Civil War field correspondents worked with few, if any, ethical standards. What do you think should be a minimum acceptable code of ethical conduct for field reporters? How would you enforce it? What problems would make this ethical standard difficult for reporters to follow? How closely do you think modern reporters follow your code of ethics? What ethical standards should apply to editors and publishers? Why? What standards apply to journalism today? Are they observed by the media?

- An important job of news reporters is to gather and publish important information as fast as possible. But what if publishing information aids the enemy during a war? If you were the publisher of a major newspaper, how would you decide what, for the sake of your readers, should be immediately published, and what, for the sake of the army and national security, should be held back? Are there situations in which you would place the interests of your readers ahead of those of the country? Are there other cases where you would refuse to publish sensitive information at all, even though your readers would be vitally interested?

Ounce of Prevention; Pound of Cure
An Army Field Surgeon, Fall 1862

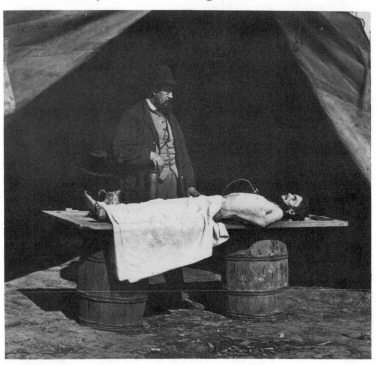

At a Glance

The Federal army had 94 medical officers in the winter of 1860. Forty-two of these defected to the Confederate army. These few army doctors represented the total military medical experience of both nations. By 1865, more than 13,000 doctors had served in the Union army, and 4,000 had served in the Confederate army. Less than one-quarter of these doctors had ever attended—much less graduated from—medical school. They learned, like all apprentices, at the knee of an established professional.

Medical school in the mid-nineteenth century was a far cry from the prestigious and rigorous schools of today. College applicants considered medical school a lowly third alternative to the more prestigious occupations of business and law. Medical school lasted only for two 12-week terms. Most medical schools were poorly equipped and woefully behind the cutting edge of medical discovery. Two-thirds of the medical school graduates never touched a stethoscope during their medical training.

The bane of Civil War surgeons was infection (called inflammation at the time). They didn't know what caused it and had no way to treat it. Inflammation was the second most common cause of death during the war (behind only disease and ahead of battlefield deaths). Many limbs were amputated only because surgeons believed amputated, cauterized limbs were less likely to become inflamed than ones that were operated on and left intact.

Doctors often went days without washing their hands because of the scarcity of water near many battlefields. At best, scalpels, probes, and saws were wiped across dirty, blood-soaked aprons between operations. Orderlies sloshed a bucket of cold water across bare-wood operating tables between patients. Operating stations were surrounded by the smell of blood and death and the screams, sobs, and moans of the wounded.

Most soldiers and commanders viewed battlefield operations as a miraculous, lifesaving advancement in war. In reality, battlefield surgeries, amputations, and cauterizations had been a real and present part of warfare for 2,000 years. The real advancements in surgical procedures came during and immediately after the Civil War, when doctors cracked open the door of modern medicine.

Meet Thomas Wallsly

Thomas Wallsly was born in 1826 in Charlotte, North Carolina, the oldest of three children, to James and Katherine Wallsly. James, born in England, had strong ties to the British East India Company, and ran an import/export mercantile.

From his earliest days, Thomas dreamed of being a doctor. In 1849 (at age 23) Thomas was accepted as an apprentice (intern) by a Doctor Hartman in Charleston, South Carolina, a Quaker doctor trained in Pennsylvania. Hartman forced his student to read every available medical and philosophical article, book, monograph, and technical paper. It was Hartman who inspired young Thomas Wallsly with the lifelong habit of study and technical advancement.

Thomas was accepted into Harvard Medical School in 1854 (at age 28). He graduated eight months later and felt that the school had been a waste of time. He had learned more advanced information and techniques from Dr. Hartman.

Wallsly returned to Charleston in 1855 and married Lilly Walters. In 1858, he moved to Atlanta and set up his first private practice.

He eagerly joined the army in the summer of 1861 and was first assigned to a Mississippi regiment for one year under General Earl Van Dorn. Wallsly was transferred to General William Hardee's division in the late fall of 1862 as that Confederate unit stumbled back south after an unsuccessful invasion of Kentucky.

Thomas Wallsly remained in Hardee's division for one year. He was then promoted to colonel and transferred to General Joe Johnston's army as a chief division surgeon. Wallsly remained with this army until April 1865, when he doctored Confederate wounded after the last battle of the war. Wallsly himself was wounded in 1863 by an errant artillery fragment that spun into his operating tent during battle. He always limped after that.

Wallsly returned to Atlanta after the war, reestablished his practice, and worked contentedly until he retired in 1884 (at age 58). He, his wife, and their three children then moved to Columbia, South Carolina, where he taught at the University of South Carolina medical school for 14 years. Retiring again in 1898 (at age 72), he returned to Atlanta, where he died in early 1900 at age 73.

Ounce of Prevention; Pound of Cure

An orderly sloshed a bucket of dirty creek water across the wood-plank table. Pink water splashed down to join the stream of red that trickled over the floor of the barn. Colonel Talgert E. Johnston sucked in a mouthful of brandy as two orderlies lifted the next screaming patient onto his table.

"Last one, colonel."

A shattered thigh bone pierced the patient's blood-soaked uniform. Teeth clenched in pain, the soldier begged, "Please don't take my leg. Please don't cut it off! Not my leg! I gotta be able to farm when I get home."

"Chloroform," ordered the colonel as he took one more mouthful of brandy and wiped his saw across a blood-soaked leather apron.

Colonel Johnston, chief surgeon for Confederate General Hardee's division, stretched and grunted four minutes later as the last patient's amputated leg was tossed casually on the day's pile of removed limbs. "Fewer than 50 wounded. Hardly worth more than a pocket case."[1]

A knee-high mound of severed limbs was piled up like a small haystack near the double barn doors. Talgert Johnston and his two assistant surgeons had set up shop in a barn just south of Carthage, Tennessee, on this dreary afternoon of November 20, 1862. Elements of General Hardee's division had rubbed against advanced units of General Rosecrans's Union forces based in Nashville.

Mixed with the decades-long smell of manure and hay was the reek of blood and vomit. Inside the barn it was close and stuffy even though outside it was bitter cold. The moans of wounded soldiers beginning to recover from the chloroform used as anesthetic during their operations mixed with the howling wind and the whimpers from two soldiers with abdominal wounds who would only be given morphine until they died. Fewer than 10 percent of abdominal wounds survived with or without surgery, and it was Colonel Johnston's policy that they weren't worth precious time on operating tables.

Major Thomas Wallsly, the newest addition to the division surgical team, said, "I'd like to work on the man with the lower abdominal wound."

Johnston snapped, "He's near death already. Never survive. Lost too much blood."

Wiping his hands, Wallsly persisted. "I've read about a new procedure for closing wounds to the intestines and stomach. I want to try it."

"No! We have 50 wounded to look after who *can* survive. Can't waste that much time on one who won't."

A red-faced, squat bulldog of a man with a bushy red mustache, Johnston sneered at Thomas Wallsly. "I performed twice as many operations as you today, Wallsly. You're too slow."

"I prefer to be careful and thorough," Wallsly answered calmly. Wallsly had been in Hardee's command only one week.

"Hogwash," Johnston snorted, reddening and glaring at his new doctor. "If this had been a battle instead of a small skirmish, you would have cost us lives."

"Practicing the most modern medical techniques *saves* lives." Both surgeons laid down the saws and scalpels they were beginning to clean and glared at each other. Wallsly was five inches taller, with a trim, dark beard. Both men wore white linen shirts, gray uniform trousers, and leather aprons. Their aprons and sleeves were now crusted stiff with a thick layer of dried blood from their afternoon's work.

Wallsly's sky blue eyes shown with bright energy, even in the dark shadows under his gray uniform hat, even as he glared, teeth clenched. Outside, a cold drizzle made the day miserable for the long lines of infantry marching south away from the battlefield. Inside, the barn was stuffy and hot and alive with tension.

Johnston jabbed a finger at his new assistant. "You waste time boiling dressings and lint."

"Boiling warms and softens the dressing. I have found it relaxes the muscles and nerves and reduces inflammation."[2]

"Nonsense!" snorted Johnston. "The regulations say nothing about boiling dressings."

"Boiling reduces inflammation, speeds recovery, and saves lives."

"It wastes time. And that means that fine young men will bleed to death waiting for a turn on the operating table. In this division we *will* treat every wounded soldier within 24 hours of injury—even in a major battle. And that, major, requires *speed*."

The third of the division's three doctors, Captain Sidney Feller, a timid wisp of a man, stood inconspicuously in a corner of the barn. The four remaining orderlies had begun cleaning up after the 90 minutes of afternoon surgeries. Wallsly extended his hand to one of these. "Thank you, Pevis. You were a pleasure to work with today."[3]

The 18-year-old boy blushed. "Thank you, sir."

Johnston growled, "Don't fraternize with enlisted orderlies!"

"Why not?" answered Wallsly. "He's a talented assistant."

"He's a *private*. Call him Private Jenkins."

Jenkins awkwardly paused near the double barn doors. "Where should we throw the pile?" The "pile" was how they referred to the mound of amputated limbs. The pile often grew to frightful size in the aftermath of major battles.

Johnston growled an answer as he and Major Wallsly circled each other like fighting cocks in the pit. "You amputated limbs you could have saved," accused Wallsly.

"I acted in accordance with Confederate regulations to save lives. But you, major, *risked* lives by not cauterizing wounds.[4] You also don't need to preserve a full flap of skin to sew over the amputation. Cauterize, sew quickly where needed, and move on."

"That's butchery," Wallsly shouted. "Tying individual arteries reduces inflammation and promotes healing—as does resetting bones and saving arms and legs."

Colonel Johnston put his face up close to Wallsly's, his eyes even with the major's chin. His voice dropped to a low, menacing growl. "I'm warning you, major. You're in Hardee's division now. *I* am the chief surgeon, and in this command we *will* follow established procedures."

Wallsly started to respond with new arguments, then changed his mind. "I must leave, colonel. I am camp sanitation officer and should reach Mumfreesboro ahead of the main body of the division."

Johnston snorted. "A meaningless title that you, as the new surgeon, get to carry. I'd ignore it, myself."

"Sanitation is anything but meaningless, sir. I found I could reduce sick-call rates in General Van Dorn's command by rearranging the camp for better sanitation."

"Poppycock," snapped the colonel. "Sick-call rates are reduced by firm leadership that punishes shirkers and loafers."

Major Wallsly's slave, a soft-spoken, intelligent man in his late fifties with white curly hair, waited patiently by the major's wagon. Wallsly had named his servant Jefferson after the president so committed to states' and personal rights. Jefferson had served Wallsly since he was a young boy. "Should I fetch your duelin' pistols, suh, or is you an' your new colonel still on speakin' terms?"

Wallsly smiled and shook his head. "The man is a butcher, a barbarian! His medical ideas are 50 years behind the times." He sighed. "We're all packed?"

"Yes, suh. I cleaned and loaded the las' of your surgical equipment whilst you and the colonel was . . . talkin'." Jefferson looked down at the ground and cleared his throat. "Why not let this-a-here General Hardee set up his camp any way he likes, suh, afore you buzz in and raise hell? He *is* the general."

Wallsly chuckled. "Afraid I'll ruffle too many feathers again as I did when I reorganized Van Dorn's camp?"

"Well, suh, the wasp that buzzes too loudly may get swatted."

Wallsly shook his head. "It's easier to set up camp correctly than to change it once the camp is established. Even Van Dorn finally admitted I was right."

"*Finally* is the exact word, suh."

"I'm the sanitation officer, Jefferson. And this wasp has a duty to protect the 4,000 lives in this division. Drive us straight through to Mumfreesboro and don't spare the whip."

Wallsly and Jefferson didn't find the division's designated camp area on the west side of Mumfreesboro until 10:30 the next morning. "Drive me through the division area, Jefferson. I want to see how camp is being laid out."

Less than a minute later, Wallsly shouted "Halt!" and sprang from the wagon's front seat. A detail of 12 soldiers digging a nearby trench snapped to attention. "Lieutenant!" Wallsly barked, storming toward the diggers like a swirling fury. "What are these men doing?"

The startled lieutenant stammered, "Digging sinks, sir."[5]

"Here?" Wallsly bellowed. His voice rose. "Sinks *here*?!"

Still in the wagon, Jefferson muttered, "Nothing like a friendly, 'How do?' greeting to our new camp."

Thoroughly confused, the lieutenant glanced nervously at Major Wallsly. "Yes, sir. It's close to the tents so the men don't have far to walk."

"And half the nearest regiment will be on sick call with diarrhea—or worse—within a week." Wallsly gazed across the field to where the division's tent city was beginning to grow. "No, lieutenant. The sinks will be at least 130 paces from the nearest tent."

"One hundred and thirty paces, sir?" repeated the lieutenant, hoping this was a joke.

"One hundred and thirty paces in . . . that direction," said Wallsly pointing toward the far tree line.

"But, sir, that'll put the sinks all the way out in the woods."

"In the woods or beyond, lieutenant. Your choice."

"*Beyond* the trees? But, sir, the colonel said . . ."

Wallsly interrupted, "I am the division sanitation officer, and for matters of health I out-rank your regimental colonel."

The lieutenant pleaded, "But, sir, this isn't health. It's just the sinks."

Wallsly growled, "Do it or face division court-martial."

Back in the wagon, Wallsly glowed with satisfaction. "Looks like we arrived just in time, Jefferson."

"In time for what, suh? To get your head chopped off on the first day here?"

"He was digging the sinks in the wrong place!"

"But, suh, did you jus' dig yourself a grave where he wanted to dig sinks?"

"This is my assigned job, Jefferson, my *duty*. Drive on and let us see what else is going on."

Jefferson slapped the reins and muttered, "Gwine see plenty disagreements, is what I 'spect we is gwine to see."

Three minutes later, Wallsly bounded from the wagon again to confront two sergeants overseeing a detail of slaves who were finishing an enclosure for the division's cattle and pigs.

"These animals must be moved," he barked.

"Moved, sir?" repeated the senior master sergeant.

Wallsly glared at the thick and burly veteran. "At least one-quarter mile from the tents."

The sergeant chuckled as if Wallsly had made a joke. "Now *that* would be very amusing, sir, since the general has specifically ordered that the animals be kept in close where he can keep an eye on them and where we can deliver the meat as fresh as possible to the troops once it's butchered."

Wallsly stood nose to nose with the sergeant. "I am the division sanitation officer, and for matters of health, my word is final. Move the animals."

The sergeant leaned back and scratched his head, still smiling. "I've heard of *commanding* officer. But I ain't never heard of no such a thing as *sanitary* officer."

"*Sanitation* officer," Wallsly corrected.

"And I never, sir," the sergeant continued, "was told to take no orders from a sanitary officer."

The confrontation was interrupted by the arrival of galloping horses. A tall, lean man with thick gold braid on the sleeves and front of his gray coat pointed at Wallsly with his riding crop. "Explain yourself, major."

"Good morning, general," Wallsly answered, leaning back from the sergeant so he could salute. "I am simply reorganizing the division camp according to the best sanitation principles."

The general growled, "*I* arrange my camp, major. And what I like is a compact camp that promotes control and security."

Wallsly was already prepared with an answer to this argument. His eyes danced. "How secure is the division, sir, if half the men are sick and can't answer assembly?"

General Hardee glowered at his new surgeon. He hissed out through clenched teeth. "My tent in 15 minutes, major." He turned to ride off, then paused and added, "The cattle stay."

Wallsly began to protest, "But . . ."

"Fifteen minutes, major!" And General Hardee thundered across the division camp on his chestnut horse.

The sergeant gloated, "Like I said, major, guess we'll just finish this here stockade where it is."

Wallsly spun on his heel and stormed back to the wagon.

Jefferson sat quietly on the wagon's seat. "Yes, suh. My mamma always tol' me that a good firs' impression is worth its weight in gold."

Wallsly dropped onto the wagon's front seat and kicked at the curved front floor board. "This one's even worse than Van Dorn. Why do generals insist on acting like it's still the eighteenth century?"

Twelve minutes later Major Wallsly swept off his hat as he stepped into General Hardee's office tent and saluted. The general studied maps and scouting reports without glancing up. "This is *my* division, major, and *I* give the orders. You *advise* for sanitation matters, not command." Hardee turned to face Wallsly. He jabbed his cigar at the major. "Countermand one of my standing orders again and I'll bust you to orderly." He leaned back in his folding camp chair, puffed his cigar, and folded his arms. "You got something to say, you say it to me, not the men who follow my orders."

Wallsly took this as an invitation to speak. "Sir, the men have to *live* in this camp. If we enforce better sanitation, it will mean that you have more healthy men for your battle line."

Hardee cocked his head and blew a billowing cloud of blue-gray smoke. "Moving cattle out of the immediate camp area means that any Union cavalry raid could make off with our primary food supply. Moving the sinks means men have to trudge through winter cold and freezing rain to relieve themselves. They won't do it. Nor should they."

"They will if you order them to," Wallsly answered. "When they live around human waste, sick rates for diarrhea and dysentery soar. Once they see that sanitation keeps them healthier, they'll be happier."

General Hardee clamped his cigar between his teeth. "You got three minutes, major. Show me your proof."

Wallsly reached into his shoulder satchel and lifted out the reports he had written on the effect on sick-call rates he had recorded in Van Dorn's camp after imposing his sanitation plan. The general puffed, read, and nodded. He leaned toward the tent flap. "Send in Colonel Williams."

As Colonel Williams, the division adjutant, came in, Hardee asked, "What would be the impact of expanding the picket perimeter?"

"Minimal, sir."

Hardee nodded, then addressed Wallsly. "All right, major. Move the sinks and livestock."

Wallsly interrupted, "Also, sir, I want the men to collect and remove garbage and grease daily."

"Daily?! It's not practical to clean the camp more than once a week."

"Daily, sir. Also, sir, you should encourage the men not to fry their food. It's bad for the intestines."

Hardee aimed his cigar at Wallsly again. "You've got one month, major, to prove to me that you're right." Then he stabbed at the air, as if the cigar were a sword, for emphasis. "One month! But you may *not* complain to anyone about how the men cook or clean. That's their business and neither I nor you will mess with it. Understood?!"

"Yes, sir! Thank you, sir." Wallsly saluted again and turned to go, victory dancing in his eyes.

"One more thing, major. You work for Colonel Talgert Johnston. He is my chosen chief surgeon and your commanding officer and establishes surgical policy. You seem to have forgotten that at Carthage. Don't forget it again."

Colonel Johnston leisurely arrived in camp two days later and "allowed" his two assistant surgeons to handle daily sick call. He himself was rarely seen in camp. When Wallsly asked why he didn't take his turn in the sick-call rotation, Johnston shrugged, "I am a surgeon, and there are no surgeries to perform."

Life settled into a hectic routine for the assistant surgeons. Mornings began with sick call. A 4,000-man division could typically expect 200 new complaints every day.

It became an unconscious habit for Major Wallsly to carry a ball of opium in one pocket for the treatment of diarrhea and dysentery, a wad of the compound called Blue Mass in the other for constipation, a bottle of quinine for fevers if accompanied by headaches, ground sassafras for pneumonia and gout, and a bottle of arsenic for fevers if accompanied by indigestion. Smallpox cases were given ammonium acetate and sent to the division hospital. Asthma and breathing complaints were treated with horseradish, ammonium, and quinine. Morphine was offered for pain. Mercurical ointment and soaks were ordered for blisters, bruises, and foot bleeding.

Each morning Major Wallsly reminded Captain Sidney Feller to keep exact logs of every complaint and to chart them beside the complaints recorded in the other divisions of the army.[6] Over the noon meal Wallsly and Feller reviewed the charts and discussed treatment for patients in the hospital.

After eating, Wallsly conducted rounds in the small division hospital where orderlies cared for sick and recovering patients. Finally, Wallsly settled into his favorite part of the day: study. He read every medical paper Jefferson could find, scrounge, or order for him. He practiced new operating techniques on fresh cadavers. He studied local plants that promised to offer some medical benefit.

On December 6, orderly Pevis Jenkins rushed to Major Wallsly as he began his daily rounds. "Sir, I can smell one of the patients."

"Gangrene?"

"I believe so, sir. Will you amputate now?"

Wallsly's face spread into a grin. "No need, Pevis. Have you collected a supply of maggots as I requested?"

Jenkins grimaced. "Maggots, sir? Actually crawling on his flesh?"

"It's the newest therapy. Maggots eat only dead, decayed tissue and won't touch what is live and healthy. They prevent the spread of inflammation and gangrene."

Jenkins frowned. "I know this man, sir. He'll never stand for it."

"Give him laudanum as a sedative. He won't care what we do."

Still Jenkins squirmed. "Just promise you'll never let maggots crawl around inside me."

That evening Colonel Johnston burst into Wallsly's tent as the major experimented with powdered starch, trying to follow an article's directions for forming the new plaster casts for setting broken bones. The colonel's bulldog face glowed red and twitched with anger.

"Major! What is this nonsense I hear about maggots?"

"It's the latest treatment, sir. I'll loan you a paper describing their success."

"We treat gangrene by amputating because that procedure has been proven to save lives."

"Maggots save lives *and* limbs, sir." Wallsly defiantly glared at his commander. "This is *my* patient."

Johnston wagged a finger at his assistant. "I'm watching you, major. If that man dies, I'll court-martial you for murder." Then he stomped out of the tent.

Jefferson, brushing a uniform coat for Wallsly to wear the next day, glanced up from his work. "I sees you and the boss has patched things up, suh."

Wallsly answered, "Next battle, Jefferson, I want to try operating on a chest wound. I just read an excellent article on techniques to close ruptures of the lung."

Jefferson rolled his eyes, "That, of course, will please the colonel no end, suh."

"I am a trained surgeon, Jefferson. I have a duty to practice the best possible technique. I will *demand* to do it."

Jefferson shook his head, returned to his work, and muttered, "Which will give the colonel the perfect opportunity to demand that you is shot."

Wallsly's report to General Hardee was delayed until two days after Christmas 1862. With great relish, Wallsly laid graphs on the general's table showing that rates of diarrhea, dysentery, and fever were significantly lower in this division than in any other in the army. He glowed with satisfaction as he folded his arms and announced that this proved his theories on camp sanitation. Finally, he noted that his maggot therapy had saved two soldiers' lives *and* limbs.

Colonel Johnston, who was also there, sneered, "I notice that asthma, smallpox, and pneumonia rates are still high."

Wallsly flushed angrily. "If I had been allowed to improve the men's diet, cooking habits, and bathing, I'm sure that these rates would also drop."

The colonel snorted, "This is an army, not a social club. Our mission is to harden the men into soldiers."

"*Our* mission, colonel, is to keep the men healthy so that they *can* be soldiers."

Johnston glared back at his unruly assistant. "We can't cater to whining weaklings."

"Enough!" shouted General Hardee. "First, battle is imminent. Rosecrans's Union army is moving south from Nashville. Prepare yourselves for a major battle. Second, Major Wallsly's recommendations for camp organization seem to be effective and will remain in place."

Wallsly beamed. Johnston reddened and began, "But, sir . . ."

"Third," continued General Hardee, talking over his chief surgeon, "we cannot and will not alter the eating, cooking, and grooming habits of my soldiers. Further, I will not have the rest of the army snickering that maggots run rampant through my division hospital. We *kill* maggots, not operate with them. They will not be used."

"At least, sir," Wallsly interrupted, "permit me to try new, advanced surgical techniques on the wounded from this battle."

"Fourth," bellowed the general, "Colonel Johnston is in charge of surgery and all surgeons will follow his policies." Before either officer could utter a word the general snapped, "Dismissed!"

Wallsly slumped dejectedly in his wagon on the ride back to his tent. "That cretin won't let me experiment with new operating techniques."

Jefferson clicked his tongue at the horse. "But the camp sanitation officer won a great victory, so I hears. Don't forget to count your wins, suh, whilst you brood 'bout how they's not lettin' you run the army."

Sadly Wallsly shook his head. "You'll see, Jefferson. Someday soon the world will laugh at the medicine we are practicing here and wonder how we could be so ignorant."

"Yes, suh," Jefferson smiled. "It must be a tiresome burden, suh, to have to single-handedly educate the entire Confederate army."

Aftermath

In early 1865 Pasteur published the first article describing his theory that microscopic organisms—"germs"—caused disease. Several months later Joseph Lister developed the concept of operating room sterilization. All surgery was instantly transformed by these two monumental discoveries. Ironically, these surgical breakthroughs first reached America in April 1865, only days after the last battle of the Civil War.

Inflammation was renamed infection and its causes and prevention were correctly identified. The boiling of dressings and surgical instruments became routine and standard practices for all surgeons. Over 900,000 limbs were amputated during the Civil War. Over a quarter million died from postoperative infection. Most of these deaths could have been prevented if sterilization had been discovered only four years earlier. Only camp-borne disease killed more men than did infection.

Notes

1. Every doctor carried a small pocket-sized case of instruments used for minor operations such as lancing boils or abscesses, minor suturing, or even amputating a toe or finger.

2. Infections were called "inflammation" in the 1860s. Inflammation was characterized by redness, swelling, soreness, and heat. Most patients developed inflammation after surgery. Doctors believed that inflammation was caused by irritation and overexcitement to tissues and nerves from the trauma of injury and operation. We now know that these infections were caused by unsterile operating conditions. However, the concept of sterilization was not discovered until 1865.

3. Every surgeon was assigned two orderlies to act as assistants. One administered anesthetic; the other held the patient still. Additional orderlies carried the stretchers of new patients in and postoperative patients out to wait for ambulances to take them to a hospital.

4. Searing the severed arteries and tissues of the remaining stub of an amputated limb (cauterizing) was accomplished with a red-hot iron, not unlike a branding iron for cattle. Cauterizing was quick and brutal. It had been the preferred medical technique for over 2,000 years. The alternative was to hook each individual artery with a curved needle, pull it out of the limb exposing one-half inch of artery, and tie it off with thread or catgut. Tying was slower but promoted faster healing.

5. "Sinks" was the common term for the trenches that served as latrines for the soldiers.

6. The second assistant surgeon was always assigned to record the name and complaint of every soldier on sick call as well as the name of every soldier upon whom an operation was performed.

Follow-up Questions and Activities

1. **What Do You Know?**
   - What were the responsibilities and functions of army doctors during the Civil War? What training did they typically have?
   - What were the common medical complaints of soldiers during the Civil War? What were the typical treatments?
   - What did doctors during the Civil War call infection? What did they think caused it? How did they treat infection?
   - What was the prevailing view of sanitation during the Civil War? Why?

2. **Find Out More.** Following are six important topics from this story for students to research in the library and on the Internet. The reference sources at the back of this book will help them get started.

- Research the history of American medical schools and medical training. What was the first American medical school? When did it open? When were women first admitted to medical schools? Compare modern medical schools and training to those of 1860. Compare the status and prestige of doctors and medical schools in each time period as well as the length of study and course material covered. When did medical training begin to resemble that of modern medical school and internships?

- Research the history, role, and prominence of doctors in America beginning with early colonial times. Trace their social status, requirements to practice, and general influence as well as their knowledge and techniques.

- Research battlefield surgical practices and medicine over time, beginning with the ancient Greeks. How have different types of wounds been treated? What success rates have doctors in different eras achieved? Chart the major advances in battlefield medicine over the past thousand years.

- The American Civil War was the first war featuring general use of anesthesia for virtually every operation. Trace the history of surgical anesthesia. What was used during the Revolutionary War? What were the plusses and minuses of each common Civil War anesthetic? What methods were used by other indigenous peoples and previous armies? How did they do surgeries without modern anesthetic?

- Research the role and history of medical orderlies. Have all armies had them? What other duties have they typically performed? Now focus your research on Civil War orderlies. How were they picked? What were their primary duties? What other duties did they perform? What was their status relative to other soldiers?

- "Triage" is the process of, first, screening incoming wounded to determine their priority for attention by surgeons, and, second, administering first aid to stabilize each patient while they wait. Research the current practice and history of triage. How did it start? Have medical priorities always been the same? How important is triage?

3. **Make It Real**

- Hold a class discussion of the injuries and operations each of you has undergone. Let each student share his or her experience and memories of the operation. What did the injury feel like? How did you feel facing an operation? Did you trust your doctor(s)? The hospital? Compare your experiences and feelings to those of soldiers during the Civil War. As an alternative, invite an appropriate hospital worker in to discuss modern surgical techniques. Or students can visit the website http://members.aol.com/cwsurgeonO/index .J.html to learn more about Civil War surgery.

- Imagine you are an army orderly during the Civil War. Pick a specific unit (division and brigade) to be assigned to. Also pick a specific date and place where your unit was involved in battle. Research the activity of your unit during that battle and write a letter to your parents describing your duties and activities on the day of the battle. Write a second letter describing a typical day in late February after almost four months of monotonous winter camp.

4. **Points to Ponder**

- Do you think it is ethically acceptable for armies to use untrained and poorly trained doctors to provide for the medical needs of their soldiers? Why do you think Civil War armies used doctors who had never been to medical school?

- What kind of ethics apply to a doctor's practice of medicine, and how are these affected by being in the military? Have military doctors in more recent conflicts faced dilemmas similar to those Wallsly faced?

1863 at a Glance

The Tide Turns

During the bitter and bloody campaign of 1863, Confederate hopes rose high and, even as late as mid-1863, victory seemed close. Then those hopes withered like yesterday's rose pedals, never to rise again. James Plimpton invented roller skates in 1863. The Confederacy must have felt that they had slipped on one of his skates as they tumbled from dreams of victory into the despair of defeat. The first "horseless carriage" was invented in France. Its maximum speed was three miles per hour—not much slower than many trains on the crumbling Southern rail system.

The noose of the blockade around the Confederacy's neck continued to tighten, slowly choking the breath and life out of the rebellion. Although Tennessee was still lost, at least Union forces were not able to continue their advance and cut any deeper into the heartland of the South.

In the West, the Mississippi River was lost when Vicksburg fell. With it, the Western third of the Confederacy, with its rich and abundant fields of essential grain, was lost.

In the East, Robert E. Lee scored yet another stunning victory and sent yet another Union general (Joe Hooker) packing in disgrace. Then Lee again turned his thoughts to offense and planned an invasion deep through Maryland and into Pennsylvania. He ventured as far as Gettysburg before meeting General Meade and 80,000 men of the Army of the Potomac.

On those three sultry days at the beginning of July 1863, Robert E. Lee stumbled and lost his magic touch. He faltered. Then he outright failed and missed his opportunities for victory. His army was defeated and fled in tatters back to Virginia.

That decisive defeat occurred on the same day that Vicksburg, Mississippi, finally fell. July 3, 1863, marks the official turning point of the war. After that day, the Confederacy lost all hope of victory. The South was running out of cards to play—along with replacement soldiers and everything else a nation and community need. The end was not here yet, not by a long shot, but it would now surely come. The tide had turned against the South.

Key Events in 1863

Date	Event
January 1	Lincoln's Emancipation Proclamation is officially issued.
January 15	The Confederate government passes the first military draft law in American history, requiring all males between 18 and 45 to register for the draft.
March 10	Lincoln signs the first federal draft law, making all males between 20 and 45 eligible to be drafted.
May 1–4	The Battle of Chancellorsville is a brilliant victory for Lee. However, Stonewall Jackson is accidentally killed by fire from his own men. It is a major blow to the Confederacy that far outweighs the victory.
May 15	Lincoln relieves General Joseph Hooker and appoints General George Meade to be commander of the Army of the Potomac.
May 17	Vicksburg, Mississippi, the last Confederate stronghold on the Mississippi River, is surrounded and cut off. The siege of Vicksburg begins.
June 10	Lee wins a small battle at Winchester, Virginia, and begins his invasion of Maryland and Pennsylvania.
June 20	West Virginia, which has been under Union control since the beginning of the war, is admitted into the Union as a free state.
July 1–3	The Battle of Gettysburg is the bloodiest battle of the war and a clear defeat for Lee and the Confederacy. Lee scurries back to Virginia. Meade fails to pursue aggressively and allows Lee to escape total defeat.
July 2–3	During the Battle of Gettysburg, Union cavalry General Philip Sheridan establishes the superiority of Union cavalry forces, a position that up until then had been held by Lee's cavalry chief, General Jeb Stuart.
July 3	Vicksburg falls. The entire western third of the Confederacy is lost as the Mississippi River comes under Union control.
July 13–16	New York draft riots rock the Union and nearly succeed in pulling New York out of the war.

September 19–20	At the Battle of Chickamauga, Union General William Rosecrans is pushed back and his army is nearly destroyed when he attempts to push south from Tennessee into Georgia. Rosecrans flees north to Chattanooga. This Southern victory is the first good news the Confederacy has had since May.
November 23–25	Union General Ulysses Grant takes command of Union forces at Chattanooga and quickly defeats Confederate General Braxton Bragg in stunning victories at Lookout Mountain and Missionary Ridge. Bragg is driven back into Georgia.
November 26	Confederate General James Longstreet attacks General Ambrose Burnside's small force outside of Knoxville and temporarily reestablishes Confederate control over eastern Tennessee. In one week of sporadic fighting, Longstreet is unable to penetrate Burnside's defenses and retreats, leaving all of Tennessee under Union control.

A Place of Freedom
Southern Slaves' Efforts to Gain Freedom, March 1863

At a Glance

By 1860, more than 4 million slaves were scattered across the South: household slaves, plantation slaves, and personal slaves and servants. Slaves worked in all manner of menial physical labor and lived in every community of the 15 slave states in the Union.

The one universal hope of these men, women, and children was freedom. But for most, freedom seemed impossibly far away. One misstep—even one misglance—could mean a beating. An insult or actual transgression could mean death or life in iron chains and restraining collars. The guns, hounds, and whips of owners were turned on any who tried to escape or assert themselves. Sheriffs, posses, bounty hunters, and the army all pledged to capture and return runaways. President Lincoln pledged not to interfere with slavery.

Still, slaves dreamed of freedom, and many did more than dream. Some 100,000 escaped to freedom in the North and Canada, either on their own or, more commonly, using one of the many routes of the Underground Railroad. Over 30,000 found ways to save the money needed to buy their freedom. A few tried (unsuccessfully) to start revolts to win instant freedom.

The one all-important question was "What should they *do* to better ensure their freedom?" Some volunteered to help the Confederate army, hoping that would help them gain freedom, or at least better treatment, after the Confederacy won the war. Some ran miles in terror to nearby Union army lines. Most had to wait for the war to fight its way to them before they had any hope of acting on their own behalf.

In late 1861, the Union army seized the Sea Islands along the coast of South Carolina. Panicked whites fled, leaving behind more than 8,000 slaves and hundreds of acres of rich cotton fields and farmlands. The Sea Islands became a magnet for Southern slaves, a place of peace, shelter, education, and food—a place of freedom.

Meet Ransom Wilson and Elizabeth Wilson

Ransom and his two brothers, Joshua (Josh) and Bartholomew (Bar'loo), were born slaves on the Wilson plantation along the shore of the Ashepoo River just west of Walterboro, South Carolina, about 30 miles southwest of Charleston. Ransom was the youngest of six children. Two died in infancy, and a sister was sold off the plantation. The three boys grew up working in the Wilsons' cotton fields.

In early 1863 Ransom was 25, had married Daisy, another Wilson slave, and had a two-year-old daughter. He lived his entire life on that plantation, going beyond its boundaries only once, on the last day of his life.

Elizabeth (called Liz'bet around the plantation) was the oldest daughter of Ransom's oldest brother, Joshua, and turned 13 in early January 1863. A thin, sickly child, she had not been forced to work in the fields and was free to play with the younger plantation children.

Elizabeth, however (with the encouragement of her mother), opted to risk her life and walk three miles each way every day to a Mrs. Thatcher, a free black living in Walterboro, who ran a secret school for black children. (It was illegal for blacks to be educated.) Elizabeth hid her school papers inside bundles of laundry in case she was stopped on her way. From Mrs. Thatcher, she learned to read and write.

It was Elizabeth who, after the family successfully crossed behind Union lines at Beaufort in the Carolina Sea Islands, wrote the family history. Elizabeth lived and worked as a teacher in Port Royal, on the Carolina Sea Islands, until health forced her to retire in 1922 at the age of 71. Eight years later, poor health forced her to move to St. Louis to live with her daughter. She died in St. Louis in 1934 at the age of 85.

A Place of Freedom

Ransom Wilson's first action when he jolted awake was to clamp one hand over his wife Daisy's mouth to keep her from screaming. Daisy seemed to relish any opportunity to cut loose with an ear-piercing wail. Ransom had awakened with a start to the sound of breathing—heavy breathing, labored breathing, just outside their dirt-floor shack.

His first thought was that it must be an overseer, one of the white men hired by Mr. Wilson to control the slaves on this South Carolina plantation and make sure they worked as hard as humanly possible. The overseers had taken over complete control of the slaves a year ago, just before the 1862 spring planting, when Colonel Wilson had ridden off in his sparkling gray uniform to fight the war.

An overseer always meant trouble for slaves. But it was especially bad to see an overseer at night. It always meant whippings.

"I hears breathin'," he whispered into Daisy's ear. "So don' scream."

She nodded, eyes wide with fright, and he relaxed his hand. The breathing sounded close enough to touch through the cardboard-thin walls of the shack.

"Sounds like he's hurt, whoever it is," whispered Daisy.

Ransom muttered, "Lawd, maybe it's Old Bones, went out diggin' again an' got hisself hurt." Old Jeremiah (white-haired and an unremembered number of years past 50) had been called "Old Bones" ever since he dug up a bone along the bank of the Ashepoo River one night and claimed that it was from an ancient human. The fuss had quickly died away, but the name stuck.

"Well, go *see*," urged Daisy in the deep dark of their windowless shack.

"But what if it ain't Old Bones?"

"Jus' go see!"

Ransom slid out of bed and grabbed a thick stick he had slowly whittled into a formidable club as he tiptoed toward the door. Ransom was a short, thick-chested black man with strong, sinewy arms and legs. The skin on his back was rippled by ridges, evidence of past whippings.

He paused at the shack door, his heart thudding hard in his chest, before he eased the door open a slim crack. A uniformed man sat slumped against the shack wall.

"Lawd a'mighty. His coat's covered in blood."

"An' it's a *blue* coat," added Daisy, peering over his shoulder after she waddled up behind him, being seven months pregnant.

The soldier's voice came out as a horse whisper, "Help me."

Ransom smelled trouble. Injured white folks coming to a slave's shack for help wasn't right at all. "You's *white*, suh. You wants to go to the Big House."

The man raised a blood-encrusted arm and grabbed Ransom's wrist. "Water . . ." The man groaned and tried to swallow.

"Mercy be!" hissed Daisy. "I'll fetch the bucket."

Ransom's head swam with how wrong this situation felt. His voice sounded like a whimpering plea. "Suh, you don' want *our* water. You want *white* folks' water. They'll fix you up jus' fine in the *Big House*."

The soldier pleaded, "I'm a Union officer. Hide me."

Ransom's eyes grew as big as the full moon, partly hidden behind scattered clouds. "Lawd a'mighty. They'll kill us all if'n they finds you here."

Ransom's older brother, Bartholomew, who served as head gardener for the plantation grounds, lived in the next shack in the line of slave huts bordering the marshland where river water pooled during the rainy season. He poked his head outside to see what the fuss was about. "Who's dat man an' what's he talkin' 'bout, brother?"

"He's a Union man—the other side in the war, Bar'loo," Ransom whispered.

"Well, what's he doin' here?" Bar'loo asked, peering down at the soldier as if he were a sack of flour. "Lookie at all dat blood!"

Daisy had returned with a bucket and wooden ladle. The Union officer poured water down his throat before explaining. "I escaped from a prison train two days ago. Been hiding and wandering south since."

"South?" asked Bar'loo. "Why south if'n you's from da' Noth?"

"Git him inside afore I scream," insisted Daisy. "Don' want the ober'seer spotting us, does you?"

After several more ladles of water, the soldier continued his story to a growing audience of half a dozen slaves who had slunk into Ransom's shack to see what was happening. Ransom and Daisy's two-year-old child woke, crying because of the commotion. Daisy cradled the child and softly hushed her.

"My company was captured in Virginia," he began.

"Virginy?" Ransom interrupted. "Lawd, but that's a far way from here."

"I was on a train to a prison camp in Georgia. As an officer—a wounded officer—I wasn't guarded as closely. I rolled off the train into a ditch as the train slowed to a stop in Walterboro and escaped."

"Is that how you got all bloody?" asked Mattie, a heavyset, white-haired woman who cooked in the Big House. She began to wash and wrap the officer's wounds with a roll of gauze.

The soldier shook his head. "Wounded in battle." Blood still oozed from his head where a musket ball had grazed his scalp and torn off part of his ear and from a vicious bayonet gash in his shoulder.

"Why'd you come *here*?" Ransom demanded. "Virginy is noth, that's the other way out o' Walterboro."

The soldier paused to drink and to stuff a slab of corn bread that Mattie had offered into his mouth. "There's a Union force at Beaufort in the Sea Islands."

None of the slaves in the room had ever set foot off the Wilson plantation or heard of places farther away than Walterboro. "Git Liz'bet," said Daisy. "She'll know where that's at."

"Tell her to bring her learnin' books," Ransom added as Bar'loo slipped out the door and started through deep shadows down the line of shacks to where Ransom's and Bar'loo's oldest brother, Joshua, lived with his family, including his 13-year-old daughter, Elizabeth (Liz'bet). Elizabeth had been hiking into Walterboro each day, hauling loads of laundry, so that she could secretly go to school to learn to read and write. She was the only educated slave on the Wilson plantation and the recognized authority on virtually every subject.

By now there were almost 20 slaves crammed into Ransom's and Daisy's shack. Midnight had come and gone. All eyes watched Liz'bet as she studied her notes and books. "Beaufort's less than 30 miles," she concluded. "Take the road south to Hendersonville, cross the Combahee River, and go south through Gardens Corner and Lobeco."

"Thirty mile?" Ransom repeated. "Lawd, a'mighty. I could walk there in a day."

"Why get a pack o' blisters jus' so you can be a slave there instead o' here?" asked Joshua, the most skeptical (and most often beaten) of the Wilson slaves.

"You'd be free if you reach Union lines," said the officer.

"Free?" repeated many of the assembled slaves. Some, like Joshua, spit it out with bitter skepticism. Many said it almost as a prayer.

"Technically, you'd be declared to be contraband by the army. Then you could live and work in the Sea Islands—free."

"It don' matter whatever you wants to call me," whispered Bar'loo, "jus' so long as I gits free."

A hushed moment of hope hung in the dull room until Joshua snorted, "An' you'd be run down by dogs, hanged, an' shot dead fo' runnin' long afore you reached Hendersonville, too."

It had happened just that way before. All the Wilson slaves believed it was the most likely fate of any runner.

Before dawn, the Union officer, fortified with water, food, and a rough map Liz'bet had drawn on one of her precious pieces of paper, slipped out of the row of shacks and headed south along the shore of the Ashepoo toward Hendersonville.

"Think he'll make it?" Daisy asked.

"I'm thinkin' mo' 'bout us," Ransom answered.

"You gwine run?" she stammered. "You'll git yo'self *killed*!"

"But that's *freedom* waitin' jus' 30 mile down the road there, Daisy. *Freedom*!"

Over the next few nights a debate raged throughout the row of slave shacks. Should they believe the Union army officer? Could they make the 30-mile run over unknown terrain to the Sea Islands? *Should* they even try?

Little Mary May, who was a seamstress and handmaiden in the Big House, said, "The Missus (Mrs. Wilson) tol' me the Yankees chain blacks to carts and make you pull like a mule 'til you falls dead!"

"That's jus' a wild pack o' lies, honey chil," laughed Mattie. "Ain't no such thing. Yankees believe that blacks is people jus' like them and wants us all to be free."

"Ain't so!" snapped Joshua. "They hate blacks up noth jus' like they do here. They jus' ain't got slaves. That's all."

Old Bones nodded in agreement. "Blacks fought in the army right 'side them Yankee whites in two old wars. My gran'daddy tol' me 'bout it. He was in one of 'em! That didn't do us no good. We still slaves."

Benjamin Tucker, the plantation blacksmith, snuffed hard to gather attention. "White folks used to sneer, 'Fix 'dis, boy!' Now they comes by an' they tips their hats, 'How do, Benjamin Tucker?' And they asks me real respectful like, 'What you think I ought do with this-a here sqeekin' axle?' I ain't a-fixin to run nowheres. Life is getting' better right here where we are."

"I ain't been whooped or beat in over three years," added Mattie in agreement. "Even when I tells the Missus how wrong she is."

"Fo' you, maybe," snarled Ransom. "But in da' fields, it's da' same as always was, and ain't never gwine get any better."

Jackson, another old Wilson plantation slave, did much of the wagon driving into Walterboro for supplies. He added, "I seen the Sechest army once." Sechest was how the Wilson slaves pronounced "secessionist," or Confederate. "They marched through Walterboro. Flags a'flyin' and a whole mess o' drums bangin' so loud it shook the wagon. Seemed they jus' marched past *forever*. There was so many, no way they's gonna lose a fight. I say, stay here, say 'Hooray fo' the South,' an' maybe Massa Wilson, then he treat us better after they win."

Ransom shook his head. "Freedom is jus' a few miles! Jus' one day walkin' and we's there! We's at a place of freedom."

"Where they like as not turns you over to a bounty hunter," said Joshua.

Eventually they decided that Liz'bet should ask her teacher. A thick pack of slaves gathered at Joshua's shack at sunset the next night to hear her report.

"Mrs. Thatcher said Contraband is what the Union soldiers call a slave when they makes him free. She also said they's thousands of free Contrabands on the Sea Islands. They got's a school an' they own farms!"

"Tha's it," said Ransom. "We's goin!" His eyes gleamed in the soft glow of moonlight.

Daisy gently laid a hand on her husband's arm. "We can't *all* go."

"Yes, we can," Ransom insisted.

Daisy's voice was gentle but firm. "Old Bones and Mattie's too old to walk 30 mile. I'm too pregnant. Little Jasmine is only two. She can't be walkin' 30 mile. And you can't be carryin' her if'n you is gonna make it."

Tears sprang into Ransom's eyes. "But Daisy, sugar, we *got's* to go together. We *got's* to be free together."

" 'Sides," added Mattie. "You can't jus' walk down the road. You's got to sneak thro' swamps and fields an' such—all at night—wid' nothin' to eats, and not knowin' which'a ways you is goin'. Hounds and men on horse chasin' you, shootin' at you, all the way . . ." She shivered. "I ain't makin' *that* walk. No, suh, I ain't!"

"But it's *freedom*," Ransom insisted. "Tha's worth *anything*."

Bar'loo suggested, "Some of us'll go an' get help to come back an' fetch da' res'."

"Like that Off'cer fetched help fo' us?" sneered Joshua. "You ain't seen any o' the help he promised, has you? He probably got hisself shot and kilt afore he got two mile! An' the same happen to you, too, if'n you go."

" 'Dis here is the mos' serious decision we ever made," said Mattie, fire and hope blazing in her eyes. "I says we votes. Either we all agree to go or we all agree to stay."

Except for Old Bones and Joshua, who believed the trip would surely fail and wouldn't help the slaves any even if they made it to Union lines, all agreed to the escape plan. The remaining questions was, who should go?

Four nights were consumed by the discussion. Always the slaves in the discussion circle glanced warily over their shoulders, knowing that such talk meant a death sentence if they were caught.

It was agreed that four men would make the initial run to Beaufort and Contraband freedom. The rest would wait for the help they would send back to fetch the remaining slaves. The chosen four were Ransom, Bar'loo, William, an older slave, and 16-year-old Robert, a quiet boy with graceful hands who spent most of his time in the woodworking shop and who was the only plantation slave who naturally smiled. William ("Will'm"), whose back was a rugged relief map of crisscrossing scars from past whippings, said, "I been whipped so much, they dun beat the fear right out o' me. I'll go."

On a cool, clear night, still a week or two before spring planting in 1863, Ransom gave his wife a final kiss on her tear-stained face. "I come back quick fo' you and Jasmine, sugar. An' I'll come back free! I swear I will." He slipped out of their shack to join the other three, hiding in the shadows by the gnarled cypress trees lining the marsh. With a final glance back at the row of rickety cabins that had been their whole world, the four turned south and started their run for freedom.

Daisy clutched their blanket around her and squeezed her eyes tight shut all that night. She wanted to scream out in terror, thinking of what might happen to her man between here and freedom. But she didn't dare make a sound for fear of giving away their escape.

The overseers exploded in rage the next morning when they discovered that four slaves had bolted. Savage and indiscriminate beating and kicking became the order of the day. Virtually every slave was attacked. Details of the escape were pounded out of each friend and family member.

Late that afternoon Bar'loo and Robert returned to the plantation, riding in the back of a wagon, their faces distorted and discolored from vicious beatings, iron collars locked tight around their necks. Bar'loo was dragging an iron ball locked onto one bloody ankle as they were dumped to the ground like sacks of trash near the slave shacks. The overseers grinned at the looks of horror on the slaves' faces.

It took an hour of intense care by Mattie before they were sure either man would live, and longer still before either man could speak. Joshua and Old Bones sat on the sidelines, sadly shaking their heads. "I tol' 'em this would happen."

"Where's Ransom?" Daisy demanded. "He made it?"

"In a manner," mumbled Bar'loo through swollen lips and missing teeth.

"Now, wha's that 'sposed to mean?" demanded Mattie. "Is he free or no?"

Bar'loo's eyes were swelled shut and hidden. Tears trickled through the tiny slits. "We was caught crossin' da' river. Ransom, he's free now in da' only way a slave is ever free—he's dead. They hanged him and William right there at da' river."

For three days straight, Daisy wept uncontrollably. The other slaves shuffled back into their work routine in hollow silence. On the Wilson plantation, the fires of freedom burned low.

Aftermath

Less than a month after Ransom and William were killed, a strong Union patrol rode through the Wilson plantation on a foraging expedition. They seized a large stock of food and livestock and allowed slaves to follow in their growing supply train back to the Sea Islands. Fifty of the Wilson's 70 slaves followed the blue coat patrol to freedom in Beaufort. The remaining 20 were apparently as frightened of the Union army as they were of Southerners and dared not leave the familiarity of their lifelong surroundings—even for a walk to freedom.

Over 500,000 blacks became Contrabands before the war ended, flooding into every Union army camp eager to work as cooks, drivers, laundry maids, diggers, construction crew, and soldiers. They brought with them only the clothes on their backs and a new sense of hope and optimism that had not been seen in their families for generations.

The Civil War wrought a revolution in black status in the North as well as in the South. In the North, citizenship, voting rights, rights to at least a rudimentary education, and desegregation of schools and transportation all followed after the blacks' contributions to the successful Civil War. The war and its aftermath created a sense of hope and possibility in blacks that they had not possessed since their ancestors were first enslaved and transported to America. Ensuing years would quickly tarnish the glitter of that hope and make painfully clear how far blacks still had to struggle to reach the equality they first believed the war had brought to them. But that disappointment cannot diminish the vast gains they made as a result of the bloody Civil War.

Follow-up Questions and Activities

1. **What Do You Know?**

   - How many slaves lived in America in 1800? In 1860? Where were they located in 1800? In 1860?

   - How could a slave gain freedom?

   - What risks did slaves face if they tried to escape to freedom?

   - Why were the South Carolina Sea Islands captured by Union forces? Why were they important to Southern blacks?

   - What was the Underground Railroad? Why was it given that name? What did it do?

2. **Find Out More.** Following are seven important topics from this story for students to research in the library and on the Internet. The reference sources at the back of this book will help them get started.

   - Research Union General Benjamin Butler, the man who first used the Confiscation Laws to free slaves and the first man to form black regiments and combat units using freed slaves.

   - What were the Confiscation (Contraband) Laws? Who passed them? Why were they passed? How were they used during the Civil War?

   - Research the life of slaves in the Confederate army. How many slaves served the Confederate army? What did they do? Compare their lives and activities to the life of Contrabands who worked for the Union army.

   - Research the daily lives of plantation slaves in the 1860s. What jobs did they perform? What was a typical day like? How often were they treated kindly and given decent food, clothing, and medical care? Why would such slaves be dejected and bitter? Compare the life of a slave to that of free blacks in the South and to that of free blacks in the North.

   - Research the life and accomplishments of Susie King Taylor, a South Carolina slave girl who learned to read and write and who was living on one of the Georgia Sea Islands when Federal troops captured the area in early 1862. She taught school, volunteered as a Union regimental nurse, and later founded the Boston branch of the Women's Relief Corps. Compare her freedom and activity in later life to that of her early life as a slave child in Georgia.

   - Research the Underground Railroad. What was it? How did it work? Who worked for it and on it? Make a map of the major routes used on the railroad to move escaped slaves north. Find out how slaves were transported along these routes and how long it took to travel them. Research famous railroad conductors (guides).

- When, why, and how did slavery begin in America? How, when, and why was it abolished in the different states and territories? Did slavery ever exist in Canada? Among the Native American tribes? If so, how did they end it?

3. **Make It Real**

- On a map, color free and slave states in 1860—free states one color, Confederate slave states a second color, and "border states" (slave states that did not secede from the Union) a third color. Now shade those free states that had ever practiced legal slavery and label each state with the year in which slavery was outlawed. Finally, write the number of slaves (as of the 1860 census) residing in each slave state.

- Imagine that you are a slave escaping via the Underground Railroad. Which route identified on your research activity map would you take? What kind of plan would you make to get to freedom?

- Make a class list of all of your freedoms as citizens of the United States. What do you have the right to do? What do you have the right to expect and to demand from your government and from other citizens? Do all citizens have the same rights? Are there rights and privileges your parents have that you don't have? Have you ever lost rights and privileges? When? How? How can citizens of this country lose their basic rights and privileges?

  Imagine losing five of the freedoms you have listed. Write a letter to a friend describing your daily life without those freedoms. How would the loss of those freedoms change the structure of your life?

- In this story four of the Wilson slaves run away. Hold a class trial to determine if they should have been punished. Appoint "lawyers" for both their prosecution and their defense. The rest of the class will act as jury. The teams of lawyers must cite as many arguments as possible to either defend or condemn the actions of these four slaves. Does the trial provide any insights into the beliefs and attitudes of white Southerners during the mid-nineteenth century?

4. **Points to Ponder**

- Do you think the Contraband Laws were good or bad for blacks? The Union army used the laws to free many slaves. However, freeing slaves in this way first required that the government acknowledge they were subhuman property. Do you believe that the end result was worth the demeaning classification?

- Do you think the Union army was morally justified in stealing someone's legal property just because they thought it was wrong for Southerners to own slaves? What if people thought it was morally wrong for you to own a dog, a bird, or a fur coat? Would they be right (justified) in stealing your pet or property? What is the difference?

Diary of Death

The Siege of Vicksburg, May–July 1863

At a Glance

While the war in the East dragged on through its long series of duels between the Federal Army of the Potomac and the Confederate Army of Northern Virginia, and while the Union effort to smash south through Tennessee into the heart of the Confederacy faltered, Federal eyes turned to the war in the West—to the Mississippi River. Admiral David Farragut steamed into the mouth of the Mississippi and began his push to conquer the river from the south in early 1862. General Ulysses Grant was assigned to push south with his Union army from Kentucky and Tennessee to meet Farragut.

New Orleans and Baton Rouge fell in Louisiana. Fort Donaldson, Kentucky, and the Ohio River fell. Memphis, Tennessee, fell. Over the course of nine months of intense fighting, every Confederate stronghold on the Mississippi fell—except Vicksburg, Mississippi.

It seemed that Vicksburg, the powerful citadel sitting on high bluffs overlooking the Mississippi, would not fall.

Grant assaulted the citadel repeatedly beginning in late 1862, but without success. Desperate for some success, Grant, in late April 1863, took his army across to the east side of the Mississippi well below Vicksburg and began a wide swing that would take him east as far as the rail junction at Jackson, Mississippi, then back west toward Vicksburg. Meanwhile, Union Admiral David Porter's fleet of ironclad river gunboats crept downriver and within range of Vicksburg.

In mid-May 1863 the residents of Vicksburg still felt so sure of victory, so confident in their military superiority, that it never occurred to anyone in town that Vicksburg could fall. They were protected by over 30,000 stout Mississippi and Louisiana troops and by almost 200 cannons.

But then, on May 15, shells began to rain down upon the city.

Meet Lucy McRae

Lucy McRae was born in Vicksburg in 1850. Her father was a prosperous local merchant who owned a dry goods store and served as a commissioned merchant, arranging shipment for goods up and down the Mississippi.

Lucy grew up in a happy and relatively carefree home. She was a good student and developed exceptional writing skills early. By the age of 10 she kept a regular and detailed journal. Excerpts from her journal describing the 47-day bombardment of Vicksburg (written when she was barely 13 years old) have been published in many books describing the Western campaigns of the Civil War. The following story is summarized from her diary accounts, augmented by the letters and diaries of three other Vicksburg women.

Lucy helped her father rebuild his merchant business after the war, but quit the business when she married the son of a prominent Memphis banker at the age of 20. By the time Lucy was 25 they had settled in New Orleans, where they developed a small but prosperous shipping company.

Lucy bore three children and died in New Orleans at the age of 55. Even to the day she died, the nightmares of her Vicksburg ordeal never faded.

Diary of Death

On the steaming morning of June 10, 1863, I woke from the sweetest possible dream, so sweet that at first I didn't realize it was a dream. I heard songbirds chirping in the trees instead of screams and screeching shells. Our house and garden still stood. The air smelled of sweet jasmine instead of gunpowder, burning houses, and death. Mrs. Jamison smiled and waved at me from her front porch.

I smiled at the delicious picture and nestled in my blankets, until I remembered that Mrs. Jamison was torn apart by a mortar shell two weeks ago. Then I remembered that the west wall of our house disintegrated in the deafening explosion of an artillery shell, and that, once the gunners had our range, our house was leveled within half an hour as my mother helplessly shrieked and cursed from the street.

I stirred and opened my eyes to the flickering light of oil lamps in this prairie dog cave where I now live with almost 200 other residents of what used to be our fair city of Vicksburg. The air in the cave is so stale and lifeless that the lamps barely stay lit and burn weak and smoky. Dust so fills the air that it is hard to breathe. This is a problem in every cave. Oh, how we long for a stiff breeze that will blow cool, sweet air into our hiding place.

My name is Lucy McRae. I am 13 and adore writing, which is good for there is little else to do in these endless days of sitting in terror as our town is blown apart. The exploding shells rain from the sky, sometimes 20 in a minute, sometimes only one or two. But they always come to torment us—all day and almost all night.

I remember the first day of the shelling—May 15, not yet a month ago and already a lifetime. I remember laughing with two friends as the first black dots of Federal gunboats crept downriver. We sat on Chestnut Street hill with the first peaches still hard lumps and scoffed at the notion that such small dots on the distant river could ever harm us. We were protected by the great guns on the bluff and by General Pemberton's mighty army that roamed the land somewhere east of Vicksburg.

We shrugged indifferently as the first shells fell harmlessly short of town. But then they found the range. Mrs. Gamble's head and arm were blown off as she stepped through her front gate. Mrs. Wilkins was killed in her carriage as she waved to friends while riding to the courthouse. The town vibrated. Peach trees around us shook with each monstrous explosion. I was given my first whiff of sulfurous exploding gunpowder, a smell that is now so pervasive that I no longer notice its pungent and stinging odor.

The first fires erupted. People screamed and raced indoors. But we soon were shown that doors and walls were no better than paper at defending us from the screeching shells. Walls evaporated as the whining shells rained down. Elegant houses collapsed into piles of worthless, smoldering rubble. And still the shells screeched through the sky. The concussion of each exploding shell took my breath away.

All that evening and night we huddled in the cellar, weeping with terror, clutching each other for comfort as the constant whistling screech of shells and rolling thunder of explosions reminded us of how fragile our city and lives really are.

By morning there came a lull in the shelling. We emerged from our hiding places to find torn-up pavement, shattered walls, rich gardens that had turned into lifeless moon craters.

There was a numbness about the people as we gaped at our beloved Vicksburg and then at the hateful cluster of black dots on the river. But still, it did not occur to anyone that we could be beaten by the endless shellings.

Over the next few days, as shells rained upon the city from the river, General Pemberton's army staggered back into Vicksburg, having been badly beaten in several battles to the east. The gaunt, lifeless look in the soldiers' eyes frightened me worse than the screeching shells. These were our protectors, and they looked as if they needed protecting more than we did.

By the 19th of May we were surrounded—Grant's army on the land side and the wretched gunboats on the river side. It was on the 22nd of May—after one week of constant shelling—that my fright turned to rage. Always a headstrong and stubborn girl, I felt I could not tolerate one more minute of this torment. I stomped to the bluffs and demanded of a soldier, a sergeant I think he was, why the monstrous rifled cannons had not driven all the hateful gunboats away.

He shrugged and said that they had tried, but that there were too many of them. I stuck up my nose and sneered something spiteful like, "If there are so many it should be all that much easier to hit one!"

As luck would have it, a Lieutenant Walters, with a Louisiana unit, had just ordered two of the great cannons under his command a short way down the line to prepare to fire. All eyes turned toward the two black barrels as they were lowered to aim at one particularly large Federal gunboat.

They fired almost as one. Fire and smoke punched 60 feet beyond the barrels. The sound was deafening. Both guns sprang back a dozen feet and were shrouded in a swirling cloud of dense smoke.

"Reload!" cried the lieutenant while the onlookers cheered when one of the shells tore a huge gaping hole in the armored side of the gunboat.

Then one of the other gunboats fired back. I saw the cotton puffball of smoke rise from its gun turret. Then a second and third ship fired. Then five more all at once. I heard the familiar whistling screech of arcing shells.

"Here it comes," groaned the sergeant still standing next to me.

The first shell struck the bluff below the two cannons that had fired. The next exploded beyond their embrasured (fortified) gun placement. The next three were direct hits. The hill and wooden barricades surrounding the two guns disappeared in a wall of flame and smoke. The concussion knocked me to the ground. Five more shells slammed into the stricken spot, carving huge gouges in the hill as if a giant pig were rooting through it for truffles.

By the time my legs had slowed their trembling enough to allow me to stand, the smoke had cleared. Two lumps of twisted, black metal marked the spot where two proud Confederate cannons had stood only a moment before. The lieutenant and all his crew were dead.

"Poor bastards never had a chance," my sergeant muttered. He wiped tears from his eyes and said, "That's why we don't fire, Miss. We need to save the cannons for when they attack."

My heart ached with grief and guilt for having yelled at the gunners. I stumbled back to the cave father had dug under mother's potting shed, feeling for the first time that we were all going to die.

Escape from Vicksburg was impossible. A vast Union army, a sea of blue, ringed Vicksburg on the eastern land side (held outside of town by Pemberton's soldiers in their deep trenches), and muddy brown river water and black dots of gunboats fenced us in on the west. Field artillery shells with their high-pitched whine and the bellowing of mortar shells now joined the gunboats in raining death and destruction onto Vicksburg. We were surrounded by a circle of fire!

For the first time, I began to wonder how much food there was here in Vicksburg with us. Enough for us *and* the soldiers? For how long?

When the shelling on May 29 completely destroyed our house and collapsed our small private cave, we moved into one of the large caves dug deep into the yellow clay hillside below Sky Parlor Hill. Mother wept all day and could not be consoled. Over and over she cried, "Why must they destroy everything I love? What have *I* done to them? Why can't they take their fight somewhere else and leave us in peace?"

No one had an answer to her questions. We sat in shock in the pitch-black cave, feeling the ground quiver with each explosion and listening to the whines, the screeches, the thunder, and the occasional screams from those hit—or almost hit—by the bursting shells.

The elderly Groome sisters moved into our cave on June 1. Both white-haired and widowed, they sat beside each other through the long days of shelling. Whenever a shell exploded near our cave, Ethel would ask, "Sister, are you killed?"

"Guess not. I can still talk," answered Eleanor. "And you?"

"Guess not. I can still hear."

Then they would both laugh at the absurdity of it all.

After two days of their unending—and unchanging—prattle, I began to wish a shell *would* strike them. Then I chastised myself for harboring such awful thoughts.

Eleanor was killed the next day by a mortar shell while carrying back a bucket of water. With vacant, lost eyes, Ethel now sits alone by the cave entrance and quietly supplies both sides of the conversation whenever a shell strikes nearby. I dare not get annoyed at her for it. I don't want any more blood on my conscience!

Mr. Cantwell, who lived down the street from us, was shaking hands with a friend one morning when an exploding shell left him splattered with blood and holding a disembodied hand. A 13-month-old girl was killed while taking her first steps. Both parents cheered as their baby girl struggled to walk, and then screamed when a shell ended her life.

Can any terror be worse than this horrible shelling? Oh, God, how I wish it would stop, just for one day, for even one hour of peace!

Wounded soldiers from the fighting along the eastern trenches pile up faster than they can be cared for. Every standing building has become a makeshift hospital.

Every morning, the sound of swishing skirts joins the thunder of the shelling. The women of Vicksburg have vowed to care for each wounded soldier and civilian. Bandages and medicines are scarce. But still they risk their lives every day to venture topside and lavish care and attention on the hurt and dying.

Mrs. Willis was changing a leg dressing on a wounded soldier when a mortar shell crashed through the wall and killed him where he lay. Later that same day she was holding the hand of a badly wounded man when a bursting shell sent shrapnel through the wall and killed him. Now she trembles uncontrollably and moans so piteously that many fear she will die of pure terror.

Mrs. Reyers had, with great satisfaction, just finished tending a row of eight soldiers lying in adjacent beds when an explosion collapsed the wall, killing all eight. She ran into the street screaming and was killed by the next shell.

And still the women proudly march out of our sanctuary caves each morning to comfort and tend the endless rows of wounded.

Deaths now happen much faster than burials. The stench of rotting, decayed flesh fills the air and threatens to overpower the ever-present odor of gunpowder.

May Green has three small children. Her husband is away with General Johnston's army somewhere in Tennessee. She has become exhausted, chasing after her rambunctious boys. With the constant rumble of shellings, they are unable to sit still. Brad, her six-year-old, got away, but couldn't have been out of the long, T-shaped cave more than five minutes when four of us ran out to search. Emma Balfour found him dead and buried under a pile of smoldering rubble. Now May can't stop sobbing and trembling. Other women have had to take care of May's two remaining boys.

And now it is June 10. I am no longer sure there is an outside world. We have been completely cut off from supplies and news for almost a month. Does the world know we are still here—and suffering unimaginable tragedies every day?

Food is critically low. No one gets more than one meal a day. Gnawing hunger is a more constant and disturbing companion than is the endless shelling.

I made a trip to the nearest well to fetch our family's bucket of water for the day. (No one is allowed to wash any longer. With 31,000 soldiers and we civilians, the wells are quickly running dry.) Along the way I noticed that all the birds are gone. Not one song, not one twitter could I hear. The traitors! They have all defected to the Union side where trees and grass still grow unmolested.

I suppose that I would like to join them. But we have all resolved never to surrender. I am now convinced that we will all eventually be killed by the shelling—a few at a time, day after day, until there is no one left to shoot at. With thousands of shells falling on us every day, it seems a mathematical certainty that eventually one will hit me.

June 11. General Pemberton encouraged all civilians to search through the town for unexploded shells. The army needs the gunpowder and explosives inside. Ten-year-old James Colby was killed when the shell he found and struggled to lift exploded in his face. His mother had been proud when he found it and had given him permission to carry it to the trenches on the east side of town. Now she has joined the legion of wailing, grieving mothers who populate so many of the caves.

June 12. There was a lull in the shelling today. Often they stop for a few hours each night. But this was at 5:00 in the afternoon. Jenny Trace, Emma Balfour, and I scrambled up onto Sky Park Hill to watch the evening clouds and breathe some fresh air. The silence was almost deafening. I became nervous and agitated. So did Emma. We realized we missed the noise and vibration of the shelling. It has become a part of us. I wonder if I will ever recover.

June 14. I heard a terrifying story today. One of the caves farther south in town collapsed last night when a shell bounced into the entrance and exploded. Every person in it either died in the explosion or was crushed and buried when the cave collapsed. No one knew it had happened until this morning. By then, relief diggers found only bodies.

June 15. There is no food. How can we survive if we can't eat? Babies chew on dirt. Mothers don't even stop them anymore. Better dirt in their bellies than nothing at all. As awful as it sounds, we have all resorted to eating mule. It's not bad, but there isn't much left. There are no vegetables. All the gardens in town have been destroyed by shelling.

We had a weed salad last night. It was spiny, bitter, and terrible tasting, and I almost gagged. But at least it was *something*. The rock-hard pea bread we have been eating and the sweet potato coffee are also gone. There was a fistfight over a single moldy apple yesterday. Two men went to the hospital because of the injuries they received. One of them later died—all for one moldy apple! The other supposedly shrugged and said, "One less mouth to feed." I am too tired from terrible hunger to go to the hospital and see if it is true.

June 17. I must be growing used to the shelling. Each evening Emma and I sneak out to sit on the hill and watch the shells explode. We pretend it is a fireworks show and applaud the bright bursts and screeching streaks of light.

June 18. I watched a funny confrontation this afternoon. Mrs. Hall has somehow managed to keep one of her dairy cows alive. It has provided needed milk for dozens of children. Two soldiers spotted the cow in a deep hollow where she has been hiding it and wanted to kill it for meat. They had dragged the cow out into the open to make it easier to butcher.

Mrs. Hall attacked them with her cane. Angry words flew back and forth. The soldiers threatened her, but Mrs. Hall became a wild woman. Her cane flashed through the air and both soldiers beat a hasty retreat. A crowd of civilians cheered.

Before Mrs. Hall could lead her cow back to its hiding spot, a shell directly hit the cow and exploded. Mrs. Hall wailed in tormented pain as if she had lost a child and dashed off toward the river bluffs screaming at the gunboats. I never found out what she intended to do.

June 20. I announced to my parents today that I cannot stand living in caves one moment longer and that I intend to sleep in my own house and bed tonight. I said I didn't care that there was no house or bed any longer, I wanted to sleep in them anyway. I am ashamed to say I made a frightful fuss, so that Reverend Jackson, who can barely walk with his wounded leg, hobbled over and told me I could sleep on his pallet near the cave's entrance.

In a huff I stormed over to his spot and spread out across the entire pallet, forcing that kind, elderly, wounded man to lie down in the dirt of the central walkway. But I was in such a state, and feeling so sorry for myself, that I didn't care.

Less than an hour later, a mortar shell buried itself six feet deep into the hill directly above our cave and exploded. We all woke screaming. The wall next to me collapsed and I was buried. Had I been sleeping on my back I would have died. But I was on my stomach and managed to keep a small pocket of air in front of my face.

The cave filled with noise and dust. Everyone choked, gagged, and screamed. The reverend was partially buried and cried for help. Men groped through the dark to the cave-in and dug their fingers raw and bloody to free me.

Sometime during that terrible commotion, a baby was born in the cave: William Siege Green. What must that baby think of the world from his first experience in it?

I trembled and refused to sit inside the cave for the rest of the night, sobbing in the soft dirt at the cave's entrance. I finally calmed down when the reverend hobbled over and thanked me for saving his life. If he had been lying on that pallet, he said, he surely would have died.

Somehow his soothing voice pierced my self-pity and helped me regain my resolve to survive and beat the Yankees. I do, however, have an overwhelming desire to take a bath. Oh, if only there was enough water!

June 22—the 38th day of endless shelling. There was supposed to be a hanging today. Two rail-thin soldiers were caught stealing a chicken that had somehow survived. They were sentenced to be hanged from a tree. The division general finally let them go, saying there wasn't a tree left standing in Vicksburg tall enough to hang them from.

The soldiers have squatted for weeks in mud and dirt trenches under constant mortar, artillery, and rifle fire. They get little water and only one scant meal a day. And still we expect them to bravely fight and struggle to protect us.

I think the general let the men go because he knows that everyone is so tormented by hunger they are going mad. There is a joke going around among the soldiers. The Union is sending in a new general who will surely conquer us: General Starvation. Ha, ha. Some joke.

The two Crandle boys (aged two and four, I think) have lost all fear of the shelling. They used to whimper at the back of the cave and would not go near the entrance. Now shelling has become a part of their normal lives and they boldly scoot outside whenever Mrs. Crandle turns her back.

They both crawled out this afternoon to play with a pair of bright yellow dandelions they spotted. Mrs. Crandle frantically raced after them. The four-year-old twisted away from her grasp, screaming that he wanted to look for butterflies.

A solid shell whined through the sky and smashed through her arm before she could reach out for him again. She stared at her missing limb and laughed, relieved that her son hadn't been holding her hand when it hit. Her children continued to wander, seemingly unaware that she had been hit. She is now asleep and deathly pale. We're not sure she will survive.

June 24. We have to buy water now. Half a bucket per family is the limit. A few sips and some for soup—if we can find anything to make soup out of. Many have collapsed from thirst. It is a terrible thing to be so dry you aren't able to swallow.

Vicksburg now belongs to bombs, death, weeds, and rats. Many have resorted to eating both weeds and rats. We have had our share of weed soup and weed salad, but have not yet stooped to eating rat.

June 26. The rank stench of death has infested every fiber of Vicksburg. Of all the sounds that now haunt my dreams—whining, screeching shells, explosions, the moans of countless wounded and dying—it is the screams of women who have just lost another child that drives me to shivers and cold sweats. I wonder how long it will be before my own mother makes that horrid wail.

June 27. It rained today! What blessed relief! We rushed outside to fill every bucket. I raised my face to the sky and let sweet water fill my mouth over and over. The grime and dirt of weeks without bathing rinsed out of my hair and off my skin.

Many started impromptu dances to celebrate the glorious rain. Mrs. Weimer and her three children were killed when a shell exploded in the midst of their dance. It is a sad commentary on our brutal existence that some asked first if the three buckets of water she had filled survived, and only second whether the people still lived.

June 29. I tried rat today. It made me sick. But I was too hungry to care. It is so frustrating to think that abundant farms with full granaries lie only a few short miles away. And here it is considered a feast to stuff a rat and a weed into the family pot.

June 30—the 46th day of our misery. I have been underground for too long. Humans were not made to endure this. I feel like a grub, like a root, that has been planted in the place of damnation our preacher tells us of. And now I must live like some tendril of a rotting plant and be tormented through all eternity.

July 1. The sun is out. Maybe I'll be lucky and find a juicy rat and we will live for one more day.

Aftermath

On July 4, 1863, at the insistence of his junior officers, who said it was better to surrender than watch their soldiers starve, General Pemberton surrendered the citadel of Vicksburg to General Ulysses S. Grant. He had negotiated the surrender the day before, but waited to make it official until the 4th, hoping that the Northerners would be more lenient on Independence Day.

Some 31,000 soldiers surrendered, with over 200 cannons and 80 remaining mules. The citizens of Vicksburg slowly began to dig out and rebuild their destroyed city under the watchful eyes of the occupying Federal garrison.

Vicksburg had been destroyed, blasted into dust by 47 days of bombardment from over 400 Federal cannons—more than 200 on land and 200 on river gunboats. For over

20 hours a day, often as many as 2,000 shells a day had rained onto the beleaguered city. Fewer than a dozen buildings remained standing. No trees remained. Cobbled streets were buckled into ruin.

Miraculously, most of the town's population survived, living in caves—some hastily dug, some elaborate and fortified with timbers like mining shafts. But the scars of that terrible 47 days never left the hearts and minds of those people.

Several Southern Civil War researchers have quipped that every Southern boy's blood stirs strongest at 1:00 P.M. on July 3, the time at which General George Picket began his fateful charge at Gettysburg. Up until the moment of that disastrous charge, the South had hope; they felt that they could win. Fifteen minutes later, with Picket's division blasted into utter shambles, the South began an unending slide into oblivion.

But actually, the tide turned forever against the Confederacy at 9:00 A.M. that same day when General Pemberton sent a white flag through the lines to begin negotiations with General Grant for the surrender of Vicksburg. Gettysburg was a disaster, but one from which both Lee and the Confederacy could recover. Not so with Vicksburg. Once Vicksburg fell, there could be no hope of a Confederate victory.

With the loss of Vicksburg, the South lost both its only connection to the lands beyond the Mississippi and its ability to deny the use of that great river and highway to the Federal army. The western third of the Confederacy was cut off, including a majority of its remaining productive agricultural lands and the last source of fresh troops to pour into its beleaguered armies.

From July 4, 1863, on, the South would slowly starve, just as the citizens of Vicksburg had during the 47 days of their ordeal. Federal forces now controlled the superhighway of the Mississippi and were free to shift troops south and north at will.

The fall of Vicksburg was truly the straw that broke the Confederacy's back. Coming on the same day as the defeat at Gettysburg, it made July 3, 1863, the bleakest of all imaginable days for the South.

Ironically, Confederate General Johnston had finally decided to come to the relief of Vicksburg. He had issued orders for his 40,000-man force to move west and attack Grant's army on July 7. On July 4, with his army already in motion toward the attack, he had to cancel the order.

Follow-up Questions and Activities

1. **What Do You Know?**
   - Why was the city of Vicksburg important to the South? To the North?
   - Why did the Union gunboats shell the town? Why not just shell the gun emplacements on the bluffs overlooking the river?
   - Why couldn't the citizens of Vicksburg get any food?
   - What is a siege? Why would an army lay siege to a town instead of attacking its defenses?
   - Why did the women of Vicksburg want to care for the wounded and sick even though it meant risking their own lives?

2. **Find Out More.** Following are four important topics from this story for students to research in the library and on the Internet. The reference sources at the back of this book will help them get started.

- Many people have written about their experiences while being trapped in Vicksburg in the early summer of 1863. Find other accounts and compare them to Lucy McRae's.

- The two commanding generals at Vicksburg were Generals Pemberton (Confederate) and Grant (Union). Research the lives, careers, and accomplishments of these two leaders.

- Research the Mississippi River in the 1860s. What was it used for? By whom? How much cargo traveled up and down this waterway? What alternatives existed? In how many places could a large shipment cross the river?

- Compare the experience of Vicksburg to those of other besieged cities during war. Two famous twentieth-century besieged are the Escorial during the Spanish civil war in the 1930s and the city of Leningrad during World War II. How many others can you find throughout history? What happened in each case?

3. **Make It Real**

- What do you think children did to pass the time during the long 47 days of the siege of Vicksburg? Did they play games? What games? Did they mostly sleep? Were they bored or frightened? Imagine being a child your own age living in Vicksburg in May and June 1863. Write a letter describing the events of one day. What would you do? What could you do? What would you want to do? What did you think and feel during this day?

- Lucy writes about the lack of water and eating rats to survive. What are some other ways people in cities under siege have dealt with thirst and starvation? What could you do to survive if you were in this kind of situation? Are there edible plants near where you live? Any accessible sources of water? Brainstorm and come up with a list of sources of food and water to use during a siege.

- Make a map of the Mississippi River showing the original Confederate and Union territories that it touched and dominated. Make a new map for each year of the war showing how parts of the river and adjacent lands changed from Confederate to Union control.

4. **Points to Ponder**

- Is it ethical to bombard a city instead of just the army you are fighting? Is it right to attack a city instead of just the soldiers who have volunteered to risk their lives in combat? Compare the siege of Vicksburg to the World War II bombing of London, Stalingrad, and German cities and to other siege bombardments throughout history. What typically happens to the civilians trapped in a surrounded city?

- Do you think 47 days of constant bombardment would have a permanent psychological impact on the survivors? What effect do you think it would have? How would it change the outlook and attitudes of the survivors?

Home Town Horror
The Battle of Gettysburg, July 1863

At a Glance

In the early summer of 1863, the all-important Confederate stronghold of Vicksburg, Mississippi, was besieged by General Ulysses S. Grant's Federal army. The Confederate government urged General Joe Johnston to rush his army west from Tennessee to directly aid General Alexander Pemberton's force trapped in Vicksburg. General Robert E. Lee was ordered to divert Union attention away from Vicksburg and back to the East.

Lee proposed a sweeping offensive north into Pennsylvania for his Confederate Army of Northern Virginia, hoping such an offensive would accomplish some—if not all—of four goals. First, it would tie up Federal forces in the East to prevent them from sending reinforcements to Grant at Vicksburg. Second, it would take the pressure of feeding both Confederate and Union armies off the back of Virginia for a summer and let the Virginia fields recover. Third, an invasion might push the demoralized Northern population to the point where they began to pressure the federal government to end the war.

Finally, if Lee could decisively defeat a Union army *in the North*, there was a *chance* that he could force Lincoln to come quickly to the bargaining table for peace talks.

With high hopes and light, confident hearts, the three corps of Lee's army swung west behind cover of the Blue Ridge Mountains and headed north through Winchester (Virginia), Hagerstown (Maryland), and up into Pennsylvania.

At the first sign of gathering Union forces, Lee ordered his scattered army (spread in a great arc from the Maryland-Pennsylvania border up to the town of Carlisle, Pennsylvania) to converge.

The easiest spot for all to reach was a small, sleepy farm town where 10 roads intersected: Gettysburg, Pennsylvania. Contact between Confederate and Union armies started when one Confederate brigade marched to the edge of Gettysburg on June 30, 1863, searching for shoes rumored to be available in town. They were pushed back by General John Buford's Union cavalry.

Seemingly within hours, 140,000 soldiers descended on the small town, swelling its population almost a hundredfold. Over the first three days of July 1863, those giant armies fought the biggest, bloodiest, and most decisive battle of the war—all while 2,400 local residents trembled and watched in horrified awe.

This battle at Gettysburg is the best known and the bloodiest of all Civil War battles. It marked the turn of the surging tide against the Confederates, the point from which they would forever retreat, diminish, and fade. Lincoln wrote and delivered his famous Gettysburg Address in memory of this epic battle.

Meet Amelia Harmon

Amelia was born in Baltimore in 1847. Her father was a lawyer who worked for a shipping company based out of Baltimore harbor. Amelia's mother died in childbirth when Amelia was six. Amelia was raised thereafter by hired nannies.

Amelia grew up as a bold and curious child. She was a good reader, but preferred to discover her answers by roaming through the teaming city of Baltimore or through the quiet woods near the spacious Harmon house. She was an erratic student, pouring her vast energy into her studies only if the subject at hand sparked her immediate interest.

Mr. Harmon held abolitionist leanings and was decidedly pro-Union. However, pro-Confederacy fervor permeated Baltimore in 1861. Mr. Harmon feared that Baltimore would erupt into street-by-street violence, and he decided to move Amelia where she would be out of harm's way until the war was over. His older sister, a widowed seamstress, lived in the sleepy farm town of Gettysburg, Pennsylvania. For his daughter's safety, he sent Amelia to live with this sister.

Amelia's aunt, 52-year-old Susan Castle, enrolled the then 14-year-old Amelia in Oak Ridge Female Seminary near her house on the west side of Gettysburg. In the afternoons, Amelia worked for a local cobbler, old John Burns, who was a veteran of the War of 1812.

By September 1863, Amelia grew deeply depressed from the unending sight, sound, and smell of suffering, pain, and death in Gettysburg. She returned to Baltimore a listless girl who rarely ventured from her father's house. She took a small job at her father's shipping company, working there and living quietly at home until just before her 67th birthday.

With World War I looming on the horizon, Amelia's antiwar fervor was stirred to action. She became a crusader against U.S. entry into the war and volunteered to work in the Washington office of Congresswoman Jeanette Rankin, an avowed pacifist.

Amelia died in 1918 at the age of 71. Some said she died just as American boys packed up to fight in Europe because she couldn't bear to see the wounded begin to stack up from another war.

Home Town Horror

Sixteen-year-old Amelia Harmon's trouble started with innocent curiosity on the morning of June 30, 1863. Amelia was the first to spot an approaching dust cloud billowing softly in the West above the trees along the Chambersburg Pike.

Maybe she should have been concentrating on her studies instead of dreamily gazing out the window. But the sleepy farm town of Gettysburg, Pennsylvania, had been buzzing with an electric tingle for a week since word had raced up from Hagerstown that the great masses of Bobby Lee's rebel army had marched through there beginning on June 23.

By the 24th, Lee's army had crossed into Pennsylvania—rebels invading deep into the North! Mile after mile of rebels stomped across the border in a towering cloud of dust that extended far back into Maryland. How could a curious girl concentrate on needlepoint, poise, and grace in the face of news like that? A small column of rebels had even marched straight through Gettysburg heading east on the afternoon of the 26th while Amelia and her aunt had been visiting down near Emmitsburg. Amelia hated having missed the chance to see what fearsome rebels looked like.

When she spotted the dust cloud, Amelia squealed and leapt from her seat, pointing out the window. Wasn't that the natural thing to do? Didn't the Oak Ridge Female Seminary value academic curiosity?

The room exploded into shrieking chaos. Miss Carrie Sheads, the seminary's head mistress, rapped her desk with a ruler and snapped, "Girls! Girls!" But her icy threat was ignored. A big dust cloud boiling over the Western hills meant soldiers marching from Chambersburg and Cashtown, just 10 miles away. It meant rebels coming to Gettysburg!

Miss Sheads aimed her pointer at Ameila. "Miss Harmon, you are responsible for this . . . this unladylike behavior. Report to my office during lunch!"

Her chilling edict could scarcely be heard over the shrieking chaos in the classroom. Many of the 30 girls in the room screamed in honest terror. But Amelia was filled with overpowering curiosity. How could she not be fascinated by these vicious fighters who spread a ripple of terror hundreds of miles ahead of themselves?

Oak Ridge, also called Seminary Ridge, lay just west of Gettysburg. The girls' seminary occupied two stately buildings just south of the larger Lutheran Seminary. Amelia lived with her aunt, Susan Castle, in an elegant two-story house farther south on the same low ridge.

Amelia was about to ask if they could go meet the rebels when Miss Sheads stamped her foot and clapped her hands. "We will act like ladies in this school! Hysterics are a sign of poor breeding. Prudence, dignity, and caution are our guiding words." As always she stood ramrod straight, chin held high, and, even when scolding her girls, sounded gracious. "Line up quickly by the door. Walk with proper decorum and grace, as ladies!"

Gettysburg's mayor, Jefferson Hampton, the short, balding newspaper and print shop owner, burst in, his face dripping with panicked perspiration. "Quick Miss Sheads! Get these girls into hiding. Take the silver. Take everything you value. Lock yourselves in the basement and pray you're not discovered."

The girls shrieked. Miss Sheads clapped her hands. "Dignity, girls."

Confused and curious, Amelia asked, "Why should we hide, Mr. Hampton?"

"My God, miss, they're *rebels*! Pardon my language, but they'll rape, murder, loot, and burn our poor town!"

Startled, Amelia asked, "Did they do that to Chambersburg?"

The mayor fidgeted. "No. . . . But the point is they're *rebels*. They *might* do . . . anything!"

Several girls turned pale and sank to the floor to keep from fainting. Others broke into high-pitched squeals. Miss Sheads clapped once. "Girls. Dignity!" She turned to the mayor. "There are many valuable books and artifacts in this school. Will you help us carry them to the cellar for safety?"

The look of a trapped animal flashed across the mayor's face. His eyes darted from the thinly smiling Miss Sheads to the window and back. His lips twitched. "Sorry . . . I . . . uh. That is . . . I can't." And he fled out of the seminary, sprinting east away from the dust cloud.

"Ladies, begin with the valuable paintings and rare books. Carry them straight to the cellar storage room. I will gather our silver collection."

Girls hurried into the halls to pull paintings from the walls. Amelia crept toward the west door. Georgiana Woolsey, a friend and fellow student, hissed, "Amelia! Don't go outside. You *know* what will happen!"

"Fiddlesticks. I don't believe a word of it." She glanced back and giggled mischievously.

Georgiana blanched and hurried with her painting toward the cellar stairs.

Out on the rolling seminary lawn, Amelia watched tiny dots of humans emerge from the dust cloud as it closed on McPhearson's Ridge, the next ridgeline to the west. Her heart pounded. Rebels!

But the rebel column stopped, sat for a minute, and then retreated back west under its slowly dissipating cloud of yellow dust.

"Fiddlesticks!" repeated Amelia, stomping her foot in disappointment. She turned back toward the school and found Miss Sheads standing sternly on the seminary steps, eyebrow arched in disapproval. "First you create a disturbance, and now you disobey my instructions and endanger all our lives." Amelia felt certain that Miss Sheads's glare was powerful enough to stop the entire rebel army. "Follow me!"

Amelia was marched to the school office and assigned a punishment sampler. She would work on the sampler in Miss Sheads's office for one hour before school, during lunch, and for one hour after school each day until it was completed to Miss Sheads's satisfaction. When finished, the phrase "Rules are a blessing to make my life better" would be stitched in bold letters and hung on the wall next to Amelia's desk.

While the other girls began to haul the seminary's treasures back up from the basement, Ameila furiously drove her needle through the coarse material as if it were a sword and the sampler was an enemy soldier. Why didn't Miss Sheads encourage her curiosity? How unfair to punish Ameila for wanting to learn, to observe.

Before she had made any real progress, Mr. Steven Simpton, a prosperous grain merchant, burst in. "Miss Sheads! Hide everything! Soldiers!" He pointed wildly toward the south.

Miss Sheads allowed a quick, thin smile to grace her face. "The rebels were in the *west*, Mr. Simpton, and they have departed."

"Not rebels, Miss Sheads. Union cavalry is riding in. A whole regiment of them!"

Amelia interrupted, "If they're Union, they're *our* soldiers. Why hide?"

Mr. Simpton gasped, "They're still soldiers, miss. And *cavalry* at that, the worst kind. Lord knows *what* they'll do. Hide everything!"

Again Miss Sheads attempted to smile. "You will help us move our remaining valuables to the cellar?"

Simpton squirmed and dripped perspiration. "I . . . can't. I have . . . responsibilities, you see." And he sprinted back toward town and the safety of his warehouse basement.

The rest of June 30 remained quiet as Union cavalry milled off to the west by McPhearson's Ridge and as the seminary girls sat huddled in neat rows in the basement hall.

Early the next morning of July 1, after an ominous blood red sunrise, Amelia jabbed at her sampler as if trying to punish the material. Miss Sheads reminded her to concentrate on her work. But how could she? Soldiers and armies roamed all about the edges of Gettysburg.

And then Amelia spotted a boiling dust cloud rising over the Chambersburg Pike off to the west. "The rebels are coming back!"

Miss Sheads arched her eyebrow in icy reproachment. "Concentrate on your sampler, Miss Harmon."

"But there's going to be a battle—right here in Gettysburg!"

Miss Sheads drummed her fingers on the desk for a moment before crossing to the window to study the dust cloud inching closer to Gettysburg. "Prudence, caution, and dignity, Miss Harmon. We should seek shelter in the cellar."

Amelia suggested, "I should go home to look after my aunt."

Miss Sheads curtly nodded, "Then good day, Miss Harmon. You are dismissed. School will be suspended until it is safe."

The tension outside was so thick Amelia could feel and taste it in the muggy, oppressive air. The overpowering reek of danger almost bowled her over. Feeling the first tremors of fear, Amelia wondered if she, too, should seek shelter in the cellar or, as her curiosity urged her, drift west to meet a rebel.

Amelia hurried to John Burns's cobbler shop. At 72, Burns was a veteran of the War of 1812 and wise about battles and war. Amelia liked old John and worked for him in the afternoons to make extra money. Surely he would know what to do.

But she found the shoe shop empty, its shelves stripped of merchandise and leather. Gettysburg looked like a ghost town. Everyone trembled deep in hiding. The streets were deserted, the stores silent, the normally busy morning commerce and activity was only a hazy memory. War had arrived, and there seemed to be no room left for normal life.

Now anxious and uncertain, Amelia raced back to school on Seminary Ridge as the first cannons roared and the first massed volleys of muskets rang through the clear morning air.

A flock of startled birds whipped the air as they bolted out of trees along the woods of McPhearson's Ridge. A family of deer galloped past Amelia, running from the din of guns and tramping feet.

Amelia's heart hammered in her chest. This was no place for an unarmed girl. This was war, and the rules Amelia had lived by all her life did not apply here. War was a place to either hide or die.

Amelia pounded up the seminary steps but the double front doors were locked and bolted. A cannonball slammed into the grass a hundred yards away with a bone-jarring crash. It tore a great hole in the lawn as it bounced once and smashed into two trees, snapping one trunk in two.

Around her the whine of bullets and the screams of the wounded filled the air. Amelia hid in thick bushes and pressed her back against the seminary's brick wall, mesmerized by the Union soldiers frantically running and galloping into the thick haze of smoke that covered McPhearson's Ridge to the west. She saw the flash of flame from every cannon blast and felt the crushing concussion of their explosions.

Her heart raced as the battle seemed to creep closer, not on McPhearson's Ridge any longer, but now spilling onto the northern end of Seminary Ridge and into the thick woods straight in front of her between the two ridges.

The 150th Pennsylvania Infantry marched past Amelia speeding toward the woods. Amelia noticed an old, buckskin-clad man marching with them carrying an ancient musket.

"John Burns!" called Amelia. "What are you doing with those soldiers?"

Burns, a bullet wound on one arm wrapped but still dribbling blood, slipped into the bushes beside Amelia as a stray bullet twanged into the seminary wall above them, spraying a shower of dust and brick chips into the bushes. "I'm fightin' fer the Union, o' course. And what are you doin' out here this close to a battle?"

"The school is locked," she answered, then added, "Have you met any rebels?"

Burns patted the barrel of his squirrel gun. "My musket here has met a few this morning in its own special way."

"But you're not a soldier."

"I fought—and even got wounded—in the War of 1812. Well, actually the wound was in 1813. . . ." He hiked one pant leg to show the scar.

"You already showed me," answered Amelia, averting her eyes, not wanting to see it again.

Burns continued. "How dare they try to split apart the Union we fought so hard to preserve? I say, kill every danged one of 'em! Besides, I heard they came here to steal shoes—*my* shoes!" Burns scampered out of the bushes and raced to catch up with the Pennsylvania Infantry.

Amelia called after him, "Is it safe for me to stay here?" The only answer she received was another musket ball that crashed through a seminary window near her, spraying shards of deadly glass across the lawn.

Amelia was terrified and fascinated at the same time. She wanted to run far away, but she was also mesmerized by this new and powerful world of guns, noise, rolling smoke, churning chaos, soldiers, and battles. She pressed her back to the bricks and stayed hidden behind the seminary bushes.

As the sun edged past noon, pelting Gettysburg with its vicious heat, units of Union blue streamed back through town, abandoning the western ridges. Firing on the west side of Gettysburg slowed to a mere trickle. A few locals cautiously drifted out to see the effect of the morning's fighting.

The first Confederate lines advanced to the seminary. Amelia rose from her hiding place and, heart pounding up in her throat, joined several students and teachers from the Lutheran seminary who were watching along the edge of the Chambersburg Pike.

Rebels! Marching straight at her. Muskets with long bayonets were carried at the ready, pointing forward. Amelia's first impression was that these rebels were frightfully lean, scruffy, dirty, and ragged. Many didn't even have shoes, advancing on bare, callused feet. But they also looked happy and confident—even cocky. How could they be so satisfied when they were obviously so deprived?

"Afternoon, ma'am." An older rebel soldier wearing a gold and blue sash touched one hand to his wide-brimmed gray hat. Amelia decided he must be an officer. Several men in the ranks following him whistled and hooted.

Amelia blushed—mostly because she realized she liked the attention from these young warriors, many looking no older than she was.

A concrete block of a sergeant barked at his men and their noise ceased.

These men and boys didn't look like evil, vicious warriors. To Amelia, they looked just like the farm boys around here and like the city boys she had known back in Baltimore.

"It's not safe for you outside, ma'am," said the officer. "You'd best get to cover."

Amelia's curiosity again overwhelmed her caution. She called, "Where are you from?"

But the unit marched past toward the fierce shooting still roaring off on the other side of town without pausing to amuse one young girl. "Virginy!" several soldiers yelled back at her and the others cheered and waved hats. The sergeant barked at them to be quiet.

Amelia was left standing at the road's edge with the first unsettling suspicions that these mighty devils of the rebel army were no different than the boys she had seen dressed in Union blue.

Amelia noticed thin wisps of smoke rising above the ridge in the south and thought of her aunt. Rushing across the fields, Amelia found the house door smashed, windows shattered, endless holes punched in the walls—several big enough to crawl through.

Bullet holes peppered the front walls as if a giant woodpecker had attacked the house searching for a tasty meal. The front porch railing was broken and lay crumpled in the trampled flower beds. Several small fires smoldered in nearby fields where exploding shells had ignited crops.

Amelia found her aunt slumped on the front lawn swing, dazed and staring aimlessly off across the trampled fields. Her voice sounded flat and listless. "A group of Union infantry stopped at the house and asked for water. It seemed so simple and harmless. . . ."

"But what happened to the house?" Amelia exclaimed.

"Then there was a fight," Aunt Susan answered vaguely, as if in a trance. "Federals inside the house. Confederates outside. Just a small fight. No more than 50 Federals and one company of Confederates . . . maybe two . . ."

"But the house is ruined!" squealed Amelia.

". . . Only lasted 10 minutes," continued Aunt Susan in an eerily calm and even voice. "It's over now. It was very noisy, though. They pushed me down—for my own protection, I suppose. I *did* hurt my arm . . ."

"But the house is ruined!" Amelia repeated as her aunt vaguely gazed at a growing bruise on her left forearm.

Aunt Susan vaguely waved toward the house. "Those that can have left, I suppose. . . . The rest will likely want something to eat. . . ."

Amelia stepped into the shattered house and gasped. The hall and both sitting parlors were covered with groaning wounded soldiers. The carpet was soaked in blood. Furniture was gouged, ripped, and ruined. The stifling stench of gore and death had replaced the scents of baking and lilac Amelia had grown accustomed to. Books had been pulled off shelves and used as pillows. Now they were stuck shut, the pages crusted in deep red blood. Every wall had been punctured by musket balls. Paintings had been hacked and punctured.

Blood stained the bottom hem of the floor-length window curtains in the parlor and crept up the silk fabric in shades of red and pink. Amelia's shoes and dress hem dragged through puddles of deep red as she picked her way toward her room, tiptoeing to avoid touching the bodies stacked in every nook and cranny.

Twice bloody arms reached up to clutch at her dress and beg for water and help. Amelia glanced down and found terror and torment etched in the young faces, the same kind of faces that had looked proud and cocky just a few short minutes before. Many faces were frozen in anguished stillness, doomed for eternity to wear a mask of pain and suffering.

It occurred to Amelia that bullets wore neither blue nor gray coats. Bullets, once released, cared not whom or what they destroyed, only *that* they destroyed. Battles were designed to unleash unspeakable destruction, and neither army seemed to care if that destruction spread out to torment the local community along the way.

Blue coats, gray coats—it made no difference. Both had been equally efficient at ruining Aunt Susan's house. Both of their blood was equally capable of destroying the carpet. Both groaned, whimpered, and died no matter whose bullet, shell, or shrapnel struck them.

The house was ruined. Nearby fields were trampled. Fires smoldered unchecked in the woods and pastures. Barns were gutted and stripped of valuables. Livestock were slaughtered or stolen to be butchered for dinner. Grass and flowers were trampled to mud. Fences were smashed. Trees were splintered.

Suddenly enraged by the arbitrary cruelty of war, Amelia stormed away from her aunt's house. On Seminary Ridge near the Lutheran Seminary, she found a Confederate colonel with gold braid crawling across his gray coat. He gazed at Amelia's angry face with soft, kind eyes sunken behind bushy beard and eyebrows.

"Who is going to repair this mess?" she demanded, waving her hand at the trampled fields, smashed and smoldering buildings, and carpet of wounded and dead.

The colonel's eyes appeared sad, even heartbroken, as he gazed around the battlefield devastation that had raged across the west side of Gettysburg. "I'm sorry, miss. I wish it were otherwise. But I'm afraid it is just the fortune of war."

"No," snapped Amelia. "It is the 'fortune' of Elmer McDade whose corn crop and fences were trampled and destroyed this morning. He now has no crop to support his family and livestock. It is the 'fortune' of Susan Castle, my aunt, whose house and furnishings have been wrecked with bullet holes and blood. She and I now have nowhere to live."

The colonel's eyes turned steely. "I care less for the houses and fields than I do for the men who died in them this morning."

"We all feel for the dead and wounded soldiers," said Amelia. "*But* we here in Gettysburg didn't volunteer and march off to war. We didn't ask for a battle. And we will have to live here long after you march off tomorrow."

The colonel glared sternly at Amelia. "First, there are 50 Virginia towns that have been ravaged far worse than this—including Fredericksburg, where I have lived all my life. No one in Gettysburg complained when Union armies destroyed my town. Second, if your town supplied soldiers, food, and equipment to the Union army, then you *did* ask for war and battle. Third, we are not leaving tomorrow. This, I'm afraid, is going to be a big fight, miss. We won't march off tomorrow, and I would find shelter, if I were you." The colonel touched his hat and turned away.

"But . . ."

"Sergeant, get this woman out of here," interrupted the colonel. Again he touched one hand to his hat. "Now if you'll excuse me."

"No, I won't," called Amelia as she was forcibly led off by the sergeant. "You have to end this awful destruction."

The colonel spun in his saddle. "Tell that to your president, young lady. He alone can put an end to this atrocity." His spurs raked back across the horses flanks and the steed galloped away, kicking great clods of dirt back at Amelia.

West Gettysburg had turned into a wasteland of destruction, looking as if it had been struck by the full wrath of a tornado. In a few short hours, war had spat out its fury. Gettysburg was covered in blood, trampled, shot up, and drowning in wounded soldiers.

Were this pain and death the true face of war? Destruction swirled in the wake of battle and glory, destruction that lingered long after the armies and glory had marched on. For armies marched to the call of their drums and after the glory that lay over the next hill and seemed not to care whose town, whose field, whose house, and whose life they trampled and maimed in their frantic search.

A thick dust cloud still boiled over Chambersburg Pike. Rebels continued to pour into Gettysburg against a glowing red sunset. Amelia sighed. So much was destroyed so quickly in battle. How could this sleepy little town ever recover? How would they survive if the armies decided to pound each other and Gettysburg again tomorrow?

And this was only Thursday, July 1. The nightmare that was called the Battle of Gettysburg was only beginning. The worst two days were still to come.

Aftermath

The three-day battle at Gettysburg was truly an awe-inspiring and terrifying event. In a town of less than 2,400 residents, over 140,000 men collided for three days of fighting. It is estimated that cannons fired more than 30,000 times and over 7 million musket balls were fired—a total of over 500 tons of lead were hurled across the fields and streets of Gettysburg.

More than 18,000 soldiers died, and 20,000 were wounded and taken away with departing armies. Another 12,000 wounded were stacked in Gettysburg for care. One-third of those died from their wounds. Over 22,000 corpses, quickly rotting in the fierce summer heat, were left for the residents of Gettysburg to deal with. Over 15,000 severed limbs were stacked to rot in great piles around the battlefield and in the town.

For over a month the town was smothered in wounded soldiers and piles of dead. The stench curled noses miles away. Disease and decay permeated everywhere in town. The water became contaminated from the decaying bodies of men and horses. The town suffered from an acute shortage of medical supplies. Food became scarce with all these extra mouths to feed.

Buildings had been damaged and burned, fields disrupted and trampled, woods stripped and chopped down for firewood. Crops of wheat, peaches, corn, and rye were destroyed for the season. Several farm families were wiped out. It took years to scrub the last blood stains from wooden floors. Some bullet holes were not fully mended for a decade.

Because of the loss of Vicksburg and the western third of the Confederacy, and because of the excessive erosion of the Southern economy, Lee's army was never able to rebuild to its former power after its devastating loss at Gettysburg. The Confederacy was reduced to two hopes: 1) Northerners (especially urban poor) would riot and revolt and force the country to quit the war; or 2) the Northern people would tire of the war and vote Lincoln out of office during the '64 election.

The glory of the Confederacy as a self-determining power was over.

Follow-up Questions and Activities

1. **What Do You Know?**
   - Why did Lee invade Pennsylvania? What did he hope to accomplish?
   - Why did the armies meet at Gettysburg? Was that one of General Robert E. Lee's targets?
   - Why was this battle so important? What would a decisive Confederate victory have meant?

- What was Pickett's Charge? Who was General George Pickett? Who was charging? What were they charging? Why was it important? Did they succeed?

- How many casualties fell on the fields around Gettysburg? How many were left there to be cared for by the local population?

2. **Find Out More.** Here are seven topics that are important to this story for students to research in the library and on the Internet. The bibliography at the back of this book will help them get started.

  - Research the Battle of Gettysburg. Why is it so famous? What happened there on each of the three days of the battle? How much ammunition was shot across those fields? How much gunpowder was exploded? How quickly after the battle did both armies leave Gettysburg?

  - Four Southern generals figure prominently in the battle of Gettysburg: Generals Robert E. Lee, George Pickett, James Longstreet, and Jeb Stuart (Lee's cavalry commander). Research the lives and accomplishments of these four prominent Southern leaders.

  - Confederate General Richard Ewell took command of Stonewall Jackson's corps after Jackson was killed (two months before Gettysburg). Many believe Jackson would have acted more aggressively and decisively and would have won the battle at Gettysburg for Lee. Research the life and career of General Ewell. Did he feel that he failed at Gettysburg? What happened to him during the last two years of the war?

  - Three Union generals (John Buford, Winfield Hancock, and George Meade) and one colonel (Lawrence Chamberlain) figure most prominently in the fighting at Gettysburg. Research these four Union soldiers and discover their lives and accomplishments both before and after Gettysburg.

  - Our annual celebration of Thanksgiving has an important link to Gettysburg. Research the history of this annual celebration to see how our modern celebration began by presidential decree after this historic battle.

  - The town of Gettysburg was devastated by the battle. One day it was a prosperous farming town; the next it was trampled, chopped down, and shot up by massive warring armies. When the armies left, the civilian population was left to tend the broken bodies, bury the mounds of dead, patch their town and shattered fields, and piece their lives back together. Research the experience of this town and other Civil War towns that were the sights of major battles (Fredericksburg, Sharpsburg, Petersburg, Atlanta, etc.). How did they each fare during and after battle?

  - Research the Gettysburg Address, a short speech made by President Abraham Lincoln. Why did he make it? Where did he make it? What was the occasion that caused him to deliver it? What was unusual—even remarkable—about this speech at the time? How was the speech received when he presented it?

3. **Make It Real**

  - Gettysburg is a famous battle in part because of its sheer size. Approximately 140,000 men collided on the fields surrounding this small town of 2,400. How big is 140,000 soldiers? If 140,000 men stood side by side in one long row, how long would that row be? (Assume each man with musket takes 2.5 feet of linear space.)

Pickett's charge involved 15,000 soldiers all advancing on one small spot in the Union line. Allowing 2.5 feet for each person, and assuming they advanced 4 deep, how wide would 15,000 men stretch? What would have to happen in order to wedge them together at one small point of attack, say one-third of a mile wide?

How many Union defenders could you stuff into position of attack only one-third of a mile wide? (Assume that the men were jammed in every 18 inches, but that only the front four rows ever hope to fire at the enemy. Men standing farther back would be firing into the backs of their own men.) Compare the size of these groups with the size of your school, your whole community, with a packed stadium at a major sporting event.

- More than 18,000 soldiers died and 30,000 were wounded during the battle. How do those numbers compare to the population of your school and your town?

- How do you think it would feel to be suddenly overrun by 140,000 soldiers? Would you feel awed, helpless to protect your own community? Terrified? Fascinated? Fearful? Imagine that you are a citizen of Gettysburg and write a letter describing what you saw, felt, heard, and experienced during those three chaotic days of battle.

4. **Points to Ponder**

- The town of Gettysburg was devastated not just by battle but by the burden of wounded and dead afterward and by the need to clean up and repair the damage. Why would an army leave its wounded in the care of a civilian population? Who should take care of battle wounded? Why do you think the military didn't do so at Gettysburg?

- Lee's invasion of the North, which ended at Gettysburg, was a great all-or-nothing gamble. Why did he take such a risk? Why did he scatter his army over 50 miles of roads and allow his cavalry (an army's intelligence) to ride off for a full week? Can you think of reasons why he would and why he shouldn't have?

- Pickett's charge was described as "beautiful" by most—even Union soldiers—with its rows of brilliant flags, countless gleaming bayonets, and eerie silence as troops started forward. It was called a glorious spectacle of might and majesty. Does it seem wrong to you to describe a gruesome and deadly battle as beautiful? Why or why not? Haven you seen paintings or movies of battles that made them look beautiful?

Striking Out
New York City Draft Riots, July 1863

At a Glance

By the summer of 1863, the Civil War had dragged on for two bloody and indecisive years. Calls for new volunteers were not meeting the needed quotas. Most willing volunteers had already enlisted. In response to these recruitment shortfalls, Lincoln instituted the first military draft in federal history. (The Confederacy had started a military draft eight months earlier.)

Politicians in Washington insisted that an escape clause be included in the draft law. A man could either pay the government $300 to buy his way out of military service or could hire an able-bodied replacement. This clause was immediately labeled the "rich man's clause" and was exceedingly unpopular with urban working poor (mostly immigrants—and, most recently, the flood of Irish poor who had settled in virtually ever major Northern city trying to escape famine in Ireland).

These immigrants typically lived in poverty and squalor, always on the brink of starvation, in abysmal tenement housing. They worked long hours at backbreaking factory and other jobs for frightfully little pay—when they could find work at all. Unemployment was high.

Democratic Party leaders decided to use this lower-class unrest to unseat Lincoln in the 1864 elections. Their tactic was to inflame urban immigrant workers against the military draft and, thus, against the war and government in general.

The efforts of the Democrats was made easier when the draft suffered from terrible timing. Scheduled months in advance to begin on July 10, 1863, the draft just happened to begin one week after the bloody fighting at Gettysburg.

The first 1,264 names of the draft were drawn on Saturday, July 11, in New York and listed in the papers on Sunday morning, July 12—right next to the first complete listing of dead and wounded from Gettysburg. Sparks of resentment were easily fanned into flames that roared through New York for three vicious days of riots and mob rule.

Meet Michael Ryan

Born Michael O'Ryan in a small town in coastal west Ireland, Michael completed his apprenticeship as a leather worker in 1856 at the age of 23. He was widely considered to be a skilled craftsman. He married Fiona, his red-haired, green-eyed childhood sweetheart, the next year and they moved to Belfast seeking work. However, business was so bad in Ireland that in 1859 they emigrated to America.

It took seven months for Michael to gather the money, papers, and tickets for the passage. The couple sailed in September 1860 for New York. They carried a few clothes, Fiona's inherited silver pieces, and Michael's leather-working tools.

However, there was no skilled work to be found in New York for new Irish immigrants, even after Michael dropped the "O" from his name to sound more American. By late 1861, their silver had all been sold to keep them alive. Michael could find work only as an unskilled "pack mule" at the docks, hauling 50-pound sacks of grain to and from waiting ships.

Conditions for migrant laborers were so dismal that, during the bitter winter of 1861–62, the whole family of Michael Ryan's best friend (the friend, his wife, and one child) froze to death when no heat was available and no open fires were allowed in their tenement flophouse. Michael was one of the thousands who joined the April 1863, New York dock strike to protest ghetto squalor. The strike was broken when free blacks were imported to do the work. Michael, and the other migrant workers, had to swallow their pride and slink back to work without raises or back pay. But the defeat lingered like bitter bile in the throat of Michael Ryan and other dock workers.

Michael's name was never drawn in the draft. He never joined the army. He worked and lived along the lower east side of New York all his life, where he died at age 53, survived by Fiona and two children.

 **Striking Out**

More than a dozen men crowded into the fourth-floor New York City hotel room. The shades had been drawn to prevent outside observation, and three armed men stood guard at the door to ensure that no one got in. The gas wall lamps cast a dull, flickering glow across the meeting. Two men sat behind a small table. Others clustered on the floor before them.

One of the two men was Fernando Wood, a U.S. congressman from New York and a known Copperhead (a Northerner who supported the Confederacy). A plump man with trim beard, he rocked back in his chair with arms folded and listened as the other man at the table, John Andrews, spoke.

John Andrews was a secessionist evangelical, who regularly spat out inflammatory speeches from street corners and pulpits. His pale green eyes glared with hate even when he tried to smile.

"Gentlemen," Andrews announced, "*this* is our moment. There will never be a more perfect time for us to strike."

The meeting had hastily convened at Andrews's insistence at 7:00 P.M., Saturday, July 11, 1863. Many of the assembled men fanned themselves with sheets of paper. Still, dribbles of sweat trickled down every face in the stuffy room and spread across their starched shirt collars.

"Why now?" demanded Congressman Wood.

Andrews smiled, a sinister glow on his face. He raised the long fingers of one hand to dramatically count off his points. "Three reasons, congressman. First, New York City is unguarded. All the militia units called up to protect the city were ordered to Gettysburg over two weeks ago. None have yet returned. New York is guarded by only a few hundred police."

The cluster of men murmured and nodded. "Second, the great mass of Irish immigrants in New York still seethe from how free blacks were used to break their dock strike in May. They will be an easy mob to ignite."

Again the men nodded knowingly. "Third, I have just been told that the first names drawn by the New York District Draft Board for the national military draft lottery will be published in the paper tomorrow."

An awkward silence spread across the room. The men couldn't see how this worked to their advantage. Andrews leaned hard upon the table. "That list will appear on page 1, gentlemen . . . right next to the first published list of casualties from Gettysburg." Andrews rose to his feet. His gesturing hands whipped the air and seemed to stir the assembled hearts into a frenzy. "The message will be clear. Once your name appears on the draftee list, it will soon appear on the casualty list!"

The men cheered. This suited their purpose perfectly. Andrews's voice rose to a fevered pitch, "Inflame the mob with fear and hate and turn them loose to cripple New York from within!"

The men sprang to their feet cheering. But not Congressman Wood. He thoughtfully toyed with the tip of his cane. "How will an angry New York mob defeat Lincoln?"

Andrews answered, "If an enraged mob can cripple New York City for one week, New York Governor Seymour, who is secretly a supporter of our cause, will declare a state of emergency and will convene the legislature to consider a motion to secede from the union. If New York secedes, the Union crumbles!"

"And how will your men sufficiently inflame the mobs?" continued the congressman.

"These mobs are made up of the most desperate dregs of the city, congressman. We will use three simple messages." His overlong fingers counted them off in the steamy air. "One: Wartime inflation is making their intolerable situation even worse. Don't put up with it. Stop the war! Two: This war is a rich man's war, but poor men's blood is being spilt. The draft exemption proves it. Don't accept the draft or the war! Three." Here Andrews paused and leered. "Three: Free black slaves will stream north to steal your jobs. Don't fight in a war to free blacks who will destroy your livelihood!"

Congressman Wood smiled wryly. "Excellent, Mr. Andrews." He jabbed a finger at Andrews's chest. "Make sure your mobs rule this city by noon on Monday!" He patted his top hat and stepped to the door. "Good evening, gentlemen, and good luck."

"We'll spread the message of fear and hate, congressman," Andrews answered. "Tomorrow's paper will be the match that ignites the fire."

Michael Ryan woke sore and grumpy on Monday morning, July 13, 1863. Not 6:00 A.M. yet and already stifling hot. Words from last night's meeting still rang in his head, buzzing like angry wasps. He shoved the thin sheets aside on their mattress-on-the-floor bed and tried to stretch. Only 30 years old and he already felt like an old man. "Too much work and too little rest," he muttered.

"Finally his lordship decides to rise," countered his wife, Fiona, already up tending to their three-year-old daughter Bridget in the third-floor, walk-up, one-room dump they rented on East 18th Street in New York City. "Maybe if you got home on time you'd be able to rise before the day's half gone."

Michael was a skilled craftsman who thought of himself as an artist and dreamer. But four years of grinding work on the docks of New York, the only work he could find in this new country of opportunity, had ground down his bubbling Irish spirit more than it had his body. "You should have been there to hear the speakers last night, Fiona."

"Maybe I should 'o. But *someone* had to look after Bridget."

Michael scooped up his daughter and spun her through the air while she laughed. "And a fine delight of a daughter she is, too." He winked and added, "Almost as fine as her mother."

"Don't sweet-talk me, Michael Ryan. You were out past midnight!"

"It was the speakers at the meeting, Fiona. And especially that one man . . . somethin' Andrews his name was. He found the exact words to say everything we've been feelin'. All our frustration, all our problems. It's the *war*, Fiona. Every speaker said the same. If we can stop the war, our troubles will be over!"

Fiona shook her flame red hair and laughed. "Oh, is that all? So you'll hustle out and end the war on your way to work this mornin', will ya?"

Michael struggled in vain to remember the speaker's words, and how they had made it sound so perfectly right. "It's the draft, Fiona. If we can stop the draft with one great protest, then the war will *have* to end and we'll get better pay and better jobs."

"So you're going to protest today instead of work, Michael?" Fiona demanded. "We could use a bit of money."

He shook his head and struggled into a pair of work pants. "I have to go, Fiona. It's my duty—the speakers said. The draft isn't fair. The war isn't fair."

Fiona rolled her eyes toward the ceiling. "And what has fair got to do with life in America?"

Michael struggled to remember the words of last night's speaker. "The rich men don't have to fight. They can *buy* their way out. That's not fair. If we win the war, free blacks will steal our jobs. And we're the poor blokes who have to bleed and die! It's *wrong*, I'm telling ya'."

Fiona shook her finger at her husband. "Sounds fine and dandy, Michael. But war or no war, there will always be boss men who try to cheat the working poor."

Michael leaned toward the wall and yelled to his friend Rory O'Bryne. "Are you ready, Rory, lad?" The walls were so thin, there was no need to pound. Rory O'Bryne had been a prized carpenter in Ireland who now worked hauling fish off boats for an eastside packing plant.

The two men, and eight others from the 24 units in their building that had been a fashionable single-family home before the owner got greedy, emerged into the summer grime of New York to an overcast, hazy day that felt like a steam bath. The rally was gathering at the corner of 3rd Avenue and 28th Street. When Michael and Rory pushed into the back row, a speaker, standing on a stage made of several packing crates, was already reaching his climax for a shouting mob of 200 men and women—mostly working immigrants from every country in Europe.

"Are you going to spill your blood while rich men pay their $300 and sit safely on the side?" The speaker yelled, "Are you going to spill your blood to free slaves who will rush to New York to steal your jobs? Are you going to let your living conditions get even worse?" The intersection rumbled with a fierce "No!" after each question.

"Then stop the military draft today! With bricks and stones and fire show your elected officials you demand *out* of the war!"

A great cheer erupted from the crowd. Bricks and paving stones were torn loose from buildings and streets with crowbars and sledgehammers. Clubs and bats were waved overhead.

"To the district draft office!" screamed the speaker, pointing north toward 46th Street. The crowd surged up 3rd Avenue. The speaker melted into the background and slid, unnoticed, down a side alley to gather a new mob a few blocks away.

The ranks of the angry mob grew to almost 500 as fed-up workers walked off their jobs in factories and packinghouses and joined the noisy crowd. Michael swelled with a feeling of power. The bricks swinging in his hands felt like votes that would finally mean something when he cast them. He felt that he and the men rushing grim-faced with him up 3rd Avenue weren't the lowly scum of the city. To Ryan, they seemed like noble crusaders for justice.

Michael bellowed at the line of 60 policemen that blocked the mob from reaching the 9th Federal District Draft Office at 46th Street and 3rd Avenue. He could feel the pulsing fury of the crowd. He was part of that fury.

"Disperse immediately and go home, or you'll be arrested!" shouted the police captain.

But Michael's valiant crowd would not be calmed. Not by threats, not by orders to disperse. Someone yelled "Fire!"

The air filled with bricks and stones. Like deadly hail, the brick missiles rained upon the police line. Fifteen policemen crumpled to the street. Others stooped to help the fallen back to their feet or to tend their wounds.

Someone yelled "Charge!" The crowd yelled and rushed forward. Michael didn't feel that they were doing anything wrong. It was like the speakers had said, this was their true duty to their families and their people.

The police scrambled back up the street to avoid being slaughtered, abandoning the draft board office where the draft lottery drawings were still in progress. Office workers tumbled out rear windows to escape as front windows and doors disintegrated in a shower of bricks and stones.

The Irish mob ransacked the building, searching for any valuables they could steal and destroying all equipment and records of the draft board. Before the crowd shuffled back into the street, black smoke curled thick from the upper floor windows. The crowd cheered as the draft building burned.

Michael found Rory deep in the crowd. "Now there's a message against the draft they won't be forgetting for a long while! I'm goin' to tell Fiona before I try for some work on the docks."

"This isn't the end, Michael. It's only the beginning," answered Rory with a fierce gleam in his eyes.

Someone yelled, "Get the blacks! They're to blame for our troubles!"

An intensity spread over Rory's usually friendly face. "Can't back out now, Michael. The job's only half done. Like the speakers said, the blacks got to get the message they can't take our jobs. And we're the ones that have to give it to them!"

"No, Rory. We just planned to protest the unfair draft," Michael began.

But another man yelled, "I know where some blacks live on Lexington Avenue. Let's go!"

The crowd cheered and surged down 46th toward Lexington.

"Rory, we've done our part," Michael pleaded.

"Either you're with us," snapped his friend, "or you're with the blacks."

Several others in the crowd turned menacingly toward Michael.

"I work on the docks and hate blacks just like the next man," Michael insisted.

"Then come on! We've got to tell them they can't take our jobs like they did this past spring."

Michael was drawn back into the mob flowing toward Lexington.

On Mulberry Street, they found a second, smaller mob confronting a line of police. Wearing gold braid on the visor of his hat, City Police Superintendent Anthony Kennedy stood behind the line, shouting orders. Michael's great mob roared around the corner, pushed aside the smaller protest, and smashed into the police line. Irish men and women lined one roof across the street, hurling their brick missiles down at the police. As the police line tumbled back in chaos, one rock struck Superintendent Kennedy. He crumpled on the sidewalk.

Before the police could regroup and push forward to rescue their chief, Kennedy was surrounded by the angry mob. For one brief fraction of a second the crowd stared at the chief, struggling to his knees, blood streaking down his face. Then someone yelled, "Kill him!"

Clubs and rocks crashed down and the police superintendent lay dead in the gutter.

Michael stared in horror at the bloody corpse as the crowd around him cheered and hurled a new volley of stones at the policemen clustered half a block down the street. "Lord have mercy! What have we done?"

Rory grabbed Michael's arm and shook him hard. "He tried to stop our legitimate protest."

"But that was . . . *murder*, lad. We *killed* him." Michael flushed with shock and shame as he said the words.

Rory snarled, "Either you join us, or you join *him*!" Again the crowd cheered and flowed back onto Lexington.

Smoke rose high into the New York sky a few blocks farther north, evidence of the work of another mob gathered and inflamed by the talented speakers. Sirens wailed farther south and east, announcing the presence of other mobs roaming the city.

Progress down Lexington was slow. There were a number of bars on this part of Lexington Avenue. The crowd flooded into every one of them demanding free drinks. If the owner refused, the place was smashed and looted.

Two men pointed at a stately, three-story house in the middle of one block. "That's the one!" A barrage of rocks smashed through the front. Torches followed on the second wave. The house caught fire as the mob, now numbering over 1,000, cheered. A few raced to the front porch hoping to slip inside and loot the place before flames drove them back.

Fire alarms sounded. The mob turned on the approaching firemen heaving rocks and liquor bottles at the horse-drawn fire engine. One horse was killed and one crippled by the barrage. The firemen fled, abandoning the rig.

Women and children crawled out back windows of the burning house. Someone cried, "They're white, not black! This must be the wrong house." Then someone yelled, "But they were rich and could pay to get out of the draft."

A new round of paving stones crashed into the burning house and the crowd danced and cheered until the house collapsed and sheets of flame spread to the houses on either side.

A 40-man detachment of the Invalid Army Corps arrived in wagons and deployed on Lexington Avenue to block the mob's progress. The Invalid Corps were crippled and maimed soldiers who still wanted to serve and had volunteered for home guard duty.

"Get 'em!" someone yelled and the mob surged forward. The corpsmen fired one warning volley just over the heads of the mob. They were answered with a massive volley of bricks and stones that left 4 soldiers dead and 13 severely wounded. The rest hobbled into their wagon and sped off in retreat.

"We need guns," someone cried.

"To the armory!" another voice yelled. The crowd cheered and turned toward the armory at 21st Street and 2nd Avenue.

The mob continued to grow like a living, hissing, out-of-control beast. A trail of shattered glass, looted stores, and ransacked bars littered the monster's path. Smoke billowed into the sultry sky from a dozen fires, evidence of activity by other mobs in the city.

Many wives joined in the frenzied crusade, chiding, pushing, urging their men on to greater acts of savagery.

William Jones, a black barber, had been walking toward his home in Greenwich when the mob found him cowering in an alley. They dragged him into the street and beat him until he dropped senseless to the pavement. Then they hanged him from a lamppost and set the corpse on fire. Many in the crowd pranced around the human torch chanting, "Hooray for Jeff Davis!"

"Who's Jeff Davis?" someone asked.

"President of the Confederacy," the answer was shouted.

Michael grabbed Rory and shook him hard, as if that could stop the madness. "For God's sake, man. He never did anything to us."

"He's black!" Rory answered. He squirmed away from Michael's grasp to run after the mob as it approached the Federal Armory at 21st Street and 2nd Avenue. Sixty-four policemen of the elite Broadway Squad stood guard at the front of the building.

A runner from another mob announced that they had burned a black orphanage at 5th Avenue and 43rd Street. The fierce cheer of the crowd, now numbering almost 3,000, reverberated off the brick high-rise buildings, striking fear into people a dozen blocks away.

Wave after wave of bricks and stones assaulted the police line. The police shielded their bodies and fired back as best they could, but the rumbling tide could not be stopped. The surviving police retreated inside the armory and out the back to safety. A third of their number lay dead on the bloody sidewalk at the armory stairs. Their bodies were kicked and trampled as the crowd surged into the building.

A thousand muskets and rifles were stored in the armory. The crowd seized every one before they burned the building. Sirens wailed across the city. But there were no reinforcements to quell the riots. Smoke hung thick over New York and blurred the sun into a dingy orange blot.

Michael grew increasingly terrified by the random and vicious violence. This was no protest. This was a wild war against all humanity. "This is a bloody revolt, Rory," he pleaded. "We have to go."

"Aye, lad," Rory answered. "We have to *go* get cartridges and musket balls for these muskets and then 'go' where they'll do some good."

Tears welled into Michael's eyes. "But we're killing innocent . . ."

"No one is innocent. Not in this city," Rory interrupted.

Someone yelled, "They caught another black!"

A great cheer arose as the crowd surged around a corner. While looting a store, some men had found Abraham Franklin, a 60-year-old crippled coachman hiding in his two-room flat upstairs. They hanged him from a lamppost and chanted "Jefferson Davis! Jefferson Davis!"

Michael pulled away from the crowd and collapsed into the street, weeping. This mob no longer stood for justice, for families, for ending the war. This was savage, brutal madness. A wild insanity had seized the city as the sun sank low in a blood red haze and had turned hard-working, honest men and women into vicious beasts.

A runner arrived to announce that a force of 300 police had been ambushed 10 blocks farther uptown by another mob. They had been trapped in a narrow street while men and women in windows and on roofs hurled deadly bricks and stones upon them. Fifty policemen had fallen before the crowd was driven back by fierce gunfire.

Another runner urged everyone to march to the *Tribune* building for a night attack to destroy that newspaper. The crowd cheered, waved their empty guns, and flowed uptown.

Michael grabbed Rory as he marched past. "Don't go, lad. This is wrong!"

Rory's eyes flashed wild and fierce. "They want a fight? Well then, come on! I'll give 'em a fight they won't forget!"

"We're slaughtering innocent women and children. No good can come from this."

"If that's what it takes to gain some respect in this town, I'll burn every building in this city before I knuckle under again!"

"But you'll all be arrested or killed," Michael sobbed. "This has gone too far. It's against the law."

"We're *making* the law," Rory answered.

Michael sat alone in the gutter for hours that night, smelling the rolling smoke of billowing fires, hearing the distant wail of sirens and the angry rumble of mobs. He wept bitterly for the brutal horror of this day and for the awful state their lives had descended to. Life wasn't fair. America wasn't fair. The war wasn't fair. But this protest wasn't fair either. It was a world gone mad, and Michael Ryan was afraid.

Aftermath

During the three days of vicious rioting in New York, 319 died including 43 blacks brutally murdered by the mobs. Over 1,600 people were injured. Over 80 buildings were burned, and over 150 were looted and ruined. Some 900 blacks had pounded on Manhattan police station doors begging to be let in to hide in jail cells. Almost all had been turned away to fend for themselves on the street.

On Thursday, July 16, John Andrews was arrested for treason and inciting a riot. The mobs created by Andrews's vision of fury and hate were never organized well enough to truly control the city. Still, for almost three days the rioters were free to roam while other citizens cowered and fled.

Michael returned to his wife and his one-room apartment, to his subsistence job on the docks, and to the miserable life he had known before, just as if the riots had never happened. Rory O'Bryne was badly wounded and captured late Wednesday afternoon and was jailed for life, having been charged with being a leader of the insurrection.

The New York draft riots were over. But the Union was badly shaken by their strength and violence. Support for the draft dipped dismally low. New York State officials begged Lincoln to postpone the draft for at least six months. The New York city council considered raising enough money to pay the $300 exemptions for all 1,264 names on the initial New York City draft list. Smaller, more peaceful protests in other cities continued for months.

While many of the New York rioters were recent Irish immigrants (having fled to America to escape the famine in Ireland), most Irish supported both the draft and the war. Almost 150,000 Irish Americans served in the Union army. One of the all-Irish brigades, the 2nd New York, became one of the most highly decorated and toughest brigades in the Army of the Potomac. Irish Americans made significant contributions to the country and to the war. It is unfortunate that their lowly position on the socioeconomic ladder left many vulnerable to the inflammatory rhetoric of John Andrews.

One positive development emerged from the New York draft riots. Most of the nation was appalled at the vicious abuse of blacks during those three days. Support for blacks in general and for abolition in particular rose markedly after the riots.

Follow-up Questions and Activities

1. **What Do You Know?**

   - Why did the New York riots occur? What were the rioters protesting? What were they trying to accomplish?

   - Who rioted? Why this particular group? Was this same group involved in any of the draft riots in other cities?

   - Why didn't the military quickly step in to quell the New York civil disturbance?

   - Why were blacks a prime target of the rioters?

   - Why did the riots fail to achieve any lasting changes?

2. **Find Out More.** Here are some topics that were important to this story for students to research in the library and on the Internet. The bibliography at the back of this book will help them get started.

   - The July 1863 New York draft riots were the biggest and most violent of the protests against the military draft, but they were far from the only protest. Research the New York riots as well as draft riots in other Northern cities. Were the complaints the same in each of the riots? Were the results the same?

   - Only a small portion of the New York draft riots is described in this story. Research the day-by-day events as the riots unfolded. What stopped them? What kept the riots from growing bigger?

   - Research New York City at the time of the Civil War. What was the population? Who was in charge of the city's government? Try to find a map of the city at the time and locate where the riots took place.

- This story describes a riot organized to protest the Civil War. Were there other social, economic, or political reasons to protest—even to riot—in America in the 1860s? What were they and how were they addressed?

- The New York rioters voiced a number of legitimate, important grievances. Make a list of these grievances and research them to see if, and how, they were addressed by federal, state, and city authorities.

- A growing antiwar sentiment existed in the North by 1863. Who still supported the war? Who opposed it? How popular was the war in 1863? In 1864? Did opposition to the war make it harder for Lincoln to continue the war effort? What effect did the opposition have?

- Research the Civil War drafts (Federal and Confederate). Why were they instituted? Why did the Federal draft include provisions for people to buy their way out of military service? Who insisted on the two "rich man's" buyout clauses? Compare the Civil War drafts with those enacted for other U.S. wars. Have other drafts caused riots? When? What happened?

- When were military drafts first used and by whom? What countries have military drafts and mandatory military service today? When was the last time the United States held a military draft? When and why was it abolished?

- Research other civil protests in America. What events and policies have sparked civil riots? What has been the outcome of those riots? See how many you can identify and document.

3. **Make It Real**

   - Are there policies at your school or in your community you would like to protest? As a class identify one law, rule, or policy you want to protest against. Carefully build your argument against this policy. What policy would you substitute in its place?

     Now design a protest to publicize your collective views and arguments. How will you protest? What will you do? What won't you do as part of your protest? Are there limits to what is appropriate behavior and action as part of a protest? How will you make sure your protest is not inflamed into a riot? Did the process of identifying, designing, and conducting your own protest help you better understand the New York draft riots?

   - Make a detailed timeline of major American events during the years 1862 and 1863. What was happening in the war and in the country that precipitated the drafts and the violent protests against the draft? Do you think Lincoln should have been able to anticipate that there would be serious opposition to the draft law?

   - Calculate what the $300 buyout amount in 1863 would be worth in today's money. If people could buy their way out of military service during a draft today, what amount of money do you think would be appropriate for a modern buyout?

4. **Points to Ponder**

- Do you think it is morally and ethically appropriate for a government to require that young people serve in its armed forces? Do you think having an all-volunteer army is preferable? Why? Can you think of advantages and disadvantages of each system?

- Riots are an extreme version of a protest. Virtually all agree that protests are legal and legitimate. Do you think that planned, intentional riots are ever legitimate and justifiable? When? Why or why not? Are they ever effective in forcing changes?

- What is the difference between a protest and a riot? Between a riot and a revolt?

Sounding Battle
The Life of a Drummer Boy at the Battle of Chickamauga, September 1863

At a Glance

Our visions of Civil War battles typically include lines of hardened soldiers, countless long muskets with gleaming bayonets, fire and smoke belching from rows of cannons, and fields covered in blood and bodies. We hear haunting rebel yells, the deafening roar of cannons, and the continuous din of massed musket fire. Yet we should include in that image drums and picture 12- or 13-year-old boys marching bravely into battle with those lines of soldiers.

Both sides of the Civil War used drummer boys. Regimental drummers were supposed to be at least 16 years old. Battalion or company drummers were often as young as 12, with a few as young as 10. Some of these boys were treated like mascots, some like regular soldiers. Regimental drummer boys were paid a regular soldier's wage. Drummer boys for smaller units were paid by the unit with whatever they could raise.

About 40,000 musicians enlisted in the Union army, 20,000 in the Confederate. Some were musicians in division and corps bands. Most were drummer boys. Drummer boys served as a communications link between a commander and his soldiers. Officers couldn't shout loud enough for 800 men to hear amid the din of battle. But those soldiers could all hear a pounding drum. Reveille, taps, assembly, chow—all the routines of camp life were announced on the drums. So were marching and drill commands as well as battle commands. Drummer boys marched into the thick of battle, armed only with their drumsticks and courage, while the long lines of soldiers and the outcome of battles depended on how well they performed their communications duties.

After the fall of Vicksburg and the defeat at Gettysburg (both in the summer of 1863), the Confederacy was desperate for a victory. Confederate General Braxton Bragg (in Tennessee) itched to provide that victory even as he retreated slowly from Tennessee, leading almost 55,000 rebels into north Georgia in early September 1863. Opposing Bragg was Federal General William Rosecrans with his 50,000 men.

Bragg was hungry for victory. But, more important, if Rosecrans was not stopped, he would cut deep into Georgia and thus the heart of the Confederacy. General Rosecrans's leading regiments stopped near a meandering creek in northwest Georgia called the Chickamauga. As reinforcements under General James Longstreet poured in to swell Bragg's ranks on September 17, he knew the time was right to strike. Battle was at hand.

Meet Ephram Dillard

Ephram Dillard was born in Biloxi, Mississippi, in August 1850. His father was a gulf fisherman and shrimper. Called "Efi" by his parents and friends, Ephram dreamed of being a soldier while perched in the back of his father's fishing boat and taught himself to drum on an oil can. He tried to enlist when he was only 10 years old, in 1861, but was laughed out of the recruiting line. Efi's father beat him for trying to enlist without permission, saying it wasted the army's time and made a laughingstock of the family.

When a great push for new recruits rolled through Alabama and Mississippi in the spring of 1863, Ephram slipped out without asking permission and tried to enlist again. This time he lied, saying that he had permission, and signed on as a drummer boy.

Three companies were formed in Biloxi that May. Ephram was brought along as their drummer boy with his parents' grudging permission. He quickly picked up two new nicknames from the soldiers: Dillweed and Shortbread. (Efi only stood 4 feet, 10 inches.)

The new companies trained for three months near Hattiesburg, Mississippi, before being shipped north to join Bragg's army as it retreated out of Tennessee into northern Georgia. Just in time for their first test in battle—Chickamauga.

Ephram's unit also saw action on Missionary Ridge and later in the defense of Atlanta. Ephram survived the war and, as a veteran soldier at the age of 14, returned to Biloxi to help in his father's fishing business.

At the age of 17, Ephram tried to join the U.S. Army but was rejected for being too young. He fished the rich waters of the Gulf of Mexico until, in 1917, at the age of 66, he volunteered to be a drummer for the army in World War I. He was rejected one last time by the army and died two years later, the last living veteran of the 18th Mississippi Infantry.

Sounding Battle

Captain Joshua Stalter rushed back into the makeshift rows of white tents occupied by his three new volunteer companies. He breathed deeply to calm himself before saying to the boy sitting outside the orderly tent, "Shortbread, sound assembly. Colonel's on his way."

Thirteen-year-old Ephram Dillard scrambled to his feet and tried to smooth his over-sized, gray uniform coat. His family called him "Efi." He had already picked up two more nicknames in the army: Dillweed and Shortbread. No one called him Ephram. Efi looped his drum harness around his neck and leveled the drum surface at his waist.

In imitation of his captain, the boy sucked in a slow breath to calm himself. Still, his heart pounded and his mouth felt uncomfortably dry. He'd only been in the army since May—less than four months—and was just beginning to feel comfortable with the army's 30-plus commands on the drum.

Now the training was over. The colonel was coming to welcome them into the 18th Mississippi Infantry Regiment. From now on, it would be *real*. Suddenly it actually felt like war!

Efi breathed in deeply one more time and pounded assembly on his drum. To Efi, his drumming this day sounded sharper, crisper, and more warrior-like than it ever had before.

Gray-clad soldiers scrambled out of tents and away from card games and cook fires. They snatched hats, caps, and muskets and jostled into line. Lieutenant Harold Packard (barely old enough to shave) stomped along the lines, barking orders. "Line up. Get yer interval. Dress right! Look sharp."

Sergeant William MacInnerny (a burly 6-foot, 5-inch giant called Mace and the jokester of the company) let the butt of his musket inch forward as he stood in his position at the end of the front rank, so that Lieutenant Packard stumbled over it and almost fell as he raced back and forth hollering at the troops. Packard glared at Mace, whose innocent face betrayed no hint of his guilt. Frustrated, Packard turned to the men next to Mace, then scowled at the interior ranks, who were struggling to suppress a laugh. "Rifle butts back next to your heel! Quiet in the ranks! Dress right!"

"That'll do, Shortbread," Captain Stalter whispered to stop the drumming, and then glowered at Lieutenant Packard. The captain bellowed, "Companies, attention!"

Three companies snapped to attention.

Efi, as always, was impressed by how the captain knew which syllables to draw out (the end of "companies" and the middle of "attention") and which to bark hard and fast.

As Colonel Samuel Wood, regimental commander, trotted his horse into the new companies' area, Captain Stalter bellowed, "Present arms!"

The soldiers' 250 left hands slapped onto their musket stocks as the rifles and gleaming bayonets were raised in salute. The officers flashed their swords up and then down in a sweeping arc.

Colonel Wood stopped in front of the companies astride his mount. His battle-hardened, steel gray eyes critically appraised these replacements for his regiment. He nodded to Captain Stalter and casually saluted.

Captain Stalter barked, "Order arms!"

Like a clap of thunder, the 250 hands again slapped the musket stocks. With a ground-trembling thud, 250 muskets simultaneously hit the soft Georgia grass. Efi swelled with pride, knowing they had presented themselves to their new commander like true professional soldiers.

Colonel Wood stood in his stirrups to speak. "You have trained well over the last several weeks. You're in General Cleburne's division now, the fastest-shooting division in the Confederacy. I expect you to uphold our standards for rapid, accurate fire." He paused for a rolling cheer from the ranks. "Men, there's going to be a scrap—a *big* scrap—within the next day or so."

To the assembled replacements, the colonel seemed to look forward too eagerly to battle. To him, these new troops seemed young, raw, and overly nervous. He cleared his throat and tried to exude bright confidence in his smile "For most of you this will be your first battle. Hold your lines. Follow commands. Listen for the drum signals. You'll do fine."

Colonel Wood paused, his gloved hands clasped on his saddle pommel, searching for something else to say that would give these new bucks confidence in his command, but couldn't find it. "That's all. Dismissed." Then he added, "Kill Yankees!" and rode off toward brigade headquarters.

The replacement soldiers whooped and cheered, waving hats and muskets as they watched the colonel's dust billow softly in the air above these fields just east of a meandering stream called Chickamauga. But they each also felt an icy fear. Battle was coming.

In camp on that brisk afternoon of September 18, 1863, the new companies were both louder and quieter than usual. Battle was coming! Every ordinary word and movement felt electrically charged. Each stale joke seemed funnier and had to be told louder and laughed at harder. Every sparkle of fall color on the surrounding trees seemed more precious and beautiful. Every musket barrel needed an extra coat of oil. Every spring needed an extra testing. Battle was coming!

Through the late afternoon Efi heard sporadic firing from fierce cavalry clashes—a sure sign of coming battle. The replacements nervously grabbed for their muskets each time the firing flared. Veterans from other companies laughed, "The armies are just closing up a bit. No need to jump out of yer skin." Then they added, "yet," and winked and laughed.

Mace ran an afternoon poker game on a tree stump they used as a table. Patrick Lyman, called Ace—a hard-drinking, card-playing son of a Mississippi Baptist preacher—was dealing the deck.

Efi sat near the raucous game, tuning and testing the stretched hide on his metal drum.

"Dillweed, come over here," called Sergeant James Peck, a tough bully feared and disliked by most in the company, as he puffed on his root-briar pipe. "You don't know the pleasure of tobacco, Dillweed. I figure you ought to get a taste in case you die tomorrow."

"Leave the boy alone," growled Mace, his brow furrowed in concentration as he studied his cards and the others spread across the tree stump.

"I don't want our drummer to enter battle without knowing the joys of tobacco," Jimmy Peck insisted. He held out his pipe, a thin stream of gray smoke curling from the bowl. "Here, Dillweed, take a puff, and know real joy."

Efi had been curious about tobacco for months. Most soldiers craved and cherished their tobacco. "I guess I just might," he said, trying to sound brave and grown-up.

The poker crowd hooted. Ace Lyman leaned back from the tree-stump table and waved a curved, metal flask. He took a long swig and said, "Might as well do it all and try a snort of moonshine as well, Shortbread."

"Leave him be," snapped Mace.

Lyman shrugged, sucked down another mouthful of liquor, and slipped the flask back inside his boot.

Efi reached out and took the pipe. He paused, unsure, while a dozen faces eagerly watched. Then he jammed the stem in his mouth and sucked hard.

A monstrous, hacking cough exploded from Efi's lungs. The pipe shot forward like a musket ball. Efi dropped to his knees, doubled over, gagging and retching. The gathered crowd roared. For a full minute no one thought of the coming battle.

Mace glared at Jimmy Peck. "I said to leave Shortbread alone. He'll face plenty enough tomorrow without you making him sick."

Peck retrieved his pipe. "I was just havin' fun with the boy." He clapped Efi on the back.

Long shadows flowed out to the rear of the Confederate camp as Efi stumbled to the canvas tent he shared with three other soldiers. He felt light-headed and nauseated and had trouble walking. He shoved his drum inside and collapsed with a deep groan onto his blanket.

Soon Efi heard Sergeant James McRae calling. Sergeant McRae had fished with Efi's father and had promised the family to watch after their boy. "Efi, get a move on. Haul up water and bring up firewood. Let's go!"

Efi struggled outside, still feeling woozy. "Why do I always have to fetch and haul?"

"You're a musician, not a soldier. It's always musicians' job to support the troops."

Efi shouldered two buckets and headed for the stream. On his way, he watched the thin lines of smoke from Confederate campfires rise like a forest of tree trunks to mingle with the fingers of growing mist. Then he froze. Farther west, beyond the Chickamauga, up against the steep western ridge, he saw other tree trunks of smoke rising into the sky. Union fires! The enemy was *that* close!

Efi's heart pounded and his hands trembled. He tried to concentrate on the simple task of carrying water to keep his mind from racing ahead to tomorrow.

"Hey, Dillweed, you finally gonna take a turn and cook something for us tonight?" Ace Lyman called as Efi struggled back into camp under the weight of the water. Lyman said it every night. Usually it was annoying. Tonight, its familiarity comforted Efi.

"I know how to cook fish and shrimp real good," Efi answered, as he always did.

"We ain't got no shrimp. Just beans, peas, corn bread, and pork."

Efi smiled and shrugged—as he always did. "I don't know *anything* about how to cook those." Lyman smiled and reached out to gently punch Efi's shoulder. "You'll do fine tomorrow, Shortbread."

The camp grew quiet as darkness settled over the valley. Men clustered closer to their fires, wondering how they'd react in battle, how it would feel to be shot, how it would feel to be frightened. Efi couldn't sleep and wandered out to sit with Mace and Ace Lyman.

Mace said, "Sorry about Peck and his tobacco stunt."

"I always wondered what it was like," Efi answered. "Now that I know, I don't reckon I'll need another puff."

Both men smiled and stared at the fire.

"Mace, will you be scared tomorrow?" Efi asked barely above a whisper.

Mace snorted as he rocked back on his log seat. "Me? Why it's just Yankees over there."

Efi pretended to carefully prod the fire with a stick. "I ain't never been *really* scared afore . . . afore now. Have you?"

"Me? Scared? Oh, why, plenty of times. Well, at least *once* I was. See, I was trapped in a bog surrounded by six bull gators—*big* gators, I mean. And . . . well, no. I take it back. I weren't scared then neither. Well, maybe I *ain't* never been scared. But, then, ain't been nothin' worth being scared of."

Several men laughed. One threw a blanket at Mace.

"What's it like?" Efi asked, still staring at the red embers deep in the fire.

"Bein' surrounded by gators?"

"No. A battle."

"Ain't rightly sure. But I reckon it's loud and hot with lots of shooting and yelling. Some'll get killed, I guess. That's about it."

Efi nodded. "I can handle that."

Captain Stalter wandered by. "Get some sleep, Shortbread. We don't want a groggy, half-asleep drummer in the morning."

It seemed only a moment later that a sentry shook Efi and said the captain wanted him to sound reveille in the pitch-black, icy-cold predawn of Saturday, September 19. Efi lifted his few possessions out of his drum, hauled it outside, and strapped it on.

Captain Stalter was already up and dressed. "Let's go, Shortbread. Get 'em up."

The brain-rattling, ear-splitting racket of Efi's reveille drum pierced every tent, head, and dream. The soldiers tumbled out fast and eager, knowing that today was the day they had trained and waited for.

The companies gulped down a quick breakfast in silence as the mist burned off to reveal a crisp, clear fall day. They packed rations, water, and cartridges and nervously assembled in the road next to their rows of tents at the call of Efi's drum. Efi glanced longingly at his simple canvas tent and wondered if he'd ever see it again or if nightfall would find him crumpled and gathering flies in some forgotten field.

Other Confederate units were also out early. The narrow country roads were clogged with hurrying troops, rumbling cannons being raced by their horse teams to the front, and rickety supply wagons. Occasionally the ground would rumble as a cavalry unit thundered past. The 18th Mississippi and the rest of General Cleburne's division lined up at the edge of the road, waiting.

By 9:30 they heard firing, first the scattered fire of pickets, then the roar of massed volleys, the earth-shattering explosions of cannons, and the continuous rolling thunder of a close-in brawl. For the hundredth time the soldiers checked their locking pins, hammer springs, and cartridge boxes. They tightened their cartridge belts and then nervously loosened them again.

And they waited. The battle seemed to flow from left to right and back again, always through the trees and across Chickamauga Creek. Always "over there" and never drawing closer. And still they waited. Efi nervously tested and tightened his drum head to adjust its tune.

The endless grind of waiting rubbed the men's nerves raw and sapped their energy like a sweltering summer day. Ace Lyman, the preacher's son, quietly handed Efi his playing cards, tobacco pouch, and liquor flask. "Hold these for me, will you? If I die, I don't want my papa finding these on my body."

"Think the Federals will attack us?" Efi asked Lieutenant Packard, who paced beside the company, glaring at the men who had stretched out in the grass to sleep while they waited. "Why do we just stand here and wait?"

Packard scowled at Efi and stormed off down the line.

"Sounds like *we're* doing most of the attacking." This came from Captain Stalter, who was quietly smoking his pipe in the shade. "I guess we're in reserve this morning."

He then rose, stretched, tapped his pipe on his boot, and came up next to Efi. "The men'll all be watching you today, Shortbread."

"Me? Why me?"

"You're the signal, the center of the unit. As long as they can hear you, they'll know they're where they're supposed to be. They'll feel safe. As long as they can hear you, they'll march, they'll stand in line, and they'll fight. You just keep playing, loud and strong, and don't let anything frighten you."

"No, sir!" answered Efi, his eyes growing noticeably larger.

The sun crept toward noon. The battle raged somewhere across the creek. Streams of wounded straggled past the 18th Mississippi, faces blackened by powder, with tight, frightened looks, their blood trickling onto the ground.

And still the 18th waited.

Sergeant Peck ambled up to Efi. "Probably nobody bothered to tell you this afore. But once we get into the fight, they'll be aiming for you, Dillweed."

"Who will?"

"The Federals, of course. If they can kill the drummer, it affects a whole regiment. You're our rally point, our communications. You and the color bearer, they'll sure be aiming for you two."

Mace sprang to his feet. "Leave him be, Jimmy Peck."

Peck shrugged and ambled back into his spot in the line. "Just trying to tell Dillweed the truth. Someone has to."

"Is that true—what he said?" Efi asked Captain Stalter.

"They'll just be shooting and hardly aiming at all, Shortbread. I wouldn't worry about it."

But Efi did. And still they waited.

At 3:30 that afternoon, Colonel Wood galloped by. "Get 'em up. Whole division is on the move. March north toward Lambert's ford. Quick now!" And he galloped farther down the strung-out line of companies.

"Shortbread, sound assembly," called the captain.

Efi's heart raced as he drummed. This was it! They were marching into battle. Real battle! Battle that turned proud soldiers into the whimpering and battered shapes that had shuffled past the 18th all day. Battle that would be the truest test of courage. Battle that would hold their very lives in its fickle hands.

"Column of fours. On the rout step. Head 'em out," called Captain Stalter.

For two hours they marched north while the fighting rumbled off to their left, across the Chickamauga. The 800 men of the 18th Mississippi stacked up behind other regiments at a ford and had to wait while the sun crept low for their turn to cross. The icy water swirled armpit deep on most of the men. Efi was submerged. Mace had to haul him up with one massive arm and carry him across the Chickamauga.

"The water looks *red*," said Efi.

"Must be the red glow of sunset," answered Mace. But they both knew it was blood from the hundreds who had fought and died along the creek's edge earlier in the day.

The division formed into line, still shivering and wet, just at sunset. Other regiments, 4, 8, even 12 lines deep, stretched farther than Efi could see. "Golly, there's a lot of us," he muttered.

The stinging, sulfurous smell of battle lingered in the air. A lull in firing made the four-mile-long battlefield seem almost too quiet. Birds flitted past, chirping. They were the first birds Efi'd heard all day.

Colonel Wood grabbed Efi's shoulder. "You know the drum signals for all battle maneuvers?"

"Yes, sir!" said Efi.

"You know the regimental call, boy?"

"Yes, sir." And Efi played it for the colonel, thinking how silly it was to have a special regimental drum call. Anyone could look around and *see* where they were.

Colonel Wood nodded. "Good enough. You'll stay beside me. The other drummer has dysentery. You are now the official drummer for the 18th Mississippi. What's your name?"

"Ephram Dillard of Biloxi, sir."

"Keep it steady and keep playing. The men are going to need the drum tonight."

"We're going to fight at *night*, sir?"

"Steady. Sound advance."

Efi pounded on his drum to signal each company in the regiment to advance. His heart was pounding far louder than his drum. He felt that his feet floated above the ground, and that the deep blues, grays, and blacks of the twilight woods and fields drifted by in a dream.

Off to his right, Efi saw the first flickering flashes of Federal musket fire. Just a few pickets, caught by surprise, and firing before they fell back to their unit lines. To Efi it looked like magical, sparkling fireflies twinkling in the night. "It's beautiful," he whispered.

"Steady, boy. Keep the beat steady."

Across a silhouetted meadow, and under increasing fire, Colonel Wood marched his regiment forward. "Close up!" shouted the sergeants and officers as men lagged behind or as gaps opened in the line where men had been hit and felled. Confederate cannon opened fire, the shells screeching overhead in great arcs like comets before exploding in brilliant star bursts of light in the woods and Federal lines.

Thick lines of firefly musket shots ahead marked the Union troops through the dark. Exploding cannon shells lit up the night like a dazzling fireworks show. The din of battle rose to a shattering roar. Still, mouth gaping open, Efi thought it was the most beautiful sight he had ever seen.

"Signal the regiment to stop and fire," commanded the colonel. "One volley only."

Efi changed the pattern of his drumming and heard company commanders down the line verbally repeat the command.

Suddenly the world exploded in a deafening thunder, a thick, choking smoke, and a blinding flash as the 18th Mississippi's 800 guns lit up the night and hurled a deadly wave of lead at the waiting Federals.

"Sound advance."

"Yes, sir," shouted Efi, to be heard over the roar of battle.

"Let 'em hear you, men," yelled the colonel.

A high-pitched, murderous wail erupted from the Confederate line, the famous rebel yell. Efi trembled at the monstrous shriek being made by so many desperate throats. It seemed to rattle the trees. Grass seemed to bend away in terror in the shadowed dark.

The rebel line advanced into the trees. Muskets exploded everywhere around Efi. He stumbled and banged into a gnarled tree trunk, unable to see. Men screamed, cursed, cried, and fought all around him. The woods were filled with firefly puffs as musket balls whined thick and deadly through the dark.

One bullet sizzled past so close to Efi's ear that he could hear it sing. But still he pounded his drum in a trance-like fury. Somewhere nearby men fought with knives and fists. The losers screamed and died. The winners just screamed. And on they marched, deeper into the Federal lines.

A crash exploded in Efi's ears and he found himself sprawled on the ground. He sat up expecting to find himself dead, or at least with a ragged and bloody hole. Instead, he found a jagged hole punched through the metal side of his drum. The bullet had even torn a hole in his gray coat.

Efi sprang back to his feet, more angry than frightened. His drum sounded tinny and raspy when he played, but play and shout he did as he stumbled forward in the dark.

All around him were flashes of light, yelling, and confusion. Men ran past him looking like gray shadows. Efi couldn't tell which side they were on. Musket balls whined through the night, searching for victims. Leaves fell like rain as deadly lead clipped through the branches.

The first icy touch of fear crept over Efi. He had no idea where he was, or where Colonel Wood was, or even where the Confederate army was. Everything was just noise and firefly flashes and chaos and the steady, wounded sound of his drum as he pounded and marched, unsure of which direction he was walking.

Suddenly Efi's drum seemed to have picked up an echo. Efi stopped when his drum smacked into another drum in the dark. He leaned forward, struggling to see who he'd run into as all around him men screamed and musket balls screeched through the trees.

Efi could just make out a cocked blue cap and blue coat that now appeared pure black. Under the cap were two wide eyes filled with a mix of terror and fierce anger. Drumsticks were raised in the boy's hands, as if he had frozen in the middle of a drumbeat.

For a long moment the two drummer boys paused, drum to drum, as the bloody battle raged around them. The Federal boy yelled and swung his drumstick, whacking Efi hard on the side of his head. Efi stumbled sideways, then screamed his miniature version of the rebel yell and lunged forward with his own stick, catching the Federal boy in the throat.

The Union drummer boy staggered back gagging. Efi screamed his rebel yell again and jumped forward, crashing into his private enemy. The two rolled on the ground, awkwardly held apart by their drums.

A lightning-bright flash and a deafening roar exploded near Efi's head. The Federal drummer gasped and slumped quietly to the forest floor.

"Shortbread, that you?" Ace Lyman peered through the dark at Efi. "You all right?"

Efi stumbled to his feet, gasping for breath, legs still trembling. "Ace, you *killed* him!"

"Him and about a dozen of his friends! I *love* this fighting!"

Colonel Wood emerged through the trees. "Where have you been, boy?"

"Sorry, sir."

"Colonel, sir," beamed Ace Lyman. "Shortbread here bagged himself a Federal drummer boy. Beat him to death with his sticks, I reckon."

The colonel nodded. "Well done, lad. Well done, indeed." He paused to assess the chaotic fighting still pounding through the woods. "It's too dark to continue. Signal regimental assembly call."

Efi pounded the regimental call on his wounded drum. Here, in the blinding dark, in the confusion and rush of battle and woods, it finally made sense to have a regimental call. It was the only way for soldiers to know where to gather.

Company commanders slowly collected around the colonel. A few fires were lit. Efi found four bullet holes in his drum, two in his coat, and a stinging red welt on his temple from the Northern drumstick. A thin trickle of blood even dribbled down his face from where a twig had gouged him.

He dabbed blood away with a sleeve, creating a red smear on his coat, and swelled with the proud feeling that now he was a *real* soldier. He felt a sudden bond, a brotherhood, a fierce closeness with these bedraggled men huddled around him.

eep here," ordered the colonel. "Get pickets (guards) out, and assemble casualty

"Sleep here? With no tents?" asked Efi.

Captain Stalter emerged from the dark. "Stay alert, Shortbread. This battle is far from over."

"But my drum's all shot up, sir."

"Then you best fix it before first light."

The night was filled with the moaning of Union and Confederate wounded scattered all about the regiment as they tried to rest. Medics stumbled through the dark trying to help and comfort. Wagons and cannons thundered past as they redeployed supplies for the next day's fight. Axes whacked steadily into trees as the Federal forces, a scant 100 yards away, built barricades and fortifications in anticipation of a renewed Confederate attack at first light.

Efi's hands trembled as he struggled to patch his drum. He tried to force his mind to concentrate on his work, but the terrified face, snarling anger, and final surprised pain of the Federal drummer boy refused to dim in his mind.

As the first hint of gray tinged the eastern sky, Colonel Wood called, "Where's my drummer boy?"

"We got no *boys* here, colonel," answered Mace, still tending a bullet wound in his arm that had soaked his sleeve with blood. "Anyone who could survive through a night like last night, why, they must be a *man*, not a boy."

Efi filled with a fierce pride as he jumped to his feet. Still, he wished with all his heart that he could go back to being a boy.

Aftermath

Night battles were rare in the Civil War. Commanders found it too difficult to control the units under their command and to follow the progress of the battle. Units found it almost impossible to keep track of where they were and where their adjacent units were. Night battles tended to quickly degenerate into uncontrolled brawls. It was the perfect formula for military disaster. So virtually all Civil War commanders refused to initiate night battles.

The Battle of Chickamauga continued all the next day, Sunday, September 20. Rosecrans's Union army was defeated and almost routed. Only the heroic acts of General George Thomas, the "Rock of Chickamauga," saved the Union forces from total destruction. The Federals retreated to Chattanooga.

Almost 85,000 men fought along Chickamauga Creek during two days of battle. Over 10,000 died. Chickamauga was a great victory and rallying point for the South, but their joy was short-lived. Union General Ulysses Grant led the Northerners in two stunning victories at Look Out Mountain and Missionary Ridge later that fall to drive Bragg's army limping back into northern Georgia again.

Over the course of the war, drummer boys in battle were gradually phased out and replaced by buglers. Bugles were easier to hear during battle. The sound of the drum was too close to that of musket fire. But drummers were consistently noted for their bravery and steadfastness in the face of the horrors of battle, even though they were usually the youngest soldiers on the field.

Follow-up Questions and Activities

1. **What Do You Know?**

   - Why did the Confederate leaders feel they *needed* to win at Chickamauga?
   - Chickamauga was the first battle in Georgia. Where had the fighting in the West taken place before September 1863?
   - Why were there so few night battles during the Civil War?
   - What was the purpose of having a regimental drummer? Why were drummers always boys?
   - Besides drumming, what other duties did drummers and musicians have?

2. **Find Out More.** Following are six important topics from this story for students to research in the library and on the Internet. The reference sources at the back of this book will help them get started.

   - Research the two-day Battle of Chickamauga. How did the Confederates almost destroy Rosecrans's Union army? What saved the Union forces?
   - Three generals led the fighting at Chickamauga: Confederate General Bragg and Union Generals Rosecrans and Thomas. Research the lives and accomplishments of these three important Civil War leaders.
   - The Confederate victory at Chickamauga was short-lived. Grant took command of the Union forces and quickly pushed the Confederates away from Chattanooga. He achieved stunning victories at Look Out Mountain and Missionary Ridge. Research the major battles in Tennessee during the Civil War. Who won? Who lost? What was gained or lost at each?
   - Repeating, breech-loading rifles were invented by Samuel Colt and Christopher Spencer in the late 1850s. These advanced new weapons were first introduced into the Union army in 1863 in limited supply. Chickamauga was the first battle in which repeating rifles saw major action. Muzzle-loaded muskets could shoot four to six rounds a minute; repeating rifles could be fired almost 60 times a minute! One man with a repeating rifle could fire as fast as 10 with muzzle loaders.

     Research the history of repeating rifles. At which other battles were they used? Why didn't every Union soldier get one? What other weapons were used during the Civil War? Research them and try to find images and descriptions of the weapons. Research other military inventions during the Civil War. Which side invented and first used them? How many worked? Did any have a major impact on the outcome of a battle?
   - Research other drummer boys, both Confederate and Union. How many were there? How many were wounded in battle? Did any go on to have full military careers? Union drummer boy Johnny Clem was the most famous of all drummer boys. He saw action at both Chickamauga and Shiloh. Research the life and career of Johnny Clem.

- Research the roll of army drummers and musicians throughout history. Have armies always had bands? Why? Have they always used drummers during battle? Why? Compare Civil War drums to the pounding drums used by Napoleon to drive his troops to victory across Europe.

3. **Make It Real**

- Learn Civil War drum codes (or invent them) and use them to signal changes of activity in the class and on the playground. Can you find advantages and disadvantages to using drum signals?

- What kind of music or songs were popular during the Civil War? What instruments might soldiers have to amuse themselves with when not in battle? Find some of the songs and perform them.

- One student in your class can attend high school for a day. A high school senior should sponsor the student and take him or her around to classes and activities. That student will keep a careful journal of how he or she felt being the youngest. Overwhelmed? Intimidated? Did the older students tease this student? Did he or she try to act older and more sophisticated?

  Imagine being at war and begin 8 to 10 years younger than anyone else in the regiment, having no one your own age to talk to. Write a letter to someone at home describing how you'd feel about being there all alone, about the other men in your regiment, and about being in battle armed only with a pair of drumsticks.

- A Civil War army was organized into corps. Corps were made up of divisions, which were made up of brigades. Brigades were made up of regiments, regiments were made up of companies, and companies usually included 100 to 120 men and worked pretty much as a unit. Research the number of each sized unit contained in the next larger unit for both Confederate and Union armies. How many men were there in a typical Union corps? In a Confederate corps?

- Create a timeline of the fighting in Tennessee during the Civil War. Begin in the spring of 1861 and track major army movements and battles in that state from then until the end of the war.

4. **Points to Ponder**

- Do you think it is right to allow children (boys) on the battlefield? Why or why not? Are there some things you would allow them to do in the army but not others?

- Why do you think armies want music when they march to war and enter battle? Why have bands and drummers always been an important part of armies?

Fast, Dark, and Quiet
Confederate Ships That Ran the Union Naval Blockade, October 1863

At a Glance

In May 1861, President Lincoln issued orders for the U.S. Navy to blockade all Southern ports and economically strangle the Confederacy into submission. The Confederacy had little manufacturing capacity. Shoes, muskets, rifles, cannons, gunpowder, etc.—even much of the army's food—had to be imported. The South had only one small nail factory. Its only large ironworks were in Richmond, Virginia, and Birmingham, Alabama.

Southerners could *fight* the war, but they couldn't *supply* it without a steady stream of ocean-borne commerce.

However, in 1861 the entire Federal navy consisted of only 69 ships, all with wooden hulls. Over half were sailing ships. This small force had 4,000 miles of coast, bays, and inlets to cover. A blockade was an impossible task.

The Southern response was to run the blockade. In 1861 it was easy; almost any ship could do it. Companies and investors sprang up across the Confederacy and in England vying for a piece of the enormous profits available from the lucrative blockade-running trade. Cotton could be purchased for $.05 a pound on the dock in Charleston and sold for $.53 a pound in England. Quinine (a popular medicine) purchased in Nassau for $10 sold for $400–$500 in Richmond, Virginia. Millions could be made in a month.

By 1862, the Federal navy had become much better at catching blockade runners. They acquired new, faster ships. Their tactics improved. Slower, heavier blockade runners were forced out of the business. Only specially designed, high-speed ships were still able to run the blockades.

One by one the Federal navy closed Southern ports by conquering the coastal forts that protected them. Port Royal and Hilton Head, South Carolina, fell to Union forces in late 1861. Beaufort, South Carolina, surrendered in December 1861. Tybee Island, Georgia (guarding the entrance to Savannah), fell in early 1862. New Orleans

213

was conquered in April 1862. The Outer Banks of North Carolina fell in mid-1862; Norfolk and Hampton Roads, Virginia, fell later that year. Morris Island (one of the entrances to Charleston, South Carolina) fell in September 1863. Mobile, Alabama, was taken in early 1864. By then, the U.S. Navy boasted 700 warships, including 180 side paddle steamers and 105,000 sailors.

With every closing of a major port, the noose tightened around the Confederacy's neck. Only the bravest and most skilled dared to run the treacherous gauntlet during the final years of the war. But the need was immense. The Confederacy could not survive without outside manufactured goods. Blockade-running became a high-stakes gambling game played by Southern daredevils.

Meet Captain John Wilkinson

Captain Wilkinson was a 16-year veteran of the U.S. Navy when he resigned to fight for the Confederacy in April 1861. He had spent seven of his navy years leading part of a national coastal survey project and knew the Carolina coast as well as any man alive. Born in coastal Massachusetts, Wilkinson was raised on and near the ocean. He was a naturally skilled seaman and had grown into a fearless and cunning tactician.

As captain of the *Robert E. Lee*, Wilkinson made a record 21 successful blockade runs in less than 15 months. During these runs, he amassed a huge fortune, both in pay (up to $5,000 per round-trip) and through the sale of cargo he personally imported in the captain's locker of the *Lee*'s cargo hold.

Wilkinson took two months' shore leave in late 1864 (during which time the *Lee* was captured) and shifted his command to the *Charlotta*. He remained one of the Confederacy's last successful blockade runners—even after the last open port, Wilmington, North Carolina, was finally closed in February 1865. Wilkinson was never captured and his cargoes were never confiscated.

Wilkinson retired after the war at the age of 42 and lived in Charleston, South Carolina, as a rich man for the rest of his life.

Fast, Dark, and Quiet

"Captain Wilkinson! Why is this ship still in port?" A slender, dainty-looking man, Mr. Barclay St. Clair was trying his best to appear outraged as he scrambled up the slanted gangplank onto the crowded deck of the *Robert E. Lee*. It had taken St. Clair over an hour to find the *Lee* along the two miles of bustling river docks in the Confederate import-export capital of Wilmington, North Carolina. The delay had only heightened his frustration.

The date was October 8, 1863. The *Lee* was moored along the crowded river docks of Wilmington, 17 miles up the Cape Fear River from the Atlantic. Because the river paralleled the curving coastline, Wilmington was nestled close enough to the ocean to smell the salt air as well as hear the clang of masts and the blasts of ships' horns on the river.

Captain John Wilkinson stood midship, just before the squat pilot's house, which was tucked in beside the *Lee*'s giant side paddle wheel. A short, neat man with a trim beard and a cold, hard look, Captain Wilkinson had been talking with his chief engineer, Jason Ivery, a plump, cheerful Scotsman born and raised in Boston. Wilkinson groaned and rolled his eyes. "So we *will* have a super on this trip." (Supercargo, or "super," was the term for an owner's representative.) Wilkinson cupped his hands to his mouth and shouted. "Good day, Mr. St. Clair. And welcome on board the *Lee*."

Dabbing at his face and neck with a handkerchief, St. Clair ignored the greeting. "As a representative of the owners of this vessel . . ." he began.

"*Half* owners," interrupted Wilkinson. "The Confederate States of America own half."

"Very well, *half* owners," St. Clair conceded. "The owners I represent would like to know why this ship didn't sail 10 days ago."

Wilkinson shook his head and muttered, "English accountants."

"If you minimized each port visit," continued St. Clair, "you could triple profits for our investors."

"No!" bellowed Captain Wilkinson. "I would *end* all profits because this ship would be captured or sunk."

"I don't understand," St. Clair faltered.

"You will be traveling with us on this voyage, will you not, Mr. St. Clair?"

"Yes, the owners . . ."

"Good. Then you will see *exactly* what I mean." Wilkinson gestured to his engineer. "Barclay St. Clair, representative of the *Lee*'s English half owners, this is Jason Ivery, chief engineer."

St. Clair again dabbed his face and chin. "Doesn't it *ever* cool off in these Southern colonies?"

"*States*, Mr. St. Clair. And it will be warmer yet when we reach Bermuda."

St. Clair glanced at the ship's engineer. "The company profile says you're a Scot, but Jason Ivery doesn't sound Scottish."

"Me da' changed the family name from McIvers and made sure each of us wee 'uns had an American-sounding name, don't you see?"

Voices flared near the bow as several deckhands squabbled. Wilkinson pushed forward through the rows of cotton bales stacked on the deck. "What's going on aboard my ship?"

"The new chap, captain," answered one of the deckhands wearing the faded uniform of a British seaman. (Many English seamen had deserted His Majesty's service to seek the higher pay of blockade runners.) "He was stuffing deck cotton bales into the hold."

The captain groaned, "Supers and new deckhands. I don't like this trip already." Wilkinson pointed at the new sailor. "Name?"

"Ned. Nedrick Stokes, sir. And if we pack these bales below, we can load more on deck."

"Aye. And have my ship grounded on the bar or on Frying Pan Shoals so the Federal navy can blow it apart!" Wilkinson drew a deep breath to calm himself. "Aces."

"Aye, sir," answered Jes Stram, a short, wiry seaman with a weathered, sea-blown face. Stram had picked up the nickname "Aces" when he bet his entire $1,000 pay for one voyage on a single hand of poker and won with a pair of aces.

"You're in charge of the new man. Make sure he doesn't sink my ship."

Barclay St. Clair had wormed his way forward. "Why *don't* you load the cargo below where seawater can't damage it?"

"You shall see, Mr. St. Clair. You shall see," growled the captain. He glanced at the sun dipping toward the thick line of trees on the west side of the Cape Fear River. Then he bellowed, "Mr. Ivery, make steam. We shove off in one hour."

"So you're *finally* ready to sail?" asked St. Clair, traipsing along at the captain's elbow.

"It is not me, but the tides and moon, that are finally ready, Mr. St. Clair. When I reach Smith Island I will need the tide just past high and running with me out to sea. I will also need a moonless, black night. Under any other conditions, we will be intercepted and sunk."

"Make a comfortable five knots, Mr. Davies," announced the captain as the mooring lines were cast off. Howard Davies had been the *Lee*'s pilot as long as Wilkinson had been her captain. The *Robert E. Lee*, at 294 feet long and only 21 feet wide, looked like a knife slicing through the water. The narrowness and shallow draft made the ship dangerously unseaworthy but gave it incredible speed. The main deck rose only six feet above waterline. The entire ship was painted a dull gray-brown to blend in with both the ocean and coastal sand dunes where it might have to hide.

All that rose above that deck were two stubby masts so that sails could be used to augment the power of the side paddle wheels, the top of the housing for the paddle wheel, and two chopped-off smokestacks. It was at the smokestacks that the captain now pointed. "*That*, Mr. St. Clair, is the problem with having English accountants try to run my ship!"

"I see no problem," said St. Clair.

"Smoke, Mr. St. Clair. Smoke. If I had been allowed to carry a smaller cargo on the last run from Bermuda and stock in more hard Welsh coal, I would not now have to burn soft Southern bituminous coal, which produces billows of black smoke. True, the ship made extra profit on the last trip. But that extra profit will make this trip more dangerous. That smoke will make us much more visible to Federal blockade ships."

"We had not considered smoke," St. Clair admitted.

"Aces! Will Bennett!" called the captain.

Jes Stram and William Bennett were the senior deckhands on board the *Lee*. Bennett was quiet, aloof, and serious, and had not picked up a shipboard nickname. Only the captain got away with shortening his name from William to Will.

"Aye, captain," answered the two seamen.

"Deck bales secure?"

"All lashed and secured, captain." Long rows of cotton bales, stacked five feet high, covered the *Lee*'s deck.

"I still don't see why we don't load it all below," whined Barclay St. Clair.

"You will, Mr. St. Clair. I fear all too soon, you will."

The *Lee* reached Smithville, a tiny fishing village at the mouth of the river, just before sunset and glided to a stop. Smith Island sat at the mouth of the Cape Fear River, splitting the river in two. From Smithville, Wilkinson would have to pick either the north or south entrance. Blockade runners stopped at Smithville to scout the placement of Federal ships along the ocean routes before picking their channel for escape.

The *Lee*'s officers gathered on deck with the captain as the sea turned from slate gray to deep purple and then to black to blend with the eastern sky. For a brief time, points of light marked the position of Federal blockade ships. Then, one by one, the lights blinked out.

"They've gotten smarter and are blacking out their ships, captain," said Quincy Dallard, an experienced English seaman who had signed on as first mate.

"Aye. But there appear to be no more than 30 ships in the line tonight," said the captain, his eye still jammed against his long, brass telescope. "We should make it through."

"Against 30 ships?" gasped St. Clair. "Shouldn't we wait for better odds?"

"These *are* better odds, Mr. St. Clair. There's a lot of ocean out there to cover, and I can run this ship both dark and quiet." The captain snapped his telescope closed and announced, "Moon sets just past midnight. Tide turns at 12:20. We depart at 12:30 for the north channel entrance."

The 40-man crew knew there would be little sleep and no peace for the next three days while they raced to Bermuda. It would have been less stressful if they had a bigger crew. But a bigger crew took up more space and left less room for cargo.

Captain Wilkinson checked the time, clicked his pocket watch shut, and extinguished the small lantern he carried. He quietly waited until 12:30, then said, "Raise anchor. All ahead slow, Mr. Davies. Make for the north side of the channel entrance."

"Bar will be rougher there, captain." Davies's face glowed faintly in the reflection of the one tiny pinprick of light allowed on the ship. That light lit the ship's compass so that the pilot could set and steer a course.

(A coastal bar is an area of naturally shallow water at the entrance to an estuary. River and ocean waters collide ferociously over this sand ridge (or bar) and churn up frightfully rough seas. It is not uncommon to sail off a glassy smooth ocean and crash into choppy, 10-foot waves swirling like a washing machine over a bar.)

"Aye, so it will. But navy ships won't be able to see us silhouetted against any lights in Smithville."

"Aye, captain. North side of the channel. All ahead slow." Mr. Davies rang the command down to the boiler room. There was no bell on the engine room telegraph. The sound of bells carried too far across the ocean. One of the boiler room crew had to vigilantly monitor the needle and watch for changes in the indicated speed.

The captain called, "Mr. Quincy, please inspect the deck and crew for rough seas. No further noise above a whisper. I want two lookouts on the bow, one ready to sound depth at all times."

"Aye, captain." The mate groped his way forward down the rows of cotton bales.

"Shouldn't we go faster, captain?" asked Mr. St. Clair.

"First, no, we shouldn't. The paddles would slap the water and make noise blockade ships could hear. We'd also create a bow wave, which often glows luminescent and could be seen. Second, I said silence on deck!"

Every porthole and hatch had been covered by heavy tarpaulins. Even though the boilers were barely making steam, the lack of ventilation made the boiler room a hellish steam bath.

Time crept by slower than a caterpillar. A few gulls lazily circled overhead, then floated off into the night, as if bored by the lack of action and prospects on the *Lee*.

"Mr. Davies, have we cleared Smith Island yet?"

"Soon, captain," the pilot whispered back. "Should be feeling the bar any minute now."

The *Lee*'s bow lurched up. The ship seemed to twist like a bucking bronco as it dipped into an unseen trough. The deck lurched and groaned. St. Clair dropped to his knees and slid across the deck, crashing into the nearest row of cotton bales. The long ship felt as if it buckled as the bow and stern climbed separate towering waves and the midships dropped into a trough. For a moment the ship's paddles spun free before grabbing back into the next wave.

"Steady," whispered Captain Wilkinson.

"I need more power to hold her, sir," hissed the pilot.

"Ring for flank," whispered the captain. "But I want the speed dropped back again before we clear the bar."

By feel alone, the pilot shoved the engine room telegraph forward one notch to flank speed. The deck vibration increased. The paddles slapped harder against the swirling waters. On the bow, Ned Stokes stared in helpless terror into the black night. Monstrous waves materialized right before him and slammed across the bow. He was washed and dragged across the deck by the mighty surge, saved only by his lifeline tied to the deck rail.

There was no sign of land, but all on board could smell it close by. The *Lee* pounded blindly through the dark, trusting to the compass and the skill of the pilot.

The groaning and twisting screech of metal deck plates eased. Barclay St. Clair was able to stand.

"Crossing the outer bar, captain," whispered Mr. Davies.

"Turn north-northeast, Mr. Davies. All ahead slow."

"Aye, captain."

The first obstacle had been passed. If the *Lee* could now creep far enough north along the coast without going aground on an unseen spit of land or on Frying Pan Shoals (which extended 10 miles into the ocean), and if the ship could do it quickly enough to have some dark left, then they could turn east for their run to the open sea, having skirted around the flank of most of the blockade ships.

Seconds crept by. Stokers in the boiler room were drenched with sweat and were still hours from any relief from the terrible heat.

"All stop, Mr. Davies. Sound the bow."

The paddles stopped. The ship drifted in the endless black. Ned Stokes lowered over the bow a weighted line marked in one-foot increments, letting the cord slide through his hands until the weight hit bottom. He marked the length of line that had passed through his hands, whispered "36 feet below the bow," to the next man, and began to haul in the line.

The depth was whispered back to the captain. He grunted and said, "Come starboard two points, Mr. Davies, and continue ahead slow."

Their progress was maddeningly slow through the dark, with dangers lurking unseen all around. Every man on board wanted to roar at full speed for open water. Yet each man also knew that would be a suicide dash. Nerve-wracking stealth was the only path to success.

It felt as if they had been crawling up the coast for days when Ned Stokes whispered back, "60 feet below the bow."

Captain Wilkinson nodded, "Congratulations, Mr. Davies. You have gotten us past Frying Pan once again. Come right to 045 and run for one hour, then right again to 090. We still have over two hours of dark left. I would like three, but two will have to do."

The paddles gently lapped at each gentle swell that rode under the *Lee*. The deck crew stood still and silent as a painting, each ear straining, dreading to hear the sound of another ship drift across the water.

A soft metal clang drifted across the water. Then a gentle cough.

St. Clair began to tremble. "Captain . . ."

A thick hand was clamped across his mouth. The captain breathed, "Not a sound" in his ear and let go.

"Mr. Davies, 10 points to port, if you please," Wilkinson whispered.

Seconds turned to hours, minutes to lifetimes. Tension grew unbearably heavy as the *Robert E. Lee* drifted at two knots, knowing a navy warship lay only a few hundred yards away in the dark.

There was a rustle of canvas near the bow, then the soft plop of careful footsteps as Mr. Quincy rushed to investigate. Ned Stokes was unwrapping the *Lee*'s one small cannon. "I can hit them," he whispered.

"Freeze!" Quincy hissed into Ned's ear.

Now they heard voices and commotion on the navy ship's quarter deck. There was a call for all lookouts to deck and topside.

"Damn!" muttered the captain. "We've been heard." He paused and added, "Steady as she goes, Mr. Davies. They may know something is out here, but they still don't know what or where."

Lanterns were lit on the navy ship, trying to pierce the dark. The ship stood out like a lighthouse. "A steamer," Wilkinson muttered. "Ironclad. Heavy armament. Good. It'll be slow. Cruising slowly southward. At least half a mile off . . . " He cupped his hands to his mouth and whispered, "Will Bennett."

"Aye, sir?"

"Prepare the flares."

"Flares?" blurted Barclay St. Clair. "Flares will give our position away."

"Silence! You'll see, Mr. St. Clair."

The wind and waves picked up, fresh and stiff out of the east. The waves began to slap against the *Lee*'s bow.

A flare arched into the night from the navy ship, glowing like a red comet.

Captain Wilkinson cursed, "Drat! They think they've spotted us." Then he barked, "Mr. Davies, all ahead full and 10 degrees port, please. We'll skirt them to the north. Mr. Bennett, three flares at right angles to our direction, please."

"Aye, captain."

When a navy ship detected a blockade runner, they shot flares across the water in the direction the enemy ship was traveling. Other navy ships in the area would steam in that same direction to intercept the runner. Wilkinson's flares, fired in a different direction, were designed to confuse navy ships and make them take the wrong heading.

One by one, the *Lee*'s flares arched to the southeast while the ship actually steamed northeast.

"That cruiser will be coming about and on our tail. I need more steam!" Captain Wilkinson tore back the tarp covering the boiler room hatchway and pushed back the hatch cover. "Mr. Ivery, I need more steam now!"

"It's the soft coal, sir," came the reply from the stifling room below. "Low heat content. Takes time to build up a good head of steam."

"We've got no time," answered Wilkinson. "Deckhands! I want five bales of cotton unlashed and carried to the engine room. Aces! Soak the cotton in turpentine and feed it to the boilers. That'll get us a jolt of speed."

The *Lee* lurched forward into the night. The bow sliced through the growing waves, spraying blasts of seawater back across the deck and crew. A shower of sparks billowed out of the smokestacks with the thick smoke.

"Mr. Davies, as soon as the bales have been burned and the sparks are gone, come 40 points to starboard."

"Into the navy ship, sir?"

"With a good head of steam, we'll cut well across her bow and leave her groping in the wrong direction."

Wilkinson turned toward the bow. "Bring me the idiot who made that noise!"

"It was the new man, sir," answered First Mate Quincy Dallard.

The deadly game of hide-and-seek had turned into a frantic race of hare and hounds through the dark.

"The quartering wind is stiff enough to help, sir," Aces Stram commented.

"Aye, Aces. It is. All hands raise the sails! We need every knot the *Lee* has in her."

"Ned Stokes reporting as ordered," said a small, nervous voice.

"Your tomfoolery will likely get us killed, man. I should have you flogged!"

"But I could have hit them, sir!"

"With that tiny gun?" bellowed the captain. "You wouldn't have dented a deck plate. We are not a Confederate navy ship, mister. We are a private ship contracted by the Confederacy. If we fire on a navy ship, we can be imprisoned for piracy. Piracy! Do you hear me?"

"Yes, sir!"

"Never fire on the navy! We can run, and we can hide. But if we ever fire, we will die in prison or on the gallows! Now get aft and help with the sails."

"Yes, sir. Sorry, sir." Ned Stokes scampered to the aft mast, fearing he'd be shot or thrown overboard by his own crew for creating the telltale noise that gave them away.

The *Lee* flew through the choppy Atlantic water, sails straining on their stubby masts. Smoke bellowed thick and black from the twin stacks. Less than a mile away, the now-glowing navy cruiser steamed hard after them. Other ships would be converging. Within an hour the first light would tinge the eastern sky and make the *Lee* an easy target.

There was nothing for anyone above deck to do but wait, staring into the endless black of the ocean. Below deck every stoker furiously flung coal into the giant twin boilers. Heat blasted off the glowing metal hard as a solid wall. Steam hissed through the pipes, driving the paddle wheel's towering pistons and rocker arm. At full speed, the engine room was a deafening din of noise as well as a blast-furnace inferno of tormenting heat.

"Storm's brewing," called the captain, as the growing wind sang in the rigging. "Good. It'll reduce visibility after dawn."

They heard the dull tha-wump of distant cannon fire.

"Watch for it!" cried the captain.

"A hundred yards to starboard," yelled Quincy Dallard, pointing at a tiny geyser of water marking where the shell had smacked into the ocean.

"Ten points to port, Mr. Davies," Wilkinson yelled, adjusting their course away from the navy ship.

Two more shells were fired. Wilkinson could see a distant speck of light marking the cannon explosion and the navy ship's location. One of the shells whined through the night and soaked the deck with spray when it hit the waves just off the bow.

"Those gunners are good," Aces commented. "Considering it's still dark."

One of the three shells in the next round scored a direct hit on the forward deck. Cotton bales exploded like ripped-up feather pillows. The deck looked to be caught in a blinding blizzard. Fluff balls of white floated everywhere, only to be snatched away by the howling wind.

"That is why we stack cotton bales on the deck, Mr. St. Clair. It is effective armor plating for the *Lee*." Wilkinson smiled in the dark. "Not to worry, Mr. St. Clair. We're a good mile and a half in front and pulling away. A storm is brewing that will cut visibility to less than half a mile. We'll be safe unless a lucky shot strikes the paddle wheel."

Two more shells struck the *Lee*. One exploded harmlessly in the rows of cotton, destroying half a dozen precious bales. One tore into stern deck plating, peeling back the iron plates as if they were paper. Molten metal shrapnel sprayed across the crew quarters below, killing all three men resting inside.

"Fire crews!" called the captain. "Make sure nothing's burning below."

St. Clair added, "Send a doctor to tend the wounded."

"We have no medic on board," Wilkinson growled. "Your owners eliminated the position to make room for cargo."

The *Robert E. Lee* raced into the growing waves and now steady rain. The ship pitched dangerously while cresting each steep swell and seemed to rocket into each trough as if it would drill straight to the ocean floor far below.

"Steady, Mr. Davies," said the captain reassuringly. "Keep her afloat." The ship made three more turns, and in the cold gray of a seething dawn storm, the *Lee* had escaped the navy's pursuit.

The deck crew took a fleeting moment to cheer as they staggered across the deck, lowering the sails and checking lash lines on the cotton cargo.

St. Clair demanded, "How can they cheer when three men died?"

"They're cheering because we didn't all die."

"Will you hold a memorial service?"

"There will be time for mourning in Bermuda," answered the captain. "And not before!"

A drenching rain pounded down in howling sheets that tore at sailors' clothes and stung their skin. Waves rose like gray monsters trying to tear the frail ship apart.

"Mr. St. Clair," called the captain. "You have studied the Federal navy in detail, have you not?"

"I have."

"In the Wilmington blockade force, do they have Clyde steamers?" (The Clyde River in Scotland was where most of the Confederate side paddle steamers had been built. Clyde steamers like the *Robert E. Lee* had a distinctive profile and look.)

Mr. St. Clair tried to concentrate his thoughts as with each new pitch and roll he feared for his life. "Yes, captain. There are at least three Clyde steamers the Northern navy has captured and pressed into service. At least one has been assigned to this sector."

Wilkinson nodded, "As I thought." He called out loudly, "Mr. Dallard, lower the Confederate Stars and Bars and raise the Stars and Stripes. If another navy ship spots us, we'll try to convince them we're part of the blockade fleet."

St. Clair stared at him in shock. "Is that legal, captain?" he asked.

"Do our investors worry about legality, Mr. St. Clair, or do they worry about getting the ship to port without being caught?"

St. Clair groaned, then asked, "Captain, the return trip will be easier and safer, won't it?"

"On the contrary, Mr. St. Clair. On the return we'll carry 900 kegs of gunpowder. If we get hit on that trip, we will disintegrate in a fireball that will be seen for 100 miles. We will also be carrying $70,000 worth of quinine, 6,000 Enfield rifles, and 400,000 rounds of ammunition—which can also explode quite handsomely, I am told."

"We'll be a floating bomb for the navy to shoot at!" gasped St. Clair.

"Aye, we will. But I don't intend to be hit. We will also carry six miles of canvass cloth, barrels of molasses, and 25,000 pairs of shoes."

"No shoes," St. Clair interrupted. "The profit margin is too low."

"But Confederate soldiers need those shoes, Mr. St. Clair, and they will be on board."

St. Clair argued, "We should carry more luxury items—silk and shawls, fine laces, Paris fashions, and French brandy. They bring more profit."

Wilkinson growled, "A well-equipped Confederate army able to win our freedom on the battlefield is what will create better profits."

St. Clair threw up his hands. "Very well. But can't we pack *some* luxuries?"

Wilkinson smiled. "There's the captain's locker." (Each captain was allocated a small cargo space to import his own merchandise. That cargo usually generated far more profit for the captain than his $5,000 pay.) "I'll be stocking lucifer matches, whalebone corset stays, coffin screws, French brandy, and champagne."

"How soon can we leave Bermuda?"

"As soon as the moon and tide at Wilmington will be again right for our approach, Mr. St. Clair, and no sooner."

Captain Wilkinson turned back to the pounding storm. "One thing at a time, Mr. St. Clair. First I have 600 miles of storm and Federal patrol ships to contend with. One thing at a time."

Aftermath

In its 15 months of cat-and-mouse blockade-running between July 1863 and October 1864, the *Robert E. Lee* made 21 successful trips, hauling out 7,000 bales of cotton worth $2,500,000 in gold. The ship also brought in 40,000 rifles, 200 cannons, 4 million rounds of rifle and musket ammunition, enough beef and pork to sustain Lee's army for two years, and 300,000 pairs of shoes, as well as countless commercial and luxury supplies. That one ship, in one year of running, produced over $18 million in profits.

Best available estimates are that a total of 1,650 ships tried to run the blockade, averaging five trips each before being caught or sunk. That is 8,250 successful cargo trips over the four years of the blockade!

All but 140 of those ships were caught or destroyed. The Union blockade captured 1,149 ships and burned or drove ashore 355. The remaining few were unaccounted for. Cargo worth $22 million was captured and sold at auction by the federal government.

Although thousands of cargoes were slipped through the blockade to Confederate ports, that amount of commerce was a small fraction of what the Confederacy needed to import during the war. Even though it appeared to be porous, the blockade slowed the inflow of cargo to the point where the Confederate army's lack of supplies became a deciding factor in the war.

There is no question that, without Union sea power and the blockade, the Confederacy would have been able to sustain its ground fight long enough to win its independence. The supply, morale, and strength of the Confederate armies would not have deteriorated as they did.

Wilmington, North Carolina, the last open Confederate port, had become more important to the Confederacy than Richmond by mid-1864. When the forts guarding the mouth of the Cape Fear River finally fell in early 1865, the Confederacy's last gasping chance died.

Follow-up Questions and Activities

1. **What Do You Know?**
   - Why did the Union forces blockade Confederate ports?
   - Why didn't the Confederates stop the blockade? Did they ever try? Why didn't they build their own fleet of warships to drive off the Union navy?
   - What was the Union plan to blockade Southern shipping? Why did the Federal navy attack and try to conquer Southern coastal forts?
   - What products were most important for blockade runners to carry, according to ship owners? Which products were most important to the Confederacy?
   - Where did blockade runners go? Why didn't they sail straight to major markets in Europe?

2. **Find Out More.** Following are six important topics from this story for students to research in the library and on the Internet. The reference sources at the back of this book will help them get started.
   - Research the *Robert E. Lee* and its famous Captain Wilkinson. Where was the ship built? How many runs did it make? Find out about the entire naval career of Captain Wilkinson. What did he do after the war? What had he done before it?
   - The *Lee* is only one of many famous privately owned blockade runners. Research others such as the *Sirus, Margret and Jessie, Cornubia, Flora, Ella and Annie, Venus, Little Hattie,* and *Little Ada.* Many of these ships used aliases to fool Union officials. How many names can you find for these famous ships? Which ports did they work out of? Who were their captains? How many runs did they each make through the blockade? Can you find an image of the *Lee* or any of these other ships?
   - The *Alabama* was a Confederate naval warship that was used to run the blockade and to harass Union blockade ships. Research the amazing and successful career of this Confederate ship.
   - Many of the specially designed blockade-running ships were financed by big Southern import/export companies. Two of the biggest were John Fraser & Company out of Charleston and the William C. Bee Company, which had several offices. Research these two influential and powerful companies. How did they build their initial wealth? How well did they survive the war and the collapse of the Confederacy? What happened to them after the war?

- Many of the fastest blockade runners were side paddle steamers built in Scotland's Clyde River. Research the history of Clyde steamers. What happened to paddle wheelers? Why and when were side paddles replaced with rear propellers?
- Research the success of blockade runners. What products did they bring into the Confederacy, and in what quantities? How much cotton did they carry out to fund the war? How much profit did they produce for their owners? Which of their products were most important to the war effort?

3. **Make It Real**

- Prepare a map showing the major Confederate ports and the coastal forts that guarded them as they existed in the summer of 1861. Draw new maps for each year of the war, coloring in the coastal areas captured by Union forces and showing the steady success of the blockade. Trace the routes of the blockade runners.
- Prepare a detailed timeline of the Union blockade. Include each coastal fort conquered and each port, river, or bay closed to Confederate traffic.
- What is a knot? Why do ships measure speed in knots instead of in miles per hour (mph)? Compare mph and knots. Why were knots developed? Who developed the idea? Convert mph to knots. Make a chart showing all of the speed limits in your town converted into knots.

4. **Points to Ponder**

- The Union blockade was intended to harm all Southern citizens, not just the army. Was that a morally acceptable thing to do? Civilians suffered and starved because the blockade prevented food from being imported. Many died from the unavailability of adequate medicines. Is that kind of general attack a legitimate part of warfare?
- The blockade "entitled" U.S. warships to intercept neutral ships in open ocean to inspect them and ensure they didn't carry war-related material that could go to the Confederacy. Do you think that was ethical? Correct?
- Was the blockade a cowardly way to win the war?

1864 at a Glance

The Endless End

In 1864 Louis Pasteur developed his theory that germs (bacteria) cause disease, and that heating and washing to destroy bacteria could prevent infection and disease during operations. Unfortunately, his discovery did not reach American battlefields in time to affect the butchery practiced by Civil War surgeons. Even if it had, it could not have helped to rescue the Confederacy.

During 1864, the Confederacy's last desperate hopes all faded into dust. The Union blockade had reduced Confederate shipping to a tiny trickle. More than 1,500 blockade runners had either been captured or sunk. Fewer than 100 were still afloat and free.

Two major Union offensives were launched. In the West General William T. Sherman aimed for Atlanta, and General Ulysses Grant bulled his way south toward Richmond. Neither general was willing to back off after battle or defeat as had previous Union commanders. Each shoved brutally forward regardless of losses inflicted by Confederate forces. Finally, the Union had generals willing to slug it out to the death. The Confederacy no longer had the strength for such a fight. By October, Sherman sat in Atlanta and prepared to burn and butcher his way across the rest of Georgia. Grant had bypassed Richmond and settled into a trench war against Lee beside the small rail center of Petersburg.

Also in 1864, Lincoln was overwhelmingly reelected. The South had hoped that General George McClellan would win, because he was willing to discuss peace.

By the end of the year nothing but stubborn pride sustained the Confederacy. There was no longer any question of victory. The only remaining questions were when and how the end would come.

Key Events in 1864

Date	Event
April 18	Union General Sherman, now in command of Union forces in Tennessee, pushes south into Georgia.
May 4	Union General Grant, now in command of the Army of the Potomac, pushes across the Rappohannock River to begin his drive to Richmond.
May 5–6	General Robert E. Lee and Grant clash at the Battle of the Wilderness. Lee holds the field, but instead of retreating, Grant slips around the Confederate forces and continues his attack.
May 8–12	Grant continues his attack at the Battle of Spotsylvania. Lee successfully defends and holds the battleground, but Grant again slides away southeast and continues his southern attack.
May 12–16	Lee and Grant continue their nonstop clash at Drewry's Bluff. The results are the same as before.
June 1–3	Grant attacks Lee at Cold Harbor, Virginia. Over 7,000 Union soldiers are cut down in less than 20 minutes of fighting. It is Grant's worst mistake of the war.
June 15	Union troops arrive at Petersburg and face Confederate defensive trenches. The siege of Petersburg begins.
June 27	General Sherman, who has been pushing slowly and steadily south toward Atlanta without major opposition, attacks Confederate General Joe Johnston at Kennesaw Mountain. Sherman is driven back, with heavy losses.
July 13	Confederate General Jubal Early tries to duplicate Stonewall Jackson's 1862 success in the Shenandoah Valley but is defeated and driven back toward Richmond.
July 24	Union General Sherman reaches the defenses of Atlanta and begins his attack on the city.
September 1	Confederate General John Hood is forced to abandon Atlanta. Sherman occupies this critical Confederate rail center.
November 10	Lincoln is reelected, ending Southern hopes of the North electing the peace-minded McClellan, who was willing to negotiate a settlement.
November 15	Before leaving Atlanta, Sherman decides to burn all military facilities. The fire rages out of control and most of Atlanta is destroyed.
November 16	Sherman begins his "march to the sea," burning and destroying everything in his path on the way to Savannah.

Date	Event
December 15	Confederate General Hood, with a small force still active in the West, attacks Union defenses at Nashville, Tennessee. He is defeated by Union General George Thomas, the hero of Chickamauga.
December 21	Sherman occupies Savannah. His destructive march to the sea is complete. He now turns north to meet Grant, still struggling against Lee in the Petersburg trenches.

Southern Shortages
Southern Women's Soldiers' Aid Society Efforts, 1864

During the Revolutionary War fewer than 100,000 men left their homes to serve in the fledgling American army and navy. Eighty years later, the population of the country had increased less than sixfold. Yet, more than 4 million men left home to serve in the Civil War armies of North and South. For every man who marched to the Revolution, 40 marched off to the Civil War.

That loss of manpower proved devastating to families and local economies—especially in the South. Every family had not one but more commonly four or five men at war. Towns were often stripped of males between the ages of 16 and 50. The Confederate army also commandeered a great force of slaves to haul and dig, depriving many plantations and communities of their basic workforce.

Women were left to sustain families and communities, to pick up the pieces, to carry on, to fill the roles of their husbands, brothers, and older sons—to perform all of their own normal duties, and to take on extra burdens to support the war. It was a grueling and daunting challenge.

This burden was especially difficult in the South, with its newer, smaller government that had to rely far more heavily on local clusters of women to fill in yet another gap—providing the material support for their men at war that the government couldn't provide.

The changes in Southern lifestyle came gradually at first. For a time war hit home only in posted casualty lists. Old men still sat in rockers in courthouse squares. Field hands still slaved from dawn to dusk. Lavish beds of roses and dahlias were still carefully cultivated. But changes soon arrived in the form of constant and increasing shortages, spiraling astronomic prices, greater labor shortages, and increased workloads for every remaining citizen of the South. By 1864, the changes had become a crushing burden that threatened to tear the fabric of the Southern society apart.

Meet Virginia DeLouise

Virginia Taylor was born in Charleston, South Carolina, in 1812 (during the opening shots of that war). Her grandfather (a brother of Robert E. Lee's grandfather) had grown wealthy in land, lumber, and plantation dealings. Virginia's father was placed in charge of the family shipping company in Charleston and turned it into the family's one money-losing venture. He lost four ships and cargoes during the War of 1812 to British warships, and he was never able to fully recover.

Virginia married a 40-year-old lawyer, Charles DeLouise, when she was only 17 and moved with him to Fayetteville, North Carolina. There she gradually assumed a position of prominence in local social circles. Charles died when Virginia was 41 (1853), leaving her a wealthy and influential widow in Fayetteville.

After the war, Virginia moved to Richmond, Virginia, to be close to other family members. She died on a visit to Fayetteville in 1871 at age 59.

Southern Shortages

A s inconspicuously as she could, 52-year-old Virginia DeLouise leaned toward a tall, elegantly dressed woman busily scraping lint from cotton towels in a circle of women huddled near the kitchen stove. The lint would be shipped to the front to dress battle wounds. These women met three times a week here in Fayetteville, North Carolina, to support the Confederate war effort. Virginia had to lean close for her whisper to be heard above the branches that scraped and slapped against the siding in the blustering wind this icy afternoon of February 12, 1864. "Mary Jane, a word?"

With a slight nod to the other ladies clustered around the table, 38-year-old Mary Jane Burton rose and followed Virginia into a back sitting room. Virginia closed the door. "I have received a letter from President Jefferson Davis himself."

Shock flashed across Mary Jane's face. Her hand sprang to cover her mouth. "They actually wrote to him?"

"Who?" Virginia demanded.

"Some in our Aid Society have grown opposed to the war. I heard that they were going to write to the president and tell him so. I assumed he wrote to you because they wrote to him."

Virginia DeLouise was a large and stately woman, a second cousin to Robert E. Lee, and every bit as much a general. Now she scowled and seemed to swell into a mighty wall. "How dare they?!"

Mary Jane blushed and shrank before this human mountain of power. "Many members of this Aid Society have said they wished the war would end."

"End in *victory*!" Virginia interrupted.

"No, just end," Mary Jane corrected.

Virginia sighed and deflated like a leaky balloon. Weary age seemed to creep over her as her fierceness drained away. "None of our members wrote to President Davis. That is not why he wrote. . . . It is bad enough that the war has turned against us. It is bad enough that we must each give our wealth, our possessions and heirlooms, our very means of livelihood to the war. It is bad enough that most of our men and many of our slaves have been taken away by the war. It is bad enough that we must endure unending and unbearable shortages of every conceivable commodity. But this. . . . We're tearing our society apart! It is inconceivable that our own women—our friends and comrades in triumph and deprivation—would lose their will and determination to carry on."

Virginia paused, head bowed. "Without steadfast determination and a cheerful countenance, what do we have? I must root out this disease." She paused again, drumming her fingers on an end table. "This makes my news doubly dangerous. President Davis wrote to say that we will no longer support the 17th North Carolina Regiment. Henceforth, we will support the 28th Regiment."

Groups of women all across the South were assigned to support every active Confederate regiment. This collection of as many as 50 women in Fayetteville met three times a week at the rambling home of Vivian Lancet, the wife of a wealthy cotton exporter, to sew, mend, and fabricate needed supplies for their regiment.

Virginia paused and glanced suspiciously at her friend. "How do you think the others will react to the news? Will it affect their resolve?"

"Why ask me?"

Exasperated, Virginia said, "It is *desertions* over this past month that have dropped the 17th under 150 men, too small to be a separate regiment."

Mary Jane's cheeks flushed bright red and she lowered her eyes. "So you know?" her voice barely above a whisper.

"That your son is one of those deserters and is hiding in a storage barn on your plantation?"

Mary Jane's eyes flashed anger. "There are other women in our group with family members who have deserted. I have heard that two of our most prominent members, Vivian Lancet and Jane Goodman, each has a deserter son hiding in the nearby hills."

Virginia murmured, "How can you bear the shame?"

Mary Jane ground her teeth together and glared at the elected head of the Fayetteville Women's Soldiers' Aid Society. "We maintain a cheerful countenance and stiffen our resolve to fight for our glorious Confederacy." In a lower tone Mary Jane added, "And take a broom and beat the stuffing out of the disgraceful derelict every chance I get."

"I fear that some of our women will feel demoralized and loose their last scrap of devotion to our sacred cause if they learn that our regiment has dissolved not because of hated Yankee bullets, but because of cowardice. And now you tell me that some have already lost heart with our cause." Virginia's eyes narrowed. Her face tightened. "Keep careful watch on our group today and help me identify those who have lost faith."

Mary Jane said, "You must announce the change, of course. But don't mention the reason. Now, more than ever, we must *all* fight on!" Mary Jane Burton owned a large plantation with 180 slaves. She had as great a personal stake in the war as any woman in the state.

Back in the living room and main sitting parlor, Virginia rang a small bell for attention. "Ladies, it is time for committee reports. But before reports, I have received some important news."

"I wish it were good news about *firewood*," said Elizabeth (Bet) Taylor, a tiny, 30-year-old woman who served as a volunteer nurse. Bet felt ridiculous in her billowing white nurse's hat, which seemed to stand almost as tall as she did.

A rare snow flurry had swept through Fayetteville the previous night, making the new shortage of firewood acute.

"Or about a new supply of pins and needles. Why must there be shortages of *everything*?" added Jane Goodman in her soft voice that usually sounded more like a whisper.

"We'll just have to pray harder," said 20-year-old Susan Harmon, wife of a Presbyterian preacher now serving with General Johnston's army in the West. "Our cause is just and God *will* support the Confederacy if our hearts are pure."

"And strike Abraham Lincoln dead!" said Jane in a voice that was loud and stirring for her. The assemblage of women applauded their agreement.

"It is news about our 17th Regiment, ladies," Virginia announced to draw the conversation back on track. All sewing, lint scraping, bandage rolling, and leather working stopped at the mention of the regiment President Davis had assigned this group of women to support.

"Ladies, the 17th Regiment has been redesignated a battalion within the 28th. We will henceforth support the 28th North Carolina Regiment."

An awkward silence blanketed the room. All were sadly aware that this change reflected many deaths of local men and boys. They also knew it reflected the recent epidemic of desertions from the army. Mary Burton blushed and lowered her eyes. Susan Harmon clasped her hands in prayer. "God save the souls of the dearly departed . . . and damn to hell every deserter!"

Virginia DeLouise again rang her bell for attention and beamed a confident smile. But her voice rumbled with an unmistakable threat that commanded every lady in the room not to question the change. "It is now our duty to accept the change with a cheerful countenance and use our energies to turn it to good."

Jane Goodman, a plump woman with a natural liquid grace and the widow of the mayor of Fayetteville who had died in battle in 1862, sighed, "So many deaths and so much dying. Can the struggle be worth so great a price?"

Susan Harmon bristled. "Our struggle is worth *every* sacrifice. I am a simple preacher's wife and do not have much. Still, I have given my entire inheritance, my brass, my silver, my jewelry, my slaves, my two wagons, and my livestock to the Confederacy. I give my time, energy, and prayers. And I will gladly give more until the fight is won. No sacrifice is too great!"

Many women in the group applauded.

Jane sprang to her feet, eyes ablaze. Her sewing tumbled to the floor. "Noble words, Susan. But I have already lost a husband, a brother, and two of my three sons in this horrid war. Must I lose everyone I love so dearly? Soon, even if we win, there won't be anyone left to live in the Confederacy."

Virginia DeLouise leaned to Mary Jane and murmured, "I believe Jane Goodman is one."

Vivian Lancet, a tall, thin woman and host of these gatherings, patted Jane's arm to ease her back into her seat.

Bet Taylor had to stand to be seen. "We have all seen so, *so* many dead and mutilated! Almost every male in Fayetteville is a maimed and crippled veteran. Surely there must be a way to preserve our nation without enduring such horrors."

Mary Jane Burton whispered to Virginia, "Bet Taylor is another." Virginia nodded as her eyebrows arched.

Jane Goodman nodded in agreement with Bet. "At some point the war will no longer be worth the price it exacts. And that moment, I fear, is rapidly approaching."

The room erupted in heated whispers, insistent murmurs, hissed warnings and threats, and occasional shouted outbursts.

"Ladies, please!" Virginia called. "We are proud North Carolina women and will maintain our cheerful fortitude. There is not one of us who does not despise every Yankee and will not rest until someone with good Southern blood spits on each of their graves! There is not one of us who is not willing to give her property, her energy—her very life—to further the Confederacy."

The women nodded and murmured their agreement with their elected leader.

Vivian Lancet wagged her finger to emphasize her point. "It is the constant shortages that irritate us and make us speak in uncivil ways. Our communities are falling apart because of shortages. Food, fuel, teachers, fashions, every luxury and necessity, preachers, dresses, bonnets . . . even firewood—all seem to be hopelessly overpriced or completely unavailable. A simple needle is so precious now it is considered an heirloom! In three short years this war has marched our society backward a century and a half."

"Bickering and complaining will not win this war," Virginia continued. "I, for one, intend for the Confederacy to win this war. And if that means that we women of Fayetteville must lead the battle cry, then lead we shall. As your elected chair, I now call on three committees to issue their reports."

The heated mob regained their composure and sank back into chairs as Vivian continued. "First, the education committee report from Jane Goodman, the committee chair."

Jane stood and dragged three clothbound books from a canvas bag draped over her shoulder. "Because teaching has never been considered an esteemed profession, most of our teachers traditionally came from the North. In 1861 they either left or were driven out. Every public school in this county was closed. Most North Carolina colleges also closed when both teachers and students enlisted in the army. For over two years our children have been growing up in ignorance."

She paused while others murmured their agreement with her assessment of the collapse of Southern education. "Recently, we have made good progress. After the calls for teachers by both the governor and the president, we have secured 15 teachers in this county alone—all of them women who are performing admirably. All but a few rural schools are now reopened." (Until 1863, only men taught in Southern public schools.)

A round of applause interrupted her report. "Even better, we have new texts available for our schools. As you know, all of the old, Northern textbooks were destroyed in early 1862. I hold here three of our new texts." Jane held up the first book. "Johnson's *Elementary Arithmetic*." She randomly opened to a page and read. "If one Confederate soldier kills 90 Yankees, how many Yankees can 10 Confederates kill?"

The women smiled and nodded their approval. Jane raised the next book. "Marinda Moore's *Geography*, which explains, for example (and I quote) 'the principal obstacle to Confederate trade is the illegal blockade by the miserable and hellish Yankee nation.' " Again the women nodded and applauded.

"Finally, I hold *The Geographical Reader for Dixie Children*, which correctly explains that slavery is not sinful because slaves are a contented people. On other fronts, we have found a Georgia company that makes pencils using coal instead of graphite. These pencils work well enough for our students. I have but one continuing problem to report: There is no paper available for the schools. Our children must learn to write and cannot do so without paper."

Virginia thanked the education committee for their work as a number of women eagerly flipped through the new books. "Now we will hear from Susan Harmon, chair of the religion committee."

Susan stood and thinly smiled. "You will be pleased to hear that both the Methodist and Baptist Conventions have confirmed the moral superiority of the South to the materialistic, mongrel North. Episcopal Bishop Stephen Elliott has proven in his Bible studies that slavery was established by God and that Southerners have been given the sacred responsibility to perpetuate it. He and other Bible scholars have found 18 specific references in the Bible that confirm the righteousness of the Southern lifestyle and the Confederate cause."

Susan paused to glare at those she suspected of not wholeheartedly supporting the war. "The Methodist Council has confirmed that failure to support the Confederate cause is sufficient reason for eternal exclusion from the kingdom of grace and everlasting glory."

Again she paused, smiling smugly. "Our only problem is a lack of preachers to conduct Sunday services. Most ordained ministers are serving with the various armies. With the colleges reopened, we are hopeful that soon ministers will again be available to every community."

Virginia thanked Susan for her stirring report as the assembled women applauded.

Jane Goodman had eased next to Vivian Lancet and whispered, "We *all* still have much to lose if the war continues." Jane paused and glanced over her shoulder before adding, "A dear brother, for example."

Vivian blanched and gasped. "What do you know of my brother?"

Jane smiled. "Only that he has made several very successful smuggling trips through Memphis."

Vivian sank lower into a chair, trembling. "Do the others know?"

Jane shook her head. "I think not. It would make you an outcast to be enjoying smuggled luxuries while the Confederacy chokes in starvation." Jane patted Vivian's arm. "But the point is, if the war continues, he *will* be caught. I believe you and I share common views."

"But we can't stop our work for the war," Vivian spluttered.

"We should support the troops, but not the war. Our voices must ring loudly in Richmond. Can we count on your support?"

Vivian blushed but silently nodded as Virginia announced, "And finally, our own volunteer nurse, Bet Taylor, and the medical committee report."

Even after short Bet Taylor stood up, many had to crane their necks to be able to see her. "All frontline hospitals continue to be critically short of lint, bandages, morphine, surgical saw blades, and chloroform. The blockade makes these items almost impossible to obtain. Many suffer and die needlessly because of these terrible shortages. Here at home, our hospitals desperately need quinine, morphine, nitric acid, bandages, lime, and volunteers. Disease is at epidemic proportions in virtually every hospital. But most doctors are away with the army and most towns have no doctors at all to care for the sick. We don't even have enough men left in town to dig the graves for the soldiers who die while under our care."

Mary Jane Burton turned beet red and blurted, "My son *can't* come in and dig. He'll be caught and hanged as a deserter. A hanged soldier does no one any good. At least this way, after the war, he'll be alive to run the plantation."

"*What* plantation?" snapped Susan Harmon. "If we lose the war because half the army has deserted, then there won't be any Burton plantation to run!"

Virginia raised her hands and bellowed, "Ladies, please! Hush with such talk. There can be no room for it in our hearts or in our voices. I thank the committees for their reports and diligent work. And now we must continue with our assigned work to support the 28th Regiment so that they can continue the glorious fight for our cause."

Jane Goodman squatted next to Bet Taylor and murmured, "The very fabric of our civilization is coming unglued, Bet. We see it right here in this room—so very different from our eager meetings in '61 and '62 filled with confidence and harmony. We need to search for other solutions than fighting and killing. Will you help me?"

Bet turned, eyes widening. "What kind of solutions . . . ?"

Jane interrupted, "We'll talk later," smiled, and patted Bet's arm.

Virginia said, "After our diligent work this blustery morning and these stirring committee reports, I think we should pause to nibble refreshments." Then she added, "These are stressful times. We do not need to add to that stress from within. From this moment on, I expect the members of this Aid Society to remember our sacred duty and to create solutions instead of complaints. After refreshments, we will adjourn for today."

Vivian Lancet rang a small bell. Three slaves emerged from a back pantry with platters of sponge cake and sugar cake. Two more carried steaming pitchers.

"Coffee?" exclaimed Virginia. "Have you been holding out on us, Vivian?"

"Coffee is over $10 a pound, Virginia. No one can afford that. With Confederate pride I serve a substitute: roasted corn meal."

"Far better than using roasted cubes of sweet potato," agreed Mary Jane. "But it *smells* like coffee."

Vivian smiled. "I added one-eighth cup of real coffee for the aroma. I *could* afford that much."

With "ahhh's" of delight, the women clustered around the pitchers to breathe in the dearly missed aroma.

Vivian pointed to the last two pitchers, "Tea with currant and blackberry leaves. Not like the real thing, but a passable substitute since no one can get real tea anymore."

Virginia DeLouise again drew Mary Jane Burton aside. "Their reaction was worse than I feared. Especially I am beginning to suspect the loyalty of Jane and Bet."

"Bet is such a compassionate and tenderhearted person," said Mary Jane. "I'm sure her heart breaks every time she tends to a wounded soldier."

"Nonetheless, I will not have members spreading the notion that the war isn't worth fighting. I will not allow us to disintegrate from within."

"When I left home this morning I thought slaves were my only problem," answered Mary Jane.

"Slaves?"

"Every plantation owner now lives in terror of slaves. We have 180 and only two hired men to control them. Five have run away and not been caught! How much do the others know of the war? Of Yankee advances and promises of freedom? Will they poison me tonight? Tomorrow? Will they revolt and slit my throat? It would be easy for them to overpower us."

"I see," murmured Virginia.

The women ate hungrily, politely ignoring the fact that the platters were earthenware instead of silver and that the pitchers were badly tarnished from lack of available polish. But, then, everything had grown shabby during the war. Worn spots and torn fabric were patched and sewed instead of being replaced. Shelves were bare of brass and silver heirlooms.

The meeting ended as the cake trays emptied. Members of the Fayetteville Soldiers' Aid Society bundled themselves in threadbare coats and scarves and drifted home in groups of twos and threes.

Virginia maneuvered her way to Jane Goodman. "Jane, a word?"

"Certainly, Virginia."

"Get your coat. We'll talk as we walk."

"But I promised to talk to Bet and Vivian before I left," Jane answered.

"I'm sure you did," said Virginia. "Nonetheless, get your coat."

Jane dutifully fetched her coat and answered the summons, finding Virginia waiting for her on the front porch, her breath hissing into frosty clouds.

Their feet crunched over a film of ice as they walked. Jane hugged her arms tight around her to ward off the biting wind. Virginia began, "A most serious and disturbing rumor has reached my ear. I hear that you are writing to President Davis urging him to end the war."

Jane sighed and nodded. "I am *planning* to write as soon as I gather more support. We must seek another way to resolve the conflict. The military is hopeless."

"Never!" Virginia barked, her voice as hard and bitter as the cold.

Jane continued, "The shortages will kill us if the Yankees don't. We have nothing left to give. I have lost my husband, a brother, two sons, and my family's wealth. The government, the society, and the army are all crumbling."

Virginia motioned toward a bench out of the worst of the wind. "We are surrounded by a sea of hardship and depravation. All that holds back the floodwaters of ruin is our unwavering resolve. We will not be defeated if we refuse to consider defeat!"

Jane explained, "I am not saying we should abandon our work, only that we urge the president to seek peace now."

"You would allow Yankees to reign victorious?!" Virginia bellowed. "If even one crack shows in that dam of stalwart Southern resolve, then the dam will split and we will be washed away—if not by Yankee guns, then by our own despair. This is 1864, for goodness sake! We can't survive on the innocent blush of '61 or '62. These are the times that try our souls. And I will not have the Soldiers' Aid Society of Fayettville found wanting!"

Jane remained resolute. "We must do *something*."

"Give me one week, Jane. Do nothing and talk to no one about this for one week. And then we will see."

Jane pursed her lips in thought before slowly nodding in agreement. The women rose to trudge home. Virginia said, "Did you know that our own Ruth Mancot just published another poem?"

Jane shook her head. Virginia smiled. "It is a stirring piece entitled 'The Godliness of Stonewall Jackson.' *That* is the attitude we must preserve, Jane. Think on it and we will talk next week."

Virginia found Mary Jane Burton waiting in her carriage when Virginia reached home on Azalea Street. "Were you right? Has she written?"

"She has not written the letter yet, but intends to," Virginia answered feeling suddenly bone tired from the effort to maintain her cheerful and confident facade.

"What happened?" Mary Jane demanded.

"I bought one week's time."

"What good will *that* do?" continued Mary Jane. "What can you do in one week?"

"Buy one more week," Virginia answered, struggling to sound enthusiastic. "And then I shall buy another, and so on until the spring campaign begins and Robert E. Lee creates a miracle victory on the battlefield to carry the groundswell of Southern pride through the summer."

Mary Jane began, "But . . ."

Virginia interrupted. "We will preserve and wait for good news from the front. Without it, I fear Jane's sentiment will quickly spread."

"But . . ." began Mary Jane again.

Virginia cut her off. "Don't dwell on problems and disagreements. Focus on our opportunity to work for the Confederate cause. We must move forward with cheerful fortitude!"

But what can we *really* do?" insisted Mary Jane.

"*Do?*" Virginia repeated. "We will do everything we *can* do. We will loathe Yankees and continue to preserve!" She sighed and added, "I fear that, for now, that is all we *can* do."

Aftermath

Southern women remained remarkably loyal and supportive of the Confederacy to the last bitter gasps in 1865. They willingly poured their family wealth, possessions, silver, brass, jewelry, granaries, and life's blood into the war effort. That generous sacrifice meant that Southern families had been stripped bare and were economically devastated at war's end. They had typically saved nothing to fall back on, having already given everything to the Confederate army, government, and cause. The loss of the war, of their lifestyle, and of so many of their men made these women especially bitter at war's end.

After the war, Virginia DeLouise moved to Richmond, Virginia, to be closer to other family members. She died on a visit back to Fayetteville in 1871 at age 59.

Follow-up Questions and Activities

1. **What Do You Know?**

   • Why did private women's groups have to support army units?

   • What services did women's groups provide for the units they were assigned to support?

   • Why did so many Southern schools close at the beginning of the Civil War? Why did newspapers also close as the war progressed?

• Why did the South suffer from so many shortages that didn't affect the North?

2. **Find Out More.** Here are seven topics that were important to this story for students to research in the library and on the Internet. The reference sources at the back of this book will help them get started.

   • Research the vast amount of work Southern women had to perform to support the war. Which tasks did they have to do because the government didn't or couldn't do them? Why wasn't the Confederate government better able to provide the support its army required?

   • Desertions were a major problem on both sides of the war. Research desertion during the Civil War. How many deserted from the Confederate army year by year? How many from the Union army? What was the punishment for desertion? How many were caught and actually punished?

   • How many slaves lived in the South in 1864? How many were freed in 1865? What happened to them?

   • Research Southern shortages during the war. What became scarce? Were there any commodities and services that remained plentiful? What effect did each shortage have on daily life?

   • Not all Southerners believed in the Confederacy. Research Southern women who remained loyal to the Union. Sarah Johnson, Nellie Taylor, Mrs. Elizabeth Grier, and Mrs. Shepard Wells are a few of the Southern women who remained outspoken supporters of the Union. Research the experiences of these and other loyalist Southern women. What happened to them during the war? After the war?

   • Research Southern literature during the war—poems, newspaper articles, textbooks, and prose. Compare it to the propaganda created by other warring regimes in the twentieth century. Why would a nation want to slant every written piece to make itself appear to be flawless and blameless?

   • Over three-quarters of all Southern newspapers went out of business during the war. Why? How did Southern citizens get news about the war and world events?

3. **Make It Real**

   • Make a chart of the Southern population. How many families lived in each state of the South? What was the population of each state? How many soldiers enlisted in the army from each Southern state? What percentage of the white male population went to war from each state? How many men died during the war? How many returned home crippled and maimed? On average, how many war dead and wounded came from each family in each state? Including cousins and uncles, how many families do you think lost no one?

   • Make a list of what was considered to be "women's work" when the war began. What new professions were taken over by women during the course of the war? What new work did women take on because most men had gone to war? What extra work did women take on to support the war? Compare women's experience during the Civil War to American women's experience in other wars (from the Revolution through Vietnam).

4. **Points to Ponder**

- Why do you think the Southerners felt such a strong need to religiously and philosophically justify and legitimize slavery and the Confederate cause? Why did they rewrite textbooks to support the Southern view? Do most warring nations exhibit this same urge? Did Northern society take similar actions during the Civil War?

- Why was desertion such a big problem during the Civil War? Why did so many want to desert and willingly risk the consequences of being caught? Why didn't all soldiers feel motivated to stay and fight for their cause?

Battle "Cries"
Women Working in an Army Hospital, May 1864

No one expected the war to last long enough to need hospitals, nurses, coremen, or convalescent facilities. Almost instantly, the demand for skilled medical personnel vastly outstripped the available supply.

After the First Battle of Bull Run (Manassas), field army hospitals shipped the wounded back to Washington and Richmond. Neither city was prepared for this on-slaught of demand for urgent care. Wounded were stacked in every available space—even in the Capitol rotunda. Many died of neglect before the few available doctors and volunteer nurses could tend to them.

In both North and South, a new breed of medical facility sprang up—small-scale, private hospitals staffed by women nurses. It was a radical idea at the time. Medical services had traditionally been performed by men. Women were considered too frail and constitutionally weak to withstand the site of blood, wounds, and disease. Polite society frowned on the women who tried to invade this man's profession.

Still, more than 3,000 women served as nurses in private and governmental hospitals during the war. It was the beginning of a new vocation for women.

The largest hospital on either side of the war was giant Chimborazo Heights in Richmond, Virginia, with 8,500 beds, 10 kitchens, two bakeries, which churned out 10,000 loaves of bread a day, a 400-keg brewery, and its own icehouse. At the other extreme, many hospitals consisted of a few beds in one or more rooms of a house.

By 1864, 13,000 doctors served in the Federal army, about 3,500 in the Confederate army. Many of these doctors had hands-on experience as apprentices but no formal classroom training. Medical school at the time only lasted for two 12-week terms and was considered a lowly, third alternative to either law or business school. Many college-degreed doctors had never used a thermometer, a stethoscope, or a syringe.

Death rates in Civil War hospitals were atrociously high. Infection and disease ran rampant through the wards. Bacteria, viruses, and germs had not yet been discovered. No one knew of the connection between cleanliness and disease. Sterilization did not exist. However, one hospital stood out far above all others for its success. It was a small, private hospital started in Richmond, Virginia, in 1862. This hospital treated 1,733 patients during the war. Only 73 died, a success rate unmatched in any facility on either side.

Meet Sally Tompkins

The Tompkins' family wealth derived from landholdings and real estate deals in the late 1700s and early 1800s. Sally was born in early 1833 and raised in the small town of Poplar Grove, Virginia, where her father owned a lumber mill. After his death in 1850 (when Sally was 16), her mother moved the family to Richmond.

Shortly after the First Battle of Bull Run, Sally volunteered as a nurse in a hospital started by the sister of Robert E. Lee. Sally's family (especially her mother) strongly opposed her volunteer work, fearing that with her frail constitution and diminutive size (she stood well under five feet tall) she would collapse under the strain of work.

By January 1862, 30-year-old Sally convinced a prominent family friend, Judge John Robertson, to give her his in-town house so that she could open her own hospital following her own ideas of care.

Sally opened a 28-bed hospital at her own expense—using her family inheritance. Before the end of the war, Confederate president Jefferson Davis awarded Sally the rank of captain as a special recognition of her extraordinary success rate. As a military officer, Sally was able to keep her hospital functioning for eight months after the war's final blows until her last patients were well enough to travel home.

Following the war, Sally lived in Richmond for the rest of her life, staying active in local charities, until becoming destitute, having spent what little family money remained after the war. She lived the last years of her life in the Home for Confederate Women in Richmond. When she died in 1916, she was buried with full military honors.

Battle "Cries"

The rain grew from a faint pitter-patter to a constant drumming during the afternoon of May 19, 1864. Wind began to rattle the windows. Thirty-two-year-old Sally Tompkins glanced outside at the spreading wetness on Chestnut Street and sighed. A thunderstorm was rolling into Richmond, Virginia.

"Louisa? You best sit with the new men. Take Cassie and Mae with you and try to keep them from tearing out their stitches again."

Forty-two-year-old Louisa Harrison had been a volunteer at this private hospital serving Confederate soldiers for 15 months, working six days a week and often staying long into the night. Sally Tompkins was founder and director of the hospital.

"I was just delivering the afternoon doses of quinine," answered Louisa, carrying a porcelain platter filled with small vials of the precious medicine. Louisa stood a full head taller than Sally. Both wore their hair pulled back in a bun and both wore dark, plain, high-necked dresses with flowing skirts. Louisa was thick-boned and sturdy. Sally, a bundle of energy, was petite, frail, and had the tiniest of waists.

Sally nodded toward the window. "Thunderstorms always bring out the worst memories for the wounded."

Louisa nodded in understanding. "I'll finish medicine rounds later." She set the tray on a table and rushed to what had been the spacious dining room where new patients were delivered and where the most critical were cared for in this 28-bed hospital. The hospital usually held more sick than wounded soldiers. But there had been so many battles lately that the wounded had pushed out all but their most serious typhoid and diphtheria cases.

Sally settled onto a straight-backed chair between the beds of two soldiers who had arrived three weeks before. One would have to learn to live without one hand and one leg. The other had lost an arm, an eye, and part of his face. Those wounds would heal. But these two, especially, could not rid themselves of the terror of battle. Their real wounds were the endless terrors locked deep in their minds and souls. These wounds, Sally knew, her medicines and bandages could never mend.

The first soldier glared with clenched teeth at the ceiling as if expecting to see lines of blue soldiers emerge from the long cracks. The rat-tat-tat of the rain pushed him back into the dense thickets of the Wilderness where, in a wild and screaming charge, he had been cut down by a fierce Federal volley.

He tensed in bed. Sally wiped the beading sweat off his forehead and patted his shoulder. He screamed for the men in his company to press forward and he cheered them on. He called for his captain to duck and moaned as he seemed to sadly count the men around him as they fell. Then he raised his missing hand and, suddenly confused, wondered why it didn't still hold a rifle.

Sally whispered, "It's only rain. You're safe here," and continued to pat his shoulder as he began to sob, then to scream, and then to begin the nightmare charge all over again. Sally moaned with him, frustrated that she could do nothing to take away his pain, afraid that she would soon be unable to stand hearing their intense sufferings any longer and would break and run herself.

On Sally's other side, the man with the heavily bandaged head tensed his body as the rain drummed harder on the windows. His one remaining eye turned wild and frantic as it darted around the former living room seeking shelter. As he had every day for three weeks, he moaned, "No, no. There's too many. No. Go away. NO!" Then he screamed, went rigid as a board, and collapsed whimpering into his soft clouds of white pillows. He had not once spoken in the hospital except for his nightmare hallucinations. Sally often wondered if his mind would ever be well enough to talk again. He simply lay in bed and whimpered, or screamed, and vacantly stared through his one terrified eye.

As the first bolt of lightning crackled nearby, Sally heard terrible screams from the back room and sighed. Storms were always hardest on the new ones.

The 12 beds in the dining room of this house-turned-hospital were used for the most critical and newest patients because the double French doors from that room led onto the back porch where army ambulance wagons deposited their cargo and picked up the bodies of those that didn't survive. There had been heavy, continuous fighting over the past several weeks, and these beds were filled with new arrivals. Overflow patients lay on straw heaps on the floor between beds.

Louisa and three of Sally's four slaves (all of whom worked full-time at the hospital) glided from bed to bed, checking dressings, trying to calm the pain and fear that wracked each body.

Louisa sat with one man who bellowed in terror. She softly sang to him, hoping the notes would soothe his tormented soul. Rain rattled the windows. Thunder rumbled down the streets. But this soldier heard only musket fire, the whine of musket balls, and the roar of cannons. Eyes gone wild with fright, he bellowed his rage and hate and tried to rise.

Louisa cried, "Mae, I need you!" Then instructed, "Help hold him down. He has fresh hip and side wounds and isn't supposed to move."

The soldier bellowed and tried to push the women aside. Louisa called to Daisey, another of Sally's slaves. "Get Joseph. We need more strength or he'll tear out his stitches."

Then searing pain exploded through the man's body like the stab of a red-hot knife as he started to roll off the bed. He gasped and sank back into the bed, shrieking.

"Check the bandages, Mae. Is he bleeding again?"

Near the double doors, a captain lay with a brutal stomach wound. His fresh bandages and his bed sheets were already stained by a creeping puddle of red. Cassie, another of the black girls, slowly fanned him through the muggy warmth of the afternoon. Eight of his soldiers were gathered solemnly, silently around the foot of his bed, rain dripping off their greatcoats onto the wooden floor.

The captain feebly asked to be raised. Cassie propped extra pillows behind his back and head. His skin was the color of gray putty, his life slipping slowly away like sand in an hourglass—a little more, a little more. His eyes rolled back as the struggle went on. And then, with a final sigh, came painlessness and death. The soldiers stood for a moment, heads bowed. Then they shuffled out to catch a wagon ride back to the fields of killing.

Cassie hurried to the front room. "Mistress Sally, you best come. There's been a calling."

Amazingly few soldiers died in Sally Tompkins's hospital. In the early months of their operation, when a soldier did die, Sally said that he had been called to God. Now the staff simply said there'd been a calling.

"Are Joseph and Tom still here?" Two male army nurses worked two hours each morning and each afternoon at the hospital to provide services that were not considered appropriate for women—such as complete patient bathing and use of the bathroom facilities by the invalids.

"Yes, ma'am."

"Run and ask them not to leave yet. They can carry the body to the woodshed until the ambulance comes tomorrow." Then Sally added, "Who was he?"

"That new captain, ma'am." Cassie turned and hurried off.

Sally sighed and let her head droop forward. That captain had arrived yesterday morning. She hadn't even had time to greet him or to introduce herself. *They come so filled with pain, misery, and terror,* Sally thought. *They come needing so much. They lie here and stare off into space with vacant, hollow eyes. Some die, some hobble off. None, I think, ever really recover.* Again she sighed and asked out loud to the walls that never answered, "Why are they so eager to volunteer for war when *this* is what awaits them?"

Sally Tompkins's hospital had treated more than 1,000 patients so far in the war. This was only the 62nd to die under her care. "I should be pleased with our successes," she thought. "But each death weighs so heavily, and there have been so many endless deaths. We mend their bodies so they can hobble out and join the thousands of other cripples begging on the streets." She cried aloud, "When will it ever end?!" startling several patients lying in the front room where she still gently rubbed the shoulder of a whimpering soldier.

"The storm's passing," called Louisa, stepping back from the dining room. "I can see blue sky off in the West. I think it's safe to finish our work."

"Our work, I fear, will never be finished," Sally answered.

Ellen Stately, another volunteer, descended from the upstairs ward. The upstairs rooms were used for those almost well enough to be discharged. "Did everyone survive the storm down here?"

Sally breathed deeply and forced herself to smile as she tried to shake her gloom. "No worse than usual, I think, except for one calling."

"Number 62," said Ellen, who had worked at this hospital since it first opened. "It was the captain, wasn't it? I knew he couldn't last."

Sally rose, breathed deeply, and turned to the only escape she knew from the death and pain that surrounded her—work. "Louisa, finish the medicines. Be generous with the morphine and quinine today. Mrs. Candell has promised a new shipment tomorrow. Cassie, fetch nitric acid and bromine.[1] I thought I smelled gangrene on one of the newer patients. Ellen, you and Mae will open windows to ventilate and change dressings . . ."

"We're running low on lint,"[2] said Louisa.

"Mrs. Candell can always get lint. I'll remind her tomorrow. The girls will start with the afternoon scrubbing and then start dinner. We have over 30 mouths to feed today."

The "girls" were Sally's four slaves, whom she had brought to the hospital with her when it opened.

"Must they scrub the floors and walls *every* afternoon?" Louisa asked.

"And change the linen twice a week," answered Sally. "It is our duty to make cleanliness a living part of this hospital. I think it shortens patient recovery time. And haven't you noticed that we have less disease here than in most hospitals? I suspect that cleanliness is somehow the reason, but I can find nothing in the medical literature to support it."

Sally joined Cassie in the dining room where the black girl had prepared a tray with linen bandages, a pile of soft lint, a bowl of water, and glass bottles of nitric acid and bromine. Sally nodded toward a bed along the south wall. "It's Isiah." Then she added, "Be strong, Cassie. He *needs* this treatment."

The black girl nodded, "Yes, ma'am. But I surely do hate this treatment."

The young soldier couldn't have been more than 16. He still hadn't begun to shave. Now, with both legs amputated above the knee, he would never walk. The boy cringed as the women approached and pressed back into his pillows, clutching the sheet tight around him. "Don't touch me! You jus' leave me alone!"

"Isiah's such a good, strong name," said Sally in her well-practiced, soothing voice. "You'll be fine. We just need to make sure your wounds are healing properly."

No one mentioned amputations or missing limbs in the hospital. Every gruesome battlefield butchery was simply called "a wound."

Cassie pulled back the sheet. Both women smelled, wrinkled up their noses at the odor of putrid flesh, and nodded. "Both legs," said Sally. Then she murmured, "It's amazing he's still alive."

Isiah began to whimper. "Oh, please, please don't do it again. It burns so bad. It hurts too much."

Cassie unwound the linen bandages over the useless stubs of his legs.

"Please don't," he sobbed. "I can't stand the pain. Oh, please let me be. Jus' let me die in peace . . ."

Tears rolled down Sally's cheeks as she thought, *He's too young to know this much suffering.* She patted his shoulder and repeated, "You'll be fine. This will only take a moment."

Cassie lifted the nitric acid bottle and a thick cotton cloth. The boy weakly tried to kick with legs that were no longer there. "No, damn you! Leave me be!"

Sally drizzled the acid onto the putrid flesh at the tip of his stubs. The flesh bubbled, sizzled, and smoked. Cassie mopped up the excess with her cloth, which also began to smoke as the acid ate through the cotton fibers. The smell of burning flesh mingled with the stench of putrification and rose in waves so thick and strong they were almost visible in the stale air. Sally and Cassie both gagged but continued their frightful work.

Isiah screamed. His body went rigid as a board, his eyes bulging in horror. Sally dripped more acid on the worst spots until the decayed flesh disintegrated.

The boy passed out from terror and pain. "Now bromine to promote healing," said Sally, wiping away her own tears. Cassie dabbed bromine on the ugly, charred scars. Then she dabbed handfuls of lint in her bowl of water and patted the damp lint against the wound and covered it all with fresh linen bandages.

Back out in the front hall, both nurses sank onto a wooden bench. Their hands trembled from the grim memory of their effort.

So much pain and torment. . . . Why are they so eager to be part of it? Sally shook her head to clear the thought and said, "Maybe Doctor Wallace is right and we should try maggots on cases like Isiah's."

Cassie shuddered. "Them little wiggly, crawly flesh-eating worms? No, ma'am! They surely do give me the creeps."

Sally smiled a tired and strained smile and patted her slave's knee. "I know, Cassie. The thought of placing maggots on the terrible wounds of our patients makes me shudder as well. But the doctor says in a week or so they work wonders."

Cassie tightened her face into a mask of horror. "We leave 'em on for a week to crawl through the patients flesh and through the bed, and . . . who knows where all?!"

Sally said, "They eat only the putrid flesh and promote healing. If we still smell gangrene in two days we'll try them." She breathed deeply and rose. "Come. Other patients need our attention."

From the outside, Sally Tompkins's hospital looked like a comfortable two-story home—painted white with dark green shutters, a picket fence, and a Virginia state flag hanging from the columned roof over the small front porch.

Inside, the parlors, dining room, sitting rooms, and master bedrooms had been converted to hospital wards. The judge's downstairs office was the medical supply room. One upstairs bedroom was saved as a rest area for the volunteer nurses and as a small office for Sally.

Storm clouds parted and the sun peered through a hazy sky. A breeze fluttered clean, sweet air through the hospital rooms, diminishing the smell of blood, disease, and fear.

Louisa finished charting the afternoon doses of medicine and said, "Sally, have you gone to the post office for mail today?"

Sally, straightening bedding and checking dressings, grimaced and slowly shook her head.

"You *have* to go Sally. You're the only one who can sign for packages and letters for the soldiers."

"Maybe tomorrow," Sally answered vaguely. "There's too much to do today."

"Nonsense, Sally Tompkins," Louisa insisted. "The men need their letters to boost their spirits."

"But there have been so many battles lately. I could not bear to find more names on the list."

Lists of the dead, wounded, captured, and missing soldiers after each battle were posted at every Southern post office. People rushed in to read the lists and left, either broken and weeping if they found a loved one's name, or joyously relieved if they didn't. So far in the war, Sally had learned of the deaths of three cousins, two uncles, and one brother from the hated post office lists. Almost worse, she had found the names of more than 100 former patients she had painstakingly nursed back to health so that they could rejoin their units.

Sally asked, "Don't I hear enough suffering here? Why must I endure it out there as well?"

"Don't read the list," suggested Louisa. "Just get the mail and come straight back."

"It's the weeping," Sally answered. "If it isn't mine, then it's someone else's who has read the list—or, more often, *many* someone elses'. I can't get near the post office without hearing the weeping and the misery."

"Think of the joy and healing the mail will bring, Sally. Focus on *that* and the trip will be easier."

"And then there are the cripples begging in the street," Sally continued. "The maimed, the amputees, with their hollow, vacant eyes, nearly starving, whimpering for a handout. And I think, 'I'm saving my patients lives for . . . *this*!' And I begin to think that it is far crueler to keep them alive than to help them swiftly die and be done with the suffering."

Louisa stamped her foot. "Sally Tompkins! You hush with such foolishness. You run the best hospital in Richmond—why, I bet the best in all Virginia. Soldiers up at the front lines say, 'If I'm shot, take me to Sally Tompkins.' You hold your head high, be proud, and get out there and let the nation thank you for saving so many lives."

Sally nodded, looped her bonnet over her head, and wearily marched to the door. "I am not like you, Louisa. I can no longer see the bright side. Wherever I look, I only see dying and suffering. That is why I am so thankful you are here."

Two days later, on the steamy morning of May 21, a new volunteer, 25-year-old Sara Pryor, arrived for her interview to become a nurse at Sally's hospital. Sara, wife of General Richard Pryor, had recently moved to Richmond from Roanoke to help care for an ailing uncle. After a brief introduction in the wide foyer that had been turned into a reception room, Sally asked, "Can you sing?"

"Sing?" Sara repeated. She had expected to be quizzed about her knowledge of medicines and medical procedures.

"We find singing often speeds patient recovery."

"Singing?" Sara asked again. "Songs heal battle wounds?"

"Few of the worst battle wounds are physical and not all our patients have been wounded."

Sara said, "I suppose I sing well enough in church. But I thought you would want to know most about my knowledge of medicines and my ability to bandage. I plan to become a doctor, but need more practical experience before I can find a doctor who will sponsor me."

Sally wistfully shook her head. "You'll learn little of advanced medicine in this hospital. We use only the basic medicines here—sulfates for fever; morphine, heroin, and opium for pain; quinine for general health and energy; nitric acid and bromine to prevent gangrene—and even they are hard enough to obtain."

"That's all?" questioned Sara.

"There are few others we can find anymore," answered Sally with a shrug. "We may start using maggots, but haven't yet."

"I'm familiar with all of the medicines you named. Do you also use mercuric derivatives? Camphor? Digitalis?" Sally sadly shook her head. Sara continued, "Wolfsbane? Arsenic?"

Sally wistfully sighed. "The blockade, Sara. What little gets through goes to doctors with the armies. We have to make do with medicines that naturally grow locally—sassafras, skull-cap, and pommegranate."

Sara pursed her lips in thought. "I have been to other hospitals. Half their patents die. Not so here. I came to learn your medical secrets, your special magic."

Sally seemed to droop. Her cheerful facade drained away. "We have no secrets and no magic, Mrs. Pryor. Come, let me show you the wards and the patients we work with."

After taking only 10 steps into the dining room ward, Sara began to stagger. Perspiration beaded her forehead. She wobbled forward another two steps. With a soft, "Oh dear," her eyes rolled toward the ceiling and she collapsed to the floor.

Two of Sally's slaves, Marie and Mae, hauled her back to a couch in the reception room. Sally dabbed a cold washcloth on her forehead until she revived. "Are you ill?" asked Sally, feeling Sara's pulse and her forehead for a fever.

"No, just overwhelmed," Sara answered, pointing at the door leading to the dining room ward. "I have seen pictures of wounds and operations. I know the prescribed treatments. But . . . but they're just boys in there—boyish faces grown old and thin from suffering. . . . And the odor was so powerful . . ." She lowered her eyes and almost whispered, "And they all seemed to stare at me, pleading, demanding comfort and relief. . . . There were just so many suffering eyes."

Sara blushed and sat up. "I feel so ashamed. You must think I'm terrible for not being able to walk through the ward."

"Not at all," Sally answered. "I feel ashamed for myself that I have grown so accustomed to these sights and smells that I do not notice them anymore." Sally added, "Perhaps you will not want to nurse here with us?"

"No, please. I am determined to serve. And if I am ever to become a doctor, I must become as accustomed as you." Again Sara pointed at the door to the dining room. "May I try again?"

Sara forced herself to walk, step by hesitant step, through the ward. She forced herself to smile into mangled faces, to pause and listen to the rantings of a fevered teenager, to offer water to a boy who had lost both legs and could not stop sobbing. She forced herself to breathe in the pungent air and to not tremble at the sight of pain and suffering.

"I don't think I could ever get used to the terrible wounds," said Sara as she and Sally talked in the upstairs office after their tour.

"Disease is our biggest enemy," answered Sally. "Daily scrubbing of everything seems to help. It may only make the men feel better, but I also think it somehow helps prevent the spread of disease."

Sara glanced curiously at her new boss. "I don't understand. Medical books say nothing about scrubbing."

"But it seems to be true. So every day we scrub—walls, floors, and patients. We spread lime around the building to prevent disease from entering. We tend to dressings and administer whatever medicines we are able to obtain. We prepare and serve food, and we listen."

"Listen?"

"Talking seems to be as strong a therapy for these men as quinine."

Sara faintly smiled and shook her head. "Talking, singing, scrubbing, listening. I thought nursing would be about medicine and bandages."

With a fresh pair of willing hands, the routine and rhythm in Tompkins's hospital continued. Volunteers and slaves washed, cooked, cleaned, begged for supplies, and listened. Patients struggled through terrible pain, fear, boredom, and fever. They talked of home, of family, of places they'd seen. Most, unless ranting in fevered delirium, never spoke openly of battle.

Each morning the nurses tackled bedsores, bandages, washing, feeding, scrounging, medicating, fevers, washing and scrubbing, and then started the cycle again.

Daily convoys of overloaded hospital wagons rolled into Richmond from the nearby fighting where Federal General Grant hammered the Confederate lines, hurling waves of blue soldiers into endless attacks. On the morning of May 28, two wagons pushed up to Tompkins's back porch.

"We have no space for new patients," said Sally to the driver.

"There's no where else to put them, ma'am."

"But we have no more beds," she insisted.

The lieutenant in charge shrugged as his men jostled the first litter onto the back porch. "Then put them on the floor."

Sally grabbed Marie and Cassie. "Both of you, run and find Mrs. Candell. She must scrounge for blankets, pillows, lint, bandages, and food—now! Tell her we are desperate. Also find Joseph and Tom. Tell them to come early and have them bring other men strong enough to move the wounded and to haul straw for beds. Hurry!"

Sally leaned against the railing at one end of the porch, listening to the rising chorus of groans, moans, and cries from the newcomers, a symphony of pain and misery. A deep bitterness swelled up in Sally. "Why won't they ever stop coming?" she hissed. Then she calmed herself with a deep, slow breath. "My duty is to ease the suffering."

But Sally's inner voice refused to be silenced. "Why must suffering and screaming for months be the way we settle disagreements?"

Sally pushed the thought aside and fetched a pitcher of raspberry tea so she could offer sips to the first of the new men, lying, bleeding, trembling on the porch. "Where do they keep coming from?" she asked to no one in particular. "How can there still be this many left to fight and shoot and die?"

Four of this batch, she saw, would never live through the day. Three others were delirious with the pain of multiple raw and gaping wounds. Most had had a limb amputated at the front and held the vacant and haunted look of those who had survived the grinding mill of the frontline surgeon's table.

"Battle must be truly awful," Sara answered. "Look at what it leaves behind."

"We fight our battle right here, every day," Sally answered, "a battle that never ends." She was forced to talk while she worked, applying a pressure bandage to slow the flow of blood from a deep thigh wound that had been crudely and quickly sewn together. "An endless river of wounded men have flowed into this hospital for two years, bringing their pain and misery for us to battle."

She finished the dressing and turned to the next man trembling on the wooden porch. "The sounds of our battle will haunt me until the day I die."

"The screams of the wounded?" asked Louisa, carrying a tray of glass medicine bottles onto the porch.

"No. Screams are angry and full of life. Screamers will recover. It is the pitiful whimpers filled with hopeless despair that haunt me. So much whimpering. So many broken men. For one moment of glory, they spend a life of hopeless whimpering."

For the first time, Sally saw the war not as a patriotic and noble struggle, but as a senseless meat grinder whose sole purpose was to create tormented patients.

There was no way for her to make sense of it. There seemed to be no way to stop it, or no one who wanted to stop it. There seemed to be no shortage of men willing to be the next round of patients.

Sally Tompkins sadly shook her head and returned to the only thing that made any sense—patient by patient, easing the suffering so many others were so eager to create.

Aftermath

Sally Tompkins and Phoebe Pember (who ran another Richmond hospital) are the most famous of the Confederacy's volunteer nurses. But they are only two of thousands of devoted volunteers for both South and North.

The quality of all aspects of medical care made great strides forward during the Civil War. Doctor training, technique, and certification improved. Professional nursing staffs were created and trained. The fundamental precepts of skilled nursing were first imported and systematically applied in the United States. The life expectancy of a wounded soldier in 1865 was over four times what it had been in 1861.

Notes

1. Nitric acid and bromine were used to burn away decayed flesh in gangrene patients and stop the spread of the gangrene.

2. Medical textbooks of the period recommended keeping wounds moist to promote healing. Lint scraped from fabrics (like the lint found on clothes dryer filter screens) was soaked and pressed against wounds to keep them damp.

Follow-up Questions and Activities

1. **What Do You Know?**

   • What kind of professional training and education did American doctors receive in 1861?

   • Why were there no women nurses at the start of the Civil War? Why were women allowed to become nurses during the war?

   • Why did both North and South develop so many small, private hospitals? Why weren't military hospitals all large, government-run facilities?

   • Why was amputation the most common battlefield surgery?

2. **Find Out More.** Here are nine important topics from this story for students to research in the library and on the Internet. The reference sources at the back of this book will help them get started.

- Research medicines used during the Civil War. Identify the medicines and what they were used for. Are any of them still used today? What are the tools that a Civil War army surgeon used?

- Quinine was considered to be a valuable medicine in the mid-nineteenth century. For what medical problems was it used? What was it supposed to be able to do? Does modern medicine still use quinine today? For what? Have you ever seen quinine? Where?

- Research battlefield surgery during the Civil War. Why were so many amputations performed? Did they use anesthesia? Did they practice sterilization? What was a typical battlefield surgeon's success rate? What were the greatest dangers for those wounded on the battlefield?

- How many soldiers died during the Civil War? How many died from disease? From infections? Directly from battle wounds? Which diseases claimed the most victims among Civil War soldiers?

- Research the Battle of Cold Harbor (and the running battle from the Wilderness to Petersburg). How many casualties piled up on both sides? How did battlefield strategy change during this three-week period?

- Research Union General Ulysses S. Grant. He was the first eastern Union general to aggressively push the war into Virginia. What were his successes and failures before he took command of the Army of the Potomac? Research his troubled life outside the army. Why did many feel he was unfit to command? How many casualties did the armies suffer under his command? How many did he inflict on the Confederate armies he faced? What happened to him after the war?

- This story is about one heroic female nurse during the Civil War. There were many other women about whom stories could be written. Five of the most famous are Mary Walker, Clara Barton, Dorothea Dix, Mary Ann Bickerdyke, and Elizabeth Blackwell. Research their lives, struggles, and accomplishments.

- The U.S. Army Nursing Corps was created and developed during the Civil War by Dorothea Dix. What were the requirements to be an army nurse under Ms. Dix? Why was she so strict with her assigned nurses? Were any such requirements established for Confederate nurses? Why or why not?

- Research medical knowledge and belief in the mid-nineteenth century. When were bacteria discovered? When was connection between bacteria and disease established? By whom? What did Civil War medical professionals believe caused disease? How did they typically treat disease? Why was bleeding used? Is it still used today?

3. **Make It Real**

- Imagine yourself lying immobile for days on end in a long ward room of an army hospital, alive but badly wounded and unable to move. Think of the sounds you would hear lying in your bed; of the small patch of wall and ceiling you could see; of the smells of medicine, gangrene and death; of the pain and memories that wrack your body. Write a letter to your parents describing your experience in this hospital.

- Make a timeline showing all major medical and scientific discoveries and inventions from 1850 to 1875. How did medical knowledge improve over that quarter century? If the Civil War had been fought beginning in 1875, how many more lives do you think would have been saved through improved medical knowledge and technique?

4. **Points to Ponder**

- More soldiers died of disease than of battle wounds in the Civil War. More wounded died in hospitals from complications of surgery than on the field of battle. Why? How do you think this changed the views, beliefs, and practices of common soldiers?

- Women were thought to be incapable of standing the stress and rigors of most professions in 1860. There were only a scattering of women teachers, nurses, postal workers, doctors, etc. Where do you think these beliefs in the frailty of women originated? Why did they persist—even among women? Do you think it was shocking for both men and women to find out how capable women really were?

Tears of Fear
Army Deserters, May–June 1864

At a Glance

Desertion is a problem for every army. That problem became epidemic during the last 18 months of the Civil War. The first recorded complaint of Civil War desertion was made by Union General Frederick Patterson in a letter dated June 23, 1861 (*before* the first major battle of the war). By early 1865, what he referred to as a "nagging problem" had become a tidal wave that threatened to single-handedly swamp the Confederate army.

Desertion occurred in many forms: failure to report for the draft, bounty jumping (only in the North), failure to report back from furlough, failure to report back from a hospital, straggling and skulking (hiding) to avoid battle, as well as outright leaving one's unit. All forms of desertion radically increased once the North and South began to draft soldiers (both in 1863). Volunteers were more willing to endure the fierce hardships and dangers of army life.

Why did soldiers desert? The most common reason was problems at home. The Confederate government annually "taxed" all farms 10 percent of their production for the army. With men gone to war, harvests were typically reduced even before the tax. Since soldiers often went months without any pay they could send to their families, belts were cinched mighty tight at home.

The second most common reason was the draft. Some resented being forcibly drafted. The drafts applied to everyone living in the country—even those born and raised on the other side, even foreign nationals with no real stake in the war. Such men grudgingly entered the army, already searching for ways to get out.

Some deserted because of camp life. Most of the time it was mind-numbingly boring. Soldiers suffered from chronically inadequate food, and what they got of it was notoriously bad. They lacked adequate clothing and lived in squalid conditions where disease stalked every soldier and took a far higher toll than did battle.

Some deserted out of fear, in the heat of battle. Some deserted because they were forced to fight outside their native states or because they didn't like and trust their commanders. Some in the North deserted for profit. Most Northern states offered cash bonuses to new volunteers. Unscrupulous men volunteered, received the bonus, and then deserted only to travel to another area and volunteer all over again. Several men were caught after joining the army more than 50 times.

Deserting was not as easy as it might seem. Most deserted to the enemy while on picket duty. But a soldier had to be extremely careful not to get shot by wary pickets on either side while he crossed between the lines. Some deserted during the confusion of a fight, using the raging battle as a convenient diversion. Some deserted while on patrol or on guard duty.

A deserter was far from free once he escaped from his own unit. Rings of pickets encircled all army camps. Infantry and cavalry patrols swept a wide area beyond the pickets. Conscript Bureau brigades patrolled the countryside in search of runaways. Professional bounty hunters eager for the $30 bounty on returned deserters roamed every region with packs of trained hunting dogs.

Yet no threat or obstacle seemed to stem the tide of desertion. Some states and units tried leniency to encourage deserters to return. Few did, and more deserted. Some states got tough. Deserters were branded on the arm or forehead with the letter "D." They were physically tortured. They were sentenced to forced labor gangs. A few were shot or hanged. Yet still men deserted. By the end of the war 1 in 7 Confederate soldiers had deserted, as had 1 in 10 Union soldiers.

Meet Edward Cooper

Edward Cooper was born to James and Carolyn Cooper in 1840 on a small family farm, second of four children. James was the third generation to farm that small piece of hilly, heavily wooded red clay soil in the rural, steep hills along the northern Georgia-Alabama border. Edward's older brother died of disease as a child. His two younger sisters both married at the age of 16. One died in childbirth in 1861. The other moved to Atlanta with her husband in 1860.

Edward never attended formal school. His mother taught him to read and write. Edward married a neighbor, Mary McRae, in 1858 when he was 18 and she only 16. He inherited the family farm after both his parents died of disease in 1860.

Edward and Mary produced two children, Lucy, born in 1859, and Edward (Little Eddie), born in late 1860. Edward joined a Georgia regiment during the winter of 1861–1862, leaving his wife and children to manage the farm in his absence. The regiment was assigned to Robert E. Lee's Army of Northern Virginia. This was the first time Edward had ever traveled more than 20 miles from his home.

Tears of Fear

S team rose from the grass on the morning of June 10, 1864, blurring Edward Cooper's view of the Moseley, Virginia, train station, making the bare platform appear more like a dream than a small and—for Edward—dangerous Confederate depot just south of Richmond on the line to Atlanta. It had rained overnight. Thunder had rattled the hills, sounding to Edward more like the cannons of battle than a glorious light show of nature. Now the moisture rose into a swirling mist of steam as the rising sun heated the day.

Corporal Edward Cooper sprawled in the grass, scarcely daring to breathe, not daring to raise his head more than a tiny inch, terrified that he would hear the click of a musket cocking behind him or see an officer's pistol pointed at his head, afraid he would be caught—and hanged.

He wished for the thousandth time that he had thought things out before he deserted, that he had taken the time to plan. But the opportunity had suddenly appeared three days before—an easy chance to duck into thick bushes as his regiment marched past. Edward had seized the chance first, and only thought of planning and the consequences later while he ran, frightened and desperate, across the Virginia countryside.

He had slipped into the bushes and run when he was posted as a bridge guard while his regiment marched west after the battle of Cold Harbor, Virginia, heading to reinforce the units fighting in the Shenandoah Valley. Edward had wandered for a day, unsure of how to get home. Then he thought of the trains. Afraid of the throngs of officers in Richmond, he skirted the city to the west and now crouched in the grass one stop down the line.

Edward drew in a deep breath, knowing he had to make himself walk down onto that train platform or he would never be able to hop a train and get home to northwest Georgia. Only home and Mary's letter felt real to Edward. Even the sun seemed a dream-like orange glow, a distant bonfire, as it slid above the eastern hills. These past three days of running and hiding—trembling at the faintest sound of human or horse, creeping through farms—felt like a child's game rather than a desperate race to avoid capture.

He drew the crumpled letter from his pocket, knowing it alone would give him strength and purpose. He smoothed the page against his leg and momentarily panicked as the dampness from his pants seeped through the rough linen to smear the delicate ink. He waved the letter and blew on it to dry it and keep the writing legible. Reading was slow, difficult work for Edward. But he had read this letter so often, he'd memorized the words:

My Dear Edward:

I have always been proud of you, and since your connection with the Confederate Army, I have been prouder of you than ever before. I would not have you do anything wrong for the world, but before God, Edward, unless you come home, we must die. Last night, I was aroused by Little Eddie's crying. I called and said, "What is the matter, Eddie?" and he said, "O mamma! I am so hungry." And Lucy, Edward, your darling Lucy; she never complains, but she is growing thinner and thinner every day. And before God, Edward, unless you come home, we must die.

Your Mary

Edward had volunteered for the Confederate army in January 1862 and had strutted off to war in his gray uniform coat as his family smiled and waved. After 28 months of endless marching and fighting in a dozen battles; of smelling sulfurous smoke, death, and fear; of terrible food and stalking disease, nothing made sense to Edward Cooper except getting home to comfort his Mary, and whispering, "Everything's all right. Don't cry," to his children.

If he could just get to Atlanta, he could walk the rest of the way. Heck, he'd run if he had to, to see his Mary and the kids and to hold them in his arms.

Peering cautiously through the tall grass, Edward scanned the station for provost officers—the military police who searched for deserters. Of course, he had no passport for a furlough, no legal excuse to leave his unit and board a train, no right to stand, waiting, on the train platform. Of course, his name would already be posted on the deserter lists with every command.

A dozen soldiers slumped in tired clusters on the platform, but none seemed to be on the hunt for runaways. Still, he hesitated. If he were caught, he'd *never* get home to save his family. He'd be branded a coward and deserter and forever shamed. He might be shot or hanged! He thought he heard the whine of a distant train. He had to act, and act fast.

Edward was filled with fear and confusion. Desperation gave birth to a bold plan. But the idea seemed vague and unfocused. He hated his inability to think through an idea and spot its hidden risks and pitfalls. He had never been good as a planner. He was a simple farmer, stuck here in Virginia, and not entirely sure where Virginia was. It had been almost effortless to walk away from his regiment. Getting home seemed to require so much thinking, scheming, and planning; it sapped his energy like summer humidity.

He shrugged and sighed. He only had one plan, and there was no time to wrack his brain for another one. He'd pretend to be a dreaded provost. No one *ever* questioned their right to board a train.

Edward scrambled out of the grass, shouldered his musket, and marched straight toward the station platform. His heart pounded and his knees felt as wobbly as the waving grass. He willed them to stop trembling. Mounting the platform he called, "Passport inspection!" trying with all his might to sound routine—even bored—instead of frightened beyond belief.

Attempting to appear authoritative and distinguished, Edward tugged at the hem of his faded gray coat, now baggy and threadbare with a maze of homespun butternut patches that never lasted long. At 5 feet, 8 inches, Edward, who was thin, wiry, and tough, looked pretty much like 50,000 others in Lee's army. But he felt like an obvious impostor. However, no one questioned his authority. Most of the men grumbled as they fished through stuffed packs. One complained, "Come on, corporal. We're not deserters."

"Then you'll each have a valid passport," Edward answered, having already checked and returned two of the brown paper scraps that became more precious than gold once they were stamped at a regimental office.

One young man backed slowly against the wall as Edward approached. With a sickening jolt, Edward realized that the man had no passport. He was a deserter. For one terrifying moment the two men gazed at each other, each seeming more frightened than the other. Then the man bolted, sprinting down the main street of Moseley.

"Deserter!" cried several of the men. One swung his rifle up to his shoulder.

"Don't shoot!" Edward shouted, haunted by the knowledge that it could so easily be he dashing headlong down the street.

Several officers on horseback rode the man down and dragged him back to the platform.

Edward's mouth turned cotton dry at the pitiful sight of this weeping deserter the officers herded back. With a jolt, Edward realized everyone expected *him* to know what to do with the prisoner. "Take him to the local jail and hold him there," he managed to stammer.

With a sharp whistle, a train rocked and lurched into the station. Southern tracks had so deteriorated in the last few years because of a lack of iron and rail spikes that trains were rarely allowed to exceed 20 miles per hour for fear of derailing. Steam billowed across the platform. Most of the cars were empty freight cars, returning south after dumping their loads in Richmond.

A few soldiers clambered off. Those on the platform shuffled on board. Edward simply stepped on with them and, to ensure that no one questioned his presence, continued his role as provost, marching through the open cars checking passports.

It took more than a day to reach the sprawling city of Atlanta, now abuzz with frantic activity. Wagons loaded with supplies rushed north. Field artillery teams raced through the streets, the chains on their limbers rattling against the cobbles. Union General Sherman was marching south to attack Atlanta. For the first time this bastion in the heart of the South felt the tingle of approaching war. There was no time for the army to be concerned with one misplaced soldier.

Edward slipped west out of town and worked his way past pickets, patrols, and the cavalry screen. Then he turned north. With every mile his spirits rose. At every crossroads, bridge, and ford, they sank again. Conscript Bureau agents roamed the crossroads. Provost guards and army outposts guarded every country ford, bridge, town, and crossroads, searching mostly for deserters. It seemed that the land was infested with Home Guard units, bounty hunters, provosts, and army units. Edward began to believe that more of the army was out scouring for deserters than was fighting the Yankees.

Once he thought he heard the distant baying of hounds used by bounty hunters. The sound drove into him like frozen daggers. He trembled, breathing hard and raspily. He felt trapped like a caged and hunted animal. Then he was ready to burst with rage. Why was his own country turning him into a hated, cowardly criminal just because he wanted to protect his family? Wasn't that his first duty? Wasn't he honor bound to provide for his family above all else? Why was he hunted and hated for doing his duty? Why did he feel like cowardly scum?

Edward dodged around the town of Rome, Georgia, tromped through the steep and thickly wooded hills of the Chattahoochee Forest, then skirted Summerville when he spotted a Union cavalry patrol there.

He passed through Menlo, really just one store and a couple of houses, and almost ran the last three miles up into the hills to the sweetest little valley under the sun—the place he called home.

As Edward first spotted the familiar fence line and pasture, he shouted, "Mary! I'm home!" He ran into the sloping front yard. "Mary! Lucy! Little Eddie!"

The murmur of a light breeze whispering through pine trees was the only response. Then he noticed that neither vegetable garden nor fields had been planted and were overgrown with weeds and trampled. Weeds stuck up through the porch planks. The barn had burned; only the west wall still stood. What few possessions and bits of furniture hadn't been taken from the house were now smashed and strewn across the floor.

His family was gone, the homestead deserted. Edward sank onto the porch steps in bewildered disbelief. He snatched Mary's letter from his pocket and frantically read and reread the words, hoping to find a line he had overlooked that would tell him what had happened, provide a clue to where they had gone.

Edward dropped his head into his hands, his mind a jumble, and he wept. He was too late; his family was gone. Maybe they had starved. Maybe they'd been killed. Maybe . . . maybe. Each new maybe tormented Edward more.

For more than a day he sat on the porch, weeping and trying to think. What should he do? Where should he go? He was a deserter. He couldn't march into town and ask about his family; he'd be captured. He couldn't go back to the army; he couldn't stay here. The sight of his home repeatedly brought a flood of tears to his eyes.

Edward had lost everything that was dear to him: his family, his farm, his friends in the army, his good name, his honor, his future, even his country. If only he had planned better. If only he could have thought it through. Why hadn't he deserted sooner? Why had he deserted at all?

His thoughts were interrupted by the sound of footsteps in the underbrush of the woods. A man staggered into the open, obviously exhausted, frightened, and barely able to stay on his feet.

The man wore a blue uniform.

Terror, anger, and curiosity all surged through Edward. A Yankee! If Yankees hadn't started the war, none of Edward's miseries would have happened. He wanted to lash out at this intruder. But then, this soldier might be part of a patrol and would capture Edward. Edward wanted to run and hide. But then, it might be better to be captured by the Union army than by the Confederates, who would surely hang him. But this man seemed drained down to his last ounce of energy, still running from something, driven only by his fear.

This man was a Yankee deserter! *That's* why he ran and why he looked so terrified.

For over a week, Edward had run from and through the Confederate army to get here, and all that was here for him was a Yankee deserter. The irony struck Edward. He threw back his head and laughed.

The Yankee stopped and cocked his head. Whatever reception he had expected, this wasn't it. He jerked his rifle off his shoulder. "Don't laugh, boy! I could kill you!"

Edward shook his head but couldn't stop—two enemy deserters meeting here to fight out the war. It was too far-fetched for even a story. Still, it made as much sense as having to become a hated and hunted criminal to save your own family.

"I mean it, Johnny Reb! I'll shoot." But the Yankee glanced nervously over his shoulder and edged closer to the porch.

Edward stopped laughing and held out his hand. "Hey, Billy Yank. What you runnin' from?"

The Yank lowered his rifle, stepped forward, and shook Edward's hand, nodding slightly. "Joseph Quincy. 23rd Illinois Infantry, out of Springfield."

Edward nodded toward the porch beside him. The Yankee sighed as he sank down. Joseph Quincy was younger and plumper than Edward, and his uniform, although mud-caked from days of running, still appeared new.

"Why'd you run?" Edward asked. "Yanks is winnin' the war and they obviously feed you better'n Lee fed us."

"I was drafted last summer and sent to a supply depot in Kentucky. Late this May I was moved forward to join my regiment—part of Sherman's army."

Edward interrupted, "You want some water? I got a well out back."

After a long drink, the two men settled back into the shade of the front porch. Quincy continued. "Kennesaw Mountain was my first battle. There was so much screaming. Lead thicker than flies on a dead horse. The men on both sides of me died. One got shot in the neck; a cannonball took the other's whole head off. Last thing I saw of him was his pipe clenched in his teeth as we advanced. Then the rebs charged. There were so many I couldn't even count. More men dropped. I panicked and ran.

"When I stopped running, I was alone in the woods and it was quiet as death. I didn't know where I was. I was terrified to look for the army. I didn't know which one I'd find. I never *meant* to desert. It just . . . happened. So I skedaddled. That must have been four . . . five days ago."

"You *what*?" asked Edward.

"Skedaddled. It means to run away."

Edward nodded. "Good word. Skedaddle. And *this* is where you skedaddled to?"

Quincy paused, staring down at his feet. "Now I'm a deserter. I can't go back. They shoot deserters in my regiment. I can't go home to Springfield. My folks knew Lincoln before he was elected. My dad is Swedish and always talks about doing your duty. They'd disown me. I heard of a town in Canada called Skedaddleville. I guess that's where I'm heading."

A lonely silence fell over the pair of deserters before the Illinois Yank asked, "Why'd *you* run?"

Without a word, Edward pulled Mary's letter from his pocket and passed it to the Union soldier.

"And they didn't give you a furlough for *this*?"

"While Grant was attacking, *no one* got a furlough."

"Where's your home?" Quincy asked.

"You're looking' at it—what's left of it, that is."

"Where's your family?"

Tears crept into Edward's eyes and he wiped a sleeve across his nose. "They were gone when I got here. And I don't know what to do."

A dozen riders emerged from the woods and trotted toward Edward's house. Quincy grabbed for his rifle, then paused. These riders were each armed with new Spencer repeating rifles.

The riders stopped at the porch, grinning down at Edward and Joseph. "Looks like we jus' found us two new members, boys."

"Members of what?" Edward asked.

An older man tipped back his hat. "You ain't never heard of the Destroying Angels?"

Edward and Quincy shook their heads. The circle of riders softly laughed.

"We own this here county and two next to it," the older man continued. "Ain't no army unit or lawman dares set foot in these hills without askin' us first. We got near 200 members. An' since neither of you asked permission to pass through, I reckon we jus' found two new members."

"This is my place," Edward protested. "I live here."

"Not if'n I tell the Conscript Bureau where you's at an' collect my $30 bounty for turning in a deserter." The ring of riders chuckled. " 'Course, it'd be easier and quicker to turn you over to the Union army since Sherman's already well south o' here. You'd like that jus' fine, wouldn't you, Billy Yank?" The older man scratched his cheek with the muzzle of his Spencer rifle. "It'd be easier yet to shoot you right now and see if'n you got any money fer us."

Quincy asked, "Are you a militia unit? Whose side are you on?"

"We're on *our* side. Every man in the Destroying Angels is a deserter—most Confederate, some Yankee. An' up here we do what we want and no one dares say anything 'cept 'please' an' 'thank you.' "

Edward said, "We don't want any trouble. I just want to find my family."

The older man gazed around the abandoned farm. "I'd say you're lookin' in the wrong place. This here place looks abandoned to me." The riders laughed again. Several horses snorted as if they, too, wanted to join in the laugh. "We got business over on the Alabama side," the older man continued. "When we come back tomorrow, you either be ready to join the Angels or be ready to die."

The riders turned and galloped away, wildly whooping. Two fired their guns into the air. Edward and Joseph sat stunned, staring after the Angels as the cloud of dust from their horses' hooves slowly settled.

"What do we do?" Edward asked, his mind whirling in its attempt to find a feasible plan. "I don't want to join a bunch of outlaws."

"Skedaddleville," Quincy answered. "I don't want to be here when Union cavalry rides through."

Edward thought a moment. "How far away is Canada from here?"

Quincy shrugged as he thought. "I reckon it's got to be a thousand miles."

"A *thousand*?! No one can walk a thousand miles." Edward wrinkled his face as he thought. "Maybe I'll stay here. Maybe my family will come back."

"And so will those riders. They'll never let you live peacefully here."

Again Edward thought. "How do you figure you'll get to Canada?"

"Can't go north," answered Quincy. "Too much army to walk through."

Edward added, "Can't go east. That's where I just come from."

"Can't go south, that's the wrong way."

"West?" Edward asked.

"It's the only other way," said Quincy. "But there's a lot of army to get through between here and the Mississippi."

Edward stammered, "How will my family ever know . . . know I tried to find 'em?" and wiped a sleeve across his nose and eyes again.

The two men, now comrades in desertion, needing to escape the armies, the law, bounty hunters, and gangs of deserters, hefted their weapons and began their long march west.

Edward paused at the tree line bordering the west side of his farm. As he gazed one last time at the valley and land he loved, he allowed a final, wrenching sob to burst from his throat and eyes. Then he wiped a sleeve across his face and turned, following his Yankee comrade into a dark and uncertain future. The war had already destroyed everything he held dear, and he still had a thousand miles to walk before he could escape its grasp.

Aftermath

Desertion had become a serious problem for both armies by 1864, but it was more disastrous for the Confederacy, which could not fill the holes left by deserters. Desertion undermined authority and support at home. It forced the army to divert needed resources and troops into the hunt for deserters and destroyed army strength and morale.

In 1862, each Confederate deserter was individually counted. By mid-1864, Confederate army deserters were counted by the score. By early 1865, they were counted by the hundreds. General Ambrose Hill complained that an entire brigade deserted en masse. Over the four months between October 1, 1864, and February 1, 1865, 82,000 men deserted from the Confederate army—more than 20,000 per month! Lee's entire Army of Northern Virginia at the time numbered less than 60,000. The equivalent of one-third of his army deserted every month.

The Union army also suffered from desertion. Some 460,000 desertions were recorded from Union ranks during the war. Of these, 60,000 voluntarily returned to service and approximately 50,000 were caught and tried. The Union army shot 285 deserters; the Confederates about the same number.

Nothing slowed the flood of desertions. Three out of every four deserters were never caught. If even one-quarter of the Confederate deserters had returned to service, Lee would have more than doubled his strength and could have easily pushed Grant back north to Washington.

Desertion was one of the four factors that crushed the Confederacy; the others were the blockade, the lack of Southern manufacturing capacity, and the continual loss of agricultural lands as the Union army closed off the Mississippi River and captured greater and greater chunks of Confederate territory. Faced with these problems, there was no way the Confederacy could maintain battle readiness and efficiency.

Edward Cooper and Joseph Quincy drifted west almost to the Mississippi before they were caught by a Confederate patrol. As a Union army deserter Joseph Quincy was released and allowed to do as he pleased. Edward was tried for desertion. As his only defense, Edward showed Mary's letter to the officers of the court-martial. Most were brought to tears by the letter, but the law was clear and Edward was sentenced to death by firing squad. General Lee, upon reviewing the case, reduced the sentence to five years at hard labor because of Cooper's two years of steadfast service before he deserted. Edward was freed when the war ended.

After the war, in 1868, Edward drifted west to Colorado, where he worked in the Cripple Creek gold mines until he was killed in a mining accident in 1883. He never found out what had happened to his family.

Follow-up Questions and Activities

1. **What Do You Know?**
   - What happened to Civil War deserters if they were caught? Were they all treated the same? What were the possible alternative punishments?
   - Why would someone desert from a Civil War army?
   - What risks did a deserter face? Which groups, units, and individuals were hunting for deserters?

2. **Find Out More.** Following are five important topics from this story for students to research in the library and on the Internet. The reference sources at the back of this book will help them get started.

- Research the rates of, and reasons for, desertion from American armies throughout history. Compare the Revolutionary War and Civil War–era information you find with that for more modern wars, such as World War II, Korea, Vietnam, and Desert Storm.

- Research civilian attitudes toward desertion throughout the Civil War. Did they change? How did they change? Why? Were civilian attitudes different in different geographic areas? How? Why?

- Research the punishments for desertion from different armies throughout history. Look for patterns and similarities as well as for differences. Do the punishments tell you anything about the societies those armies represented?

- Research the lives of Civil War deserters. Where could they go? How did they live? How many deserters left the country? How many just went back home? Was it easier to desert when the fighting was near a soldier's home? Compare what you find with information for the Vietnam War. How many deserted during that war? Where did they go? How did they live?

- The story mentions one gang of deserters, the Destroying Angels. Did other groups of deserters form? What did they do? Did they all act the same? How many were there? Where were they concentrated? How long did they stay active after the war?

3. **Make It Real**

- Play a class game either outdoors or in the school gym. Three students will be designated deserters. The rest of the class will be provost officers. The goal of the provosts is to catch the deserters and bring them back to the spot designated as jail. However, if three deserters touch a provost for the count of three (1, 2, 3) at the same time, that provost has to desert and join the deserters.

  At what point do the provost hunters begin to back off and fear hunting the deserters? How large does the gang of deserters have to get before they stop fearing the provosts? Does this simple game give you any insights into the interaction between deserters and Home Guard units during the last year of the Civil War?

- Imagine that you are a Civil War deserter. Invent a situation that causes you to desert. As a class, discuss the mix of feelings you could have as you run away. Relief? Fear? Shame? Guilt? Excitement? Now write a letter to a friend justifying your desertion and describing what you plan to do.

- Hold a trial for a Civil War deserter. Either find a real deserter from historical records or create one for your class to use. As a defense lawyer, what arguments and evidence would you use to try to keep your client from being shot or hanged? What arguments will the prosecuting attorney use to support the death penalty? Which specific arguments sway the rest of the class, who will act as jury? Why?

4. **Points to Ponder**

- How would you propose to stop desertion if you were in charge of the Civil War army? Why do you think your plan will work?

- Desertion is a personal and moral decision. In your opinion, is it ever justifiable to desert? When? Why? Would you support allowing people to desert only from an army? From what else could you desert? What would *you* desert from? What might make you do it? Do U.S. Army soldiers ever desert today? What happens to them?

- Do you think it is morally and ethically acceptable for an army to kill its own soldiers when they have done something wrong? Is it good or bad for army morale and discipline? In this regard, do you think an army is different from a society as a whole?

- Many families were separated and scattered by the Civil War. Using only the technology available in 1865, how would you find your family again? Do you think it still happens that families permanently lose track of each other during war? Can you find twentieth-century examples of this?

Unsung Heroes
Black Union Regiments and the
Battle of the Crater, July 30, 1864

At a Glance

The Union army hired 200,000 African Americans as laborers, teamsters (those who drove teams of horses), cooks, carpenters, servants, nurses, scouts, and so on, during the Civil War. Almost half of the black males in the North worked for the army.

At the time of the Civil War, prejudice against blacks was rampant in both North and South. Abolitionism notwithstanding, most whites looked upon blacks as inferiors. Few whites would consider arming blacks, let alone allowing them to serve as uniformed soldiers—until war's necessity forced the Union to consider black regiments.

The first African American units were formed in Louisiana in the spring of 1862 from freed New Orleans black regiments first organized in 1803. Next came units of escaped slaves—Contrabands—who found their way to the captured Sea Islands along the South Carolina coast. The creation of black regiments in Ohio, Kansas, Indiana, and Massachusetts followed in the summer and fall of 1862. Illinois and Rhode Island added black regiments before the year was over.

By mid-1863, every Northern state except New York had formed black regiments. New York's governor held strong pro-slavery leanings, and many feared continued violence in New York City if African Americans were accepted as soldiers and citizens.

More than 75,000 Northern blacks responded to the initial call for recruits. They came from every corner of the Union and from every conceivable profession and station in life: cooks, waiters, barbers, printers, blacksmiths, carpenters, tinsmiths, ironworkers, engineers, teamsters, mail carriers, stockmen, sailors, butlers, coopers, fishermen, rope makers, glassmakers, slaves, chaplains, surgeons, and sawyers.

These black regiments were organized into the United States Colored Troops (USCT). The first USCT units to actually fight were three regiments from New Orleans who joined in the assault on Port Hudson, Louisiana, on May 27, 1863. The commanding Union general in his report on the battle wrote, "The brigade of Negroes behaved magnificently and fought splendidly. They are far superior to white troops in discipline and just as brave."

On June 7, 1863, USCT troops distinguished themselves during the defense of Milliken's Bend, a Union outpost along the Mississippi. On July 18, the 54th Massachusetts USCT regiment made a famous, incredibly brave, and nearly suicidal attack on Battery Wagner, South Carolina.

The myth of black inferiority was shattered. Black troops could fight every bit as well as any other troops on Earth. They made excellent soldiers.

However, acceptance of black soldiers by white Union soldiers and officers was slow and bitter. White officers of black troops were ridiculed and stigmatized and were rarely promoted as fast as other officers. White troops threatened to desert if ordered to fight alongside blacks. USCT units were supplied with substandard equipment and supplies and with the worst food and the weakest, sickest horses and mules. Virtually no medical care was provided to USCT regiments, who were therefore struck hardest by typhoid and cholera.

Black soldiers were paid $10 per month (the rate of a nonmilitary laborer) instead of the standard soldier's pay of $13. That policy was not changed until June 1864.

By June 1864, Generals U. S. Grant and Robert E. Lee settled into a trench-war standoff along the east side of Petersburg, nestled along the shore of the Appomatox River. With the Southern rail system already in shambles, Petersburg was the all-important last Southern rail hub in Virginia. While Lee's men starved on quarter-rations, more than four months' full rations for 60,000 men sat rotting at rail depots in Charlotte and Weldon, North Carolina, and in Danville, Virginia, because the Confederate rail system couldn't transport the food to where it was desperately needed. The loss of Petersburg would be a death blow to the Confederacy. That meant that the trench war around Petersburg would be the make-or-break showdown between Grant and Lee.

The two great armies faced off not for a day but for nine grueling months, separated by 150 yards of open ground, living in gopher cities of trenches; rifle pits; bomb-proof shelters; log, plank, and dirt forts; endless sandbags; sleeping holes; and covered transverses. The armies dug in deep and offered the world a glimpse of warfare to come—the trench warfare of World War I.

Meet Private Alfonse Mathews

Alfonse Mathews was born in New York City in 1838, the second child of Hiram and Ann Mathews. Ann took in wash, and Hiram worked as an assistant in a cobbler's shop. In the evenings he unloaded fish on the lower eastside docks. The family moved to Providence, Rhode Island, when Alfonse was a boy of seven or eight. Hiram had a brother there who had said that there was less trouble for blacks in Providence than in New York. In Providence, Hiram continued his work in cobbler shops, working part of the time in a shop owned by another black man.

When Alfonse turned 12 he landed his first job, delivering newspapers. When he was 16, Alfonse sold books door-to-door. He learned to read and write from a lady who worked at the publisher's distribution office. Alfonse liked this job and was good at it, being one of the district's three top salesmen, even though he was paid only half of what the white salesmen got. He was the only black man on that region's sales force and so was the first to be released when sales slowed. Alfonse was fired when he was 23, in the summer of 1861, shortly after the First Battle of Bull Run.

For the next two years Alfonse drifted through various odd jobs, filling in for whites who had enlisted in the army, until, in the summer of 1863, he decided to enlist himself. He joined a Rhode Island regiment of the USCT, was trained in Massachusetts, and shipped to Virginia in the spring of 1864 to join General Grant's Army of the Potomac. The Battle of the Crater at Petersburg was Alfonse's first major action. His unit was in the thick of the action between then and the end of the war.

Alfonse stayed in the army after the war, joined the cavalry, and was assigned to the Southwest Territories where he rode with the famous Buffalo Soldiers and was active in the Indian Wars. Alfonse retired from the army as a master sergeant in 1898 at the age of 59 and worked in the Colorado gold mines for five years before health problems forced him down to Denver to the more sedate job of a hotel butler. He retired from work altogether in 1909 at the age of 71 and died in Denver three years later, having never married.

Unsung Heroes

"Don't be askin' to use *my* kepi," growled Private Alfonse Mathews. (Kepi was the common name for the small Union army uniform caps.)

"We *gots* to. It's da' only one got no holes," replied Sergeant Cyrus Wilson.

The two soldiers hunched against the dirt and sandbag front wall of their rifle pit just past noon on Friday, July 29, 1864. Mathews and Wilson were part of a six-man detachment on guard duty for a four-hour shift. The men were part of General Ferrero's division of black troops that had recently moved to the front as part of General Burnside's IX Corps in General Grant's Army of the Potomac.

Their rifle pit looked like little more than a raised bump, one of hundreds of raised bumps along the hastily dug line of Union army trenches that stretched like a giant scar across the earth, meandering up the east side of Petersburg, Virginia. About 150 yards west, a higher, deeper, more extensive line of trenches, rifle pits, covered artillery positions called redans or redoubts, covered walkways, bombproofs, dugout sleeping borrows, sandbags, logs, and planks marked the Confederate army's position. Bristling lines of vicious *abatis* (rows of angled sharp stakes driven into the ground like a forest of spears) were wedged into the ground the entire length of each trench works to discourage the enemy from thoughts of attack. Both lines of trenches extended for more miles than anyone stuck in the rifle pit could imagine.

"We don't march, we dig. Don't use muskets, jus' use shovels," lamented Private Davis Paggett, an escaped slave from the Shenandoah Valley who had joined the army in early 1864. "We don't fight, jus' crawl through trenches tryin' not to got shot by snipers. This sure ain't what *I* thought the army'd be like."

Davis Paggett added, "Too danged hot for crawlin'. Too hot for anythin' 'cept sittin'. Nothin' gwine move in dis' heat 'cept mosquitoes."

A blistering hot, dry spell had turned eastern Virginia into a suffering wasteland of dust. With no shade in the pits, main trenches, and connecting transverse trenches, every soldier seemed to shrivel into a pitiful lump in the relentless heat. For 100 yards before and behind the trenches, no grass or flowers grew; all the trees had been chopped to stumps. It was an evil, alien world of trampled dirt heaps like an open, festering sore on the land.

Sergeant Wilson, an escaped slave from a Virginia farm, pushed out his hand and snapped his fingers. Alfonse sighed and passed over his new, blue army cap. Wilson's ebony face spread into a wide smile. "All right, gents. We's open fo' bets."

"How long?" asked Sergeant Jefferson Danforth, the senior soldier in the three rifle pits to which this company was assigned.

"Five seconds," Wilson announced. "I'll count 'em out wid' no cheatin'."

"Shouldn't someone watch the rebs?" This from Private Washington Jefferson Monroe, a free Georgia black who had been forcibly pressed into service for the Confederates until he escaped during the Second Battle of Bull Run. His mother had named him for every president she knew, hoping it would make his life easier.

Wilson laughed, " 'That's what Al's cap's fo'." He laid his own hat on the ground. "Ten cents a bet. Winner takes da' pot. I say, one." He plopped a dime into his cap.

"Two," said Danforth, plopping his coin into the hat.

"Them rebs is all trigger happy," said Davis Paggett. "They'd a-gwine shoot fas' and true. Three."

Alfonse Mathews shook his head. "You're all wrong. That's my *lucky* cap. No bullet gonna' touch that cap." He flung a dime into Wilson's hat.

"All bets in?" Wilson asked. He balanced Al's kepi on the tip of his bayonet and slowly inched it higher until the top nosed above the sandbag lip of their protected pit. "One . . . two . . . three . . ." Crack! Crack! Two Confederate rifles exploded from a raised bunker. Puffs of smoke drifted over the log lip. Alfonse's cap spun like a top on the bayonet point. "Four . . . five."

Crack! Another shot lifted the cap into the air and flung it against the back wall of the pit. The men roared in laughter.

Rifles in two adjacent Union rifle pits exploded. Private Monroe spun to watch through a crack between sandbags. "They plugged one of the rebs! I seen him flung his arms up like he's dead!"

Wilson scampered after the cap. "Lookie there! Two big holes clean through it! Two's the winner."

Sergeant Danforth scooped up the money with a proud smile.

"My beautiful cap!" wailed Alfonse wiggling one finger through a ragged hole before he flopped the tattered blue back on his head.

The others laughed. But it was a nervous laugh. Thirty to forty soldiers died every day in the trenches when they raised their head just a bit too high and created a target for Confederate marksmen.

Colonel Joshua Connie, commander of this regiment of USCT troops, scurried into the rifle pit from a covered transverse passage. A short, sour man of 40, Connie, like many of the white officers assigned to USCT units, resented being forced to lead black soldiers. Now he bent way over, as if his chin were tied to his bootlaces, to stay well below the pit's protective lip.

Colonel Connie hissed when he spoke, as if afraid that if he spoke too loudly it would draw Confederate fire. "I want no horseplay in the front trench line. I don't care what other units allow. In my regiment, you save games for off-duty time. You hear? I don't mind flogging the lot of you. You're on *duty* up here! Rebs could storm over those breastworks any moment!"

With a final glare, Connie scurried down the trench line to the next rifle pit.

Davis Paggett shook his head and laughed. "Ain't *nobody* dumb enough to be a-chargin' cross dat no-man's-lan' into fortified breastworks. Bullets and canister sho' 'nuff kill you, if'n this heat don't do it first."

"The rebs *did* once," said Sergeant Danforth. "A mile or so farther down the line. Busted clear through the trenches and took three artillery bunkers before we pushed 'em back out."

"*We* didn't push nobody nowheres," corrected Alfonse. "We was way in the rear. We never seen real action yet. This here fight I heard is comin', that'll be our first."

The cluster of soldiers grew quiet. They had all heard the rumors. The Union army was going to attack. Ferrero's USCT division was going to lead and make the suicide charge across no-man's-land, where a lizard couldn't crawl without getting plugged by a musket ball or canister fire.

But this attack was supposed to be different. Some Pennsylvania miners just up the line had been digging a tunnel for over a month, a long, straight tunnel that ran right under the strongest of the Confederate redoubts. That stronghold was a massive fortification that bristled with a dozen cannons, 12-foot walls, a deep front ditch, lines of *abatis*, and easy lines of fire for the thousands of Confederate rifles each Union soldier believed were jammed tight behind their thick log and sandbag walls. No soldier who saw it wanted to attack that place.

Cyrus Wilson leaned forward. "I heard we's gwine to crawl through 'dat tunnel and pop up way back inside a Petersburg church."

Davis Paggett sadly shook his head. "Firs', they got us livin' like rats in 'dis maze of tunnels barely fit for a gopher. Now we's a-creeping like moles through tunnels to attack the rebs." He reached under the back of his cap to scratch his matted hair. "This sure ain't what *I* thought the army'd be like."

"That is just wrong, wrong, wrong," sneered Jefferson Danforth. "I heard from the captain himself that they stuffed gunpowder in that there tunnel. Gonna blow that Confederate fort to kingdom come. Then we just prance through the gap and say howdy-do to the fine ladies of Petersburg!"

"Can't be done," insisted Washington Monroe. "I done a heap of diggin' for the Confederates, an' ain't no way you can dig a tunnel that long. Air runs out. Diggers'd die afore they got to the end." He leaned back and slid his cap down almost to his nose. " 'Sides, who'd ever light the powder? They'd be blowed up theirselves."

Sergeant Danforth started to argue, so Monroe pointed with his thumb back toward the Confederate fort and quickly added. " 'Sides again, that's 20 feet of packed dirt with logs and sandbags. Ain't no explosion gonna' blow that mountain up!"

Sergeant Danforth scowled. "That's not the way I heard it . . . And I'm a sergeant!" He folded his arms and turned west, pretending to be occupied watching the Confederate position.

All six soldiers settled into silence, trying to rest and still pretend to be watchful while they inwardly fretted about the impending battle.

Colonel Connie returned, loping crab-like down the trench. "On General Burnside's orders the tunnel will be exploded tomorrow at 3:45 A.M. Our division will lead the charge through the gap. This regiment will be second in line. Company commanders will have detailed orders by midnight." His finger stabbed in turn at each man. "Anyone in my regiment who stops or even slows down during this attack had better already be dead because I'll shoot you myself!" He grunted and loped off down the frontline trench to the next rifle pit and bunker.

"See? I told you," smiled Sergeant Danforth. "Next time maybe you'll listen when your sergeant talks."

Alfonse Mathews pulled off his cap and fingered the two new holes. Then he peered through a crack in the pit's sandbags at the Confederate stronghold. "We really gonna' attack *that* place?"

Sergeant Wilson also stared through a crack at the redan and at the Confederate flag hanging limp overhead, and he smiled fiercely. "I come from a plantation jus' 10 mile beyond Petersburg. My wife and chil' still there. So close it's like I kin smell her cookin'. We bust through da' reb line tomorrow mornin', I'll be holdin' 'em both afore da' sun sets. Then, wid this here musket an' bayonet in my han', I gits to say how-do to my ole' plantation massa."

The other soldiers chuckled—some grimly, some fiercely—at the thought of Sergeant Wilson (in uniform and with a loaded musket and a bayonet) facing his terrified former owner. "I would like to see that!" said Alfonse. "I surely would."

The men of Ferrero's division milled quietly around camp that night, one-quarter mile behind the twisting maze of trench lines. Subdued, they huddled around cook fires and muckets (hinged, tin cook pots), even though it was a warm night and no one needed the fire's heat. Somehow its familiarity comforted their unsettled imaginations and blunted their terrifying images of tomorrow morning.

"Whas we got in the mucket?" asked Sergeant Wilson as he elbowed his way into the circle between Alfonse Mathews and Davis Paggett.

Alfonse smiled. "I made us some bully stew 'stead o' plain ole' lobcourse." Lobcourse was a general name for a thick, stewlike soup made from hardtack, pork, potatoes, and whatever vegetables were available. When ginger and wine (or hard liquor) were added, it was called bully stew.

Wilson tilted back the lid and breathed in the aroma. "Ummm-umm! Somethin' *special* afore da' fight!"

Staring at the fire's glowing embers, Paggett said, "I's changin' my name."

Alfonse laughed, "You can't go changin' names without the general's permission."

"My massa named me Davis, not my momma. Well, I ain't goin' into battle named for no reb pres'dent. No, sir, I ain't. I's changin' my name to Abraham. Abraham Paggett. If'n anyone asks, dats what you tell 'em tomorrow in da' fight."

Sergeant Wilson rocked back and laughed, his teeth sparkling in the firelight. "Ain't no one gwine stop me in da' middle of a battle and ask your name—'Scuse me, suh. Afore I shoots, what's his name?' " The men howled in laughter at Cyrus Wilson's antics. "Tomorrow," he continued, "your name either *live* soldier or *dead* soldier. That's yo' name!"

Alfonse asked of no one in particular, "Are you glad to be a soldier?"

Sergeant Danforth snorted. "Soldier, New York dockworker, carpenter, or garbageman. It don't make no difference. If you're black, you are automatically nothin' until you prove otherwise a dozen times. Then they say, 'Well, *maybe* you ain't all dumb and worthless.' If you're white it's the opposite way. They get the benefit of the doubt and we get a kick in the teeth. I only joined so I could kill white folks—legal like. I 'spect that'll feel mighty good tomorrow."

Washington Jefferson Monroe had been tucked up quietly with his arms wrapped around his knees. "I's mighty glad to be a sojer. I kin walk the street without no fear, without havin' to always step aside and give the sidewalk, without havin' to always look humble and look down, without havin' to bow and tip my hat every two feet. No matter what happens tomorrow, it's worth it fo' me."

Abraham Paggett nodded in agreement. "I were a-thinkin' and a-bein' a old man on da' plantation. Old an' feelin' feeble an' ready to die. Now I gits these beautiful new clothes, an' this-a-here shiny belt buckle and musket, and my blood feels so young and brave. Wid this uniform on my back this ebenin', I knows da' rebs fears me. Leastwise, dey better. 'Cause I's a-comin! An' I is young and fired wid da' almighty force of freedom! An' das somethin' dey jus' can't stop."

"Amen, brother. You tell 'em," Alfonse laughed.

Sergeant Wilson wrinkled his brow searching for the right words. "My son is a short 10 mile away, jus' over there. An' this-a-here war is gwine set him free. An' I *has* ta be here so that no one will ever say to him that he don't deserve his freedom 'cause his daddy didn't do his part ta earn it."

Silence settled over the soldiers and they turned back to stare at the fire, which slowly ebbed to the faintest speck of red. Dark and quiet settled across the USCT camp.

It seemed the night had hardly begun when the men were roughly awakened. "Everybody up. Fill yer' canteens. No fires. Eat what you can cold. Parade in 15 minutes."

Blinking and yawning in the dark, they shuffled in long lines into the trenches. "Quiet!" snarled sergeants and officers. "You want to wake up the whole reb camp?" Hearts pounded and hands trembled as feet shuffled through billows of dust down the maze of zigzag trenches. As they shuffled past a bombproof ammo pit, a colonel whispered, "Sixty rounds for every man. Make sure you have 60 rounds. . . ."

As the vast array of units were crammed into the forward trenches for the attack, the USCT division was ordered off the front line and back to the reserve trench. "It's 'cause we're black," muttered Danforth.

"I heard it's 'cause we's green," said Wilson.

"Green?"

"You know. Untested. Never been in battle. Grant didn't want a green unit to lead the charge."

"He didn't want to give black men a chance to show we're as good as whites," Danforth snarled.

"Quiet!" hissed a captain, ending the conversation.

In a second line trench the regiments of the USCT waited . . . and waited. The sky paled and shifted toward the oranges of sunrise. Still they waited.

Then, in the twilight gray the ground trembled beneath their feet. Several men toppled against the trench wall. Birds screeched and flapped into the dark. A dog howled somewhere behind the lines.

The massive Confederate redan seemed to hop, to lift several feet into the air. As it settled with a giant thud, a monstrous grinding roar belched from the Earth. The dirt of that redan mountain exploded and boiled in a swirling fury of a dust cloud that rose 250 feet into the sky and spread like an open umbrella before sprinkling ominously back to Earth.

Every soldier gaped in fear and trembling awe. "Lawd, amighty!" "They blowed up the world!" "They must all be dead over there."

Debris and dirt sprayed into the Union trenches. Some in the forward trenches screamed and fled. So horrifying was this massive explosion that many dropped to the ground and prayed.

Union cannons, 160 of them, opened fire with a deafening roar and with flashes of fire that belched 50 feet into the predawn sky. The Union cannonade poured a hot iron storm onto the Confederate lines around that giant hole that, only minutes before, had been a massive redoubt.

The lead divisions were called to advance. It took precious minutes to get them back on their feet and then more time was wasted cutting paths through the ditches and *abatis* protecting the Union trenches. Some 12,000 blue-coated gophers crawled out of their trenches and tramped across no-man's-land. The rising sun shone on a forest of battle flags as the first sporadic fire from the stunned Confederates found their targets.

The redan was gone. In place of the massive fort that dominated the sector lay a crater, a great hole in the Confederate lines 170 feet long, 80 feet wide, and 20 feet deep at its center.

The first Union troops paused at the crater's lip, gaping in wonder at the explosion's awful effect. But sheer momentum from the moving mass of blue behind pushed them over the lip and they tumbled into the crater's powdery depths.

Soon thousands of Union soldiers milled about inside the crater, stuffed shoulder to shoulder and unsure of what to do. No generals cried "Forward!" and led their troops into the Confederate rear to win the war. No leaders rallied and organized the mass of humanity jammed into the moon-like crater.

By the time the first union troops awkwardly clawed their way up the far edge of the crater, the Confederates had recovered from the shock of the explosion. Regiment-sized battle lines formed in several adjoining trenches. Cannons lobbed exploding canister shells into the crater, killing dozens with every shot.

With thousands of Union soldiers jammed into the powder-soft crater, it was impossible for the rebels to miss. Union dead piled three and four deep near the forward edge of the crater. A few bravely scrambled over the crater's front lip and formed to advance, only to be mowed down by fire from entrenched lines of Confederates. Some made it into the vast maze of Confederate trenches beyond the crater and fought hand to hand at every twist and turn of the passages.

Many turned to flee and scrambled back out of the giant pit. But fire from adjacent Confederate positions mowed them down as they reached the top. Some 12,000 soldiers were trapped in the wasteland of the crater.

Into this hellish nightmare, the USCT division of 2,500 was ordered to charge.

With a fierce cry of pride and joy, the black soldiers bolted forward out of their protective trenches. "Git out my way! I'm goin' home!" screamed Sergeant Wilson.

Alfonse gaped at the horror before them as his company wormed through a gap in the Union *abatis* and rushed across no-man's-land. Acrid smoke rolled in thick clouds across the field. The ground was littered with fallen blue soldiers. Cannon explosions, musket roar, and human screams filled the air.

"Forward!" cried the captains and sergeants.

" 'Dis here surely ain't what I thought war'd be like," Paggett muttered as he gulped in the bitter air in heaving pants.

Other Union divisions were advancing both to the left and right of the crater to draw Confederate fire away from the men trapped inside.

Ferrero's division lost fewer than 100 men before they reached the crater's lip. By now, the dead were piled six and eight deep in the pit. Many had thrown up their hands to surrender, but there was no one to surrender to. Many stood packed so tight they couldn't have lifted a rifle to fire even if they'd wanted to. And all the while the Confederates poured a constant fire from cannon canister and musket into the pit of death.

"Forward!" cried the USCT officers. "Take that rise beyond the crater! Move forward!" And the black soldiers of Ferrero's eight regiments *did* advance. Along the lip of the crater, through the edges of the crater, worming their way through packs of terrified white soldiers, the black division steadily advanced.

"Don't stop to sightsee!" bellowed Sergeant Danforth. "Keep moving. Colonel Connie will shoot you."

"Colonel Connie ain't here this mornin'," answered Alfonse as he followed Sergeant Wilson around the lip of the hellish crater.

Washington Monroe closed his eyes and screamed to block out the terror around him as they jogged through the smoke, the glare of explosions, and the din. Monroe stumbled and tumbled partway down the loose slope into the crater. Alfonse dove and grabbed his arm to stop his slide. They clawed back up to the lip and rejoined the company.

"Down there's only death," called Alfonse thumbing toward the crater.

"Ain't no picnic up here," Monroe answered.

Almost 20 percent of the division fell before they formed on the Confederate side of the crater and began their attack. Not one white soldier followed the USCT division and joined their advance. Not one white unit forced their way forward and joined the attack. Ferrero's division attacked alone.

"This way!" cried Sergeant Danforth. "Follow your sergeant!"

"I'm goin' home!" cried Sergeant Wilson. "Git out my way!" And he bounded forward, musket and bayonet thrust toward the Confederates.

Alfonse and Abraham Paggett marched side by side, teeth clenched, eyes wide with fright. A forest of Confederate muskets seemed to be leveled against them.

The black regiments formed and advanced. Their battle flags fluttered in the morning sun. Their long lines seemed parade-ground sharp. Their voices roared in challenge. And they charged.

And they were slaughtered. The proud ranks disintegrated in horror and chaos.

Outnumbered by Confederates firing from entrenched positions, the division was mowed down like Kansas wheat. Survivors stumbled back toward the crater.

Captured whites were proudly marched off by Confederate guards. Any black soldier captured by Confederates was immediately clubbed, stabbed, and killed. The remnants of Ferrero's division poured down into the crater to escape the rampaging rebels and struggled alongside the rest of Burnside's corps to claw their way over the thick carpet of dead and stream back toward the safety of Union trenches.

By 2:00 P.M. that afternoon, the battle was over. The Confederates were already busy constructing a new trench line and redan in front of their old position.

About 15,000 Union soldiers had charged the crater. Forty percent were either killed, wounded, or taken prisoner. Two-thirds of all Union casualties that fell on the Confederate side of the crater (those who had crossed the crater and attempted to advance) came from just one of the four divisions sent into the crater—the USCT division.

Sergeant Danforth was dead. Cyrus Wilson had been shot in the hand and lost three fingers. Alfonse Mathews was gashed in the arm by shrapnel and in the leg by a Confederate bayonet. Abraham Paggett had been nicked in both legs by bullets. The wounds, though not serious, had spread thick stripes of blood down his blue pants.

To the jeers of Confederate sharpshooters and the constant crunch of Confederate shovels, Wilson, Mathews, Monroe, and Paggett huddled together in bandaged shock in their rifle pit as a pink sunset washed across the hazy sky.

They had watched a great opportunity ineptly turned to disaster. They had watched thousands of helpless men slaughtered like cattle. They had watched their friends and comrades butchered faster than they could reach out to help. The men hung their heads in bitter silence. There seemed nothing to say that could describe the horror they had lived through.

This surely wasn't what any of them thought war would be like.

Aftermath

General Ulysses Grant said that the Battle of the Crater was "the saddest affair I have witnessed in the war." He later reported, "Such a splendid opportunity for carrying a battle I have never seen."

The attack was doomed from the outset by terrible lack of management and leadership. The attacking corps commander and three of his four attacking division commanders never showed up for the assault, but stayed in their tents, drinking themselves into a stupor. The attack could have and should have easily succeeded in driving a giant wedge through the heart of Lee's defenses—if anyone above the rank of junior officer had been present to take command of the 12,000 milling troops at the crater. Generals Burnside, Ledlie, Ferrero, and Wilcox were all censured and relieved of command, the only time in the war so many senior officers were court-martialed for failure in battle. Only one medal of honor was issued for the fighting at the crater. It went to Sergeant Decatur Dorsey, a black man of the USCT.

The trench war standoff continued for eight more months through 50 miles of trenches around Petersburg plagued by flies, mosquitoes, mud, disease, death, and boredom. On the last day of March 1865, General Philip Sheridan's Union cavalry finally turned the southwest end of the trench line and forced the Confederates to withdraw. A black regiment led the Union army march into Petersburg. Blacks in town lined the street to cheer and weep for joy.

Only one of the five men in this story survived to march in that parade. Sergeant Danforth died in the crater on July 30. Cyrus Wilson was shot and killed by a sharpshooter in November. Davis (Abraham) Paggett died from typhoid in January. Washington Jefferson Monroe lay in an army hospital also with typhoid fever when the Union army finally stormed through the Confederate trenches and took Petersburg on April 1, 1865. Alfonse Mathews marched proudly into Petersburg.

After the Battle of the Crater, Grant said, "I wish I had 100,000 colored troops. I'd put an end to this war tomorrow." In 1864 and 1865, USCT troops saw major action in every engagement. There were 220 USCT regiments with 200,000 men in uniform by war's end. African Americans represented 1 percent of the Northern population but 12 percent of the Northern army. USCT units distinguished themselves at the Battle of Honey Hill, Chaffin's Farm, Darbytown Road, and Fair Oaks.

From mid-1864 through the end of the war, Union forces battered the Confederates, in large part because of the infusion of USCT troops to bolster and reinvigorate Union forces.

In early 1864 Robert E. Lee proposed that the Confederacy create and arm black units. Jefferson Davis refused to consider it. He couldn't admit that they needed blacks or that blacks were equal to whites at anything above the most menial and demeaning of tasks. That decision and philosophical belief helped spell doom for the Confederacy.

Follow-up Questions and Activities

1. **What Do You Know?**

   - Why was Petersburg so important to the Confederacy? Why was it important to the Union army?

   - What was the USCT? Why were blacks collected in segregated units?

   - Why did Lee's and Grant's armies build trenches, redans, etc., and allow themselves to get locked into a prolonged trench war? Which side benefited most from the trench stalemate?

   - How did the Union army plan to attack the Confederates at the Battle of the Crater? Did the plan work? Why didn't Union forces smash through the Confederate lines? What happened at the crater?

   - Why did the Union attack at the crater fail? Whose fault was it? What happened to the Union commanding generals after this battle?

2. **Find Out More.** Here are seven important topics from this story for students to research in the library and on the Internet. The reference sources at the back of this book will help them get started.

   - Research the history of the USCT. Who were the first black units in the Union army? The first combat units? Which units fought first? The Louisiana black units and the Massachusetts 54th and 55th black regiments were the most famous regiments of the war. But USCT regiments fought in many battles through 1864 and 1865. Research the action and contributions of USCT regiments to the Union war effort.

- Research the treatment offered to USCT troops by the U.S. Army. Were they paid the same as white troops? Where they issued the same quantity and quality of weapons? Of food? Of horses and wagons? Of medical services? Were captured USCT soldiers treated the same as other soldiers by the Confederate army? Research the Fort Pillow massacre. Why do you think blacks still wanted to be in the army and fight in the war?

- Research the development of trench warfare at Petersburg. What did the trenches look like? What were all the parts of an entire trench system? Compare the Petersburg trenches with those that spread across France during World War I.

- Gambling was a popular form of entertainment for Civil War soldiers. What else did they do to amuse themselves in camp? What games did they like to play? What songs did they like to sing? Compare Civil War games to those of American soldiers during the Revolutionary War, World War II, or Vietnam.

- Research the 1864 and 1865 battles where African American soldiers played a significant role—Honey Hill, New Market Heights, Chaffin's Farm, Fair Oaks, Darbytown Road. How many more can you find? How did black troops perform at each of these battles?

- Identify and research the life, struggles, and accomplishments of the African American medal of honor winners: Sergeant Decatur Dorsey, Sergeant Major Christian Fleetwood, Milton Holland, and eight others.

- Research the history of black soldiers in American wars. Begin with the French and Indian War and discover how many African Americans served in the American army in each war and what contribution they made to the war effort. Also compare the percentage of African Americans in the army to that of the whole American population during each of those wars.

3. **Make It Real**

- As a class, discuss and then make a chart of the motives, fears, problems, and risks of being a black soldier during the Civil War. How do you think the soldiers felt? Why did they join? Did blacks desert as fast as whites in 1864 and 1865?

   Chart African American soldiers' experience in the U.S. Army, war by war. Interview black soldiers and see if their experiences are different from those of black soldiers in past wars. Why or why not? What else has (or hasn't) changed?

- Create a schematic map of a Civil War–era trench system (trench line, rifle pits, artillery redans, transverses, communications trenches, regimental bombproofs, sleeping borrows, etc. Compare the system you create to maps of Federal and Confederate systems at Petersburg. Then compare your system to maps and drawings of World War I trench systems in France.

4. **Points to Ponder**

- Confederates refused to acknowledge the articles of war for captured black soldiers and either sold them back into slavery or killed them on the battlefield. Why? How did they justify their position?

- The Union attack at the crater failed because of the total absence of senior leadership. Why would Civil War generals fear going into battle? What were they afraid of? At what level were officers still expected to *lead* their soldiers into battle rather than just to command them from the rear? Is the expectation for officers different today? Why? Should it be different? Why or why not?

- Why was the Civil War in the East such a disaster for the Army of the Potomac? Why did Union forces succeed in the West and along the coast as part of the blockade, but consistently failed to win in the East where they had the greatest superiority in numbers?

A "Fair" Fight

Northern Women's Efforts to Support the Sanitary Commission, September–November 1864

Initially, the Northern public was not passionately involved in the war to the extent that the Southern populace was. In the North, the war was viewed more as a grim necessity. Soon, however, soldiers' aid became the primary unifying force for Northern society. Prominent citizens sponsored drives for food and clothing for locally enlisted units and privately arranged for these necessities to be shipped to the front. Over time, public loyalty spread to link local support groups with *all* Union soldiers instead of just local units.

Many soldiers' aid groups began to specialize. New York had a Slipper Circle that just produced slippers, a Handkerchief Circle, and the Ladies Military Blue Stocking Association, which knitted over 200 pairs of regulation stockings each week. Teams of boys with names like the Sawbuck Rangers and Wood Cadets chopped wood for wives of men in uniform and to raise money for the war.

Once they had gained sufficient political power to persuade the president of the necessity for a formal aid society, Elizabeth Blackwell (America's first female doctor) and George Templeton Strong (a New York lawyer) created a soldiers' aid society that grew into the official U.S. Sanitary Commission in July 1861. They chose the commission's name from the British agency created during the Crimean Campaign (in the 1850s) by Florence Nightingale.

The women who volunteered for the Sanitary Commission sewed clothes, tents, and battle flags; knitted socks; secured and packaged food and medical supplies; distributed fruit and vegetables; and staffed feeding stations at train depots. Whereas Southern women's groups had to struggle to find resources to do their jobs, in the North resources were readily available in abundance. The Sanitary Commission's challenge was to rally, secure, and organize those resources. Northern aid organizers were concerned not with surviving and grimly persevering (as in the South) but with marshaling the available resources, maintaining public enthusiasm and willingness to give, generating and directing new enthusiasm, and developing expanded support facilities and structures.

Meet Mary Livingston

Mary Chadwig was born in Chicago in 1826. Her father owned a small retail clothing store. The family lived a comfortable life in a prominent section of town. Mary married 28-year-old banker George Livingston when she was 19 years old. He was quickly elevated to upper management and became prosperous.

Mary was a busy and industrious Chicago charity volunteer by the age of 25 and worked independently as a volunteer to raise support for local army units before joining the Chicago office of the U.S. Sanitary Commission in September 1862.

In February 1863 she was elevated to the position of volunteer director for the Chicago office, the largest office in the Northwest Sanitary Commission.

After the war, the Sanitary Commission continued in a scaled-down form for several years before being disbanded and folded back into the army. Mary continued to direct the Chicago office until it was finally closed in 1866. She remained active in Chicago local charity work until she died at age 88 in 1914.

A "Fair" Fight

September 18, 1864, dawned as a delightful day in Chicago, with the rich smell of arriving autumn and a brisk hint of the coming chill in the soft breeze off the lake. It would have been the perfect day for 36-year-old Mary Livingston to walk from her fashionable house on Irving Park along the shore of Lake Michigan to the Chicago office of the Northwest Sanitary Commission just north of where Halsted Street crosses the sluggish North Branch of the Chicago River. But there was no time for enjoying the weather these days. Mary hurried to the office in her carriage just as the sun rose, expecting not to leave the office until long after sunset.

Mary, the volunteer director for the Chicago office, was surprised to find the office doors unlocked when she arrived at 7:00 A.M. She heard noises from inside. Three overloaded drays (horse-drawn delivery trucks) were lined up at the rear loading dock. Mary stepped inside, relocked the door for security, and raced through the empty reception area and past her office, her satin dress swishing along the hardwood floor.

In the vast, dimly lit warehouse room beyond, she found half a dozen volunteers struggling to sort through a mountain of bags, big boxes, little boxes, bundles, sacks of letters, and baskets. "Eight wagonloads of donations arrived from Springfield at 4:00 this morning," one weary worker murmured.

"Why didn't you send a runner for me?" Mary asked.

Forty-two-year-old Jane Hoge, Mary's friend and a longtime volunteer at the Commission, stood up behind a mound of packages she had been sorting. "Because you didn't leave here until 11:00 last night. You've got to sleep *sometime*, Mary."

The great battle at Gettysburg in July, which had brought deep grief for Mary (who lost a brother during the battle), had also spawned a surge of patriotic fervor that had translated into increased donations to the Sanitary Commission. Now rumors of an upcoming battle along the Tennessee-Georgia border seemed to have shaken donations loose from the countryside like a fall wind shakes leaves from the trees. For three days, a steady stream of food, clothing, blankets, tents, shoes, and even paper, stamps, and combs had flooded into the Sanitary Commission for distribution to the various Union field armies.

"There's no place to *put* anything," complained Jane Hoge. "We can't even find space to sort it!"

In one grim glance Mary assessed the 10- to 12-foot-high peaks of boxes and barrels, the tumbled hills of baskets and rolled bundles. She drew in a long breath while she considered how to handle this tidal wave of goods before they were all buried underneath it.

"Set up staging areas for each army command in the empty lot. (An empty lot behind the Commission office backed up to the Chicago River.) Stamps we'll keep and distribute from here. Perishables in danger of going bad bring to the reception room. We'll take them to local hospitals. Use this room to sort donations into piles by kind of item before distributing them to the various commands. I'll be in my office or in the reception room."

The weary volunteers in the long, brick warehouse attacked the stacks of goods with renewed vigor.

Back in her small office next to the Commission's reception room, Mary stared at a mountain of paperwork rivaling the crushing load of goods back in the warehouse. She had to keep track of the rosters, needs, activities, and location of 80 brigades and army forts, over 100 Commission agents in the field in the Western region, 100 wagons and trainloads of supplies on their way to the field or on their way back, 40 hospitals scattered throughout the region, and, of course, the dozens of volunteers who staffed this central office for the Northwest region. It seemed that for every action she took, letter she wrote, or supply request she filled, 10 new letters, reports, and requests landed on her desk.

She breathed deeply to recharge her energy. Where to begin today? She sighed and chuckled, "I guess with that incessant pounding on the front door."

A thin man was hammering on the front door with his fists. Mary unlocked the door and he rushed inside, blowing on his hands as if he'd been standing in a snowstorm. "May I help you?" she inquired.

The man looked around for a pot of hot coffee. "Lady, I've been riding since midnight, and I'm freezing cold. Who's in charge, and where's the coffee?"

"I'm Mary Livingston, the office director. Coffee won't be here until we open at 7:30."

"Ten wagons of donated supplies will arrive from Wisconsin this afternoon. I rode ahead to see where you want 'em unloaded."

Mary stared. "Ten wagons? Today?"

The man snapped, "What? You don't want the stuff, lady? We've been collecting for the war effort for weeks!"

Mary shook her head to dispel the image of being crushed under a mountain of donations. She forced a smile and extended her hand. "We are eternally grateful and will look forward to your wagons. They should unload at the back of this building."

The man left, still shivering, and Mary sagged against a wall. *Ten more wagons! How can we possibly handle this flood of donations?* Her lips tightened and she nodded. "I'll have to meet with Mr. Overland this morning."

Edwin Overland was the director of the Northwest Sanitary Commission, located in the two-story brick building next door to the Chicago office. Mary directed the Chicago office, the largest Commission office in the region. Mr. Overland was in charge of the entire eight-state Northwest Region of the Commission.

Before Mary could turn back to her office, two elderly couples hesitantly stepped in the door. "May I help you?" Mary asked.

One of the women nudged her husband, who slid off his cap. " 'Scuse me, ma'am. But I was—well, we was *all*—wonderin' if you had any news on the 23rd Illinois."

Mary knitted her brow in thought. "The 23rd Illinois . . ."

"With Rosecrans's army, ma'am. We heard there was going to be a fight—a *big* fight. We got boys in the 23rd."

Mary nodded, "Ah, yes. Rosecrans has crossed into northern Georgia and is due for battle. But I haven't heard anything. Lydia, the office receptionist, will be here soon. She tracks military movements for me. Perhaps she'll know more." Mary gestured at the row of straight-backed chairs lining the reception room walls. "You're welcome to wait. Coffee and donuts will be here at 7:30 when we officially open."

"Thank you, ma'am." The couples settled into four corner chairs. The man who had spoken nervously slid his cap through his fingers.

Mary dashed back to her office to gather figures to present to Mr. Overland. She would just have to convince him to provide more wagons and drivers, and probably more train space as well.

At five minutes to eight, Mary sneaked out the back to avoid having to fight her way through the reception area crowd. Five soldiers had already wandered in, all wounded and slowly recovering in Chicago convalescent hospitals. Two had wanted stamps. One came hoping for a comb. Two had simply wanted to get out of the hospital and needed a place to sit and talk. The two couples in the corner were busy talking to one of the soldiers who hobbled in on crutches, his left leg missing below mid-thigh.

Many soldiers congregated at the Commission office. A few were home on leave; most were recovering from disease or battle wounds. Some wanted a pencil, a stamp, a needle, a comb, a piece of paper, or a cup of coffee. Most really wanted someone to talk to.

Three other people had come in to deliver news that they had received in letters and update Commission files. They all crowded around Lydia's reception desk. The ones that tore at Mary's heart the most were the parents, wives, and children of dead and missing soldiers. These poor people drifted in to dull their grief by talking to anyone wearing a uniform—especially anyone who reminded them of their loved ones they would never see again.

The reception room was like this every morning, and it would only get worse as the day wore on.

One woman had also wandered in alone and was softly crying while talking with a soldier. Mary had sighed at the sight of her. A war widow. Five or six drifted in every day needing a place to let their grief drain away through tears. So did many wives of soldiers, feeling overwhelmed by loneliness and the constant fear that their husbands would be killed. So Mary had scurried out the back to go to Overland's office, feeling frustrated that there was nothing she could do to help and comfort these people.

"Enter," boomed Mr. Edwin Overland at Mary's knock. Overland was a short, thick man with a window-rattling bass voice.

Mary swept in and laid her pages of figures on Overland's desk. "We are in desperate need of extra transportation." Mary had learned long ago not to waste time with pleasantries when talking to Edwin Overland. "Eight wagons came in last night. Ten more are due today. The warehouse is already bursting at the seams. Our assigned wagons are not due back from their circuits for two more days. We need wagons and drivers. We need train space. And we desperately need both now."

"What you need," Overland countered, rocking back in his high-backed chair, "is more volunteers. You've already lost 10 since you became office director. If you can't handle the job . . ."

"That's not my fault," Mary angrily interrupted. "They had to take paying jobs, sir."

"Jobs?" Overland leaned forward across his desk. "What are they doing with *jobs*? They *are* women, right? Wives of soldiers, right?"

"Exactly. Soldiers get terrible pay. Sometimes they don't get *any* for months on end. And even when they do, precious little of their pay reaches home for many of these families. They need money." Overland started to argue, so Mary quickly added, "Plus there are so many new factories that have opened lately. The economy is booming, and there's no one left to work in them *but* women and children."

Overland scowled. Mary went on. "Some women have had to reluctantly stop their volunteer work for the Commission, so our office only has 30 active volunteers instead of the 45 or 50 we once had. The women who had to leave are now working in factories for the war effort and getting the pay they need and deserve."

"We can't pay our volunteers," snorted Overland. "This region of the Commission has sent over 30,000 boxes of supplies to the front. Our treasury is depleted. The Commission is hanging on by a thread as it is. So, if you want more wagons and train cars, you're going to have to find a way to pay for them yourself."

"Me? Raise money? But we need the wagons today!"

Overland rubbed his chin. "I can borrow from future payroll to fund your wagons today. But you'll have to raise the money to replace those funds before regional employees come pounding on your door for a paycheck!"

"Me? Fund-raising?" Mary repeated.

"There's plenty of money in Chicago," Overland reiterated. *"Money's* what this Commission needs most."

Mary nodded. "Then we'll do it . . . somehow."

As she turned to leave, Overland added, "And drum up more volunteers. Muscle and money—that's what your office needs!"

All heads turned as Mary marched back through the reception area toward her office. The room rippled with the soft conversation of a dozen gaunt and pale soldiers and more than 20 civilians. They sipped coffee, nibbled on donuts and cakes, waited for news, and sought comfort in each other's company.

"Sorry, no news," Mary automatically announced to the sea of upturned faces and eyebrows raised in hopeful question. "No visitors, Lydia," she continued. "I have big planning to do."

"But there are five nurses and six field agents already in your office waiting for their orders."

Mary groaned. She had forgotten the new field agents. This meeting would take well over an hour. With a frustrated sigh like the hiss of a steam engine, Mary said, "Then, after *them*, no interruptions."

The Sanitary Commission had hundreds of agents in the field, traveling with every major unit and at every fort and outpost. They conducted sanitary inspections; badgered and coerced field commanders into improving sanitary conditions; oversaw the distribution of Commission supplies and donations; distributed mail; arranged for the transportation of the wounded; gathered statistics for Commission reports on the physical, social, and moral condition of soldiers; and disseminated health education information. It was a mammoth job and fell mostly to volunteer nurses and other, nonmedical field agents.

One of Mary's responsibilities was to arrange for the commissions, assignments, and travel orders for these volunteers as well as to provide them with vouchers for cash, letters of introduction and authority, and a Commission notebook of regulations and information. She had to provide maps and explain their individual duties. She also had to instill in them a sense of the urgent necessity of their work.

Two of this group of agents were being assigned to direct "flying depots," mobile Commission supply centers located close to the front and able to quickly respond to emergencies. The rest would spread out with army commands.

While Mary talked and answered questions for this eager group of new field volunteers, her thoughts were elsewhere: *Somehow I have to raise money to pay for it all!* It was almost noon before Mary could send the volunteers out to their waiting carriage for the ride to Chicago's train station.

Jane Hoge walked into Mary's office during the sorters' lunch break, rubbing her sore back.

Mary asked, "How's it going?"

"We're making headway. A couple of days and it will all be sorted, *if* my back and arms hold out."

Mary grimaced, then blurted out, "Ten more loaded wagons arrive this afternoon."

"What?! We have nowhere to put the supplies. There's no one to work on them!"

"And there's even worse news."

Jane exclaimed, "What could be worse than *that*?"

Mary helplessly spread her hands. "We have to raise the money to pay for this and future transportation."

"How?"

Mary sadly shook her head. "Ask for donations? Chicago is a wealthy city. We'll just have to pester the wealthy until they give us what we need."

Jane asked, "How can we spare volunteers to do fund-raising when we're already short-handed here?"

Mary lowered her eyes to the figures on her desk. "That's our first job—find another 20 volunteers to work here."

Jane demanded, "And who will sort and pack today's 10 wagonloads of donations while we hunt for money and volunteers?"

Mary shrugged helplessly, "I don't know."

They stepped into the hall and automatically glanced at the subdued reception room crowd, hanging around hoping for news. Jane brightened, pointing toward the packed room. "Just soldiers and families," shrugged Mary.

"No. *Volunteers*," Jane corrected. "Volunteers who need a job."

Within three days 40 new names had been added to the regular office volunteer roles, and the primary office volunteers fanned out to raise money. In 10 days they had raised a little less than $100.

Edwin Overland stomped into Mary's office. "You haven't *begun* to replenish my payroll fund. Where is your fund-raising?!"

"People are depressed," Mary explained. "They're tired of the war and its endless death and grief. It's harder than I thought to drum up enthusiasm for giving."

Overland growled, "I don't want to hear problems. I want to see cash or I want to see a new director!" And he stomped out.

"People are tired of dwelling on death and losses," Mary repeated to Jane Hoge later that morning.

"But wars *are* sad and depressing," Jane answered.

Mary's expression tightened as she said, "So we need to get wealthy Chicago society excited. We need to make them *want* to come out in their finery and give."

"You mean host a party? A dance?" Jane offered.

"No. . . . Something that will bring in more money but still seem festive and party-like." There was silence for a few minutes while both women tried to come up with a scheme to raise the money they needed. Suddenly Mary brightened and said, "A fair!"

"With rides and livestock shows?" asked Jane.

"No. With auctions and sales. We'll ask for donations and sell the proceeds. We can charge admission and offer meals to each fair goer to keep people there longer."

"We should have entertainment, too, then," added Jane.

"Perfect! And a great parade through Chicago to kick it off."

"Do you think it will work?"

"It had better. Mr. Overland says I have to raise $10,000 by the end of October, or else."

Mary pitched the idea to the full Northwest Sanitary Commission Board on September 30, 1863, asserting that the fair would net $25,000. Overland was skeptical but agreed to the scheme because Mary had presented no other plan for raising money.

The women had only one month to pull off a miracle. They mailed out more than 30,000 notices to newspapers, church groups, governors, ministers, teachers, civic groups, and government officials. Each letter and notice begged for the donation of articles and memorabilia to be sold or displayed for charity.

Throughout the first week of October the women held their breath, waiting to see if their appeal would bring some meaningful response.

On October 6 a young woman in tattered clothes came in and held out a clenched hand to Mary. "I don't have anything to donate to your fair—I'm just a poor seamstress. So I decided to donate all the money I made from one week's work to the Commission instead." She opened her fingers to proudly reveal a small pile of coins. "It's $5.13. Here."

Mary protested, "Do you have children?"

"Three."

"Then you need to keep the money."

The young woman slowly shook her head, her solemn eyes never leaving Mary's face. "No. It's for you." She closed Mary's fingers over the money, turned, and quickly left.

On the next day Lydia rushed into Mary's office to announce that she had received news that nine regional cities had organized "City Fair Meetings" to encourage support for donations.

And then donations for the fund-raiser began to pour in: silverware, pianos, flowers, wreaths, clothing, silver plate and silver services, farm equipment, knitwear, sacks of grain, barrels of cologne and brandy, and five horses.

"Horses?" stammered Jane. "What do we do with horses?"

"Ask the Chicago fire house to care for them until we auction them on the 27th."

Jane asked, "Do we *have* to open on the 27th? We still need to find 100 society ladies to serve meals at the kitchen and a traveling kitchen that can serve 300 at a time."

Mary responded, "The army will supply the kitchen. They're used to feeding large groups."

Jane continued, "We also need 100 ticket takers and ushers. We need another 100 for sales. We still need to find an available building, for goodness sake!"

"At the rate donations are rolling in, better make that two—or even three—buildings," Mary answered. "And, yes, we *have* to open on the 27th. I have to give the money to Overland for his October 30 payroll."

The flood of donations continued, including memorabilia from every battle of the war, swords, muskets, eight cannons, uniforms. Crates of cartridges, shells, cannonballs, and canisters were piled up in long rows. Confederate flags and souvenirs filled up an entire building. The Eagle Works Manufacturing Company sent a complete steam engine.

One black woman sent a pair of socks she had knitted for her son, who would never need them because he had been one of the first black soldiers killed in the war. One ex-slave woman sent nine small blankets that she had knitted—one for each of her nine children who were still plantation slaves in the Deep South. The women of Dubuque, Iowa, sent hundreds of cooked ducks, chickens, and turkeys for the fair meals. Paintings, sculptures, and furniture overflowed in a newly rented warehouse.

President Lincoln sent an early draft copy of the Emancipation Proclamation. His accompanying letter said that he had a "strong desire to retain the paper. But if it shall contribute to the relief and comfort of the soldiers, that will be better."[1]

Suddenly enthusiastic and eager, Overland rubbed his hands together when he and Mary met. "You did it, Mary. You found the right chord to strike, the right sentiment to pluck! Your fair is exactly what Chicago—and the Commission—needs."

By October 25, the items for the fair filled six giant warehouse buildings.

On October 27, trains offered discount tickets to fair goers. A three-mile-long parade opened the fair. Military bands boomed, their music rattling the city. Businesses, courts, and schools closed for the day. A vast hum of happy and excited voices filled the city, the first such joyous noise in the long months of war. More than 100 farmers drove their wagons in the parade, decorated with flags and stuffed with all kinds of produce for sale at the fair. Flags flew from rooftops and church steeples. Two militia regiments marched to thunderous applause from the bulging crowd. Behind them a line of carriages carried wounded soldiers from Chicago hospitals. The crowd roared and showered the men with flowers. The soldiers wept at this overwhelming show of gratitude.

Wagons filled with a massed children's choir sang "John Brown's Body," and every captured Confederate flag that was wheeled proudly past merited a giant cheer from the spectators.

The massive crowd followed the parade to the six warehouse buildings of the fair, where Mary's volunteer army of almost 1,000 women had been working nonstop for weeks. Flags flew everywhere. Bands played inside each building except for those featuring war items. Entertainers performed and sang on five different stages. For $.75, a person could view all six buildings, bid on any items, and get a free meal.

The buildings were so crowded that ticket sales had to be suspended four times during the opening afternoon. Long lines hovered near the dining hall, and none of the 300 seats was empty until closing time. Outside thoroughbred horses, oxen, and fine art were auctioned off. Lincoln's draft alone brought in $3,000.

Mary and Jane were too harried and too tired to realize the extent of their success. They only saw the problems, the long lines, the complaints about long waits and not having enough Confederate memorabilia for sale, the difficulty in organizing all the needed volunteers. On closing day a week later both women were amazed when Overland proudly announced that they had raised over $100,000.

They both sank happily into chairs. Then Overland asked how soon they could hold a second fair. The two women looked at each other and groaned.

Aftermath

After the amazing success of the Chicago fair, scores of cities organized their own "Sanitary Fairs." Even beyond the money they raised, these fairs seemed to rejuvenate the spirit, morale, and convictions of a people weary from almost three years of bloody war. The biggest fair was held in Philadelphia in June 1864. It raised $4 million. The New York fair, in April 1864, raised $2.5 million.

The Sanitary Commissions raised over $30 million for their war effort, a third through fairs and a quarter from California donations. (That one state donated far more than any other single state and, during the last 18 months of the war, provided the majority of all Sanitary Commission donations.) In addition to cash donations, the Commission raised and distributed untold thousands of tons of essential food and supplies and organized an army of volunteers both in the field and in every Northern city to coordinate local efforts to support the armies and the war.

Referring to the lessons learned by the success of the Sanitary Commission's war effort, Edwin Overland said, "Neighbors and neighborhoods must come to respect each other more, to depend on each other more, and to wonder that they have missed finding each other for so long."[2]

The need for neighbor to help neighbor extended far beyond simply supporting active army units. In Connecticut three-quarters of all charity cases in 1864 and 1865 were families of soldiers (captured, wounded, or killed). Every Northern city was flooded with disabled veterans who were unable to work or support themselves and were no longer eligible for army pay. There were no guaranteed benefits for veterans (disabled or not). The problem of how to support them was left to state and local resources. The Sanitary Commission evolved at war's end into a social service agency to assist in caring for war-distressed families and individuals.

Northern civilian and industrial support, funneled mainly through the Sanitary Commission and the War Department, propelled the Union army forward from 1863 through 1865 in a way that the limited and uncoordinated Southern support could not match for the Confederate army. The Confederates were badly outclassed in the last several campaigns by the incredible Northern industrial and social support machine.

Notes

1. Quoted from Webb Garrison, *Amazing Women of the Civil War*, p. 138.
2. Quoted from Carl Lowe, *Civil War Storyteller*, p. 64.

Follow-up Questions and Activities

1. **What Do You Know?**

   • What were the differences between Northern and Southern women's war experiences? Why?

   • What was the function and mission of the U.S. Sanitary Commission? Who performed the work of the Commission? How was it funded?

   • In what ways did the work of the Sanitary Commission improve the army's ability to fight in the field? How did it improve morale? Health?

   • What were the motives and rewards of volunteering to work with the Sanitary Commission?

2. **Find Out More.** Following are six important topics from this story for students to research in the library and on the Internet. The reference sources at the back of this book will help them get started.

   • Research the U.S. Sanitary Commission. How did it start? Why was it created? Who started it? What was it initially designed to do? How did the Commission and its role grow and evolve during the war? What happened to it after the war ended?

- Research prominent Commission volunteers: Elizabeth Blackwell, Mary Livingston, Dorothea Dix, Mary Bickerdyke, the volunteer Hospital Transport Corps, etc. You can find prominent Commission volunteers in every major Northern city.

- Research medical and sanitary beliefs and practices of the mid-nineteenth century. What was known about scurvy, typhoid, dysentery, diphtheria, infection, and gangrene? One of the Commission's roles was to fund and direct medical research and sanitary information. Research medical advances funded by the Commission during the Civil War.

- Compare the Civil War U.S. Sanitary Commission to the combination of the Red Cross and the USO today. How and when did those organizations start? What services do they routinely perform for people in the armed forces?

- Why was California's donation to the war effort so much larger than that of other states? Why didn't this Western state take a neutral position in the war? Research state policies in California or your own state during the Civil War.

- Industrial and agricultural inventions and advancements during the Civil War in the North significantly aided the Northern war effort. Research mechanical and scientific discoveries and inventions during the period of the Civil War.

3. **Make It Real**

- Make a list of all the charitable support agencies in your community. List what help they provide, to whom they provide it, how they provide it, and how they raise their funds. Total the amount and value of aid given in your own community. When was each of these agencies founded? What happened to the needy in the community before that?

- Create and run a donation program of your own. As a class, pick a charitable need and decide how you will collect donations to help meet that need. Prepare your donation campaign and decide how you will publicize it and manage, inventory, sort, and distribute your donations. As a class, keep a detailed journal of the struggles, problems, and successes of your campaign. After you have finished your donation campaign, write an essay describing how your experience sheds light on the mammoth job taken on by Sanitary Commission volunteers.

4. **Points to Ponder**

- The Union army dumped the responsibility for most personal care, much of the feeding, entertainment and mail, and much of the medical care of the army's soldiers on the Sanitary Commission. Why? Was this a good idea for the country? For the army? Does the army use anything like the Sanitary Commission today?

- Why do you think there was so little recorded about the efforts of women to support the armies during the Civil War? Those efforts were critically important to the war's success, yet they are often completely ignored in histories of the period. Why do you think that happened? Does the same thing happen today?

Sweet Potatoes, Cotton, Tobacco, and Quinine

A Wealth of Smuggling, October 1864

The Protestant work ethic, which decried conspicuous consumption, seemed to be giving way to the pursuit of wealth by any means as the Civil War blossomed. Everything, it seemed, was for sale. This pursuit of wealth quickly bred corruption. Bribes to government and army officials became commonplace to secure lucrative government contracts to deliver everything from rifles to boots to straw hats to pickles to salt.

Commonly, the price paid by the government under these contracts was 2 to 10 times what the going price had been before the contract was awarded. Massive fortunes from kickbacks, bribes, and excessive profits piled up faster than battlefield casualties.

Enterprising businessmen on both sides of the war soon began to gaze beyond their own borders for profits. Northern and Southern states had been tightly interdependent before the war. The North needed the cotton grown in the South, and the South needed the manufactured goods produced in Northern factories. Those markets still existed; the products still existed. The supply lines had simply been severed.

Both governments officially forbade trade with the enemy in any form. However, agents for both governments often looked the other way to allow badly needed supplies to dribble across the shifting boundaries between the warring armies. Of course, a well-placed bribe or two didn't hurt a businessman's chances of pushing merchandise across the border. General Ulysses Grant said in 1863, "Many fortunes have been made in west Tennessee this past year. Yet, no honest man has made any money at all."[1]

There is a name for illegal trade across national borders: smuggling. Smuggling had become a multimillion-dollar industry by 1863. Smugglers sold their illegal wares at auction, to the government, to wealthy clients, and to sutlers. Sutlers were traveling convenience stores that followed the armies and supplied small necessities and luxuries to soldiers. Sutlers, it was said, "swarmed like bluebottle flies" in the wake of every army. Smugglers often made the best sources for sutlers to obtain the goods that soldiers were most willing to pay for.

The most lucrative region for smuggling was along the forested Mississippi Valley, with its countless sloughs and bayous, and especially through New Orleans and Memphis, with easy access to both Northern and Southern transportation systems. Senatorial staffers estimated that over $20 million a year in supplies were funneled to the Confederacy through Memphis alone!

Smugglers were typically not motivated solely by greed. Many felt deeply patriotic and were eager to supply their country with the goods it needed (as long as there was a good profit in the transaction for them). The commodity each government needed most was information. Smuggling and spying soon went hand in hand. If businessmen could cross the border to smuggle, they might just as well gather a little intelligence along the way to sell back to their own government. This practice increased profits and made it easier to obtain future necessary permits. It also increased the risk of doing business. Smugglers were often fined and released, but spies were hanged.

Meet Jedediah Turner

Born Joseph Turner in January 1812 at his parents' small farm along the bayous of the lower Mississippi Delta, Joseph changed his name at 16 to Jedediah while working as a roustabout on Mississippi River barges. Joseph's parents raised rice and chickens and fished the rich delta waters. As a two-year-old, Joseph witnessed the American victory at the Battle of New Orleans. He said that he never forgot the sound and smell of battle and claimed that he could sense a coming battle two days and 50 miles away.

At age 12, Joseph hitched a ride on a passing ship and left home for New Orleans, never to return. Joseph (turned Jedediah) worked the busy New Orleans docks until, as an 18-year-old, he slipped on a quay (small dock). His leg jammed between the dock and a barge and was crushed, leaving him with a permanent severe limp in his left leg.

Jedediah took a job as a clerk with a New Orleans importer/exporter where he learned both the vast profits available in the business world and how to create a successful business network.

In 1861, Jedediah, at age 49, went into business on his own to go after lucrative government supply contracts with the Confederates. In 1862, Union naval and army forces captured New Orleans, and Jedediah realized incredible profits from smuggling while the war lasted. A highly successful smuggler, Jedediah worked the lower Mississippi from New Orleans to Memphis until he was arrested as a spy in March 1865 and jailed. He was transferred to a federal prison in Ohio, where he died of pneumonia in late 1868.

Sweet Potatoes, Cotton, Tobacco, and Quinine

"Kill the engine," 52-year-old Jedediah Turner grunted as he eased his ponderous body out of his chair and opened the door from the pilot's house to the gently rolling deck of his 50-foot gulf shrimping boat converted into a cargo ship on Louisiana's Lake Pontchartrain.

The ship's 20-year-old pilot groaned and hesitated before throwing the lever that would stop the engine. "But Mr. Turner, if we keep going, we'll reach the other side sooner and safer. Besides, we stopped to listen just 10 minutes ago."

"Kill the engine *now!*" Turner ordered, leaning out into the steamy October night.

The pilot sighed and pulled a lever. The engine spluttered and fell silent. The *Bayou Angel* drifted through still waters in the black night, tiny wavelets softly lapping against the bow.

Turner limped to the side rail and strained to listen. "See, boss? All quiet," said a deck-hand sitting idly against the pilothouse.

"Shhhhh," Turner hissed, cupping his hands around one ear to hear even the faintest hint of another vessel on the lake's flat night waters.

All eyes of the five-man crew were fixed on the rotund man who had leased the ship to transport 100 barrels of salt and a dozen boxes stuffed with vials of precious quinine. It was illegal to transport this cargo from Turner's New Orleans warehouse (in Union-held territory) across the lake to Confederate docks. It was also immensely profitable. A bag of salt that cost $1.25 in New Orleans would fetch $70 to $80 in Alabama. The markup on quinine was even greater. The Confederacy was willing to pay the inflated prices because its army was desperate for these vital commodities.

Turner frowned and shook his head. "I don't trust the lake tonight." He turned to the crew idly lounging on deck to escape the stifling heat below. "We'll use sails for a time, both fore and aft."

"There's hardly any wind. We'll barely make three knots."

"But we'll do it silently and will reach Houltonville without being caught. Now move!"

Two deckhands scampered toward each of the ship's two stubby masts and hoisted the small sails, designed more as backup than as primary propulsion for the ship.

Turner limped back to the pilothouse and flashed a wide smile at his pilot that revealed his famous two gold teeth. "Relax. We'll make it. I always do—because I'm cautious. I haven't lost a load yet along this line." Smuggling routes and the necessary contacts to ease across guarded borders were called lines. This trip across the lake on October 12, 1864, would be Turner's eighth along this line.

Turner's left leg had been crushed between a New Orleans dock and a jostling barge when he was 18. It never healed properly, and he always dragged the leg behind him when he walked. Some described Turner as "portly." Some simply called him fat. Turner didn't care; he used another term to describe himself: rich. He had amassed a fortune rumored to be nearing a million dollars in less than two years of smuggling.

Turner eased back into his bolted deck chair and fished a gold watch from his vest pocket. Still five hours of dark. Plenty of time to glide past any Union patrol boats. Turner's baggy, patched pants and faded, outdated coat made him appear poor and shabby. It was all part of his disguise to appear like a lowly, hired middleman if stopped by a Union patrol.

Dawn had broken across the low eastern hills as the *Bayou Angel* eased against a quay on the edge of Houltonville, Louisiana, eight miles up the Techeluncte River, which flowed into the north side of Lake Pontchartrain. A small Confederate post, manned by fewer than 100 men, stood watch over this port in the eastern corner of Louisiana.

A young captain, the Confederate port master, waited with four armed guards as the *Bayou Angel*'s crew looped mooring lines over dockside bollards. Turner limped to the rail and waddled his way down the gangplank. "Captain Letcher. Good to see you again," he said, beaming cordially.

"Mr. Turner. Glad to do business with you again."

Turner grimaced at the use of the word "business," a well-known euphemism for a bribe. He motioned to the trim building that served as Letcher's office. "Perhaps you and I could talk inside." Turner motioned back to one of the deckhands and eased the captain toward indoor privacy. The deckhand followed, lugging two bags filled with clinking metal. Both bags were lifted onto Letcher's desk, and the hand returned to the ship under the watchful gaze of the guards.

"I managed to scrounge a few supplies that General Van Dorn (the regional Confederate army commander) will want."

"You have a manifest?"

Turner smiled. He had gone through this drill many times before. "Let me show you what I *do* have." He opened the bags and allowed a dazzling collection of silver and brass plates, goblets, pitchers, and place ware to tumble onto the desk. Several clattered onto the office floor. "These are the true valuables of my inventory," Turner confided. "I feel I should . . . donate these to the army. I'll gladly leave them with you."

Letcher made a fast mental calculation of the precious metal's worth. His eyes widened with the thrill of the profit he was being offered. "My guards and I should personally escort these items back to my . . . I mean, army headquarters."

"No need to trouble yourself with an inventory of the ship, captain. Just a few paltry items for army supply. I'll unload and be out of your way in no time."

The captain reloaded the sacks and marched off with his guards in tow, leaving Jedediah Turner alone on the dock. Deckhands started hoisting heavy salt barrels onto the deck and rolling them down to the dock. Within 15 minutes four wagons were galloped down the access road, raising a cloud of dust high into the air. The drivers yanked their teams to a stop and sprang down to help the deckhands load and lash the barrels for their overland trip to market.

A squat, balding man climbed down from the lead wagon and waved. "Jedediah!"

"Amos! Right on time," replied Turner, clasping the shorter man's hand. Amos Weatherall was one of the complex network of "associates" Jedediah Turner had cultivated on both sides of the border.

"I gather there weren't any problems," Amos said, gesturing at the empty dock.

"Captain Letcher was thrilled with two bags of silver and brass."

"It doesn't seem right to have to bribe port officials. We're *all* Confederates."

Turner shrugged. "It was stolen Yankee merchandise anyway. Only cost me pennies on the dollar. The real valuables are in the wagons."

"You're a good Confederate, Jedediah, risking your life to supply our glorious army with critically needed supplies."

Turner thought, *As long as I get my $65,000 profit.* But he said only, "Anything for the cause."

"Did you hear that Frederick Collin was *hanged* last week?"

Turner's eyebrows arched. "What for?"

"Spying. He was spying for the Yankees while he smuggled goods into the South." Jedediah grimaced.

Weatherall thumbed toward the wagons. "Taking these to Jackson (Mississippi)?"

"To Birmingham (Alabama)," Turner corrected.

"Why? Van Dorn's headquarters is in Jackson."

Because salt will sell for $80 a bag in Birmingham and only $50 in Jackson, you fool, thought Turner. But he said, "General Bedford Forest is operating in that area. I heard he's in great need of salt and quinine."

Amos Weatherall gazed with admiration at his associate. "You are an inspiration to all true Confederates! They should give a medal to you instead of just to soldiers."

Turner thought cynically, *It's dollars, not medals, I'm after,* but said nothing.

Amos Weatherall circled each wagon, checking tie-downs and the security of canvass covers, then mounted the lead wagon. "You coming with us, Jedediah?"

Turner shook his head and sighed. "As much as I hate horseback riding, I'll use *that,*" he said, pointing at the horse Amos had brought tied to the rear wagon, "to ride to Van Dorn's headquarters. I have some business there. Store this load in my Feller Street warehouse until I arrange for its—er, transfer." Turner pumped Weatherall's hand. "And thank you, Amos. I'll send word when I need your assistance again."

Weatherall blushed at the compliment. "Anytime, Jedediah. Anytime."

Turner hoisted himself up onto the rear wagon and used that platform to launch himself onto the horse. He waved, "A safe and pleasant journey, Amos," and rode off. Weatherall waved back as he motioned for the four drivers to whip their teams into action.

Twenty-four hours later, Jedediah Turner wearily dismounted in front of the hotel in Jackson, Mississippi, to which General Van Dorn had recently moved his headquarters. Stopped by two guards at the front door, Turner muttered, "Colonel Milton is expecting me." Colonel Walter Milton was Van Dorn's staff intelligence officer. Turner had been useful to the colonel as a source of both intelligence and wealth. The colonel, in turn, had provided the permits and passes necessary to a successful smuggler.

One guard motioned the big man up a flight of stairs. Colonel Milton sat in a small corner office behind a wobbly desk covered with sprawling charts, maps, and hastily written reports. He glanced up and offered only a quick, thin smile as Turner came through the door. "You're a week late."

"And it's good to see you, too, colonel," replied Turner. He opened a leather satchel and dropped two dozen sheets on top of the maps Milton was studying. Turner paused for effect and announced with a sweeping gesture, "Detailed reports on every Union post along the Mississippi from below New Orleans to Natchez (Mississippi). Unit identification, strength, capacity, armament, number of wagons, reserve supply levels—everything. And it is all less than 10 days old."

Jedediah flashed his gold teeth and waited for the expected praise. Milton thumbed through the pages with his glasses perched on his upturned nose. "Nothing new. Nothing particularly interesting." He shoved the pages aside. "Is that all?"

Turner was not deceived. Of course Milton was vitally interested in these reports; they would reveal the Union strength and strategy in the region. Milton's feigned indifference was calculated to increase the price Turner would have to pay for the permits he needed. Turner asked smoothly, "The cotton permits I requested?"

Milton threw up his hands. "The permits! So difficult to arrange these days."

"Of course I am prepared to pay."

Milton pretended to search for the paperwork. "Ah, yes. Ownership and transport permits in the name of a Frenchman for 800 bales of cotton—My goodness, 800 bales!" He fidgeted with the printed permits. "$2,000 *should* cover the cost of permit preparation."

Turner knew the permits—if legal—were free. He counted out $3,000 and slid it in an envelope across the desk. Milton glanced at the bills and handed back the permit forms. "When is your next trip?"

"Very soon. But I'll be returning overland through Memphis next time." Turner glanced at the stamped permits. "Jacques Pasqueral? Is that a real French name?"

"It is now," Milton said glibly, returning to his work as Turner stepped back into the hotel hall.

It took the rest of the day for Jedediah to buy a carriage and horse and four days to make the trip to Birmingham, Alabama, the second largest manufacturing center in the Confederacy. A pall of factory smoke hung over the city as forges worked nonstop to meet the Confederate demand for metal goods.

Turner was startled to find Amos Weatherall waiting in the office of his Feller Street brick warehouse. The plan hadn't called for Amos to wait in Birminghan, and plans that changed were always dangerous. "Amos, I expected you to leave as soon as the salt and quinine were unloaded."

"Your warehouse manager is ill. I volunteered to stay and arrange your next trip."

This didn't sound right to Turner at all. Had Amos been assigned to watch him? Did he suspect something beyond simple patriotic smuggling? Turner nervously cleared his throat. "*You* have arranged for the wagons?"

"Ten. Out back. Loaded with 800 bales as you ordered."

"All 40 of the bales with red tags are in the lead wagon?"

"Stacked in the front part of that wagon." Amos asked, "Why the red tags?"

Turner improvised, "Uh . . . different plantation. Wanted to keep the trading separate."

Amos nodded and picked up a handwritten note. "A Major Atkins called yesterday. He wanted to see you."

Turner glanced sharply at him, suspecting a trap. "I know no Major Atkins."

"He's on General Bedford Forest's staff. I assumed he worked for supply and was here to arrange pickup of the salt and quinine."

Turner turned pale and interrupted, "You didn't give it to him, did you?"

"No. Turns out he is with intelligence and only wanted to know if you can delay your departure for two weeks until the general can arrive to discuss his intelligence needs."

Jedediah let out his breath with a hiss. "The salt is still here? Good." Then he thought for a moment and shook his head. "Tell Major Atkins I can't wait but will be back in *three* weeks and will gladly meet the general then." Turner turned to leave, then paused. "Has Susan Shelly arrived yet?"

Weatherall nodded. "She'll meet you here at 7:00 tomorrow morning."

Jedediah Turner did not like the idea of another agent and smuggler snooping through his warehouse and files. Not at all. "I can't pay you to stay, Amos. You should go back home."

Weatherall smiled. "I don't mind. Just a few more days 'til your manager is back on his feet."

Fear and suspicion seized Turner's stomach. Amos Weatherall was becoming a serious problem. Then he set the matter aside. He would hire two other associates to "handle" Weatherall. Turner would miss him, but something odd was going on with Amos, and "odd" always meant trouble.

On the crisp morning of October 18, Turner led his caravan of 10 cotton-filled wagons west, away from the rolling hills of Birmingham. For six days he headed southwest to reach the Mississippi at St. Francisville, Louisiana, a little north of Baton Rouge. Boats waited to ferry him across to the Union side of the river, where an associate in New Roads had already bribed local Union army officers to facilitate the shipment's off-loading. The phony permits issued by Colonel Milton would allow the cotton's transport and sale through Federal territory. (Foreign nationals were allowed to own, transport, and sell Southern cotton in Union territory.)

Susan Shelly rode in the lead wagon with Turner. He had hired Susan, an Alabama actress, to play the part of his wife and assist on his planned smuggling operation back into the South.

"Do the boats all have plugs?" Turner asked at the wharf in St. Francisville. (Plugs allowed a small boat to be quickly sunk to prevent its capture.)

"Plugs and all lanterns are hooded—as always, Mr. Turner," answered his local associate, who had arranged the transport. Unhooded lanterns could easily be seen a mile away and draw unwanted attention. "And I personally guarantee that the crews can be trusted," the man added when it appeared that Jedediah Turner was not satisfied.

Turner nodded and shrugged, "Never hurts to be overly cautious."

They crossed the Mississippi in quiet and unloaded the cotton on an abandoned dock outside of New Roads. At dawn 12 wagons arrived for the cotton with one well-bribed army officer, who stamped all the transport permits for the cotton to be shipped to Cincinnati, Ohio, and sold at auction. Before the loading was complete, a buckboard wagon arrived. A lean, scruffy man climbed down. "Jedediah? I hear you've got some things to show me?"

Turner beamed and stretched out his hand, "Thomas! Good to see you, old friend. I've been saving 40 special bales on the dock. How's the sutler business these days?"

Sutlers ran traveling convenience stores for soldiers. Their wagons followed an army wherever it went and sold everything from food (fruits, potatoes, onions, etc.) to paper and stamps, to tobacco, to jewelry, gifts, and liquor. Sutlers and smugglers worked hand in hand to supply luxuries soldiers could not otherwise obtain. Thomas Casting had followed the Union Army of the Mississippi for three years, becoming a wealthy man from his three sutler's wagons.

Turner cut the straps holding the first of the red-tagged bales together. Inside an eight-inch-thick layer of cotton, the bale was stuffed with bootleg liquor and chewing tobacco. Turner waved a tobacco plug under Casting's nose "Strong *Southern* chewin' tobacco. Not that weak Northern smoking tobacco."

"I thought so," Susan nodded. "I knew you'd smuggle something besides cotton."

The second and third bales were stuffed with giant sweet potatoes. Casting beamed. "Ahhh! These will bring a fortune!" He lovingly pawed one of the potatoes. "A 50-50 split? I'll pay as soon as it's sold."

Turner laughed in the cool morning light. "With none of my representatives to confirm the sale price? I think not. A flat fee."

The sutler shrugged. "Eight thousand dollars upon your return."

"Nine thousand dollars now."

Castings glared at the big man. Perspiration beaded his upper lip despite the fall chill. "You're in Union territory now, Jedediah. I could have you arrested."

Turner rocked back on his heels and laughed again. "And lose your best source of high-profit Southern merchandise? I think not. More likely, I'll find another sutler willing to trade honestly."

"Eight thousand dollars now," Castings proposed.

"Eight thousand five hundred dollars."

"Done!"

The deal was struck and shook on. Money and goods exchanged hands.

After all the wagons had departed except for the one that would carry Turner and Susan Shelly to New Orleans, Susan asked, "I saw him finger a gun under his coat. Weren't you worried he'd kill you and *take* the shipment?"

"No. He needs me more than I need him. He's a good associate and willingly paid most of the bribes to district officials to ensure our landing would go unnoticed. It's all a game, really. We both knew where the bargaining would end before it began."

As they plodded southeast from Baton Rouge toward New Orleans, Susan asked, "How many associates do you have?"

Turner smiled, flashing his gold teeth in the hazy afternoon. "Never enough, Susan. Fifty or so on each side, I suppose. But more is always better for business."

Susan asked, "Are you in business just for the money, or are you loyal to the South—to the Confederacy?"

Turner grunted, shifted in his seat, flicked the reins, and studied this woman he had hired on two previous smuggling operations. It wouldn't do to offend a true Southern patriot. Finally he shrugged. "I hold a deep fondness for the South—the people and the culture. But the Confederacy—the government—is a disaster. Has been since the very beginning. Now it's dying, and dying fast." He sighed and adjusted his hat to block the sun. "In 1861 I had hopes, grand hopes. But now there is nothing anyone can do but try to survive and prosper while the Confederacy crumbles."

New Orleans was a vibrant, bustling city, crammed with ships, soldiers, muggy heat, and life. Turner met in a secluded park with George Denison, Special U.S. Treasury Agent for Import and Export Trade. "And what will you do with 1,000 surplus government muskets, Mr. Turner?"

Jedediah tried to look pious and patriotic. "I know of a regiment of blacks trying to form in Wisconsin. They have a benefactor willing to fund their equipping."

"Blacks, eh?"

"They desperately want to train and join the USCT."

Denison stroked his pointed goatee. "Since it's for a good cause, $5 a musket."

"They have *very* limited funds," Turner answered. "And I do have to pay for transportation, even if I don't make a penny on the transfer."

Denison pulled on the goatee hairs while he thought. "It will cost me $4 each to get them out of the warehouse," he mused.

"Done!" And the men shook hands.

Both knew Denison would pay nothing for the muskets and would officially list them as destroyed. Both also knew that Turner would resell them at a handsome profit. When Turner and Susan drove the 34 wooden crates to Baton Rouge for shipment to Memphis, Turner told her, "I have a buyer in Memphis at $14 a musket."

"That's $10,000 profit!" Susan exclaimed.

Turner nodded, "Lovely, isn't it?" Then he added, "He's going to sell them to the government for $22 each."

Susan threw up her hands in disbelief. "The government sold you muskets for $4 each so you could resell them to someone who will sell them straight back to the same government for $22—the same government that didn't want them in the first place?!"

Turner slapped the reins and chuckled. "War is an amazing enterprise. It surely is!"

Susan asked, "Why not sell them yourself to the government for $22 and make extra profit?"

"He has the Memphis government contact, not I," explained Turner.

After selling the muskets in Memphis, Turner contacted another local associate, who had secured the merchandise Turner and Susan would carry south and had it loaded on an eastbound train. That arranged, the two smugglers strolled the Memphis streets while waiting for their train—until they were stopped by an army squad led by a captain.

"Uh-oh. This smells like trouble," Turner muttered.

The captain tipped his hat to Susan. "Excuse me, ma'am. But I have orders to bring this gentleman into headquarters."

"There must be a mistake," Jedediah protested. "Perhaps we could discuss this over brandy? My treat."

"This way, please, Mr. Turner. I have orders."

Jedediah was led into a small unmarked room in a side building in a walled fort on the outskirts of town. Turner glanced desperately around the windowless room, fearing the worst. One man sat inside on a single straight-backed chair. "I am James Allen, district agent for Allan Pinkerton, chief of intelligence for the army."

Jedediah began to relax. He sounded like a businessman. "Jedediah Turner, businessman."

"Smuggler would be far more accurate," Allen snapped. "And a very prosperous one, I understand."

Turner feigned surprise. "Smuggling, sir, is illegal."

"My point exactly," smiled Allen. "I have a proposition for you, Mr. Turner. I could arrest you now for trafficking in stolen army muskets."

Pretending to be shocked, Turner gasped, "Stolen, sir? I had no idea."

Allen waved his hand to indicate that there was no need for theatrics. "*Or* I could allow you to go about your business."

Turner smiled. "And what could I do in return to make your life easier, Mr. Allen?"

Allen ignored the suggestion of a bribe. "If, on every trip you make north, you bring me valuable intelligence, you may continue to gouge obscene profits from both sides of the war. Should you ever fail to deliver timely, accurate, valuable information, you will be arrested as a spy and rot in prison."

Turner began to search for an easier out. "You want me to *spy*? They hang spies."

Allen shrugged and lit a thin Northern cigar. "Every profitable business venture has risks."

"Surely if I made a . . . contribution to your intelligence network . . . ?"

"I don't need money," Allen barked. "I need information, and I want to get it from you." Mr. Allen paused to blow out smoke. "A deal or jail, Mr. Turner. Which will it be?"

Turner seemed to shrink as he nodded and whispered, "Deal."

Allen smiled. "Now as a demonstration of your good faith, tell me about the distribution of Van Dorn's forces."

"Now?"

Allen crossed his legs and puffed out a ball of blue smoke. "I'm in no hurry."

After Turner's recital, Allen said, "Now, tell me where Bedford Forest is."

"What is the date?"

"October 30."

Turner tried to remember Amos Weatherall's words as he described Major Atkins. "Tomorrow he is due in Birmingham. That is all I know."

"Good. Be back here within three weeks, Mr. Turner, or my agents will hunt you down."

Two days later Turner and Susan stepped off a train in Fayetteville, Tennessee, and loaded their baggage and merchandise into a specially designed wagon featuring four hidden compartments. The next day they rode south toward Alabama and the border between Union and Confederate forces.

Turner sat quiet and pensive for most of the ride, periodically flicking the reins to keep their mule moving.

Smuggling in both directions, and now a double agent spy. Business was becoming complicated and dangerous. He sighed heavily and mused, "An unfortunate characteristic of war . . ."

"What is?" Susan asked.

Ignoring her question, Jedediah brightened. "On the other hand, danger always creates opportunity."

"What are you talking about?"

Turner beamed. "Susan, if I work it right, I think I just found a way to vastly increase the amount of high-profit merchandise we can carry south."

Her eyes widened. "I can't carry any more! I'm not sure I can even stand up now." Susan wore a specially designed hoop skirt with heavy bands of steel for hoops attached to a body harness. A dozen pairs of boots were hooked to the wire loops of the wide-hooped petticoat. (Boots were a valuable commodity in the South.) More important, each boot was stuffed with vials of quinine.

More medicine was stashed in three of the wagon's four secret compartments. Four bottles of liquor lay in the fourth. A coffin in the back of the wagon contained layers of medicine bottles underneath a badly decomposing corpse. More quinine vials had been stuffed down the mule's throat, a handler forcing the poor beast to swallow each one.

"One or more vials will likely break and kill the mule," admitted Turner. "But hopefully not before we cross the border. Either way, by Thursday we'll have the quinine back again—with or without a mule to sell."

At the border crossing, the smugglers were stopped by Union guards. With well-rehearsed sorrow, Jedediah thumbed toward the coffin. "Taking my uncle back home to be buried beside his dear wife beneath the dogwood trees."

The lieutenant in charge, obviously new on the job and barely old enough to shave, gazed suspiciously at Jedediah and the coffin. He turned to the guards. "Open up that coffin and see if there's really a body. You," he pointed at Jedediah, "step down to be searched." Susan's job was to act innocent and coy and, if required, stand with grace under her heavy load and avoid all suspicion.

Jedediah dutifully complied as two soldiers used their bayonets as crowbars to lever up the coffin lid. The rank odor of a decaying body poured out like a visible wave and drove them back. "It's a body all right, sir," they called and pounded the lid shut.

The lieutenant's search of Jedediah's pockets, shoes, hat, and coat lining also turned up nothing suspicious. "Search the wagon!"

As if on cue, Jedediah began to act flustered and guilty. "I do have a secret compartment in the wagon, sir. Just some liquor for the funeral." He rolled his eyes sorrowfully at the officer and lifted a false floor under the driver's seat as Susan demurely rose to her feet, flashed a seductive smile, and blinked her eyelashes at the lieutenant. Turner sighed as if his heart would break. "But I *could* offer these four bottles of liquor to you as a small token of my appreciation for the superb work of the army."

The entire squad of soldiers stared wide-eyed at the four full bottles and then turned to gaze at their lieutenant. "You can pass," said the lieutenant. "But I'll keep these." He scooped up all four bottles. "Someone might think it was contraband being smuggled across the border."

Down the road just out of earshot, Susan whispered hoarsely, "Four bottles?! Why so much?"

"Never scrimp on a bribe, Susan. It will always come back to haunt you. Notice that he never searched for the other three secret compartments or poked at your dress."

With his merchandise sold and his grand profit banked, Jedediah Turner bowed as he was introduced to General Bedford Forest at a fashionable hotel in Birmingham. "It is an honor, sir, to meet a true hero of our glorious Confederacy."

Forest had come to request that Turner scout out the rail stops along two south Tennessee rail lines now held by Union forces. "I want unit identifications and strength as well as barrack locations at each stop. I need to know where Union supply depots sit. Everything."

Turner bowed and eagerly agreed. As he carefully memorized each request from this famous Confederate cavalry raider, Jedediah Turner thought, *Mr. Allen will appreciate this report. And a good report will merit Union passes and permits—even more valuable than Confederate ones.*

Jedediah Turner smiled broadly as he left the room with a final sweeping bow. Life was good for a businessman who could see the opportunities.

Aftermath

Smuggling, bribes, and illegal activity continued almost unabated throughout the war and even long after the war officially ended. The ruin of the Southern economy reduced profits on merchandise carried south but did not stop the flow. The Southern economy was slow to recover, and networks like Jedediah Turner's were the most efficient ways to move high-priced goods to the South and to move Southern products to Northern markets. Many of these agents and smugglers became the infamous carpetbaggers, who preyed on a crippled Southern economy after the war during the ineffective and often violent Reconstruction period.

Notes

1. From Time-Life Books, *Spies, Scouts and Raiders*, p. 73.

Follow-up Questions and Activities

1. **What Do You Know?**

   • Why was smuggling so profitable during the Civil War? Why didn't everybody want to smuggle during the war and make money?

   • What products were most popular with smugglers going south? Going north? Why?

- Why were prices so different in the South and in the North? Which products were cheaper in the South? Which were cheaper in the North? Why?
- Why didn't officials try harder to stop smuggling?
- Why did smuggling and spying tend to go hand in hand?

2. **Find Out More.** Following are three important topics from this story for students to research in the library and on the Internet. The reference sources at the back of this book will help them get started.

   - Research Civil War smuggling: the common products, routes (lines), profits, probability of getting caught, fate of captured smugglers, etc. Who were some of the successful Civil War smugglers?
   - Compare and contrast smuggling to blockade-running during the Civil War. What kinds of products were brought in by blockade-running ships that couldn't be smuggled across a land border? Did smugglers bring in supplies that ships could not transport? How much money did it take to set up a blockade-running business? A smuggling business? What size crew was required for each?
   - Research graft and official corruption during the Civil War. Why were so many officials willing to receive bribes? Compare graft during the Civil War to wartime graft throughout history. Can you find examples of governments whose every action required bribes? How have those governments fared?

3. **Make It Real**

   - Smugglers often made "fortunes." How much money did a person have to have in 1860 to have a "fortune"? Research how much money was considered to be a fortune in different eras in American history. See if you can find an estimate for every war period beginning with the Revolution. Also include the Great Depression of the 1930s. Present your findings on a graph and chart. Alternatively, write an essay on the fluctuating value of Union and Confederate money and how it affected people. Try to find images of the money to illustrate your essay.
   - Research the price of common, everyday items during the four years of the Civil War. Pick a dozen common household items and find documentation of their prices in 1861, 1862, 1863, 1864, and 1865 in Richmond, Virginia, and in Washington, D.C., then graph your results. These cities were less than 100 miles apart. Why were the prices so different in the two cities?

4. **Points to Ponder**

   - Smuggling is illegal. If someone is smuggling to benefit your side, should you stop that person? Why or why not? How much of a bribe would you require to allow someone to continue to smuggle valuable goods into your country?
   - Do you think it is morally and ethically right to make large profits off the suffering and misery of a war? Who else does this besides smugglers? What about large weapons manufacturing companies? What about food suppliers to the army? Have companies and individuals always made huge profits from wars? Who profits from our military today, and how?

Johnny Comes Marching Home . . .

The Confederacy did not die with a great and cathartic bang, but rather with a prolonged and bitter whimper. The two functioning Confederate armies were both reduced to rags and quarter rations when even full rations were on the skimpy side. There was too little feed for horses. There was no longer a working rail system. Desperately needed food rotted on distant train station platforms because there were no trains or wagons to move it to where it needed to go.

Lewis Carroll's *Alice in Wonderland* was published in 1865. The Confederacy itself was beginning to seem like a mythical wonderland, a glorious dream very different from the reality of the South in 1865. Mark Twain's "The Celebrated Jumping Frog of Calaveras County" was also published in that year. Gregor Mendel discovered the basics of heredity, and John D. Rockefeller opened the world's first oil refinery.

Neither Robert E. Lee nor Joe Johnston (the two remaining Confederate commanders) had enough strength to effectively stop, much less defeat, the superior Union armies they opposed. All they could do was try to avoid decisive combat and backpedal to stay alive.

The last working Confederate port, Wilmington, North Carolina, was closed after naval bombardment destroyed the two forts that guarded its river entrance. Confederate currency was worthless. The government was in shambles and had ceased to effectively govern. In an ironic twist, Joseph Lister published his theories on antiseptic surgery less than three weeks after the last battle of the war, just a few weeks too late to save a single life in the Civil War.

In early April, General Lee was no longer able to hold back the tide of Grant's army. For one week, his army streamed west along the Appomattox River until General Philip Sheridan's Union cavalry trapped the diminished force at Appomattox Courthouse, Virginia. Johnston surrendered to General William T. Sherman two weeks later. The war was over.

During the war 700,000 had died; 1.4 million had been wounded. But the bloodshed wasn't over yet. President Lincoln was shot and killed on April 14, just five days after Lee surrendered. Three days later, the river boat *Sultana* sank in the Mississippi, killing 1,700 weakened prisoners of war who had been carried out of Andersonville prison and were on their way home.

To many it seemed that the suffering and dying would never end. On May 19 President Andrew Johnson declared that the insurrection was at an end. But the suffering did not stop. The Southern economy and society had been destroyed. Plantations, fields, lives, and communities lay in ruins. There was no money, no produce, and no commodities of commerce. Four million freed blacks suddenly had no support and nowhere to turn. The violent and bitter Reconstruction period was just beginning, and the misery would continue.

Key Events in 1865

Date	Event
January 15	Confederate Fort Fisher falls, closing the last open Southern port at Wilmington, North Carolina.
January 20	Sherman marches north into South Carolina on his path of destruction.
Feb. 14	Sherman burns and ransacks Columbia, South Carolina.
April 1	Union General Philip Sheridan defeats Confederate General George Pickett at the Battle of Five Forks, forcing Lee to abandon his Petersburg trenches.
April 2	Lee abandons Petersburg and Richmond to Union forces and attempts to flee west to join General Joe Johnston in North Carolina.
April 9	Lee surrenders to Grant, effectively ending the Civil War.
April 14	John Wilkes Booth assassinates President Lincoln at Ford's Theater.
April 17	The *Sultana* sinks in the Mississippi River, killing 1,700 Union prisoners of war.
April 25	Booth is trapped and killed by Union troops.
April 26	After a battle at Durham Station, North Carolina, Confederate General Joe Johnston surrenders the last active Confederate army to Union General Sherman.
May 12–13	A skirmish between 80 Confederates and 300 Union soldiers is the final engagement of the Civil War.
May 19	President Johnson declares that the "insurrection against the federal government" has come to an end.
June 19	The last slaves in the Confederacy are forcibly freed in east Texas.

United We Fall
Lee's Surrender, April 1865

At a Glance

By early 1865, there were functionally only two Confederate armies left, Joe Johnston's (about 35,000) and Lee's (about 60,000 including the Home Guard units protecting Richmond). Both were terribly outnumbered and short of supplies and equipment.

Confederate hopes for a negotiated settlement evaporated with Lincoln's reelection. The Union blockade closed the Confederate's last open port (Wilmington, North Carolina). Lee wrote that he was not sure he could march his army back into the field because there was not enough feed for his horses and mules.

Confederate soldiers existed on half (and more commonly quarter) rations. By March 1865, the Confederacy was quickly crumbling, with no money, no transportation system, and three-quarters of its original territory under Union control.

But surrender was not an option. The strong Southern heart still counted on Robert E. Lee for a miracle. In truth, Lee *had* performed brilliantly, holding off Grant for months with less than half as many troops.

On April 1, 1865, Lee's fragile dam finally broke. Union General Philip Sheridan's cavalry, supported by one Union infantry corps, turned (went around) the end of Lee's trench system at the Battle of Five Forks. In response, Lee had to send too many of his thin troops to the southwest end of his lines to be able to hold the main trench fortifications. On April 2, Union forces stormed the Confederate trenches, piercing the defenses at a dozen points.

Lee's army streamed west in tatters, keeping to the north bank of the Appomattox River (often little more than a wide creek). Lee hoped to reach one of the few remaining rail junctions and take trains south to join General Joe Johnston (in North Carolina) where he struggled to hold off General Sherman.

The once-mighty and fearsome Army of Northern Virginia fled in shambles, disorganized, confused, unsupplied, unfed, weak, and badly demoralized as they streamed west, trying to get beyond the reach of Sheridan's relentless Union cavalry.

Meet Captain James Fielder

Born the second son (and fourth child) of a Methodist minister in Cherokee County, Georgia, in the summer of 1838, James grew up in a stern but carefree rural environment. His older brother, Matthew, followed in his father's footsteps and joined the ministry. In 1861, Matthew volunteered as an army chaplain with the Army of Northern Virginia.

James and Matthew had always been close. James mustered into (volunteered for) the army at his first opportunity (in early 1862) as part of the 14th Georgia Volunteer Infantry, a regiment in Lee's Army of Northern Virginia. A natural leader, he was promoted to lieutenant in 1862 during the Battle of Fredericksburg. Ironically James was promoted on the same day his brother was badly wounded by a stray bullet. Matthew spent six months in a convalescent hospital before returning to Georgia to take over his father's ministry when the senior Fielder died of disease in 1864.

James was devastated by the loss of his brother as a regular companion and source of comfort and strength. He became withdrawn and despondent. Over the course of the next year he slowly shook off his depression and became a passionate and zealous Confederate optimist. Even in the dismal trenches of Petersburg, James Fielder was a ray of light, a bubbling and eager proponent of the Confederate cause in whose eyes General Lee could do no wrong.

Fielder was promoted to captain and company commander in December 1864. He spiraled into bitter depression when Lee surrendered and the Confederacy collapsed. Refusing to accept the end, he traveled west hoping to join Colonel William Quantrill's raiders, still active in Kansas.

James got as far as Memphis, Tennessee, before he turned back, retracing his steps to Georgia to care for his mother, who had become an invalid. He entered the study of law in 1868 and never left Cherokee County again, practicing law and hopefully awaiting the call to return to arms and continue the Civil War to the day he died in 1893.

United We Fall

"Captain Fielder! Pull in your pickets in and prepare for march!" Colonel Alfred Brumby's horse splattered soft clumps of dirt across the huddled cluster of soldiers that was the remnant of D Company, 14th Georgia Volunteers.

"He's down to the crick, colonel," called Sergeant Billy (Buck) Crelander, jerking his thumb toward the thick line of trees 40 yards below the company's cluster of fires. At 35, Crelander was the oldest man in the company. A strong, unflappable soldier, he would have been promoted to officer long ago if he had been able to read and write.

Colonel Brumby, a 44-year-old plantation owner, had started the war as a major. He had been promoted as, over time, those above him were killed. However, he was never comfortable (or proficient) at command, and he hated the eternal struggle of having to lead. When the enlisted men of D Company failed to stand and salute in respect to his rank and orders, his face reddened and he scowled so that his bushy mustache seemed to hide his whole face. "Well, find him . . . and hurry!"

"Did someone find food?" asked Private James (Jimmy) Doolan. "I *would* hurry for somethin' to eat."

"Move!" yelled Brumby, and spurred his horse off toward the next of his six remaining companies strung out along the north bank of the Appomattox River on this predawn morning of Thursday, April 6, 1865.

The 14th Georgia Volunteers had entered the war in early 1862 with 1,097 eager volunteers. Of these, 184 were still alive and present. The original 10 companies had been consolidated to 6. Union bullets and disease had shrunk D Company from 121 to 23.

Twenty-six-year-old Sergeant Bernard (Deets) Hoffman shook his head as he brushed dirt and mud clots from his tattered coat. "Even a month ago we would'a stood and saluted when a colonel rode in. Now it just doesn't seem to matter much."

"If he can't feed us, why should we?" complained Private Doolan.

Showers had rumbled through overnight. The men were soaked. Their wet firewood smoked and radiated little heat. Hunger tormented them.

The 14th was part of Hill's corps of General Robert E. Lee's army. The army had abandoned their long-held Petersburg trenches on April 2 and raced west to escape the clutches of General Grant's much larger Union army.

Four days later they were still marching west, with Sheridan's Union cavalry nipping at their heels like hounds cornering a desperate fox. This was the mighty Army of Northern Virginia, in name only, barely a ghost of the cocky and eager tigers who struck fear into every Yankee heart in 1863. These men had been beaten too often in the last year, had been punched too hard. They carried their defeats like heavy packs. Hunger sapped their scant energy so that they shuffled, eyes locked forward on the man in front, seeing nothing, feet dragging through dust and mud.

Buck Crelander scratched his stubble of a beard and chuckled. "We have seen it all, ain't we? We pranced into Pennsylvania. We must o' fought 30 battles. We have surely done it all. And now look at us."

"Where we goin', Buck?" asked Jimmy Doolan. "They gonna get us somethin' to eat?"

Deets Hoffman rose and kicked dirt onto the fire. "I'll tell you where we're going, Jimmy. We're marching from hell to nowhere, and for no reason either—other than just to march and be hungry." He straightened and raised his voice. "Let's go! Gather your gear. On the road in 10 minutes. Albert, hustle down to the river and round up the pickets and the captain."

Albert Contour was barely 18 and still had an innocent, rose-colored faith in Robert E. Lee and the Confederate cause. As he jogged toward the tree line (to collect the four guards posted at night to protect against a sneak Union cavalry attack) the remaining dozen and a half men of the company grumbled to life.

Captain James Fielder marched up from the trees through the steamy predawn gray light, a buoyancy in his long strides and his face shining as if he alone knew a secret reason to be excited about this day. "We'll get 'em today, boys!"

"You mean food, sir?" asked Jimmy Doolan.

Fielder laughed as at a good-natured joke. "Sheridan first, food second, right boys?"

"The lads *could* use a bite, sir," muttered Sergeant Crelander. "Most of us ain't et since that hardtack yesterdee mornin'."

"There'll be food aplenty at Farmville, boys. Train cars of it! And that's only four miles ahead."

Doolan leaned toward Deets Hoffman and whispered, "He said that about Amelia Junction two days back, and all we found there was Yankees."

"And about Jetersville yesterday," Hoffman added.

The captain tugged and smoothed on his uniform coat, as if expecting General Lee to ride past. "All pickets in, Sergeant Hoffman? All men present?"

"All 23 of us, sir."

Colonel Brumby barely slowed down as he galloped past. "Quickly, captain! Join with companies E, F, and H just ahead and proceed along this road to catch the main body of General Ferro's division."

Company D was a pathetic excuse for an army unit. It had one officer, three sergeants, and 19 privates. Only four still wore official uniform coats, and those were threadbare, tattered, and patched. The rest wore whatever they had found to cover themselves. Fourteen still carried muskets. The other eight enlisted men just shuffled along, having conveniently dropped the eight-pound weight of their muskets days before. Only 10 still wore shoes; only 2 still carried haversacks (backpacks), but both of those were virtually empty because there was no food, and blankets and heavy coats had been dumped miles back. The company had not washed in five days. No one had eaten more than a scrap of hardtack in 36 hours. They had not seen even half rations in more than a week.

Just one more day, Fielder thought as he gazed west along the narrow road. *If I can hold us together one more day, then Lee will tell us what to do and give us the strength to do it.* He nodded and joked confidently with his handful of men. *Ignore the hunger. Block everything out except keeping us together and marching forward to Lee. Lee is the future, if I can just get us there. . . .*

Standing beside this scruffy mob, Captain Fielder drew and shouldered his sword as if on a parade ground. "Sergeant Crelander, rout step, if you please. Lead us off."

With only a vague shrug, Buck Crelander turned away from the rising sun along the rough ruts that the colonel had called a road. The others shuffled after without smile, song, or emotion other than the dull shock of being part of a dying army that still refused to lie down and give up.

Ahead they heard the all-too-familiar rolling thunder of musket fire. Deets Hoffman groaned. "I don't want a fight—not here, not now."

"Leastwise, not on an empty stomach," added Jimmy Doolan.

Hoffman shook his head. "Naw, Jimmy. I mean, I'm tired of slugging it out for Virginia. We're from Georgia. Why aren't we down there fighting Sherman? I heard he's plannin' to burn all Georgia. I say we ought to *give* 'em Virginia and fight for Georgia."

Private Albert Contour hissed, "None of that talk, Deets! We fight for Robert E. Lee, the greatest general on Earth!"

Hoffman said, "Right now I don't care much for *any* general. I think we'd be better off fightin' for *our* homes in Georgia, not Bobby Lee's here in Virginia."

Captain Fielder nodded to himself. *Grumbling is good. It gives them an outlet and shows they've still got spunk. Soldiers need to grumble. It takes their mind off their troubles. Just keep 'em marching and encourage grumbling.* He cleared his throat and said, "What about it, Jimmy?"

Jimmy Doolan clutched his growling stomach. "If I knew the Yanks would offer me food, I'd sure 'nuff surrender right now to get it. Why not? I don't have a musket or uniform anymore. What good am I to Bobby Lee?"

Fielder forced a chuckle. "Just keep marching . . ."

A mounted staff major pounded his horse down the trail and stopped next to Colonel Brumby, riding at the head of his tiny column. They talked while the staff major pointed wildly this way and that. Then the major spurred his horse off to the north.

Colonel Brumby turned in his saddle. "Sheridan's taken Farmville and is marching up the tracks from there."

Many in the company groaned. Doolan mouthed their common dread. "No food!"

"Quiet!" bellowed the colonel. "Three Carolina regiments are holding off his lead units just ahead. We're to slam into the flank of the Union line." He drew his sword and pointed southwest. "We'll march at the double-quick in column through those trees. Then into battle line by companies."

Sergeant Crelander called, "Captain Fielder, what are we supposed to fight with when we get there, sir? They got repeating rifles, half of us just got rocks."

As if stepping out of a blissful fog, Captain Fielder truly saw the decrepit state of his command. He couldn't block out reality with his tunnel-vision optimism. His buoyant eagerness dimmed into a frown. *Look at us. We're not an army.* Then he clenched his fists as if to tighten his resolve. *No. Hold it together. Bobby Lee can make us back into a real army. Just hold it together.* He breathed deep and forced a confident smile back onto his face. "Raise your hands if you have any rounds."

Eight lonely hands inched into the air.

Captain Fielder nervously rubbed his chin. "Private Contour, jog ahead to E and H Companies and see how much they can spare."

Before Albert could start, runners from both of those companies arrived, sent to see if D Company could share ammunition with the others.

Colonel Brumby yelled, "Forward!"

Captain Fielder said, "If we slam hard into their flank, we won't need to fire. We'll scare hell out of 'em and drive 'em off like in the old days, boys."

"Those were the days," sighed Sergeant Crelander. "We sure were *somethin'* in the old days. Now I guess we'll just have to *yell* 'Bang! Bang!' We *are* a sight . . ."

Driven by the well-drilled and mindless habit of obeying orders, the regiment shuffled toward the trees and battle beyond even though they weren't equipped to attack a squad. Sergeant Hoffman veered left to jog up beside his company commander. "Sherman's burning his way across Georgia—*our* Georgia, sir. No reason to stay here and fight a fight we can't win. Let's go home and defend our houses!"

Fielder spun around, jabbing his sword point at Hoffman's throat. "That's desertion, Deets. You run and I'll shoot you myself."

Hoffman gently pushed the captain's sword away and smiled wanly. "I would never desert, captain. I'm just talking about changing commands to where we can do some good." He paused for effect. " 'Sides, you don't want to waste a bullet on me. You'll need every one this company has for those Yanks."

Through the deep shade of the tree line the 14th Georgia wheeled into a pitifully thin battle line. So bone weary and numb were these men that few of the unarmed ones bothered to ask what they were supposed to do. They simply marched and turned as ordered. A deer stopped nibbling in the shaded edge of the trees and watched the men file into battle line, its ears and nose twitching curiously.

Sergeant Crelander nudged the captain. "Ain't we a sight, captain! Do you remember Second Bull Run? Our ranks stretched for miles, flags flying. We stomped through woods and fields, and drove terror into every living thing within 50 miles that day! Now we don't even scare one deer."

Sitting tall on his horse as if commanding a mighty brigade of several thousand, Colonel Brumby hollered, "Forward!" and pointed his sword at the thick lines of Union infantry slugging it out across the field with the Carolina regiments barricaded behind a log and earthen wall.

The ragged line of the 14th Georgia advanced. With barely 50 loaded muskets they marched to attack a Union force of over 1,000.

The 14th had advanced fewer than 30 paces when Union infantry, a sparkling, crisp regiment with buglers and a drummer, bright flags, and 800 loaded rifles, emerged from the trees 300 yards to their left. Two batteries of cannons whirled into place with this new threat. The ground trembled when the four cannons fired, sending billows of smoke and flame 60 feet across the battlefield.

Ten men in Brumby's tiny command crumpled to the ground as this first cannon volley slammed home. The rest turned and sprinted north toward the safety of Lee's main army. There was no order or discipline; it was not an ordered retreat. They fled in terror. Each man's feet moved only to save his own life from the horrors of the next round of cannon explosions.

Captain Fielder sank back into a befuddled fog as he ran with his men. *What's happened to us? We are the Army of Northern Virginia. Enemies hear our name and tremble! We are invincible. Lee told us so! So, why aren't they afraid? Why are we afraid and running?*

Colonel Brumby yelled, "Stop! Reform!" No one even slowed in the race to safety. Desperate to issue an order his men would follow, Brumby pointed his sword ahead of the men and yelled, "Reform beyond those trees!"

Deets Hoffman paused, gazing toward the distant Southwest and his home in Georgia. He gazed back at his fleeing brothers of these past three years who sprinted north toward General Lee and the struggle to hold Virginia. A look of sorrowful apology spread across his face. He yelled, "I have to see Georgia . . ." although no one heard him. Then he turned and dashed south toward a thick tree line. Two others followed him.

Captain Fielder cursed and drew his pistol. "Deets, come back!"

A Yankee sharpshooter fired first. Deets threw up his arms, spun, looking like a ballerina, and pitched facedown into the soft dirt. The other two men sprinted into the tree line and safety. The tattered 14th streamed off the battlefield, abandoning the Carolina regiments and their duty.

Safely away from the battle, the men of the 14th shuffled onto a wide road that led generally west and north, the direction they had been marching these past four days. They walked not in formation as a military unit but in a cluster, as weary field hands might on their way home after a grueling day of work.

Colonel Brumby rode proudly at their head. "I think we did well, men. We certainly did all we could. . . . Good fight, boys."

Captain Fielder walked stiffly, apart from his tiny company, muttering to himself. "I almost shot Deets. We've been together three years. I almost shot him." Louder and to his men Fielder said, "Deets shouldn't have run. He had no right to run off and leave us."

"He was just homesick, captain," said Jimmy Doolan.

"Well, it wasn't right," snapped the captain. A shocked numbness settled over the soldiers of the 14th. They had run from battle, given the field to Yankees without a fight. They would never have done such a terrible thing before.

It's all falling apart, Fielder thought. *How can our army collapse?* Then the captain scowled. *No! I won't allow it! We will hold together.* He seemed to tighten every muscle as if trying to hold on to the past. "Straighten up! Get in ranks. March like soldiers, like the heroes you are!"

Most tried halfheartedly but with little success as if the request saddled them with a burden too great, a task too mammoth.

In these last few days everything felt different. It no longer felt like they were *supposed* to win their fights. There was no conviction, no power of will behind their muskets, no confidence in their ultimate triumph.

"It's all slipping away," said Sergeant Buck Crelander with a deep sigh.

Albert Contour answered, "It'll be fine, sarge, as soon as we regroup with the main army."

"Won't matter. We don't *believe* anymore. That's what Lee gave us, belief in ourselves. Now it's dried up like dust and gone. Grant has already won. Oh, we had ourselves some fine times. But it's all over now."

"No! Don't talk like that!" Albert snapped. Buck shrugged and shuffled on.

Captain Fielder called, "Next time we'll whoop 'em good for payback. You'll see." But there was a shrill desperation in his voice and none of the steamroller conviction that used to spread out to blanket the men and push away all their fears and doubts.

The 14th followed a trail of discarded litter, the trash of a dying army—muskets, coats, cartridge boxes, belts, and haversacks. Mules and horses that had fallen from hunger lay bloated beside the road in clouds of flies. Abandoned wagons and cannons blocked the path where they had been left because there were no animals to pull them. Soldiers collapsed and fell out by the roadside, sitting with vacant, unseeing eyes, no longer caring what happened. No one jeered and belittled them. The 14th quietly shuffled past.

Suddenly Jimmy Doolan's face relaxed into a serene smile. He stepped out of the line of march onto the Virginia spring grass and sat down with a deep, contented sigh.

Captain Fielder called halt. All six companies stopped and faced Jimmy, lounging on the grass. "What's the problem, Jimmy? You need help?"

"No, cap'n. I quit."

"What kind of nonsense are you talking? Don't you go mad like Deets!"

"Cap'n, I'm tired of marching." He paused. "I'm tired of biting cartridges open, of loading, of shooting, and of fighting. I'm tired of hardtack and tired of being hungry. I'm tired of spitting hate between clenched teeth. I'm too tired to do it anymore. So I quit." The he raised his voice, "And let me tell you, boys, it feels grand! No struggles. Just sittin'."

Fielder begged, "Please, Jimmy. We're the 14th. We have to hold together. You'll see. Lee will make it work out."

Doolan shrugged and smiled.

Three others plopped down beside Jimmy Doolan. Two of then tossed away their muskets as they did.

Colonel Brumby dismounted and stomped back to the four sitters. "Get up and march or I'll shoot you as deserters!"

Buck Crelander said, "You can't shoot 'em just for sittin' here."

Brumby drew his pistol and cocked it. "Back in line," he growled. "All of you."

Doolan and the others still sat.

"I'm warning you, I'll shoot!"

Doolan shook his head. "I'm too hungry and tired to care, colonel. Shoot if you want."

"Put the gun away, colonel," said Captain Fielder. "We're not going to shoot our own."

Brumby's face glowed beet red with rage. "You make them march, captain, or I'll have you court-martialed!"

"They just need a rest, colonel," Fielder answered. "They'll sure 'nuff fight again with a little rest."

Someone at the back of the regiment pointed to a ridgeline a half-mile behind them. "Look! Yankee cavalry!"

Brumby's face twitched with indecision. Then he stomped back to his horse. "Let the Yankees have you, then!" He mounted and called, "Forward, march!"

Albert Contour pleaded, "Please, Jimmy. Don't leave us."

"Sorry, Al. But I quit."

"But, Jimmy, what about us? I mean, if you can just *quit*, what's gonna happen to us?"

Sorrow and regret were etched in Jimmy's eyes. "Sorry, Al."

The 14th shuffled on, many glancing back over their shoulders. With tears in his eyes, Jimmy Doolan called a final "Good-bye" and sat calmly in the grass, waiting for the Yankees.

The remnant of Georgia's finest walked past a mule collapsed in the road, still tied into its harness traces and wagon, faintly kicking where it lay too weak to stand. Albert Contour poked through the wagon and found some cornmeal and a tub of fatback. The men fell on it like wild animals and stuffed it into their parched mouths raw.

"Just 10 minutes, boys," announced Captain Fielder. "Then back to the march. Lee's depending on us."

"Well, ain't this a pretty picture?" said Sergeant Crelander. "Munchin' raw cornmeal and fatback. I guess now we have done it all!"

"Too bad Jimmy Doolan couldn't be here," said Albert Contour. "He'd appreciate this." But no one was willing to run back half a mile toward the hated Yankees to take him some food.

With the gnawing demon of hunger momentarily at bay, the 14th ambled on, always west and slightly north, hoping to catch the rest of Hill's corps and Lee's main army. A rider sped past them, then circled back to shout that the Confederate rear guard, General Ewell and 8,000 men, had just surrendered at Saylor's Creek, that the Yankee cavalry was closing fast, and that they had better hurry if they wanted to reach Lee at Appomattox Courthouse in time. Then he sped off to deliver his dire news to others farther ahead.

Colonel Brumby turned in his saddle. "Don't believe it, men. It's a lie. Ewell would never surrender."

Crelander nodded, "Eight thousand rebs could hold off half the Yankee army if they had a mind to."

Even as he said it, Crelander realized that everything was different now. There weren't 8,000 Confederates left who "had a mind to." He sadly shook his head and mumbled, "Would you take a look at us now? It surely ain't like the old days."

A small Yankee cavalry patrol of no more than two dozen riders broke through the trees 300 yards from the 14th. Colonel Brumby screamed for a battle line, but no one moved. They stood and stared at the intruders as if in a trance. The cavalry quickly drew their carbines, fired two quick volleys, and retreated beyond the tree line, fearing the 14th would form for a deadly volley of their own.

Four men fell from the cavalry fire. One was Colonel Brumby, who slouched in his saddle as smears of red crept wider across his shoulder and pant leg.

"Well, I'll be. Yankees," someone muttered, as if surprised to see them here. With a slow groan, Brumby pitched sideways and tumbled to the ground.

Several soldiers with long-range Enfield rifles shouldered their pieces and belatedly fired at the tree line, as if to warn the Yankees not to come back.

"Hey, the colonel's down!" shouted someone from E Company, the leading group of soldiers. No one immediately rushed to his aid. Instead they gazed down at their crumpled commander as they would at a museum curiosity. It was incredibly difficult for the men to focus, to think like soldiers. The nightmare of the past week had been too disorienting. They deeply felt the loss of their sense of invincible unity, of their identity as Lee's fighting machine. It seemed almost more trouble than it was worth to think of what they were supposed to do.

"Think he's dead?" one soldier asked.

An E Company sergeant stooped to feel for a pulse. "Losing too much blood. He'll be dead in minutes."

Sergeant Crelander rubbed his bristly chin. "You know, captain, you're the senior officer now. That makes you the new colonel of the 14th, captain."

"Should we chase the Yankees?" Albert Contour asked.

Fielder scoffed uncharacteristically, "To do what? Yell at them?" He, too, rubbed a stubbly chin as he watched the colonel's life ebb fast away and was filled with a bitter sense of betrayal and failure. "We're no regiment, and I'm no colonel. Deets Hoffman's gone. Jimmy Doolan's gone. The colonel's gone. A hundred others we started with are all gone. We barely got 15 of us left."

"But we're still D Company of the 14th Georgia!" Contour insisted.

"We're *nothing*," Fielder answered. "Just lost soldiers walking on a rutty road."

Everything was falling apart, and it was hard to see the point of going on. Then he tightened his grip and pulled in a deep, slow breath. *No! The point is not to fall apart, to hold on just a little longer.* "In column. Back on the road."

"We're goin' to walk on, then colonel-captain?" Buck Crelander asked. "See what sights we can see?"

"Lee's up ahead somewhere. If we can just get there . . . "

"Take the horse, colonel-captain?" asked another sergeant.

Fielder shrugged. "Might as well. Let's go, boys. I'm sure Lee has a plan. He's got to have some kind of plan."

Hold it together . . . Just one more day . . .

The motley crew that had been the mighty 14th Georgia Volunteers straggled forward. Showers hung in the West, heading their way, blocking their view of the setting sun. And still the 14th shuffled on, past the thick clutter of a disintegrating army, litter strewn across the Virginia countryside, now only discarded souvenirs of the once-mighty pride of the Confederate nation.

Aftermath

On Thursday, April 6, 1865, General Richard Ewell and his 8,000-man corps surrendered at Saylor's Creek, Virginia. On Saturday, April 8, General John Gordon and his force of 12,000 (Lee's leading corps) were blocked by 40,000 Union troops just west of the tiny town of Appomattox Courthouse. The Confederate government had disintegrated and gone into hiding. Starving, surrounded by a Union army almost six times the size of his, with no food and almost no ammunition, Lee was finally forced to admit the inevitable. He concluded that, "There is nothing left for me to do but go and see General Grant, and I would rather die a thousand deaths."

Many units, like the 14th, had simply disintegrated along the weeklong trail from Petersburg to Appomattox, so Lee was only able to gather 20,000 half-starved waifs on the last day of his command. On Palm Sunday, April 9, Lee surrendered to Grant at Appomattox Courthouse. His remaining soldiers stacked arms one last time in a field washed by bright sunshine, awkwardly said good-bye, and simply walked off into the surrounding pastures and woods.

Lee's surrender effectively ended the Civil War. Church bells rang in every Northern town from Maine to California. But the war was not completely over. Ten days after Lee's surrender, one last formal battle was fought in North Carolina between Generals William T. Sherman and Joe Johnston. Johnston surrendered and the Confederate army ceased to exist. Sporadic skirmishes continued until the last shot of the war was fired in late May near Palmetto Ranch, in east Texas.

The Confederates had held out to the bitter end, refusing to yield, to admit the obvious, to relinquish the faintest glimmer of hope. Their economy was destroyed, their currency worthless. Their entire social and economic system had been destroyed. There were no goods to sell in Southern stores, no transportation system to move goods to market, and no money with which to buy goods even if they had been available. It would take decades of bitter and ruthless reconstruction to rebuild the basic infrastructure of a functioning society in the battered South and to begin to rebuild a sense of unified national identity.

Follow-up Questions and Activities

1. **What Do You Know?**

   - Why did General Lee feel he had to defend Petersburg? Why did Grant feel he had to conquer Petersburg before he moved on?

   - Why did Lee finally have to leave his trench fortifications?

   - What other Confederate forces were still active in March 1865? Where were they? What had happened to the rest of the Confederate forces?

   - When General Lee abandoned Petersburg and started west, what was his plan? Did he still think he could win?

   - Why were Confederate forces so underfed and underequipped in March and April 1865? Why weren't they better able to fight during the first week of April?

2. **Find Out More.** Following are seven important topics from this story for students to research in the library and on the Internet. The reference sources at the back of this book will help them get started.

- What happened to the Confederate government over the last two months of the war? To President Davis, his vice president, and cabinet members? To the government's official records? Why do we never hear of them officially surrendering to the Union?

- Research the events and struggles of the eight-day last march of Lee's army from Petersburg west to Appomattox Courthouse. Why did he surrender there? Why couldn't Lee keep marching west? Where was he trying to go?

- Research the roll of army pickets in battle, while on the march, and in camp. Why have them? What did they do? Where did the name "pickets" come from? During the Civil War, did the cavalry for both armies serve "picket duty"?

- What happened to the Confederate officers and soldiers after the war? Once Lee and Johnston had surrendered, what did their soldiers have to do before returning home? Was there any official duty they had to perform or outprocessing they had to go through?

- Many Andersonville prisoners were carried by train to the Mississippi River to be transported north by boat. Most were too sick and weak to walk or stand and would need months of care to recover. Some 1,700 were jammed onto the riverboat *Sultana*. In the middle of the night, the *Sultana*'s boilers exploded. The ship sank, and all 1,700 former prisoners drowned only a few yards from shore because they were too weak to swim. Research the tragic sinking of the *Sultana*.

- The last two active generals in the Civil War were the Union's William Sherman and the Confederacy's Joe Johnston. Research the careers and rise of these men to positions of prominence during the last years of the war. What happened to each after the war?

- Research Colonel William Quantrill and his raiders. What did they do, and why? How did Southerners feel about Quantrill?

3. **Make It Real**

- During the last year of the war, the Confederate infrastructure collapsed. What does that mean? Use your city as an example and make a chart showing the basic infrastructure that supports your community. What systems allow the orderly and timely movement of goods, services, money, and information? Who supplies water, power, roads, sewers, fuel, rules and social order, and maintains the social fabric? How do food, clothes, school buses, and other supplies arrive when you need them?

- Draw maps showing the Confederate- and Union-controlled territory in America for each of the five years of the war. Remember to include the far West. Do the maps help you understand why the Confederacy had to struggle so hard to provide basic support services to its army and population during the last years of the war?

- What was in an army ration during the Civil War? What was in a half ration? A quarter ration? Prepare an army meal and see how long you think you could stand eating that kind and quantity of food.

4. **Points to Ponder**

  - How do soldiers and the general population know when a war is over? How did people know that the Revolutionary War was over? How did the German people know that World War II was over?

    Why did most people think the Civil War ended when Lee surrendered? Why not when General Johnston surrendered 10 days later? His was the last active Confederate army.

  - The Civil War was followed by a bitter and corrupt period in the South called Reconstruction. If you were in charge, how would you handle Southern reconstruction? The region is in economic and political shambles. The population is broken and starving. How would you try to reintegrate them into the United States? Most Southerners felt like a conquered, invaded nation, still bitter and defiant. How would you make these people a constructive part of America?

  - In this story Sergeant Crelander said that Lee gave his soldiers a belief in their ability to win. How important are beliefs in relation to the weapons and tools of war? Do you think the beliefs of soldiers can overcome a disadvantage in hardware? Do you think that is always true? Does the same concept apply to daily life, or just to military operations during war? Do you think that the beliefs of Lee's soldiers (their confidence) affected the outcome of any battles in the East during the Civil War?

Skeleton Heroes
Prisoners of War, April 1865

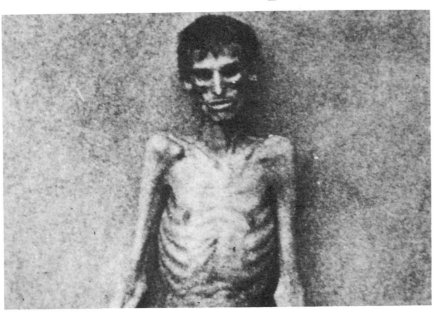

At a Glance

Traditionally, captured soldiers were paroled (sent home without weapons on the promise that they would never fight against their captors again). Higher-ranking officers were often held until they could be ransomed for cash or exchanged for other captured officers of equal rank. The British use of prison hulks (demasted ships used as floating prisons) during the Revolutionary War represented a new and cruel departure from this generally accepted policy. The British claimed that the colonists, not being professional soldiers, couldn't be trusted to abide by the terms of a parole.

For the first two years of the Civil War, captured soldiers were routinely interrogated and then paroled by being exchanged en masse at designated neutral sights along the shifting border between the armies.

Union General Grant was the first to complain that paroled Confederates often rejoined their units (some voluntarily and some by force) and continued to fight. In early 1863, he stopped all paroles and ordered that prisoners be shipped north to federal prisons for the duration of the war.

Most Union generals disagreed with Grant's policy, saying that it was important for soldiers' morale that they know that they would be quickly brought back home if captured. Grant prevailed by using two key arguments. First, the Confederacy was running short of new recruits. Not returning captured soldiers would hurt the South's ability to field effective armies far more than it would hurt the Union's ability. Second, the

South was running short of food. Laws in both North and South required that captured soldiers be given the same rations as the country's own soldiers. If the Confederacy held 100,000 captured Union soldiers, the mandate to feed those extra men might, like the straw that broke the camel's back, collapse the Confederacy's entire food supply system and hasten the end of the war.

Prisons had to be hastily built in both North and South. All became almost instantly overcrowded. In the South, disease ran rampant through the poorly constructed camps. Food supplies were chronically low. Prisoners got the worst of what little food reached the army.

The worst of all prison camps was Andersonville, in rural southern Georgia, a prison designed to house up to 4,000 men. Within four months of its opening in March 1864, more than 33,000 prisoners were crammed inside its walls. Some 13,000 died from starvation and disease before the overcrowding could be relieved beginning in October 1864. By December, the prison's population was down to 4,500, but conditions were still appalling. There were no shelters for the prisoners to live in. There was no firewood, so for months they had to eat their scanty portions of fatty pork (sowbelly) and cornmeal raw. Their sinks (latrines) routinely overflowed into the small creek that was their only source of drinking water.

It is hard to imagine a more deadly and horrifying environment. Yet, even in this hell, men survived, emerging as walking skeletons when exchanges were restarted in February 1865. Many of the last prisoners removed from Andersonville in April 1865 were so emaciated that every contour of bones and joints showed through their skin. Gangrene and scurvy had claimed most fingers, toes, and teeth. Many were almost too weak to stand. Most were exhausted by a slow walk of only a few yards.

Yet they still clung to life, and, as heroes, were rushed to the prisoner exchange point near Vicksburg, Mississippi, to be carried north on river steamers to a hero's welcome home.

Meet Chester Lumpkin

Chester Lumpkin was born in the summer of 1841 on a Michigan farm 80 miles north of Detroit, the fifth of six children. As a child, he was fascinated by nature and plants. He loved long walks through the countryside far more than helping on the family farm. Chester was described as carefree, one who loved to laugh. His father called Chester a dreamer when he was in a good mood and irresponsible when he was in a bad one.

Chester wanted to go to college to study botany. However, before he was accepted, Mr. Lumpkin and all three sons volunteered into Michigan Infantry regiments to fight the war. Mr. Lumpkin was killed fighting in Missouri. One brother was killed at Gettysburg. One returned home in early 1863 missing his right foot. Chester, the youngest, was captured at the Battle of Chancellorsville (April 1863). He was sent to Belle Isle prison and stayed there for a year before being transferred to Andersonville in early April 1864.

Skeleton Heroes

On the warm afternoon of April 9, 1865, Confederate Captain Walter James slapped his riding gloves against his threadbare uniform pants and wrinkled his nose. "How can you stand the stench?"

Resentment flashed in the eyes of Henry Wirtz, the Swiss-born director of Andersonville prison. "We do our best. Running this camp has always been . . . difficult."

Captain James shrugged and unfolded a paper from his uniform pocket. "I have train space for 300 today." He grabbed Wirtz by his shirt collar. "I want walkers this time. I don't have the crew to carry more half-dead corpses like you gave me last trip."

Wirtz gulped and shrugged. "Take any you like. Just report the names to my clerk before you leave."

James released his grip and again wrinkled his nose as he sniffed the air. "I couldn't live one day breathing this stench of death every minute, everywhere." Captain James was an escort officer, designated by the Confederate government to escort Union prisoners of war to the exchange place, Camp Fisk, Mississippi, near Vicksburg. This would be his third load of Andersonville prisoners to escort over a complicated series of rickety rail lines to Fort Fisk.

"Any personal effects to collect?" James asked.

Wirtz snorted, "For these scabbers?"

James and his six-man detail crossed the Andersonville road and train tracks to the grim stockade built of 12-foot-high poles rammed vertically into the ground and tied together. As they paused at the outer North Gate, James tugged out his pocket watch, then glanced at the clear sky.

"Spread out. Find ones who can walk. I'm tired of having so many die along the way. But grab them fast. We need 300 assembled here in one hour ready to board."

The enlisted men saluted, steeled themselves for the horrendous sight and smell beyond the gates, and marched inside. Captain James tried to force himself to stroll casually—unaffectedly—through the North Gate. The ghastly spectacle and stench were so overpowering that he swore he could actually taste them once inside the wall. His knees wobbled and he had to grasp a gatepost to steady himself while he gulped the foul air and tried to settle his stomach. "Good God, I couldn't survive three days in this horrendous pit. How did these men survive a year?"

He clenched his jaw and forced himself to walk along the beaten dirt trail called Broadway past Market Street—an area near the gate prisoners had set up for trading and selling the pitifully few items they possessed. Union army coat buttons, called hen buttons, were the most popular currency of exchange.

Not a blade of grass, not a weed, not a living thing survived here save the prisoners, the carpet of maggots, and the clouds of green horse flies that lived off the human waste and cook-fire grease that seemed to have permeated every corner of the miserable camp.

A few lucky men lived in the three small barracks that had been built in November. Most men, even now that the prison population was under 2,000, lived in the open. Some built hovels out of scrounged or stolen scraps of board, tin, and canvas. Some lived like moles in scooped-out holes next to the fetid creek that trickled past the sinks and through the prison yard.

James breathed shallowly through his mouth, as if afraid of the very air, and determined to grab his human cargo and escape this pit of horror before its poison infected him.

He stopped before a wispy shadow of a human, a mere skeleton wrapped with a tissue-thin cover of skin who squatted next to a shredded lean-to that would offer scant protection from the elements. Every curve and line of every bone and joint stood out as clearly as if he were a museum skeleton.

The man stared at James through sunken, hollow eyes that held no more glimmer and spark of life than would dead lumps of coal.

"Name?" asked Captain James.

The man continued to stare, now warily as if he sensed the approach of a predator. "They call me Squats, 'cause, see, that's what I do." His voice crackled like dried leaves and he lisped because all his teeth had fallen out.[1] Then he threw back his head and cackled gleefully. "Squattin's the secret, see. No one else figured it out. But I did, 'cause I watch. I watch and I learn." And he smiled a wide, toothless grin that sent shivers up Captain James's back.

"I need your real name."

The man paused, as if the question didn't make sense, as if this Confederate must be trying to trick him out of his treasure. "What's wrong with Squats?"

"Last chance," James barked. "Tell me your name if you want out of here."

Squats struggled to dredge up images from his long-forgotten past. "There was a fella who used to call me Chester. But he died back at Belle Isle. That's where I lived before this place."

James scanned a prison roster sheet. "Chester . . . Chester Danforth?" The name drew no reaction from the man before him. "No? Chester Irwin? . . . Chester Lumpkin?"

Chester's eyes flashed at the name from his distant past, a past that swirled as a dreamlike fantasy alien to the reality of life in Confederate prisons—the only reality Squats could still recall.

Captain James read from the roster sheet, "Chester H. Lumpkin. Age 24. Captured, April '63. One year at Belle Isle prison. Transferred here last April."

The squatter wore a few tattered rags. Thin clumps of filthy, wispy hair sprouted from his head. His skin was weathered, wrinkled, and frail like an old man's. "Can you stand, Lumpkin?"

Now Squats seemed truly frightened. "Why? It ain't food time. I can't go on wood detail since I busted this leg. But that don't matter, see. 'Cause I figured out the secret. Standers die, see. So do sitters—especially sitters. I know." Again he cackled and grinned, as if immensely proud of this accomplishment. "I learned how to survive. It's *squatters* that live."

Captain James nervously slapped his riding gloves against his pants. "I don't have time to chat, old man. Can you walk?"

Squats flushed angrily. He raised his frail fists, curling his few remaining fingers into a crude ball. The rest had fallen off from poor diet and bad circulation. "I ain't going to no hospital. Men die in there. I hear it's worse than down on South Street where the sinks overflow and everyone screams in the night and dies." Again he cackled. "See, I watch, and I figured out the secret. Squat and build a good shebang[2] up here above Broadway."

Satisfied, James nodded. "You got enough spunk left to live. You'll do. Line up by North Gate, Chester Lumpkin. You're leaving."

He had started to walk on when Squats began to weep. Salty tears ran down the grime on his sunken cheeks. "Please don't transfer me to a new prison again. I can't stand startin' over. I know the system here, see? This is all I got, and I can't give it up. But that's the secret, see. Always know you got *somethin'*. You're nothin' without somethin'. And this spot is my somethin'. Men with nothin', they always die."

Tears were replaced with a knowing cackle and grin. "I'm smart, see. I learned the secret! I got me a shebang, a spot to squat—not like the north end where the gangs rule. But not down by the sinks and creek neither."

Chester leaned forward in his squat, as if sharing a secret. "See, I watch and I learn. I got my spot in the food line—they give us *cooked* food now—and I learned how to eat cornmeal without getting sick."[3] He nodded knowingly. "That's what does most of 'em in, you know. They don't know the secret about eating cornmeal—hold it for an hour under your arm to soften and warm it. That's the secret, see? And because I figured it out, now I'm rich!"

"Rich?" asked James, startled to think that such a pitiful waif could consider himself wealthy—especially in this pit of misery and torment.

Squats raised his eyebrows and then winked. "Rich!" He cackled before saying, "I used to think teeth was the secret. 'Course, you needed a few teeth when the sowbelly weren't cooked and we had to eat it raw. But now they cook it real good, so you don't need 'em. That's not the secret. Some men used all their hen buttons buying vegetables, hoping to save their teeth." Squats cackled and winked. "They wasted their buttons, see. Teeth ain't the secret. They died anyway. And now I got all their hen buttons, and I'm rich."

James again started to walk on, but stopped when it was clear that Chester Lumpkin was not going to stand and walk to the North Gate as ordered. Frustrated, James snapped, "Do you want to go home or do you like living in this rot?"

Tears welled up in Chester's eyes. "I hate this place. Each morning I weep when I wake to find myself still here. But I don't dare leave now, see? It'd be worse to go somewheres new and have to start all over and have to learn a new secret.

"See, I know the rhythm here, 'cause I watch and I learn. During the day they bring new bodies in, marching numbly through the gates, all fearful. I laugh, and watch, and show them how to squat. But they're too afraid to learn the secret. Each night I have to listen to the screams and the moans and the dying. Most die at night, you know. Quieter, in private. And that's the secret. I watch for those who can't make it to the sinks when they have to go, all doubled over and holding their guts. Then at night, I know they'll die, see. So I sneak over in the night to see if they're dead yet, and, if they are, I get their hen buttons. I got a bagful!"

Warily, Chester Lumpkin reached into the shadows of his flimsy shebang and pulled out a stained leather bag. Pleadingly, desperately, he opened the bag and stretched it toward Captain James. "I give you eight buttons, mister, if you don't transfer me to another prison and make me start over. All right, I'll give you 10! Ten that are still *shiny*! See, I don't know if I could learn a new secret in a new place all over again."

Disgusted and terrified, James shrank back. "Get up, Lumpkin. You're going home."

Confusion spread across the prisoner's face.

"*Home*," James repeated. "Where's your home?"

Confusion vied with anger on Lumpkin's face. "I told you, mister, this here shebang's my home. It's mine, and as long as I can raise a fist, no one's going to get it. See, I know the secret— smile sweet at the guards, never go near the deadline,[4] learn how to eat the cornmeal, give anyone who comes too near my spot an evil eye, and squat. That's why I survived, why I never screamed and cried in the night. I watched and I learned the secret."

Again he cackled, pleased with his superior understanding of the Andersonville system. "Some days hundreds died. Some days it seemed like hundreds every hour. Them shovels was a-flyin' trying to make the trenches long enough to throw 'em in. New boys come and they cry and they die, 'cause they never watched and learned like me."

Captain James tried again. "The war's over. You're being set free. You're going north."

Lumpkin squinted, still unable to understand. "Free? You mean I get to pick a new spot? Do I get a new shebang? I ain't a-givin' up all my hen buttons for a new spot. No, sir-ee. That's the secret, see? I used just three buttons for the tin in my shebang. I used one for an onion once. But I watched and I learned the secret. Be *ready* to trade your buttons, but don't *actually* trade 'em. Men who lost all their buttons, see, they always died. So I hold 'em, horde 'em. I got me more hen buttons than anyone. I got hundreds if I ever need 'em, see."

"You're leaving. Now line up!" ordered James. "*That's* the new secret."

"A new secret?" Lumpkin repeated eagerly. "I could use a new secret." He staggered as he forced his bony legs to stand, as he tried to find dignity in draping his few, disintegrating rags about his grotesque form of bone wrapped in an ineffective covering of near lifeless skin and the grime of years in prison without proper washing. With a slow and shuffling gate, he wobbled toward North Gate, muttering, "I could use a new secret, see?"

A shiver made James's shoulders twitch. "Good God! How could anyone allow this— even worse, *cause* this—to happen to another human? How can any goal or war, no matter how noble, justify the torment of this place?"

Chester Lumpkin's eyes darted nervously about the train car as the prisoners were herded in like cattle. Distraught and frightened, he pressed his back against the heavy wood slats of the closed cattle car where 80 former prisoners had been prodded on board by musket barrel and bayonet. Lumpkin had turned pleadingly to the 18-year-old corporal who supervised the loading party. "I don't know the secret here, see? I don't know my spot."

"Climb in!" ordered the corporal, stepping back, revulsion on his face, afraid to be touched by the walking death of a prisoner.

Chester whispered to the man next to him, "I gotta know the secret. Two hen buttons for you if you tell me. See, I still got my buttons, so I can survive."

With tears streaming down his face, the man turned back, seeming to stare straight through Chester as he held out the stubs of his hands that looked just like Chester's. "Look at me. Look at what they did to me."

"Four buttons," Chester pleaded. "See, I'll die if I don't learn the secret. You need your spot, you need to squat, and you need the secret!"

The man next to him stared at his pencil-thin arms and moaned, "How can I face my family . . . like *this*? What can I *say* to them?"

Some slept. Some laughed in giddy delight at being released. Some raged and cursed at the terrible suffering they had endured.

"It's all gone upside down," Chester told a man near him, who giggled constantly even though both of his legs had been amputated below the knee to prevent the deadly spread of gangrene. "We used to hate Confederates. Now we're thankin' them and waving out the train car like they are our long-lost brothers. We used to respect Union officers. In prison we hated 'em 'cause they led poorly and let us get captured. I used to love sunrise and mornings. Last two years I've hated sunrise more than anything. See, that's the secret. You got to be willing to let everythin' turn upside down if you want to survive."

The train crept over a maze of small rickety tracks and lines. Often food did not arrive at stations as it was supposed to. The freed prisoners endured two and a half days without anything to eat and scant water to drink, packed inside the oven-hot and stifling cattle cars. Forty of the 300 died during the six-day trip to Fort Fisk.

Chester squatted in his adopted spot in the train car and listened to four men talk about home and family. They painted pictures of love, peace, and joy. They described places of unsurpassed beauty.

"They say that's where we're goin'—home," said Chester. "All I see when I think of home is my shebang just off Broadway and I sort o' have a fuzzy picture of a cell in Belle Isle."

"But where are you *from*?" asked one of the men. "Where's your family?"

"Michigan, they tell me," said Chester. Then he shrugged because the words meant nothing to him. "I try to think back, but there's no picture before Belle Isle, just a haze. Maybe that's the secret. Men who remembered home and wept to be there, they died first. I learned the secret, see? Shut out the past, and you'll survive the present. Still, I wish I could remember now. Some say they're real excited about goin' home. I wish I was." He cackled and grinned. "Maybe if I could remember, I *would* get excited. Maybe that's the new secret."

At Fort Fisk, Mississippi, former prisoners were officially turned over to the Union army. Civilians, Sanitary Commission agents, and Union officials wept at the sight of these men from Andersonville, so far beyond gaunt, no longer looking human, surely looking worse than death. It took this batch of prisoners three days to walk the final 12 miles from Fort Fisk to Vicksburg, where they would be loaded on river steamers heading north. Another 29 died on that grueling 12-mile march.

Chester Lumpkin stumbled through the snail's-pace march in dazed fascination. A spring mockingbird followed them for over half a mile, flitting from branch to branch, singing its repertoire of a dozen songs. It was the first bird Chester had seen in over a year. Wildflowers dotted the green, rolling hills around them. Grass! Flowers! He had forgotten what they looked like, how they radiated joy and beauty.

And trees! Real trees with branches and budding leaves. A profusion of trees lined each meadow they trudged through. How lovely the color green looked and smelled! It stirred other distant memories Chester Lumpkin had locked away to survive the reality of Andersonville. They swirled like vague dreams just beyond his grasp.

Each breath was a joy of sweet freshness, each sparkling vista a delight that tugged at ancient memories, trying to drag them back into Chester's consciousness.

A four-deck side paddle steamer, the *Sultana*, puffed lazy, black smoke as it waited for its tragic cargo at the Vicksburg docks. The *Sultana* was a luxury ship—staterooms, luxury suites, two bars, an elegant dining room, four wide decks from main up to the panoramic river views on the top promenade. Four giant boilers down below powered the massive side paddle that stretched 40 feet high. The exhausted soldiers wobbled on spindly legs and gaped in awe at the majesty of this floating palace.

Rifle-toting Union sentries herded the men on board as afternoon shadows lengthened on April 24, 1865. The talk alternated between a gleeful buzz over the surrenders of Lee and Joe Johnston and the mournful wail over the death of President Lincoln. It was clear to almost everyone that the war was over, a horrific memory to be erased and forgotten, and they were going home.

But not to Chester Lumpkin. He heard the words, but what he saw was prisoners being herded into a new prison, this one a floating prison. In despair he cowered on the top (promenade) deck behind the flag-bannered pilothouse. As more and more prisoners jammed into the overcrowded ship through the evening hours, Chester frantically scurried across the wide top deck, searching for a spot to claim as his own, for a place to own and roost—to squat—a place where he could watch and learn.

At 1:30 A.M. on the still morning of April 25, deckhands cast off the mooring lines. George Clayton, the head pilot, blasted three toots on the ship's horn. Chief engineer Joshua Wintrenger levered the gears to forward, and jets of high-pressure, superheated steam shoved the giant rocker-arm pistons around the overhead crank shaft, driving the paddle wheel. The *Sultana* muscled her way into the stiff current, bound upriver for Cairo, Illinois, with a quarter moon glistening like liquid silver off rippling waters of the big river.

On board this ship (designed for 460) were a crew of 85, 100 civilian passengers (including 14 volunteers from the U.S. Sanitary Commission there to oversee the care of the released prisoners), and 2,400 former prisoners, most of them from Andersonville, crammed into every inch of open deck space.

Afraid for his life, Chester Lumpkin's eyes darted across the deck as he squatted, searching for a sign that another spot might be better. His shoulders shook in silent terror as those around him whooped with joy at this voyage to the land of freedom.

Food and drink were regularly delivered to the soldiers at virtually every port of call. The Chicago Opera Company boarded and performed Steven Foster songs on the bow. Word spread that a seven-foot alligator was on board in a storehouse cage. A long line of eager soldiers jostled for a chance to see the beast. An atmosphere of jubilant celebration spread throughout the ship.

By the second day of their voyage north, even Chester Lumpkin began to relax. He found a spot that suited him. The food and rhythm of this new prison seemed a vast improvement over Andersonville. Still he warily watched, as on their first day out six men succumbed to the rigors of travel and their long suffering in prison and died. Six more died the second day.

"I don't know the secret, see? I got a spot and I watch. But I don't know the secret yet. Without it I could be the next to die. If I don't know the secret, how am I going to remember home and be excited?"

Sometimes, in a frustrated rage, he yelled, "I don't know the secret!" The men around him laughed and waved at the shore or at passing boats as if they had not a care in the world.

The *Sultana* plowed slowly north, boilers straining to fight the swollen Mississippi in its raging spring flood.

Then, at 2:00 A.M. on the cold and pitch-black night of April 27, the *Sultana*'s boilers exploded. Untreated corrosion pitted some pipes, allowing river water to trickle against superheated boiler plates, corrosion had blocked other pipes, creating a backup of supercharged steam. Hovering rain clouds reflected the eruption's crimson glow. The explosion's deafening roar echoed off the bluffs of Memphis, seven miles away.

A volcano of supercharged hissing steam, flame, and molten metal blasted 500 feet into the air, carrying wood, metal, and bodies high into the starless sky. The explosion and deadly geyser ripped through cabins, staterooms, the barroom, the dining room, and open decks. Metal fragments like shrapnel from an exploding bomb tore wood and flesh apart.

The *Sultana* was virtually cut in two amidships where the boiler room had been. River water surged in through a gaping hole. Within seconds, a thousand men were scalded and burned by billowing steam and flame. The pilothouse was demolished. The crippled ship drifted, lazily swirling with the current. Debris rained onto the river over a half-mile circle.

The rumble of smaller explosions and the screech of collapsing gangways and twisting metal filled the air. The fire spread onto the river with burning debris and spilled kegs of oil. Roaring flames raced through the ship. Waves of searing heat blasted fore and aft, setting men on fire, driving those who could walk screaming to the red-hot rails.

The proud side paddles sat idle and limp in the water. Then, one by one, they burst into flame. Men unable to stand were burned to death on the decks. The screams and cries of the suffering carried like a banshee's wail across the black waters. The burning ship lit up the river with an eerie red glow.

Plantation owners, small farmers, and citizens of Mound City, Arkansas, heard the explosion, saw the burning hulk in center channel, and raced to their rowboats to launch a rescue effort.

In a dreamlike daze Chester Lumpkin was hurled from the promenade deck into the bitter cold river, the left side of his face and body scalded by steam. He struggled for a time to stay afloat but quickly exhausted his meager reserve of energy. As he bobbed, gasping for breath in a fog-filled dream, his mind drifted. Like the churning river water, images began to swirl and flood into his mind—dreamlike images of peace and joy and unsurpassed beauty.

His grasp slowly slipped from the small board that kept him afloat. His body gently sank into the choppy waves. In the moment before death, in a vivid flood of memory that he had bravely denied himself all through his captivity for fear that these images of home would tear him apart and break his heart, Chester Lumpkin clearly pictured his family farm, his brothers, sister, father, and mother.

He sobbed, shedding the first real tears in two years of brutal captivity, and cried out "Doris! Doris!"—his mother's name—in a clear, loud voice that drew the attention of a small rescue boat.

"Doris!" But as eager hands reached for his frail arms to haul him on board, Chester Lumpkin drowned and died.

He was only 24 years old.

Aftermath

The wreck of the *Sultana* still stands as the worst ship tragedy in U.S. history. Over 1,700 lives were lost. Bodies were scattered over 50 miles of Mississippi floodwaters. Yet few Americans ever learned of the terrible tragedy because newspapers were still featuring coverage of the Lincoln assassination and the capture and sentencing of John Wilkes Booth. Little or no room remained for a burning riverboat filled with prisoners of war.

The burning hull of the *Sultana* drifted eight miles downriver before lodging against trees over a field flooded by spring melt. Of the 2,600 who set sail from Vicksburg, 800 died on board from the explosion and fire. The rest were thrown into the river. Only half of that number were pulled out alive by rescue boats. Almost 900 drowned in a vast field of floating debris, mostly because they were too weak and frail from captivity to hold on to floating scrap until help could reach them.

Andersonville prison was also an underreported tragedy. Almost 30 percent of the prisoners assigned to Andersonville died in the prison. Thousands more were near death when released and died either on the way home or shortly after arrival. Over 1,200 Andersonville prisoners died on the *Sultana*. Overall, more than half the prisoners forced into the squalid death camp died because of their confinement there. There was no prison, either North or South, that came anywhere close to that atrocious record.

A total of 220,000 Confederate soldiers were held as prisoners of war (POWs) in Union prisons during the Civil War, and 127,000 Union soldiers were held in the South. Those prisoners were spread out among six major prisons in the South and eight in the North.

Of the captured Union soldiers, 22,600 died while in prison (18 percent of those captured). Over half of those deaths occurred in just five months at just one prison camp—Andersonville, even though that camp held less than one-quarter of all captured Union soldiers. Twelve percent of the Confederate POWs also died while in captivity, but those deaths were spread more evenly among the various Northern prisons. Moreover, many of the deaths in Union prison camps were the result of battle wounds occurring at the sites of Union victories (e.g., Gettysburg).

Notes

1. With no fruits or vegetables, scurvy ran rampant through the prison. A loss of teeth is one of scurvy's effects.

2. Shebang was the prisoner's name for a small, hand-built lean-to or tent used as a one-man shelter. Shebangs were usually fashioned out of scraps of wood, tin, and fabric covering (usually canvas).

3. Food was so scarce in late 1864 and 1865 that corncobs and stalks were ground up with the corn kernels to create more bulk in the cornmeal given to prisoners. The coarse and indigestible cob and stalk granules literally shredded prisoners' intestines. Many of the Andersonville deaths were caused by intestinal lesions and the dysentery they caused.

4. The deadline was a rope barrier surrounding the prisoners' area eight feet away from the stockade wall. Anyone who touched or crossed that rope was shot as an escapee.

Follow-up Questions and Activities

1. **What Do You Know?**

   - Why were captured soldiers initially released during the Civil War? Why were they later held in prison camps? Who began the practice of holding POWs?

   - Why did Andersonville prisoners have to eat raw meat during the summer of 1864? Why didn't they have wood for cook fires?

   - Why did so many deaths occur at Andersonville prison camp? How many prisoners did it hold at its peak? How many was it designed to hold?

   - What are hen buttons? Why did prisoners value them? What was a shebang? What did a prisoner do with one?

   - Why were there so many deaths when the *Sultana* sank in the Mississippi River?

2. **Find Out More.** Following are five important topics from this story for students to research in the library and on the Internet. The reference sources at the back of this book will help them get started.

   - Research Andersonville prison. Try to find out what daily life was like in the camp. Why did so many die in that camp? Why didn't the prisoners try to escape? How many guards were stationed at Andersonville? How did the prison get its food? What rules and laws governed operations at the camp? How was food delivery to the prisoners changed over the one-year life of Andersonville? Why and how did the guards fare better than the prisoners?

   - Research other Civil War POW prisons. There is a website for one Civil War camp, the Elmira Prison Camp in New York, at http://www.innova.net/~vsix /elmiradoc/html. Compare your findings with conditions in POW camps in other American wars—the Revolution, World Wars I and II, the Korean War, and Vietnam.

- Research two important people at Andersonville prison: Dorence Atwater (a Union prisoner, and some say, the hero of Andersonville) and Henry Wirtz (director of the prison).

- Research the *Sultana*. When and where was the ship built? What did this ship usually carry? What routes did it sail? What happened on the night of April 27, 1865? Did the crew have any warning of a problem with the boilers? What happened to the *Sultana* after the fire?

- Research side paddle steamers, the grand ladies of the river. When was the first one built? How many were there in the heyday of river steaming? What fueled these ships? How did the side paddles work? What is the difference between side paddle steamers and rear paddle steamers? Was there an advantage to either? What happened to the side paddle ships? Why did shipping companies stop using them?

3. **Make It Real**

- Hold a class debate about the treatment of POWs during the Civil War. Divide the class into teams, one arguing in favor of POW camps, the other in favor of releasing POWs. As you argue the successes and failures of the Civil War POW system, see if you can gain an appreciation for the difficulty and burden of having to care for such great masses of new prisoners after every battle.

- Hold a classroom trial for Captain W. Mason, captain of the *Sultana*. Assign teams of defense and prosecutors who will research and argue the case. Was he responsible for the overloaded condition of the ship? Why did he permit it to sail? Could he have stopped to fix the boilers? Why didn't he? Why didn't he organize the soldiers to put out the fire right after the explosion? Let the classroom jury decide as the two teams argue their case.

4. **Points to Ponder**

- Do you think the parole system of releasing prisoners would work today? Why do you think it did work well up through the early 1800s? What has changed in society that would make it harder to parole POWs now?

- When the South was running out of food, was it right to starve their own soldiers to feed Union prisoners? Would it be right to let the POWs starve? Did prisoners fare better or worse than Confederate soldiers during the last year of the war?

- How do you think POWs should be handled? What if resources, like food and shelter, are scarce for your own troops?

Epilogue

The Road to Reconstruction, April–June 1865

On April 9, 1865, Lee surrendered. Northern telegraphs raced the news to every city and town from Maine to California within hours of the event. Church bells rang. Crowds danced and cheered.

However, the South had no comparable communication system. Richmond had been abandoned by the army and the government. The Confederate government had ceased to function, and its officials had scattered, going into hiding. News had to spread by word of mouth from citizen to citizen, from village to village. Many isolated spots in the South did not learn that the war was over until mid- to late May.

The last formal battle of the Civil War was fought on April 19, 1865, in North Carolina between Union General Sherman's army on its return north from Savannah and Columbia, South Carolina, and Confederate General Joe Johnston's beleaguered forces. Johnston was outnumbered by over two to one and surrendered. The last skirmish of the war was fought in late May in Texas between a couple of hundred Texans and 80 Union cavalry. The last shot of the war was fired in August by a Confederate whaler north of the Arctic Circle when it approached a Union whaler. The Confederate ship had not heard that the war was over.

As the various Confederate commands surrendered, Southern soldiers stacked up their arms and simply walked away, most toward home, a few toward the West and away from the devastation of war. It was time to assess the effects and damage of the war.

Four million blacks had been freed, most having no idea of what freedom would really mean—and not mean—for their daily lives. Most stayed where they had always lived, in the South and on plantations. They became either poorly paid hired hands or sharecroppers, not much better off than when they had been slaves. Some headed north, having heard that life was better there. Most were bitterly disillusioned by their reception there. A few drifted west to settle on the new frontier.

Some 1.4 million wounded, crippled, and maimed ex-soldiers were dumped back onto the mercies and care of their hometown communities. Fully half of them were unable to work and support their families. Another 700,000 men would never come home at all and were remembered only by the endless rows of white crosses on a hundred battlefields and behind a thousand hospitals across the country.

The North's booming wartime economy hit the top of its roller-coaster ride and slid quickly into recession as war-related orders and spending dropped off. Factories laid off workers and refused to rehire returning soldiers who had worked in the factories before the war.

Northern soldiers were proud of what they had accomplished. But the war was not a glorious memory to be lingered over and held on to. The entire region was eager to get on with living, to put the misery and grief of war behind them. Unfortunately, many were just as eager to hold the South responsible for the terrible suffering of the war and to punish Southerners for it. Lincoln's call before his assassination to embrace the returning South with open arms fell on deaf ears.

325

Northern soldiers were expected to lay down their rifles one day and return to the life they had known four years before on the next. Instead of answering to reveille, pounded out on a drum, the boys who had served in blue were now expected to answer to the calls of cows needing to be milked and of weeds choking the corn and tomato vines. For many it was a difficult and tormenting transition. Many reported that they felt they had more in common with rebel soldiers, with boys from Mississippi and Georgia who had tramped with the army, than they did with their families and neighbors who had stayed home. They were heroes and outcasts at the same time.

Everyone wanted to forget the war and put it behind them. No one wanted the millions of photos taken during the war. Over 99 percent were destroyed for lack of interest.

Returning from war was hardest on the soldiers who were urban poor and on black soldiers, many of whom went home to find no jobs waiting for them at all. Civil War veterans received no severance pay, no GI benefits, no medical benefits, no assistance of any kind. (Ninety percent of the Federal army had been dismissed by June 1865.) They were simply dumped out of the army and many landed hard—no jobs, no money, no means of support.

But compared to the South, the Northern returning troops had it easy. It is hard to imagine the extent of the devastation in the South.

The South was literally in ruins. It had no functioning economy, no money, no societal infrastructure, and no trains. There was no means of transportation for what food might exist. There were no jobs and no support for the disabled. One-quarter of the Southern male population aged 16 and older was dead. Another quarter were crippled. Four million freed slaves had no means of support. There were few factories, no building materials to repair homes, businesses, and factories, and no lumber or nails with which to rebuild. Entire cities had been burned to the ground. Richmond, Petersburg, Atlanta, Charleston, and Columbia were all gone. Large sections of a dozen other cities lay in ruin.

Harvests had been heavily disrupted for the past two years. Food was almost impossible to find. Precious few people had any money with which to buy the food even if they could find it.

Farms had been looted and stripped of all livestock. Fields had gone to weeds during the years of neglect. Fences and barns were gone. Farm machinery lay rusted, broken, and stripped for parts. There were no replacement parts to make them work again. Seeds were almost nonexistent to plant the 1865 crop.

Communities were scattered, having been driven out by advancing Union armies. Families were broken apart; hearts were shattered. What was not destroyed was fierce Southern pride and hate. For many, hate was all they had—in abundance.

Southern soldiers universally felt that they hadn't really been beaten. They had been starved, tricked into submission. Most felt that they could still beat any Yankee army if given an equal chance.

But there was no chance for revenge, for a new round of battles. Survival in the South became a full-time job for everyone. "One cow is a great economy," became a common saying. It meant that, in 1865, one cow created enough wealth and sustenance to allow a family to survive. A family with a cow was suddenly wealthy—if they could find enough hay to keep the cow alive.

Southerners blamed the North in general, and the federal government and blacks in particular, for their misery. Racial strife and friction increased. Poor whites, whose lives had drastically worsened, bitterly resented the gains made by freed blacks and fought to undercut any elevation of blacks' status. Blacks killed some whites, mostly plantation overseers. Gangs of whites lynched many more blacks.

It was clear to all that the South would not pick itself up and reintegrate into American society without massive assistance, guidance, and control. The Federal army established forts and garrisons throughout the region. The federal government appropriated billions for Southern aid. Government agents (often poorly screened, poorly trained, and motivated more by greed than compassion) rolled, rode, and walked south carrying their few possessions in soft-sided cases covered with carpet material. The era of Southern Reconstruction and the infamous carpetbaggers had arrived.

Glossary

Some of the military terms in the stories included in this book may not be familiar to all readers. Following are a few definitions.

Names

Confederate. Confederate soldiers were routinely called rebels, Southerners, rebs, Confederates, or Johnny Reb. The terms may be used interchangeably. Confederates named their armies for geographic areas (e.g., the Army of Tennessee, the Army of Northern Virginia). They preferred to name battles after towns or general geographic features (e.g., the Battle of Manassas, the Battle of Missionary Ridge, the Battle of Sharpsburg).

Union. Northern forces were routinely called Unionists, Federals, Yankees, Northerners, and Billy Yank. The terms may be freely interchanged. The North tended to name both armies (the Army of the Potomac, the Army of the Ohio, etc.) and battles after rivers (the Battle of Bull Run, the Battle of Antietam Creek, etc.).

Weapons

Basic. A musket or a rifle carried by every soldier. At the beginning of the war, all of those weapons were muzzle loaders. They were loaded by dropping powder and a lead ball down the muzzle and tamping them into place at the breech end of the barrel. Later in the war, Union forces introduced breech loading rifles and bullets (repeating rifles), a much faster and more efficient way to fire. The Confederacy never used breech loading rifles.

Bayonet. A short sword (usually 16 to 20 inches long during the Civil War) attached to the muzzle end of a musket or rifle. Some bayonets were sharpened on both edges; some had only one sharpened edge. When attached to a musket or rifle, a bayonet was a stabbing weapon rather than a slashing weapon such as a cavalry sword.

Breech Loader. A new firearm invented during the Civil War. (Now all firearms are breech loaders.) The key to the development of breech loaders was the invention of bullets, a single metal casing with a built-in powder charge and projectile (pointed or round). Bullets could be quickly loaded at the breech end of a rifle. Together, bullets and breech loading rifles revolutionized infantry warfare.

Carbine. A short rifle (either breech or muzzle loading) used by cavalry forces. Carbines, although less accurate than longer infantry rifles, were much easier to draw and handle on horseback.

329

Enfield Rifle. A rifle manufactured by the Enfield Company. For the first half of the nineteenth century, Enfield rifles were the most accurate long-range rifles on Earth.

Musket. A long-barreled, personal weapon with a smooth bore (as opposed to a rifle that has spiraled grooves cut into the inside surface of the bore). Muskets were faster to load than rifles but were far less accurate.

Muzzle Loader. Any weapon, rifle, or musket that is loaded by pouring powder and balls into the muzzle. Until the time of the Civil War, all muskets and rifles were muzzle loaders.

Rifle. A long-barreled weapon with spiraled grooves etched into the inside surface of its bore. The grooves force the rifle's ball to spin. Spin makes the balls fly much straighter and, thus, be more accurate over a greater range.

Sharps Rifle. A rifle produced by the Sharps Company. The preferred long-distance rifle of the 1850s and 1860s.

Shot

Caisson. A box that holds shot and powder for an artillery piece. The caisson rode on a limber, a separate, two-wheeled wagon that attached behind the artillery piece for transport.

Canister (Case Shot). The most common close-in type of cannon shot used during the Civil War. Instead of using a solid cannonball, the cannon was loaded with tin containers or bags of shotgun pellets (or rocks or nails). This turned a cannon into a giant shotgun, particularly lethal up to 200 yards.

Minié Ball. A soft lead, conically shaped rifle ball that expanded when fired to grip the rifled grooves in the barrel. Minié balls were invented in 1848 by a Frenchman, Claude Minié. The high-speed spin of a minié ball significantly improved long-range accuracy.

Solid Shot (Round Shot). Solid cannonballs, most often fired at bodies of infantry more than 300 yards away. They could fly more than one mile after being fired. These high-speed balls of 12 to 64 pounds could tear through a line of 6 to 10 men, killing them all.

Fortifications

Abatis. A defensive barrier originally made of fallen trees with the branches pointing toward the enemy. Later they tended to be built from angled, pointed sticks jabbed into the ground in long, tight rows.

Breastworks. Any quickly dug and assembled wall to use as protection during battle. Generally, breastworks were waist to chest high and made from branches and dirt.

Redoubt (Redan). Technically, a small fort that lacks sleeping and storage rooms. Usually, a redan was a raised platform for 2 to 10 cannons with thick dirt walls and spaces for firing rifles. Wall height varied from 6 or 7 feet to over 20.

Trench. Any slot dug in the ground capable of sheltering and protecting soldiers. Some trenches were shallow and temporary. Some, as at Petersburg, were more like underground cities.

Camp Calls, Terms, and Maneuvers

Butternut. The color, variously described as brownish gray or yellowish brownish tan, which became the most common uniform color of Confederate enlisted men wearing homespun uniforms.

Double-Quick. A jogging pace used by units of soldiers.

Hardtack. A double-baked, hard, dried bread that traveled well without crumbling or breaking. It was a dietary staple for both armies.

Haversack. A leather, cloth, or canvas bag about one foot square, hung by a shoulder strap. Union army haversacks were usually coated with tar to make them waterproof. Confederate haversacks typically were not. Haversacks were used to carry food (hunks of fresh meat, sugar, chunks of bacon, potatoes, vegetables, etc.) and personal items.

Impress. To force into service (often illegally). Southern free blacks were impressed into the Confederate army as early as the spring of 1861. Sailing ships were notorious for impressing men in port towns to fill out their crews. This form of impressment was often called Shanghaiing.

Knapsack. A larger canvas or leather bag used to carry blankets, coats, and tent halves. After a few months on the march, haversacks and knapsacks often became interchangeable.

Parade. To form into ranks and come to attention. The command to parade did not imply that the unit would march (as in a parade). Marching was called "to review."

Picket. A soldier stationed a short distance away from a body of soldiers as a guard and early-warning system against enemy attacks. Pickets usually marched one-quarter mile in front of a marching army and one-quarter mile to each side. Cavalry patrols would ride at a wider perimeter beyond pickets. At night pickets were usually stationed in a wide perimeter several hundred yards out from their units.

References

More than 57,000 books and 15,000 magazine articles have been published on the Civil War. Every public library owns shelves of books on this bloody conflict, far more than they have on any other American war. There are a dozen or more books focusing exclusively on each and every one of the major battles in the war. Biographies have been written on every significant leader during the war.

In this book, I have tried to focus on aspects of the war not often written about. The references below are ones I believe are dependable titles to expand your reading on the topics covered in this book. Your local library will have an extensive section on this cathartic chapter in American history. Ask your librarian for help finding additional reading.

Nonfiction Resources

Abbott, Richard. *Cotton and Capital: Boston Businessmen and Anti-Slavery Reform, 1854–1868*. Amherst: University of Massachusetts Press, 1993.

Aimone, Alan. *The Official Records of the American Civil War: A Researcher's Guide*. West Point, NY: U.S. Military Academy Library, 1993.

Bakeless, John. *Spies of the Confederacy*. New York: J. B. Lippincott, 1985.

Barry, Joseph. *The Strange Story of Harpers Ferry*. Shepherdstown, WV: *Shepherdstown Register*, 1988.

Bearss, Edwin. *The Campaign for Vicksburg* (4 vols.). Dayton, OH: Morningside Press, 1985.

Beller, Susan. *Cadets at War*. Whitehall, VA: Shoe Tree Press, 1995.

———. *Confederate Ladies of Richmond*. Brookfield, CT: Twenty-First Century Books, 1999.

Berlin, Ira, ed. *The Black Military Experience*. Cambridge, England: Cambridge University Press, 1992.

Black, Wallace. *Blockade Runners and Ironclads: Naval Action in the Civil War*. New York: Franklin Watts, 1997.

Blashfield, Jean. *Mines and Minnié Balls: Weapons of the Civil War*. New York: Franklin Watts, 1997.

Blewett, Daniel. *American Military History: A Guide to References and Information Sources*. Englewood, CO: Libraries Unlimited, 1995.

Bowman, John, ed. *The Civil War Almanac*. New York: Facts on File, 1982.

Breihan, Carl. *The Killer Legions of Quantrill*. Seattle, WA: Superior Publishing, 1981.

Brocket, L. P. *Women at War: Civil War Heroines*. Stamford, CT: Longmeadow Press, 1993.

Burns, Ken. *The Civil War* (nine-part video series). Washington, DC: PBS Video, 1996.

Calkins, Chris. *Lee's Retreat: A History and Field Guide*. Richmond, VA: Page One History Publications, 1998.

Carter, Samuel, III. *The Final Fortress: The Campaign for Vicksburg, 1862–1863*. New York: St. Martin's Press, 1990.

Castel, Albert. *William Clarke Quantrill: His Life and Times*. New York: Frederick Fell, 1979.

Catton, Bruce. *Grant Takes Command*. Boston: Little, Brown, 1968.

———. *Never Call Retreat*. New York: Washington Square Press, 1965.

———. *Reflections on the Civil War*. New York: Berkeley Books, 1981.

Chambers, William. *Blood and Sacrifice: The Civil War Journal of a Confederate Soldier.* Huntington, WV: Blue Acorn Press, 1994.

Chang, Ina. *A Separate Battle: Women and the Civil War.* New York: Lodestar Books, 1991.

Channing, Steven. *The Civil War: Confederate Ordeal.* Alexandria, VA: Time-Life Books, 1985.

Clinton, Catherine. *The Other Civil War: American Women in the Nineteenth Century.* New York: Hill & Wang, 1984.

Cole, Gerald. *Civil War Eyewitnesses: An Annotated Bibliography of Books and Articles.* Columbia: University of South Carolina Press, 1988.

Colman, Penny. *Spies! Women in the Civil War.* Cincinnati, OH: Betterway Books, 1992.

Colton, Ray. *The Civil War in the Western Territories.* Norman: University of Oklahoma Press, 1993.

Cox, Clinton. *Fiery Vision: The Life and Death of John Brown.* New York: Scholastic, 1997.

Cussler, Clive. *The Sea Hunters.* New York: Pocket Star Books, 1996.

Damon, Duane. *When This Cruel War Is Over: The Civil War Homefront.* Minneapolis, MN: Lerner Publications, 1996.

Dannett, Sylvia. *Noble Women of the North.* New York: Thomas Yoseloff, 1979.

Davis, Burke. *The Civil War: Strange and Fascinating Facts.* New York: Wings Books, 1996.

——. *The Closing Struggle of the Civil War.* New York: Harper & Row, 1993.

——. *Runaway Balloon.* New York: Wings Books, 1994.

Davis, Kenneth. *Don't Know Much About the Civil War.* New York: Bantam Books, 1998.

——. *Kansas.* New York: W. W. Norton, 1986.

Davis, William. *The Civil War: Death in the Trenches.* Alexandria, VA: Time-Life Books, 1988.

——. *The Civil War: First Blood.* Alexandria, VA: Time-Life Books, 1986.

Dawson, Sarah. *A Confederate Girl's Diary.* Bloomington: Indiana University Press, 1960.

Denny, Robert. *The Civil War Years: A Day-by-Day Chronicle of the Life of a Nation.* New York: Sterling, 1992.

Dudley, William, ed. *The Civil War: Opposing Viewpoints.* San Diego, CA: Greenhaven Press, 1995.

Esposito, Vincent. *The West Point Altas of American Wars, Volume 1.* New York: Praeger, 1967.

Foote, Shelby. *The Civil War: A Narrative* (3 vols.). New York: Random House, 1974.

Fox-Genovesse, Elizabeth. *Within the Plantation Household: Black and White Women of the Old South.* Chapel Hill: University of North Carolina Press, 1988.

Garrison, Webb. *Amazing Women of the Civil War.* Nashville, TN: Rutledge Hill Press, 1999.

——. *A Treasury of Civil War Tales.* Nashville, TN: Rutledge Hill Press, 1997.

——. *Unusual Persons of the Civil War.* Fredericksburg, VA: Sergeant Kirkland's, 1996.

Glatthaar, Joseph. *Forged in Battle: The Civil War Alliance of Black Soldiers and White Officers.* New York: Free Press, 1990.

Golay, Michael. *A Ruined Land: The End of the Civil War.* New York: John Wiley, 1999.

Goodrich, Thomas. *Black Flag: Guerrilla Warfare on the Western Border, 1861–1865.* Bloomington: Indiana University Press, 1995.

——. *War to the Knife: Bleeding Kansas, 1854–1861.* Minneapolis, MN: Stackpole Books, 1998.

Gray, Hank. *A Time to Be Remembered: The Juneteenth Story.* Palo Alto, CA: AJH Video Productions, 1993.

Greenspan, David. *American Heritage Battle Maps of the Civil War.* Tulsa, OK: Council Oaks Books, 1992.

Hansen, Joyce. *Between Two Fires: Black Soldiers in the Civil War.* New York: Franklin Watts, 1993.

Harlow, Alvin. *Brass Pounders: Young Telegraphers of the Civil War.* Denver, CO: Sage Books, 1982.

Haskins, Jim. *Black, Blue & Gray: African Americans in the Civil War.* New York: Simon & Schuster Books for Young Readers, 1998.

Hauptman, Laurence. *The Iroquois in the Civil War: From Battlefield to Reservation.* Syracuse, NY: Syracuse University Press, 1993.

Haven, Kendall. *New Years to Kwanzaa: Original Stories of Celebrations.* Golden, CO: Fulcrum Resources, 1997.

——. *Voices of the American Revolution: Stories of the Men, Women, and Children Who Forged Our Nation.* Englewood, CO: Libraries Unlimited, 2000.

Heartsill, W. *Fourteen Hundred and 91 Days in the Confederate Army.* Wilmington, NC: Broadfoot Press, 1987.

Hicks, Roger, and Frances Schultz. *Battlefields of the Civil War.* Topsfield, MA: Salem House, 1989.

Hoehling, Adolph. *Vicksburg: 47 Days of Seige.* Englewood Cliffs, NJ: Prentice-Hall, 1979.

———. *Women Who Spied.* New York: Dodd, Mead, 1977.

Holsworth, Jerry. "Winchester, VA, in the Civil War." *Blue and Gray Magazine* 15 (December 1997): 6–28.

Horner, Dave. *The Blockade Runners.* New York: Dodd, Mead, 1988.

Hunt, Harrison. *Heroes of the Civil War.* New York: Military Press, 1993.

Hutton, Paul. *Soldiers West: Biographies from the Military Frontier.* Lincoln: University of Nebraska Press, 1987.

Jackson, Donald. *The Civil War: Twenty Million Yankees.* Alexandria, VA: Time-Life Books, 1985.

January, Brendan. *The Emancipation Proclamation.* New York: Children's Press, 1997.

Johnson, Ludwell. *Red River Campaign: Politics and Cotton in the Civil War.* Baltimore, MD: Johns Hopkins University Press, 1978.

Kent, Zachary. *The Civil War: "A House Divided."* Hillsdale, NJ: Enslow Publishers, 1992.

———. *The Story of the Surrender at Appomattox.* Chicago: Children's Press, 1987.

Kirchberger, Joe. *The Civil War and Reconstruction.* New York: Facts on File, 1991.

Korn, Jerry. *The Civil War: War on the Mississippi.* Alexandria, VA: Time-Life Books, 1985.

———. *The Fight for Chattanooga.* Alexandria, VA: Time-Life Books, 1985.

Latham, Frank. *The Dred Scott Decision: March 6, 1857.* New York: Franklin Watts, 1978.

———. *Lincoln and the Emancipation Proclamation.* New York: Franklin Watts, 1979.

Leonard, Elizabeth. *All the Daring of the Soldiers: Women of the Civil War Armies.* New York: W. W. Norton, 1999.

Linderman, Gerald. *Embattled Courage: The Experience of Combat in the American Civil War.* New York: Free Press, 1987.

Lowe, Carl. *Civil War Storyteller.* New York: Mallard Press, 1992.

Lytle, Andrew. *Bedford Forest and His Critter Company.* Nashville, TN: J. S. Sanders, 1984.

Marten, James. *The Children's Civil War.* Chapel Hill: University of North Carolina Press, 1998.

Massey, Mary. *Ersatz in the Confederacy: Shortages and Substitutes on the Southern Homefront.* Columbia: University of South Carolina Press, 1993.

Mathless, Paul, ed. *Voices of the Civil War: Vicksburg.* Alexandria, VA: Time-Life Books, 1997.

McDonald, Cornelia. *A Woman's Civil War: A Diary of the Reminiscences of the War from March, 1862.* Madison: University of Wisconsin Press, 1992.

McKissack, Patricia, and Frederick McKissack. *Frederick Douglass: Leader Against Slavery.* Hillside, NJ: Enslow Publishers, 1991.

———. *Rebels Against Slavery: American Slave Revolts.* New York: Scholastic, 1996.

McPherson, James. *Battle Cry of Freedom.* New York: Oxford University Press, 1988.

———. *The Negro's Civil War.* New York: Pantheon Books, 1985.

———. *The Struggle for Equality: Abolitionists and the Negro in the Civil War and Reconstruction.* Princeton, NJ: Princeton University Press, 1974.

Mitchell, Reid. *Civil War Soldiers: Their Expectations and Their Experiences.* New York: Viking, 1988.

Moe, Richard. *The Last Full Measure: The Life and Death of the First Minnesota Volunteers.* New York: Henry Holt, 1993.

Murphy. Jim. *The Boy's War.* New York: Clarion Books, 1990.

Naden, Corinne, and Rose Blue. *Why Fight?: The Causes of the American Civil War.* Austin, TX: Raintree/Steck-Vaughn, 2000.

Neary, Donna. *Civil War Heroines.* Santa Barbara, CA: Belerophon Books, 1994.

Oates, Dan, ed. *Hanging Rock Rebel.* Shippensburg, PA: Burd Street Press, 1994.

Oates, Stephen. *To Purge This Land with Blood: A Biography of John Brown.* New York: Harper & Row, 1980.

Parish, T. Michael. *Confederate Imprints: A Bibliography of Southern Publications from Secession to Surrender.* Austin, TX: Jenkins Books, 1984.

Phelan, Mary Kay. *Mr. Lincoln Speaks at Gettysburg*. New York: W. W. Norton, 1986.

Poe, Clarence, ed. *True Tales of the South at War*. Mineola, NY: Dover Publications, 1995.

Pratt, Fletcher. *A Short History of the Civil War*. Mineola, NY: Dover Publications, 1997.

Quarles, Garland. *Occupied Winchester, 1861–1865*. Winchester, VA: Winchester Historical Society, 1991.

Quarles, Garland, et al. *Diaries, Letters, and Recollections of the War Between the States*. Winchester, VA: Winchester Historical Society, 1997.

Ray, Delia. *Behind the Blue and Gray: The Soldier's Life in the Civil War*. New York: Dutton Children's Books, 1991.

———. *A Nation Torn*. New York: Lodestar, 1990.

Rhodes, James. *History of the Civil War*. Mineola, NY: Dover Publications, 1999.

Ruchames, Louis. *The Abolitionists: A Collection of Their Writings*. New York: G. P. Putnam's Sons, 1973.

Russell, Sharman. *Frederick Douglass*. New York: Chelsea House, 1988.

Scott, John. *John Brown of Harpers Ferry*. New York: Facts on File, 1998.

Seagrove, Pia. *The History of the Irish Brigade*. Syracuse, NY: Syracuse University Press, 1997.

Seymour, Reit. *Behind Enemy Lines*. San Diego, CA: Harcourt Brace Jovanovich, 1988.

Simmons, Marc. *New Mexico: A Bicentenial History*. New York: W. W. Norton, 1983.

Steins, Richard. *The Nation Divides: The Civil War (1820–1880)*. New York: Twenty-First Century Books, 1993.

———. *Shiloh*. New York: Twenty-First Century Books, 1997.

Strangis, Joel. *Lewis Hayden and the War Against Slavery*. New York: Linnet Books, 1999.

Surdam, David. "The Union's Navy Blockade Reconsidered." *Naval War College Review* 51, no. 4 (Fall 1998): 85–107.

Symonds, Craig. *Gettysburg: A Battle Atlas*. Baltimore, MD: Nautical and Aviation Publishing Company of America, 1992.

Time-Life Books, eds. *The Blockade*. Alexandria, VA: Time-Life Books, 1988.

———. *Spies, Scouts and Raiders*. Alexandria, VA: Time-Life Books, 1988.

———. *Voices of the Civil War: Chickamauga*. Alexandria, VA: Time-Life Books, 1988.

Varhola, Michael. *Everyday Life During the Civil War*. Cincinnati, OH: Writer's Digest Books, 1999.

Ward, Goeffrey. *The Civil War*. New York: Alfred A. Knopf, 1990.

Washington, Versalle. *Eagles on Their Buttons: A Black Infantry Regiment in the Civil War*. Columbia: University of Missouri Press, 1999.

Watkins, Sam. *Co. Aytch: A Side Show of the Big Show*. Wilmington, NC: Broadfoot Publishing, 1994.

White, Richard. *"It's Your Misfortune and None of My Own": A New History of the American West*. Norman: University of Oklahoma Press, 1991.

Wilbur, Keith. *Civil War Medicine: 1861–1865*. New York: Globe Pequot Press, 1998.

Wilkeson, Frank. *Turned Inside Out*. Lincoln: University of Nebraska Press, 1997.

Wise, Stephen. *Lifeline of the Confederacy: Blockade Running During the Civil War*. Columbia: University of South Carolina Press, 1988.

Historical Fiction

Adams, Richard. *Traveller*. New York: Dell Books, 1988.

Bartoletti, Susan. *No Man's Land*. New York: Scholastic, 1999.

Cornwell, Bernard. *Battle Flag*. New York: HarperCollins, 1995.

———. *The Bloody Ground*. New York: HarperCollins, 1996.

———. *Copperhead*. New York: HarperCollins, 1994.

———. *Rebel*. New York: HarperCollins, 1993.

Coyle, Harold. *Look Away*. New York: Simon & Schuster, 1995.

Crane, Stephen. *The Red Badge of Courage*. Philadelphia: Running Press, 1992.

Fowler, Robert. *Jim Mundy*. New York: Harper & Row, 1977.

Hunt, Irene. *Across Five Aprils*. Boston: Berkeley Publishing Group, 1991.

Mitchell, Margaret. *Gone with the Wind*. New York: Charles Scribner's Sons (reprint), 1996.

Optic, Oliver. *The Blue and Gray Series: On the Blockade*. Boston: Lee & Shepard, 1939.

———. *The Blue and Gray Series: Taken by the Enemy*. Boston: Lee & Shepard, 1930.

———. *The Blue and Gray Series: Within Enemy Lines*. Boston: Lee & Shepard, 1936.

Shaara, Jeff. *The Last Full Measure*. New York: Ballantine, 1998.

Shaara, Michael. *The Killer Angels*. New York: Ballantine, 1974.

Stowe, Harriet Beecher. *Uncle Tom's Cabin*. Pleasantville, NY: Reader's Digest Press, 1991.

Primary Electronic Resources

Enter "American Civil War" into any major search engine and it will locate as many as 100,000 websites. Many of these sites change URLs; many come and go. Many are unreliable and not factually correct. Those listed here are accurate, dependable, and good links to other informative sites. Last accessed January 2002.

http://amillionlives.com
> Good information on different groups of people.

http://homepages.dsu.edu/jankej/civilwar/civilwar.htm
> A Civil War homesite.

http://jefferson.village.virginia.edu/vshadow2/
> Interesting site that tracks two communities through the war.

http://lcweb2.loc.gov/ammem/cwphone.html/
> Over 1,000 Civil War photos.

http://lcweb2.loc.gov/ammem/gmdhtml/cwmhtml/
> Civil War maps.

http://memory.loc.gov and http://lcweb2.loc.gov/ammem/ndpedu
> Library of Congress American History Sites; includes the LC Civil War collection.

http://scriptorium.lib.duke.edu/women/cwdoes.html/
> Information on Civil War women.

http://showcase.netins.net/web/creative/Lincoln.html and http:////www.members.aol.com/RVSNortow/Lincoln2.html
> Two good sites for information on Lincoln during the war.

http://sunsite.utk.edu/civil-war/
> Good general site with many good links.

http://users.erols.com/kfraser/
> Poetry and music of the Civil War.

http://www.acwa.org
> American Civil War Association site.

http://www.americancivilwar.com/civil.html/
> Good general site with links to other Civil War information.

http://www.blarg.net/˜dhhill/
> Good general Civil War site with strong links.

http://www.bluegraymagazine.com
> *Blue and Gray Magazine* (over 400 articles and links).

http://www.campbellsvil.edu/cupage/centers/civil%20war/acwi1.html
> Site of the American Civil War Institute.

http://www.civilwardata.com
> Good site for Civil War–era genealogical research.

http://www.civilwarhome.com
    Good general site with links to other Civil War information.
http://www.classicals.com/federalist/theCivilWarhall/messages/1279.html
    Good review of the causes of the war.
http://www.cr.nps.gov and, more specificially, http://www.cr.nps.gov/seac/civilwar.htm
    National Park Service (maintains over 20 Civil War sites, each with extensive information).
http://www.cwc.lsu.edu/
    Good general Civil War source site.
http://www.cwc.lsu.edu/civlink.htm
    Civil War Web Links Index.
http://www.furman.edu/~benson/docs/
    An excellent source of original nineteenth-century source documents.
http://www.harpweek.com
    Good site for general information on life in the mid-nineteenth century in America.
http://www.hist.unt.edu/09w-amw2.htm
    Good general site with links to other Civil War information.
http://www.historybuff.com
    History Buff homepage.
http://www.home.earthlink.net/~obbie/cwsites.htm
    Good general Civil War site with strong links.
http://www.itd.nps.gov/cwss
    Information on Civil War soldiers (especially African Americans).
http://www.lib.ua.edu/smr/south3.htm
    Good site for information on the South and Southern life.
http://www.members.nbci.com/acw_women/
    Information on Civil War women.
http://www.militaryhistory.about.com/cs/americancivilwar2/
    Good site for general military history of the period.
http://www.mirkwood.usc.indiana.edu/acw
    Good general site with links to other Civil War information.
http://www.nationalcivilwarmuseum.org
    National Civil War Museum.
http://www.nationalgeographic.com/features/99/railroad/j1.jtml
    Information on the Underground Railroad.
http://www.reenactment.about.com/cs/americancivilwar/
    Reenactment group ready and willing to research any Civil War question.
http://www.ruf.rice.edu/~pjdavis/
    Good site for the Confederate government and Jefferson Davis.
http://www.searchboat.com/civilwar.htm
    Good general Civil War site with strong links.
http://www.suite101.com/articles/article.cfm/3848
    Monthly articles on the Civil War plus extensive links.
http://www.us.civilwar.com
    Good general Civil War site with strong links.
http://www.usafa.af.mil/dfeng/cwarres.htm
    Accurate reference for Civil War resources.
http://www.vmi.edu/~archtml/jackson.html/
    Good site for information on Stonewall Jackson and the Shenandoah Valley campaigns.
http://www2.prestel.co.uk/simonides/links/wars/wars-1800/1861-acw/acw.html
    Good general Civil War site with strong links.

Index

Abatis, 330
Abolitionists
    Dred Scott and, 2
    follow-up questions/activities about, 26
    Harmon, Amelia, and, 180–87
    Lincoln, Abraham as, 31
    "Righteous Raiders" and, 15–25
    "Sister Spies: Life in Occupied Winchester,
        Virginia, March 1862" and, 75–83
African Americans
    follow-up questions/activities about,
        114–16, 272–74
    "Patriotic Pride and Prejudice: Northern
        Blacks' Efforts to Enlist, 1862" and,
        106–14
    reconstruction and, 325–27
    "Striking Out: New York City Draft Riots,
        July 1863" and, 190–98
    "Unsung Heroes: Black Union Regiments
        and the Battle of the Crater, July 30,
        1864" and, 262–72
Agriculture
    advancements of, xii, 285
    reconstruction and, 326
Aid groups
    "Fair Fight, A: Northern Women's Efforts
        to Support the Sanitary
        Commission, September-November
        1864" and, 275–84
    Massachusetts Aid Society, 4, 13
    New England Aid Society, 4, 7, 13
Alabama, xi, 2–3, 31
Albemarle, follow-up questions/activities
    about, 127
Alianjo, Hector Manuel, 87–94
Amnesty Proclamation, xiv
Anaconda Plan, 30
Andersonville prison
    follow-up questions/activities about,
        322–23
    "Skeleton Heroes: Prisoners of War, April
        1865" and, 313–21
Antietam, Battle of, xii, 61, 63, 139–40
Appomattox, 310

Arizona, "Turn Coat, Turn Coat: The Civil
    War in the Far West and the Battle of
    Glorieta Pass, February–March 1862"
    and, 86–94
Arkansas, 2, 29–30
Arkansas, 118
Arkansas, xi
Arkansas
    follow-up questions/activities about,
        127–28
    "Iron Might: Ironclad Naval Battle on the
        Mississippi, June 1862" and, 119–26
Army of the Potomac
    Battle of Bull Run and, 29–30
    Burnside, Amos as commander, 63
    commanders of, 59
    reporting for the, 130
    Second Battle of Bull Run and, 61
    "Supper, Shoes, and Shovels: Supplying a
        Civil War Army, February 1862"
        and, 64–73
Army pickets. *See* Pickets
Atlanta, 225–226
Atwater, Dorence, 323

Baltimore, Maryland, 29, 39–40
Barton, Clara, 249
Basic, 329
Battery Wagner, South Carolina, 263
"Battle "Cries": Women Working in an Army
    Hospital, May 1864, 239–48
Bayonet, 329
Beaurigard, Pierre, 59
Belle Isle prison, 314
Benton, 125
Bickerdyke, Mary Ann, 249, 285
Black Brigade of Cincinnati, 114
Black Cincinnati Volunteer Militia, "Patriotic
    Pride and Prejudice: Northern Blacks'
    Efforts to Enlist, August 1862" and,
    108–14
Blacks. *See* African Americans
Blackwell, Elizabeth, 249, 276, 285
Bleeding Kansas, 2

Blockade runners, xiv, 214–24
Booth, John Wilkes, 300
Brady, James, 118–26
Brady, Matthew, 141
Bragg, Braxton, 63, 159, 202
Breastworks, 330
Breech loading guns, xiv, 329
Brown, John
    follow-up questions/activities about, 25–27,
        26–27
    "Free or Slave?" and, 12–13
    Harpers Ferry and, 2, 15–16
    impact of, 2–3
    "Righteous Raiders" and, 15–25
Buchanan, James, 2–3, 32
Buford, John, 188
Bugles. *See* Musicians
Bull Run, Battle of
    Army of the Potomac and, 29–30
    as first major battle, xiv
    "Tea Cakes, White Lace, and Bloodshed:
        First Battle of Bull Run (Manassas),
        July 1861" and, 51–60
Burnside, Amos, 59, 62–63, 159
Butler, Benjamin, 115, 167
Butternut, xii–xiii, 331

Caisson, 330
California
    California Brigade, 95–96
    donation to war effort by, 285
    as free state, 2
Camouflage, 330
Camp calls/terms/maneuvers, 331
Canister (case shot), 330
Carbine, xiv, 329
Carondelet, 117, 122–24
Carpetbaggers, 296
Carson, Kit, 96
Chaffin's Farm, Battle of, 272
Chamberlan, Lawrence, 188
Chancellorsville, Battle of, 158, 314
Charleston, South Carolina, 29. *See also* Fort
    Sumpter
Charlotta, 214–23
Chickamauga, Battle of, 159, 201–12
Children during Civil War, "Diary of Death:
    The Siege of Vicksburg, May–July
    1863" and, 169–78
Cincinnati, 108–14
Civil War
    demographics of, xi, 237, 261
    key events in 1861, 30

key events in 1862, 62–63
key events in 1863, 157–59
key events in 1864, 226–27
key events in 1865, 300
postwar effect on African Americans,
    166–167
reconstruction and, 312, 325–27
Civilian reaction to war, 59
Cold Harbor, Battle of, 226, 249
Command structure of army, 74
Communication
    documentation of war and, 129–31, 141–43
    follow-up questions/activities about, 236
    reconstruction and, 325
    "'Reporting' for Duty: Civil War Field
        Reporters, September 1862" and,
        132–40
    telegraphs, 74
Compromise of 1850, 2
Confederate States of America, 3
Confederates
    early war strategy of, 30
    follow-up questions/activities about, 40–41
    names of, 329
Confiscation Law, 115
Conscript Bureau, 252
Contraband Laws, 115, 167–68, 262–72
Cooper, Edward, 252–59
Cornubia, 223
Cotton. *See also* Agriculture
    cotton gin and, xii
    follow-up questions/activities about, 49–50
    "Growin' Cotton'; Killin' Yankees," 42–49
    importance of, 1, 42
    "Sweet Potatoes, Cotton, Tobacco, and
        Quinine: A Wealth of Smuggling,
        October 1864" and, 286–96
Crater, Battle of, 271–72, 274

Darbyhill Road, Battle of, 272
Davis, Jefferson
    on African American troops, 272
    follow-up questions/activities about, 311
    inauguration of, 3
Dean, Meriam, 16–25
Delaware, xi
DeLouise, Virginia, 229–36
Demographics
    follow-up questions/activities about, 237,
        261
    numbers of soldiers, xii–xiii
    placement of battlefields, xi

Department of Justice, 330
Desertion
    follow-up questions/activities about, 238,
        259–261
    "Tears of Fear: Army Deserters, May–June
        1864" and, 251–59
"Diary of Death: The Siege of Vicksburg,
    May–July 1863," 169–77
Dickson, Charles, 5–12
Dillard, Ephram, 202–10
Dix, Dorothea, 249, 285
Documentation of war
    communication and, 129–31, 141–43
    efforts of women and, 285
    "'Reporting' for Duty: Civil War Field
        Reporters, September 1862" and,
        129–40
    traveling press corps and, xiv
"Dodging the Bullet: President Lincoln Moves
    to Washington, February 1861," 31–40
Dorsey, Decatur, 271
Double quick, 331
Douglas, Stephan
    Lincoln, Abraham and, 31
    Nebraska Territory and, 4
Douglass, Frederick
    follow-up questions/activities about, 115
    Harpers Ferry and, 15
    volunteers and, 106
Draft law
    follow-up questions/activities about,
        198–200, xiv
    passing of, 158
    "Striking Out: New York City Draft Riots:
        July 1863" and, 190–98
    "Tears of Fear: Army Deserters, May–June
        1864" and, 251–59
Dred Scott, 1
Drewry's Bluff, 226
Drummer boys, 201–12
Durham Station, North Carolina, 300

Economics
    costs of telegraphs, 130
    desertion and, 251–52
    effect of Southern port blockade, 213,
        222–23
    effect of Western gold/silver mines on, 62
    escape clause of draft law and, 190, 199
    follow-up questions/activities about, 49–50,
        296–297
    loss of manpower and, 228
    payment to African American soldiers, 263

reconstruction and, 325–26
slavery/cotton and, 42, 48–49
"Sweet Potatoes, Cotton, Tobacco, and
    Quinine: A Wealth of Smuggling,
    October 1864" and, 286–96
U.S. Sanitary Commission and, 283
Edmonds, Sarah, 98
Education
    follow-up questions/activities about,
        236–38
    of nurses/doctors, 248–49
    "Southern Shortages" and, 228–36
Elkhorn Tavern Battle, 62
Ella and Annie, 223
Emancipation Proclamation
    African American volunteers and, 114
    issue of, 158
Enfield rifle, 330
Ethics
    attacking cities and, 178
    business practices during the war and,
        286–87, 297
    children as battlefield drummers and, 212
    Confederates' treatment of Black soldiers
        and, 273
    desertion and, 260–261
    documentation of war and, 142–43
    draft law and, 200
    justification of war and, 238
    medicine and, 155
    of Southern port blockade, 224
    stealing of legal property and, 168
Ewell, Richard, 188, 310

"Fair Fight, A: Northern Women's Efforts to
    Support the Sanitary Commission,
    September–November 1864," 275–84
Fair Oaks, Battle of, 272
Farragut, David, 63, 117–18, 169
"Fast, Dark, and Quiet: Confederate Ships
    That Ran the Union Naval Blockade,
    October 1863," 211, 213–23
Female war participants. See Women
Field reporting. See Documentation of war
Fielder, James, 302–10
Flamethrowers, xiv
Flora, 223
Florida, xi, 2–3, 31
Food. See Supplies
Fort Craig, 91
Fort Fillmore, 86–94
Fort Fisher, 300
Fort Pulaski, 63

Fort Stanton, 86
Fort Sumpter, xiv, 2, 29–30, 51, 106
Fortifications, 330–31
Fredericksburg, Battle of, 63
"Free or Slave?," 4–12

Georgia, 2–3, 31
Gettysburg, Battle of, 158, 178–87, xii
Gettysburg of the West. *See* Glorieta Pass,
    Battle of
Glorieta Pass, Battle of
    follow-up questions/activities about, 95–96
    as key event of 1862, 62
    "Turn Coat, Turn Coat: The Civil War in
        the Far West and the Battle of
        Glorieta Pass, February–March
        1862" and, 88–94
Grant, Ulysses S.
    Cold Harbor, Battle of, and, 226
    command of Union forces by, 159
    follow-up questions/activities about, 178,
        249
    Look Out Mountain and, 210
    Missionary Ridge and, 210
    on prisoners, 313–14
    Richmond and, 226
    siege of Vicksburg and, 169–70, 176–77,
        179
    Tennessee/Kentucky victories by, 62
Greeley, Horace, 13, 141
"Growin' Cotton'; Killin' Yankees," 42–49
Guerrila warfare, 84–85
Guns, xiv, 211, 286–96, 329–30

Hancock, Winfield, 188
Hardtack, 74, 331
Harmon, Amelia, 180–87
Harpers Ferry
    Brown, John and, 2–3, 15–16
    follow-up questions/activities about, 25–27
    "Righteous Raiders" and, 15–25
Hartford, 125
Haversack, 331
Home for Confederate Women, 240
"Home Town Horror: The Battle of
        Gettysburg: July 1863," 178–87
Honey Hill, Battle of, 272
Hood, John, 226–27
Hooker, Joe, 63, 157
Hooker, Joseph, 158
Hot air balloons, xiv
Huster, Walter, 65–73

Impress, 331
Indian Wars, 96
Industrialization
    advancements, xi, 285
    reconstruction and, 326
Infection. *See* Medicine
Inflammation. *See* Medicine
Infrastructure, 311. *See also* Communication;
    Transportation
Invalid Army Corps, 196
Irish immigrants, 190–98
"Iron Might: Ironclad Naval Battle on the
        Mississippi, June 1862," 117–26
Ironclads. *See* Navy
Iroquois, 125

Jackson, Thomas J. "Stonewall"
    Battle of Winchester and, 63
    as brilliant/quirky general, 59
    death by own men of, 158
    Gettysburg, Battle of, and, 188
    Shenandoah Valley campaign and, 84
    Valley Campaign of, 62
    Winchester, Battle of, and, 77–83
John Fraser & Company, 223
Johnson, Andrew, 300
Johnston, Joe
    Battle of Bull Run and, 59
    command of, 301
    follow-up questions/activities about, 311
    last battle of the war and, 325
    surrender by, 299–300

Kansas
    Dickson, Charles and, 5–12
    follow-up questions/activities about, 13–14
    freedom conflict in 1856–1857, 1–2, 4–5
Kentucky, xi, 63
Knapsack, 331

Land mines, xiv
Lane, James, 13
Langston, John Mercer, 107–14
Laurel Hill, 125
Lee, Robert E.
    on African American troops, 272
    defeat of, 157–58
    follow-up questions/activities about,
        310–12
    Gettysburg, Battle of, and, 179–80, 187–89
    Second Battle of Bull Run and, 61
    surrender of, 300

"United We Fall: Lee's Surrender, April 1865" and, 301–10
Wilderness, Battle of the, and, 226
Lincoln, Abraham
  African American volunteers and, 106
  Amnesty Proclamation of, xiv
  assassination of, 300
  blockade of Southern ports, 213
  call for volunteers by, 29–30
  "Dodging the Bullet" and, 31–40
  draft law and, 158
  election of, 2–3, 31–32
  follow-up questions/activities about, 40–41
  Gettysburg Address and, 188
  reelection of, 225
Literature, Southern, 237
Little Ada, 223
Little Hattie, 118, 223
Little Mac. *See* McClellan, George
Livingston, Mary, 276–84
Longstreet, James, 159, 188, 202
Louisiana, xi, 2–3, 31
Lumpkin, Chester, 314–21

Manassas (Second Battle of Bull Run). *See also* Bull Run, Battle of
  Parker, Thomas, and, 43
  "Tea Cakes, White Lace, and Bloodshed: First Battle of Bull Run (Manassas), July 1861" and, 51–59
Margret and Jessie, 223
Maryland, 39–40, xi
Massachusetts, 1
Massachusetts Aid Society, 4, 13
Mathews, Alfonse, 262–72
McClellan, George
  indecisiveness of, 61–62
  Peninsular Campaign of, 63
  relieved of command, 63, 140
  replacement of General McDowell by, 59
  "Supper, Shoes, and Shovels: Supplying a Civil War Army, February 1862" and, 66–73
McDowell, Irving, 59
McRae, Lucy, 170–77
Meade, George, 158, 188
Medicine. *See also* Supplies
  "Battle "Cries": Women Working in an Army Hospital, May 1864" and, 239–48
  follow-up questions/activities about, 153–55, 248–50, 285

"Ounce of Prevention; Pound of Cure: An Army Field Surgeon, Fall 1862" and, 144–53
Merrimac, 62, 117, 128
Milliken's Bend, 263
Minnié Ball, 330
Mississippi, xi, 2–3, 31
Missouri, xi
Missouri Border Ruffians, 4, 13
Missouri Compromise, 2
Monitor, 62, 117, 128
Murfreesboro. *See* Stone's River, Battle of
Musicians, xiv, 201–12
Muskets, 330
Muzzle loaders, 330

Names of Confederates/Unionists, 329
Native Americans, 96
Navy
  "Fast, Dark, and Quiet: Confederate Ships That Ran the Union Naval Blockade, October 1863" and, 213–23
  first use of ironclads, xiv
  follow-up questions/activities about, 127–28
  "Iron Might: Ironclad Naval Battle on the Mississippi, June 1862" and, 117–26
  ships of, 62, 117–18
Nebraska, xi
Nevada, xi
New England Aid Society, 4, 7, 13
New Mexico, 62, 86–94
New York, xiii, 190–98
Newspapers. *See* Communication
Nightingale, Florence, 276
North Carolina
  effect of Southern port blockade, 214, 223
  secession and, xi, 29–30

Oregon, 2
"Ounce of Prevention; Pound of Cure: An Army Field Surgeon, Fall 1862," 144–53

Parade, 331
Parker, Thomas, 43–49
"Patriotic Pride and Prejudice: Northern Blacks' Efforts to Enlist, August 1862", 106–14
Patterson, Ambrose and Abigail, 52–59
Pember, Phoebe, 248
Pemberton, 178

Peninsular Campaign, 63
Perryville, Battle of, 63
Petersburg, Virginia
    beginning of siege, 226
    follow-up questions/activities about, 272,
        310–12
    "Unsung Heroes: Black Union Regiments
        and the Battle of the Crater, July 30,
        1864" and, 262–72
Photography, xiv, 141, 326
Pickets, 311, 331
Pickett, George, 188–89
Pickett's Charge, 188
Pinkerton, Allan, 32–40, 103–4
"Place of Freedom: Southern Slaves Efforts to
        Gain Freedom, March 1863," 160–67
Presidential assassinations, 41, 300. *See* also
        specific president
Prisoners of war
    follow-up questions/activities about, 322–23
    "Skeleton Heroes: Prisoners of War, April
        1865" and, 313–21
    websites for, 322
"Private Petticoat: Female Army Spy, May
        1862," 97–104
Protests of war, 190–98

Quantrill, William, 13–14, 302, 311
Quinine, 249

Rations, 312. *See also* Supplies
Reconstruction, 312, 325–27
Redoubt (redan), 330
"'Reporting' for Duty: Civil War Field
        Reporters, September 1862," 129–40
Resources
    electronic, 337–38
    historical fiction, 336–37
    nonfiction, 333–36
Rifles, xiv, 330
"Righteous Raiders," 15–25
Robert E. Lee, 214–23
Robinson, Charles, 13
Rosecrans, William, 63, 159, 202
Ryan, Michael, 191–98

Sanitary Commission. *See* U.S. Sanitary
        Commission
Savannah, 226–27
Saylor's Creek, Virginia, 310
Sciota, 125
Secession. *See also specific states*
    "Dodging the Bullet" and, 31–41

Sharps Rifle, 330
Sharpsburg. *See* Antietam, Battle of
Shenandoah Valley campaign, 84–85
Sheridan, Philip, 158, 300
Sherman, William Tecumseh
    Atlanta and, 225–26
    capture of blockade ports by, 30
    follow-up questions/activities about, 311
    Johnston's surrender to, 299
    last battle of the war and, 325
    reporters as spies and, 140
    Savannah and, 226–27
    South Carolina and, 300
Shiloh, Battle of, 62
Shot (types), 330
Sibley, Wilfred, 86
Siege of Vicksburg. *See* Vicksburg,
        Mississippi
Sinks, 153
Sirus, 214–23
"Sister Spies: Life in Occupied Winchester,
        Virginia, March 1862," 75–83
"Skeleton Heroes: Prisoners of War, April
        1865," 313–21
Slavery. *See also* Abolitionists
    follow-up questions/activities about, 49–50,
        167–68, 237
    historical aspects of, xiii
    "Place of Freedom: Southern Slaves'
        Efforts to Gain Freedom, March
        1863" and, 160–67
Smalley, George, 130–31
Smuggling, 286–97
Soldier's aid groups. *See* Aid groups
Solid shot (round shot), 330
"Sounding Battle: The Life of a Dummer Boy
        at the Battle of Chickamauga,
        September 1863," 201–10
South Carolina
    "Fast, Dark, and Quiet: Confederate Ships
        That Ran the Union Naval
        Blockade, October 1863" and,
        213–23
    follow-up questions/activities about, 167
    secession and, 31
    secession of, xi, 2–3
    Sherman's march through, 300
"Southern Shortages," 228–36
Spies
    follow-up questions/activities about, 84–85,
        104–5
    "Private Petticoat: Female Army Spy, May
        1862" and, 97–104

reporters as, 140
"Sister Spies: Life in Occupied Winchester,
    Virginia, March 1862," 75–83
smuggling and, 297
Sports and war, 60
Spotsylvania, Battle of the, 226
States' rights, xiii
Stone's River, Battle of, 63
"Striking Out: New York City Draft Riots,
    July 1863," 190–98
Strong, George Templeton, 276
Stuart, Jeb, 141, 188
Submarines, xiv
Sultana, 300, 311, 319–23
"Supper, Shoes, and Shovels: Supplying a
    Civil War Army, February 1862,"
    64–73
Supplies
    female war participants and, 97
    follow-up questions/activities about, 73–74,
        310–12
    Lee's surrender and, 301
    necessary, 64, 73–74
    North vs. South, xii
    prisoners of war and, 313–14, 322–23
    reconstruction and, 326
    "Supper, Shoes, and Shovels: Supplying a
        Civil War Army, February 1862"
        and, 64–73
"Sweet Potatoes, Cotton, Tobacco, and
    Quinine: A Wealth of Smuggling,
    October 1864," 286–96

Taylor, Virginis. *See* DeLouise, Virginia
"Tea Cakes, White Lace, and Bloodshed: First
    Battle of Bull Run (Manassas), July
    1861," 51–59
"Tears of Fear: Army Deserters, May–June
    1864," 251–59
Telegraph. *See* Communication
Tennessee, 127
Tennessee
    Battle of Stone's River and, 63
    Longstreet's attack on Burnside, 159
    secession and, xi, 29–30
    Union occupation (1862) of, 62
Texas, xi, 2–3, 31, 86–94
Tompkins, Sally, 240–48
Transportation
    advancements of, xi
    blockades of shipping ports, 30
    "Fast, Dark, and Quiet: Confederate Ships
        That Ran the Union Naval
        Blockade, October 1863" and,
        214–23
    necessary supplies and, 64
    railroad artillery and, xiv
    Sultana and, 311, 319–23
    warships, 62, 117–26
Trench warfare, xiv, 263, 273, 302, 331
"Turn Coat, Turn Coat: The Civil War in the
    Far West and the Battle of Glorieta
    Pass, February–March 1862," 86–94
Turner, Jedediah, 287–96

Underground Railroad, 161, 167–68
Union forces/names, 329
United States Colored Troops (USCT)
    Black Brigade of Cincinnati, 114
    follow-up questions/activities about,
        272–74
    "Unsung Heroes: Black Union Regiments
        and the Battle of the Crater, July 30,
        1864" and, 262–72
"United We Fall: Lee's Surrender, April
    1865," 301–10
"Unsung Heroes: Black Union Regiments and
    the Battle of the Crater, July 30, 1864,"
    262–72
U.S. Army Nursing Corps, 249
U.S. Sanitary Commission, 73, 276, 284–85,
    319
USCT. *See* United States Colored Troops
    (USCT)

Valley Campaign, 62
Valverde, Battle of, 62
Venus, 223
Vicksburg, Mississippi
    "Diary of Death: The Siege of Vicksburg,
        May–July 1863" and, 169–77
    follow-up questions/activities about,
        177–78
    importance of, 118–26, 157–58
    prisoners of war and, 314
    Sultana and, 321
Virginia, 62
Virginia
    secession and, xi, 2, 29–30
    "Sister Spies: Life in Occupied Winchester,
        Virginia, March 1862" and, 75–83
Volunteers
    African American, 106, 167
    Davis, Jefferson, and call for, 3

Volunteers
  "Fair Fight, A: Northern Women's Efforts
    to Support the Sanitary
    Commission, September–November
    1864" and, 276–84
  follow-up questions/activities about, 40,
    114–16, 284–85
  Fort Sumpter and, 106
  Lincoln, Abraham and first call for, 29–30

Walker, Mary, 249
Wallace, 116
Wallsly, Thomas, 145
Weapons, 329–30
Websites, 322, 337–38
West Virginia, xi, 158
Wilderness, Battle of the, 226
Wilkinson, John, 214–23
William C. Bee Company, 223
Wilson, Elizabeth, 161–67
Wilson, Ransom, 161–67

Winchester, Battle of, 63
  "Sister Spies: Life in Occupied Winchester,
    Virginia, March 1862" and, 75–83
Wirtz, Henry, 323
Women. *See also* Abolitionists
  "Battle "Cries": Women Working in an
    Army Hospital, May 1864 and,
    239–48
  "Fair Fight, A: Northern Women's Efforts
    to Support the Sanitary
    Commission, September–November
    1864" and, 275–84
  follow-up questions/activities about, 104–5,
    236–38, 248–50, 284–85
  "Private Petticoat: Female Army Spy, May
    1862" and, 97–104
  "Sister Spies: Life in Occupied Winchester,
    Virginia, March 1862," 75–83
  "Southern Shortages" and, 228–36
Wood, Sam, 7–11, 13
Wright, Rebecca, 76–83